PENGUI̶N̶
UNFORGET̶T̶

Eamon Dunphy is an Irish writer and broadcaster. He writes a regular column for an Irish Sunday newspaper and appears frequently on Irish television. He played professional soccer in England for fifteen years and is the author, with Peter Ball, of the classic football book *Only a Game?* (1976) published in Penguin in 1979.

LIVERPOOL JMU LIBRARY

3 1111 01451 9951

EAMON DUNPHY

Unforgettable Fire

THE STORY OF U 2

PENGUIN BOOKS

For my mother
Margaret
and my children
Tim and Colette.
For the love they've given me.

PENGUIN BOOKS

Published by the Penguin Group
Penguin Books Ltd, 27 Wrights Lane, London W8 5TZ, England
Penguin Books USA Inc., 375 Hudson Street, New York, New York 10014, USA
Penguin Books Australia Ltd, Ringwood, Victoria, Australia
Penguin Books Canada Ltd, 10 Alcorn Avenue, Toronto, Ontario, Canada M4V 3B2
Penguin Books (NZ) Ltd, 182–190 Wairau Road, Auckland 10, New Zealand

Penguin Books Ltd, Registered Offices: Harmondsworth, Middlesex, England

First published by Viking 1987
Published in Penguin Books 1988
Reprinted with an Epilogue 1993
1 3 5 7 9 10 8 6 4 2

Copyright © Eamon Dunphy, 1987
Epilogue copyright © Bill Graham 1993
All rights reserved

Grateful acknowledgement is made to the following for permission to reproduce copyright extracts: U2/Chappell International and Blue Mountain Music for lyrics from the following U2 songs: 'Bad', 'Shadows and Tall Trees', 'Twilight', 'I Will Follow', 'Fire', 'Gloria', 'Rejoice', 'Is That All', 'Tomorrow', 'A Celebration', 'Sunday Bloody Sunday', 'Surrender', 'Two Hearts Beat as One', 'A Sort of Homecoming', 'Silver and Gold', 'Running to Stand Still', 'Bullet the Blue Sky', 'Out of Control'; *In Dublin* magazine for 'Deus Ex Machina' by John Waters; *Magill* magazine for 'Don't Believe a Word' by Fintan O'Toole.

Printed in England by Clays Ltd, St Ives plc
Typeset in 10/12pt Lasercomp Garamond

Except in the United States of America, this book is sold subject
to the condition that it shall not, by way of trade or otherwise, be lent,
re-sold, hired out, or otherwise circulated without the publisher's
prior consent in any form of binding or cover other than that in
which it is published and without a similar condition including this
condition being imposed on the subsequent purchaser

Contents

Acknowledgements

Two years ago Paul McGuinness asked me if I would write a U2 book. I agreed provided the band exercised no veto over the final manuscript. They have been as good as their word. They are remarkable people who have had the courage to be known at a time in their lives when mystique may well have served them better.

I am indebted to many people for the help I received researching this book. No acknowledgement here can fully express my gratitude. I thank especially the families of Paul McGuinness, Bono, Adam, Edge and Larry: Bobby and Norman Hewson, Jo and Brian Clayton (Jo was particularly kind and brave), Garvin and Gwenda Evans, Dick and Gill, Larry Mullen Sr and Cecilia, Mrs Sheila McGuinness, Kathy McGuinness, Ali, Ann and Aislinn. All were sympathetic as I burrowed into their lives. I am deeply grateful.

The same applies to Anne-Louise Kelly, Barbara Galavan, Dennis Sheehan, Joe O'Herlihy, Tom Mullally, Tim Buckley and Steve Iredale whose working day I frequently interrupted. They were unfailingly courteous and sympathetic. Ellen Darst and Keryn Kaplin in New York were similarly patient. To Caroline, Bridget, Suzanne and Jackie in the U2 office I can only say thank you.

Frank Barsalona, Owen Epstein and Ossie Kilkenny gave me some of their valuable time. Thanks, gentlemen. Thanks too to Barbara Skydel and in spades to Chris Blackwell of Island Records.

John Clark who looks after security allowed me to breach the system a few times. Thanks, John.

Colleagues closer to home were generous beyond the call of duty;

ACKNOWLEDGEMENTS

without Fintan O'Toole, Ferdia MacAnna and Dave Fanning I would not have understood as badly as I did the city described. Bill Graham was wonderfully cooperative. He is a special man in a business that hardly merits his gifts.

Donald Moxham and Steve Averill provided vivid memories of the beginnings of this story. Brush Sheils and B. P. Fallon provided interesting perspectives which were invaluable to me.

I never met Neil McCormick but I picked his brains all the same. Likewise other *Hot Press* writers who contributed to the *Hot Press* File which was essential to my researches.

Steve Lillywhite was a patient, good-humoured guide who only laughed the odd time at my questions. I am especially indebted to Danny Lanois for allowing me to hang around Danesmoate during work on *The Joshua Tree*.

Journalists Eamonn McCann, Sam G. Smyth and John Waters placed my enthusiasm for the subject in some perspective and provided valuable contributions to the U2 story. Paul Tansey and Shane Ross had forgotten most of the Trinity years, but they were fun whilst trying to remember. Both owe me dinner.

I spent happy and productive weeks at the Tyrone Guthrie Centre in Linnamakerrig, Co. Monaghan, working on this book. To Bernard and Mary Loughlin, I am, like so many others, deeply in debt.

The Village were always eager to help despite denying me membership. To Gavin, Guggi, David, Strongman and especially Pod, a very heartfelt thanks. Maeve O'Regan provided a special insight into the Mount Temple years. Barry Devlin's memories of the Hard Times were similarly priceless. My thanks also to Terry O'Neill who 'knew them when they were nothing'. Patrick Brocklebank produced the photograph of the first meeting between band and manager at the Project in 1978.

All of these people and many more gave me encouragement and assistance over the past two years.

Veronica Farrell did much more than her job, which was to type the manuscript. Without her patience, intelligence and conscientiousness I dread to think what this book would be like. Aengus Fanning, editor of the *Sunday Independent*, was a good and generous friend. I hope to repay that generosity.

My thanks to Tony Lacey, Viking's Editorial Director, for substantially improving the manuscript I originally sent him. I thank also Clare Harington, Carol Heaton and Tessa Strickland at Viking for their encouragement and conviction.

Finally, this is perhaps the wrong place to do it, but I must acknowledge the love extended to me during this difficult project by my family and friends. In this regard nobody was kinder than Inge Eulitz. For that I am eternally grateful.

Eamon Dunphy
12 September 1987

Prologue

LIVE AID

In March 1985 *Rolling Stone* magazine featured the Irish rock band U2 on its cover. The headline read: 'Our Choice : Band of the '80s'. This was rock 'n' roll's ultimate critical accolade. In U2's case it could be argued that the honour bestowed on them was a trifle premature: it would be fully two years before the band justified the claims made on their behalf.

Live Aid took place four months after *Rolling Stone* hit the news-stands, at the beginning of the creative process that would produce their magnificent 1987 album, *The Joshua Tree*. U2 were not a stadium band. They had much to lose as they waited to take their place on the greatest rock 'n' roll bill of all time. They had fifteen minutes and three songs to attack with. This was not a U2 audience, there was no residual fervour, no long-established relationship to justify a passionate, personal embrace. But they were determined to go for it, expose themselves as they had that first time at Mount Temple School, pouring everything – fear, hope, 'fucking desperation', as Adam would irreverently describe it – into those three songs, that fifteen minutes, as if there would never be another show, another chance.

It hung on Bono. At moments of acute need like this it was

as if he was the vessel into which all their fears and hopes, ideas and emotions dissolved. In him and through him the pool of accumulated sadness, joy, anger and yearning swelled and began to flow – from Edge's guitar, through Larry's drums and Adam's bass the music gathered force, bursting out through Bono whose task it was to give it words, meaning, substance on a day like this. He was the medium for their message. When Bono prayed that day, as he always did backstage, he asked for strength. Adam prayed silently that the sound system would work.

Geldof's rule was that nobody from the audience should come on stage. There was a no fans' land between audience and stage to ensure that the rule held fast. U2's planned set was 'Bad', 'New Year's Day' and 'Sunday Bloody Sunday'. But Bono blew the plan right out of the window. And with it went the rules of the day, even one Geldof hadn't thought worth imposing: nobody would want to go from stage to audience. Nobody would be that crazy. Nobody would have time.

Paul McGuinness, their manager, sat down to watch on a television monitor backstage. He felt unusually tense. Normally he didn't doubt Bono's ability to deliver, but this was Big. The band went straight into 'Sunday Bloody Sunday'. No spiel. Bono looked deceptively calm. His fear had had the curious effect of slowing him down. Concentrate on the music. It was good, intense, controlled, McGuinness thought. Looking out at the vastness of Wembley, his tension began to drain away. Bono was introducing 'Bad': 'We're from Dublin.' The crowd roared acknowledgement. 'Like all cities it has its good and its bad. This is a song called "Bad".' The intro was crisp, clean and no bullshit. Bono had judged the mood correctly.

'Bad' was Paul's favourite U2 song. Often he would privately choke up while watching them on stage from the shadows. Now he felt an uncontrollable rush of emotion. Geldof had pulled up a seat beside him. The sight of that familiar lanky figure, subdued now, as Paul watched the kid he'd known on Grafton Street rouse and inspire this huge audience and the millions round the world, suddenly made the fantasy that was this day real. For Geldof the effect was much the same. McGuinness and U2 evoked Dublin, its sights and sounds, the failures and minor victories – all that passionate bickering about nothing.

'Bad's' opening passage was a stunning evocation of the frightening power and, yes, beauty of those moments when the heroin surged through your bloodstream, erasing all pain, all weakness. There was a glimpse – brief but powerful – of invulnerability, of harmony between mind and spirit. That beauty was captured by Edge's calm, Adam's poise, Larry's handsome innocence and by the sweeping sensuality of the melody they played. It was Bono who evoked the pain that lies in wait on the other side of heroin's beauty. This was as far as rock 'n' roll could go in its struggle to express the conflict, irony and ultimate futility of human experience. If you never touched heroin you were still engaged on the deepest, most private emotional level by 'Bad'. For you were reminded of how fleeting beauty is, reminded of the reality heroin cannot erase. Face pale and gaunt, body still, no longer strutting, Bono sang:

> *Dislocation*
> *Separation*
> *Condemnation*
> *Revelation*
> *Intemplation*
> *Isolation*
> *Desolation.*

'Bad's' lyric laid bare the illusion of power and beauty proposed by its melody. 'Bad' was a bitter lament, a reminder that the beautiful moment is often the loneliest, the most deceiving. Hearing a rock 'n' roll band play like this you understood deep within you why man is moved to tears when confronted by beauty.

Paul was crying. Geldof too. They hugged each other, half laughing, half crying. 'I never liked you, you bastard,' Geldof croaked. 'I didn't much like you,' Paul admitted. But they understood each other enough to know what this day meant to both of them.

Onstage Bono had claimed the audience. When he held the microphone out the response was lusty, frantic. This was his private way of assessing how things were going. He ventured to the front edge of the stage. It was now a U2 concert. He picked a girl out from the surging mass of bodies in front of him. He beckoned. Several girls moved forward. But he knew which one he wanted. She was pretty, dark haired, with a white sweater.

Backstage McGuinness looked at his watch. Time was running out. There'd be no third song. What was Bono at?

There was a deep pit in front of the stage. Bono stood poised now to jump into it. 'Bad' was adaptable, its variations of pace and intensity flexible enough to allow Bono to do whatever he wanted. But here? On *this* day?

The girl was at the outer edge of the pit now. Bono leaped down. The security men scrambled to contain the crowd closest to the stage who fought for a sight of the singer. Now the dark-haired girl reached him. They embraced.

Jesus, McGuinness thought, he's really blown it this time. Bono had disappeared. Nobody in Wembley Stadium could see him except the security guards and the few people on the barrier's edge. But the millions watching on television could follow every move. To them the scene was intimate, an elaborate TV spectacle that for sheer theatricality overshadowed anything else on that momentous day.

This symbolic bonding of performer and audience, music and people, captured the mood. As it was felt in Wembley

Stadium – that unique atmosphere, part compassion, part rock concert, part coming together of the young people of the world – was now by a stupendous piece of showmanship conveyed to the millions watching at home. Bono had taken the ultimate performing risk. It could have seemed gimmicky, a gauche intrusion, a breach of the spirit of Live Aid. But his animal instinct for an audience, for the occasion, had helped him get it right. The difference between cynical manipulation and great performer was in this case the degree to which performer believed in the cause and the music. The degree to which he was committed to his work.

Accepting congratulations afterwards, Paul McGuinness harboured doubts about what he had seen. Had it worked? A month later he watched a video of the performance and understood why it had worked, and knew that his band could play anywhere.

Chapter One

BONO'S STORY

On 6 May 1960 an American aircraft carrying electronic surveillance equipment was shot down whilst on a spying mission over the Soviet Union. The pilot, Gary Powers, was captured and produced in Moscow before the world's press. Powers was to become a pawn in the Cold War being waged between Krushchev's Soviet Union and Eisenhower's United States. The international scandal that followed his capture became known to the world at large as the 'U2 Incident'. The specially fitted intelligence-gathering planes used by the Americans were known colloquially as 'U2's. Two years later, in 1962, intelligence gathered by a similarly equipped aircraft led to the Cuban Missile Crisis which brought the world as close as it has ever been to nuclear confrontation.

On 10 May, four days after the Soviets shot down the U2, Paul Hewson was born in the Rotunda Hospital in Dublin. He was a second son for Bobby and Iris Hewson, whose other boy, Norman, was seven years old.

Bobby and Iris were Dubliners, real Dubliners, born and bred, as Bobby would proudly declare whenever he was asked where he came from. They came from the Oxmantown Road area of the city where they had grown up together. To say you

came from the Oxmantown Road conveyed something specific about you and yours. It meant you were city, *not* suburb. It meant you were Dublin, not Irish, not from the country, the rural heartland, the green fields. To be a 'Dub' the way Bobby meant it when he proclaimed it, was to be different, separate from any of the stock Irish characters of world renown. Dubliners were hardy and wise and ambivalent about many things, things that were said to matter to the Irish, like religion and nationalism. Yes, in a corner of their hearts they subscribed to both – yet the head argued differently and the head ruled Dubliners' lives.

Bobby Hewson liked to tell a story that reflected his and perhaps most native Dubliners' attitude to the Republican movement. He'd gone to Brunswick Street Secondary School, run by the Christian Brothers. The Brothers were powerful men for Republicanism. Sometimes when Bobby and his pals were bored, in danger of chastisement or otherwise looking to divert a teaching Brother's attention away from the business of the day, they would raise the question of the North and the British. His Republican blood stirred, Teacher would, as Bobby described it, 'be gone, marching up the Whitehall Road (which led to Belfast) to fight for Ireland'. And thus, to a classroom of thirteen-year-old Dubliners, Republicanism was a way of passing painlessly through a history lesson. This was in De Valera's Ireland of the early 1940s.

Reflecting, years later, on the subject of Ireland United and Free, Bobby spoke for most real Dubliners: 'While I am a Republican at heart, I could never see myself shooting anybody. There's a line in a play that I'll always remember: "Ireland – what the hell is Ireland – Ireland is just the piece of ground that keeps my feet from getting wet." And there's a lot of truth in that.' Yet still Bobby felt 'Republican at heart'.

For Dubliners like Bobby the question of identity was far from simple. They were Irish and as such shared with their

fellow countrymen and women a sense of outrage about the crimes committed over the centuries by British Imperialists. No Irishman or woman could reason away the suffering of past generations, the famine, the religious persecution, the economic rape, the naked and unrelenting contempt that had characterized the British occupation of Ireland. *Thus*, the Republicanism in Bobby's heart.

But no Dublin man or woman could escape from or deny the cultural and aesthetic influences that had formed them. Dubliners live in a beautiful Georgian city built by the British. They speak the English language, read English books and daily newspapers and listen to the BBC. Through music-hall, cinema and gramophone records they absorb popular English culture. Their children read English comics. Elsewhere in Ireland the Irish language and Gaelic culture had together with Catholicism served to preserve the national identity through centuries of British occupation. Dubliners are a different breed. They had resisted invaders by absorbing the new influences, whether Norman, Viking, Huguenot or British. New crafts, customs and ideas were adopted. Resistance was not over – but it was constant. Worldly, pragmatic and independent, the best Dubliners, the real Dubliners, placed the quality of life, their own personal lives, above church and state. The cause was survival, for you and yours. A good job, a place to live, the welfare of your family. Dubliners were not so much cynics as agnostics about causes and movements, cultural or religious, that demanded the ultimate sacrifice, yourself, your own individual identity.

They were as a result separate from their fellow Irishmen and women. When, on St Patrick's Day 1943, De Valera addressed the Irish people, he expressed more powerfully than ever before the vision of Ireland and Irishness that propelled the struggle for National Independence from the British: 'That Ireland we dreamed of would be the home of a people who valued ma-

terial wealth only as the basis of right living, of a people who were satisfied with frugal comfort and devoted their leisure to the things of the spirit – a land whose countryside would be bright with cosy homesteads, whose fields and villages would be joyous with the sounds of industry, with the romping of sturdy children, the contests of athletic youths and the laughter of comely maidens, whose firesides would be the forums for the serene wisdom of old age. It would in a word be the home of a people living the life that God desires that man should live.'

It would be difficult to conceive a definition of Irishness further removed from the everyday experience of Dubliners. Indeed, in his landmark speech, Dev (as he was rather cryptically known) didn't mention Dublin at all. Yet despite their scepticism and the degree to which their values were at odds with the official Catholic-Nationalist ethos, Dubliners were, in their hearts, Irish. They had on the whole remained indifferent to the 1916 rising. When Pearse and Connolly and the other heroes of that adventure were taken from the General Post Office by the British, they encountered hostility on the streets of Dublin on their way to Arbour Hill. Three weeks later, after the British had executed their captives, Dubliners wept as the coffins passed along those same city streets. A less profound, but no less significant, manifestation of Dublin pragmatism could – and indeed still can – be witnessed at closing time in the city's pubs. Here the singsong is part of tradition. And you can hear on any Friday or Saturday night the songs of Vera Lynn, England's wartime heroine, Frank Sinatra and, rendered with particular passion, Irish ballads that tell of British persecution, songs that celebrate James Connolly, Kevin Barry, 'who gave his life for the sake of lib-er-ty', and The Men Behind (The Long Kesh) Wire. This is in a city from which tens of thousands went as volunteers to die in the British army in the Great War. Dubliners joined up not for the cause but for the job and the pension that went with it.

Oxmantown Road lay on the Northside of the River Liffey. Just. It was close to everything. In ten minutes you could walk to O'Connell Street to the east. Behind you and to the north and west the Phoenix Park offered space and a sense of being in the country. The river rested a few minutes below and south. The Dublin that Bobby Hewson grew up in during the 1940s and 1950s was grand and squalid in equal measure. Oxmantown Road was neither but, in its modest, decent respectability, somewhere in between. The house Bobby was reared in was two-bedroomed, terraced and clean. If he turned left on leaving home and walked to the top of Oxmantown Road he was on the North Circular Road amid the middle-class grandeur of red brick Georgian villas. If however he turned right and headed down towards the commercial district of Stoneybatter, Bobby was just as quickly confronted by the teeming Georgian tenements that lay by the river bank. Thus, between grandeur and squalor, Oxmantown Road stood as an oasis of lower-middle-class respectability and aspiration.

But because this was Dublin the area possessed a vitality that was absent from lower-middle-class existence elsewhere. Town, with its dance-halls, cinemas and music-halls, was but a walk away. The park offered sport and in summer evenings a lingering sense of carnival. There was always *something* happening in Stoneybatter, where the shops, pubs and markets drew their cosmopolitan crowds. Life was rich and close at hand.

Bobby Hewson's father worked as a technician in the General Post Office. In the Dublin of his time this was a good job, permanent and pensionable. In his spare time Hewson and his wife were members of an amateur music-hall group based in the Father Matthew Hall, where he did a stand-up comic act and played the Dame in pantomimes. At home he was a serious man who suffered greatly from bronchial troubles that were exacerbated by the damp and cold of the halls he loved to play.

Bobby's memory of his father is of him singing all the old music-hall songs in the tiny bathroom in Oxmantown Road.

When he left Brunswick Street Secondary School at fourteen with his Intermediate Certificate, Bobby followed his dad into the Post Office. He was sturdily built, cheerful and gregarious. He stood out from the crowd, was never shy or lost for a word. He played cricket in the park and when the boys he knocked around with started going to dances, Bobby was usually first on the floor. The Second World War had just ended, money was tight even for those with good jobs, and rationing was a fact of life. Essential foods like meat, sugar, tea and dairy produce were doled out in ounces to those who produced their blue ration cards. Sometimes money could get you what you wanted on the black market, but more often extra money, disposable income, was spent in dance-halls, cinemas and pubs. Escapism was in vogue in Dublin.

Bobby loved music. He loved Al Jolson, Bing Crosby and especially the operatic stuff, the arias he listened to on the wireless, sung by Tito Gobbi, Mario Lanza and Richard Tauber. He loved to wander downtown to the 'pictures' to see the great musicals starring Crosby and Jolson. In the dark privacy of the cinema, the Bobby Hewson that lay behind the Post-Office clerk indulged in romantic notions that had to do with a life somewhat grander, more fulfilling than the one he lived behind a desk in the GPO. There was someone else he wanted to be other than the extrovert, wisecracking sportsman, someone who might express in music or song feelings deeper, darker, more profound than those allowed to clerks. If there was melancholy in Bobby's young life it derived, as in his father's case, from a sense of having more to say than working life permitted.

Bobby was a member of the Catholic Young Men's Society, the CYMS, which was more social club than religious institution. And it was there at the CYMS in Aughrim Street which ran parallel to Oxmantown Road that he first got talking-and-dancing with Iris. They'd seen each other around as they'd grown up. She was dark, pretty, petite and reserved. Iris, beneath this reserve, was fun, less rigid than she seemed. She liked Bobby's exuberance, his extrovert zest for life. One Saturday they danced, and afterwards he walked her home to Cowper Street, which was just around the corner from his home. They were nineteen. Soon they were in love.

Iris Rankin was the second of eight children. Her father Alec was a fitter with Coras Iompair Eireann, the national transport company. Iris was small and slender, almost waif-like, but stronger than she looked. When she left school at sixteen she went to work for Premier Dairies as a wages clerk. She was sacked within a week: the staff had complained that handling the weekly wages was no job for a child. She went to work instead for Kelmac Knitwear as a book-keeper.

Beneath his bluff façade Bobby was sensitive, soft, more than a little romantic. Iris was more fun, less prudish than she seemed. Together they explored Dublin. They went to the pictures in town at the Metropole, the Carlton, the Savoy. They went dancing on Saturdays, often at the Crystal Ballroom across town in South Anne Street. Occasionally they would get a bus in College Green and venture out to Bray to dance at the Arcadia Ballroom. They were happy, in love and more than good companions.

There was only one cloud on the horizon, but it was large, black and unlikely to pass. Bobby was Catholic, Iris Church of Ireland Protestant. They now knew they wanted to marry. Alas, in the Ireland of 1949 the prospect of marriage between Catholic and Protestant was shocking, scandalous even. In both communities. De Valera's Ireland was a Catholic state of just under 3 million people. That that population included 125,000 Protestants, mostly Church of Ireland, was disregarded by Dev's 1937 Constitution in which the Roman Catholic ethos was enshrined. Divorce was not simply illegal, it was unthinkable. Birth control was similarly a heathen practice, not so much forbidden as despised. With such things Protestantism was associated and, on another level, with the Imperialist persecutor, Britain. That many of Ireland's greatest men, from Wolfe Tone to Yeats, from Edmund Burke to Parnell, were Protestant mattered not a whit to the newly ascendant Nationalists. That most of what was glorious in art and literature emanated from the Anglo-Irish tradition made no difference to the Catholic Nationalist ruling class. The God that De Valera eulogized in 1943 was the Catholic God. 'Right living' was Catholic living and that most certainly did not include marriage to Protestants. It couldn't.

Catholic dogma laid down that theirs was *the one true Church*. Only Catholics went to heaven. Only *good* Catholics. In order to ensure your goodness, your fitness to enter the kingdom of God, you made your First Communion when you were seven. When you were eleven you were confirmed. These were special, unforgettable childhood days when you dressed like a prince or, if you were a girl, like a bride. You were afraid yet elated, wondering how it would feel to be made truly holy. After the service you would be taken for a special meal, followed by visits to relations who would fill your pocket or purse with money. From the day of First Communion on you would every week receive the sacraments of confession and holy communion. If you missed a week you'd feel bad. You confessed your sins, bad thoughts (sex), impure actions (sex), stealing, lying or swearing. Every Sunday, and on holy days, of which there were many, you went to mass. You were one of God's flock. Your priest was the shepherd.

Protestants were different. They were *nice*, respectable and decent. But they didn't belong to *the one true Church*. Because of that they were stigmatized in some strangely ill-defined way that nobody ever bothered to figure out. Growing up in

Drumcondra, just up the road from Stoneybatter, in the relatively enlightened sixties, ten or fifteen years after Bobby and Iris, I felt like this about Protestants. Felt rather than thought. Our bigotry was, like our Republicanism, a thing of the heart rather than a rational response, the inevitable consequence of an Irish-Catholic upbringing.

Protestant resentment at all of this was cloaked in politeness. They remained dignified and distant. They were, by and large, better off, more likely to be employed and middle class, although neither of these assumptions could be etched in stone. There were 'Protestant' employers like Guinness and Premier Dairies. There were Protestant enclaves – the Dublin suburbs of Malahide, Dundrum and the Borough of Dun Laoire out towards Bray, parts of rural Ireland, notably the counties of Offaly and Laois – where those not accounted for in De Valera's pastoral vision could draw together to create a sense of community. Their identity they took from their outlawed faith. It found no expression in the constitution of the country they called home. It presumably struck them as ironic that less than one hundred miles away in Northern Ireland the minority community, Catholic and Nationalist, agitated with murderous conviction for its civil rights.

Almost forty years on, the Republic of Ireland's constitution remains deeply sectarian in nature. A half-hearted attempt at reform to allow divorce and re-marriage, undertaken by the rather unconvincingly liberal Taoiseach, Garret Fitzgerald, was rebutted by the people in the 1986 referendum by a majority of two to one. The only constitutional change of recent times has come in relation to abortion, which in accordance with Catholic dogma is now further than ever beyond the reach of Irish women.

Mixed marriages such as the one proposed by Bobby and Iris were rare. The all-pervasive influence of the Catholic Church ensured that from schooldays on, the Catholic and non-Catholic communities lived separate lives. *The one true Church* ran the schools and colleges that 95 per cent of the population attended. In these educational institutions the prevailing ethos was Catholic and was the cornerstone of a curious, distinctly Irish form of apartheid which divided the community along religious lines.

Catholics and non-Catholics spoke the same language, looked alike, read the same newspapers, shopped in the same shops, worked for the same companies and in matters of popular culture music, films, books, sport and the comics read by their children – the two communities were identical. Yet between people who used the same 'piece of ground' to keep their feet from getting wet, people who lived side by side on the same street, there lay the impenetrable barrier of religion.

If, as sometimes happens, a precocious youngster challenged Catholic dogma by posing awkward questions about the alleged differences between *our* God and *theirs*, the child would be referred to the immaculate conception, papal infallibility and, the most damning indictment of all given a Catholic upbringing, the fact that non-Catholics didn't even go to worship *every* Sunday. *They* were different. They didn't accept that Mary, whom we knew as the mother of God, had remained a virgin. Neither did they accept that the Pope was infallible, incapable of error in his pronouncements. These disturbing revelations about non-Catholics were delivered more in sorrow than in anger. Pity rather than hostility was evoked. *They* were good people, *in their own way*. Alas, their way wasn't our way. It wasn't Ireland's way.

That view was propagated everywhere, from constitution to parish school. No politician with real ambition, nor any political party that aspired to govern Ireland, was unmindful of the primacy of the Catholic ethos. The Bishops' writ extended to the most unlikely corners of Irish life. No Catholic could attend Trinity College, Dublin, without first receiving a dispensation from his church to do so. Established in 1591 to train young men for the Protestant ministry, Trinity was now one of the world's most respected seats of learning. Nevertheless, it was deemed by the Catholic hierarchy to be a likely source of contamination for Catholic scholars. Unless granted a special dispensation on the grounds that what Trinity had to offer academically could not be obtained elsewhere – *anywhere in the world* – Catholic students who studied there were automatically excommunicated from their Church. Trinity remained out-of-bounds to Catholic students until 1971, when the government, eager to get a greater return for the grants paid out to the university, and to ease the pressure on the city's only other comparable institution, University College, urged the Catholic Church to reconsider its policy of academic contamination. After some considerable fuss, the hierarchy, mindful of public opinion, gave way.

Bobby Hewson and Iris Rankin guessed that news of their proposed marriage would shock and distress their families and friends. They were right. Oddly enough, it wasn't God who posed the major problem; it was his representatives on earth and, more specifically, his Catholic representatives in Ireland. The distress those who loved Bobby and Iris felt on hearing of their plans was occasioned more by practical considerations than the fear of God. As long as people were decent God would understand, remain on their side. And nobody doubted that Bobby and Iris were decent. The Protestant Church of Ireland was, in the spirit of God, mature enough to trust its people. Or at least to be more trusting, tending towards the view that individual conscience rather than Church law was the ultimate safeguard against sin.

God could be answered and the Church of Ireland appeased, but the Roman Catholic Church had devised a man-made obstacle course designed to intimidate members of its flock who dared to join in holy matrimony with those who did not belong to *the one true Church*. Mixed marriage was permitted, but the Catholic Church's attitude to such union was made clear from the moment they were proposed. The Catholic party would be apprised by his or her priest of the dangers of marrying a non-Catholic. It would be advisable in the interests of preserving one's faith to persuade one's partner to convert to Roman Catholicism. If this advice went unheeded the non-Catholic partner was invited to take a course of instruction in Catholic teaching. This was the kind of invitation you couldn't refuse.

Meanwhile the Catholic partner petitioned the Pope in Rome for permission to marry his or her beloved. Then the non-Catholic was asked to sign a document pledging that the children of this marriage would be raised in the Catholic faith. This procedure was overtly contemptuous of values other than those promoted by the Catholic Church.

But what really troubled Bobby and Iris were the practical, everyday consequences of the love and friendship they shared. Where would they marry and how? Where would their children worship? Where would they go to school? Was marriage not difficult enough without embarking upon it under the added burden of fundamental social and religious differences?

When he realized he was in love, Bobby began to reflect on these and other matters that threatened to undermine the happiness he and Iris had found together. He was at first troubled by the imminent confrontations with family, priests and, indeed, from where he stood in Dublin in 1949, the world at large. Slowly a conviction formed behind his gregarious mask. He *would* marry the woman he loved. *And* he would marry Iris in her own Church – properly. For the fact was that even after the humiliations inflicted on the non-Catholic partner of a mixed-marriage by the preparation for the event, there was one further insult to endure: the ceremony of marriage would take place before an altar bereft of flowers, candles or any other symbols of celebration. The Church would remain dark to signify the

17

Bishop's disapproval of the union. Bobby decided that he would not allow this to happen to Iris.

The wedding day was the woman's day, Bobby thought. It was one day in a lifetime when all should be right, when a girl's dream should come to life. There would be no darkness on the day he married Iris.

Bobby was a more serious man than he seemed. He was a 'character' all right, always at the centre of the crowd, laughing, dancing or sparring verbally with friends and acquaintances alike. But there was a streak of melancholy in him buried beneath the *bonhomie*. Like most young men born and bred in Stoneybatter in the 1920s, 1930s and 1940s the script had been written for Bobby, not by him. Life was about getting a job, marrying a girl, having kids, settling down and dying. In Catholic-Nationalist Ireland how you felt about life's larger questions was likewise determined for you rather than by you. There was little scope for dreaming. Bobby had his job, life was good, but never grand. Melancholy was perhaps a longing for some grandeur, for another script, a larger role to play than the one of Post-Office-Clerk-cum-Saturday-Night-Character. Melancholy was possessing more imagination and sensitivity than could properly be expressed behind a Post Office desk or within the confines of lower-middle-class life in Stoneybatter in the late 1940s.

Dublin, especially the part of the city Bobby lived in, was no place for the artist manqué. The sin of pretentiousness was likely to draw a contemptuous 'Who the fuck does your man think he is?' from the good citizens who had taunted better men than Bobby in their time. If Dubliners could laugh at Shaw, Wilde, Beckett and Joyce, and they did, the Who-The-Fuck rule applied even more ruthlessly to 'yer man down the road'. Long after he was passé to Dublin gurriers, Brendan Behan took his drunken broth-of-a-boy act to London and New York where he was celebrated as a great original. Later on in life, the artist manqué tossing restlessly within Bobby Hewson would emerge as a star of the Musical Society and amateur dramatic groups, and as a part-time dabbler in oil painting.

'Lovely' was the word most often used when people talked about Iris Rankin. Her dark hair and sallow skin gave her a faintly foreign look, but it was her quiet, reserved personality, a stillness about her that amounted almost to serenity, that set Iris apart from other girls around Oxmantown Road. She and Bobby were opposites, intrigued by each other at first, then as time passed each drawing on the other's personality to become more self-assured, more complete. Bobby drew her out, prompted her to laughter, and when Iris laughed, the deep and lusty sound was a delightful surprise. She slowed him down a little, made it seem less important to him to be the centre of attraction.

It was on this new found self-assurance as much as his hardy Dublin spirit that Bobby relied as he braced himself for family and Church reaction to his decision about the wedding. To *marry* a Protestant was one thing, to do so in a Protestant church uniquely defiant. Viewed objectively, in the context of Ireland at that time, Bobby's defiance was generous, courageous, a profound declaration of his love for Iris.

They were married on 6 August 1950 in St John the Baptist Church of Ireland, Church Avenue, Drumcondra. Later on Bobby and Iris were formally blessed by a Catholic priest, thus enabling Bobby to make his peace with his own Church.

They lived in rented accommodation for a few months before buying a house in Stillorgan, six miles out, on the Southside of the Liffey. Norman, their first son, was born two years later. Bobby and Iris made their own pact about how any children they were blessed with would be brought up; the boys would go to the Catholic Church and any girls to the Church of Ireland. But when Norman was born, Bobby thought again.

Iris had the bearing and the rearing of Norman. The relationship between mother and child was important. It would be wrong to separate them on the question of religion, so Norman would go to church with Iris on Sunday mornings, while Bobby went to mass.

They were very happy. Iris was a natural homemaker. She enjoyed cooking, sewing, knitting. She'd go to town occasionally to meet her younger sisters, Ruth and Stella. They'd shop, have morning coffee in Bewley's Café; Iris could hear the latest gossip from the Northside, which she missed. She would always insist on getting home to make Bobby's lunch. 'Don't mind him,' Ruth would tease her. 'Let him get his own lunch.' Iris never would. Bobby joined the drama group that started up in the Post Office. He played golf and began to paint. They still went dancing, often with Ruth and her boyfriend Ted, preferring the great Dublin treat of those innocent years, an ice-cream in Cafollas Ice-Cream Parlour, O'Connell Street, to the drink-induced euphoria of public houses. In the Post Office Bobby had been promoted to the position of survey overseer. Norman was diligent, well behaved and healthy.

Six weeks after Paul was born, Iris and Ruth were out walking the new baby when they came across some houses being built in Ballymun, where Ruth now lived with her new husband, Ted. Happy though she was, Iris still felt drawn to the Northside. She wondered if Bobby would agree to move. He did. They bought 10 Cedarwood Road the following week.

Although only a few minutes' drive from Stoneybatter, Ballymun was on the boundary between countryside and city. Between it and Dublin Airport there were only fields. At the beginning of the 1960s Ireland was edging towards prosperity. The old fear of unemployment, which dated back to the twenties and before, receded now. There was more work, the money was better. Skilled tradesmen, shopkeepers, the humblest of the white-collar workers, all could now aspire to homeownership. A ribbon of housing developments began to appear around Dublin and its established suburbs. The houses were three-bedroomed, semi-detached with a garden back and front. The new suburbs would have shops, schools and churches. The suburban dream was of space and cleanliness, of family life lived decently, away from the dirt and noise of the city, away from the public-house temptations. The promise of Cedarwood Road, Oak Drive and Willow Park was of a better life in the better world that seemed to spread before them.

Paul was a cranky baby. He cried most of the day. Peace only settled on the new house after he went to bed where, exhausted from the trauma of his waking hours, he slept long and soundly. Iris tried all known methods to still the noise coming from the cot. Her sister Ruth would come over to lend a hand. Onagh Byrne, a sympathetic neighbour from two doors along, was also enlisted to help pacify Paul. Norman, who was now a sensible eight-year-old, often walked his young brother around the block to give Iris a break.

Iris was sure there was something wrong. *Nobody* would cry like that just for attention. When he was two, Iris took Paul to Dr Lee Kidney, a noted specialist at Crumlin Children's Hospital. Dr Kidney couldn't find anything wrong with his young patient but suggested he stay in hospital for a week for observation. The good news, seven days later, was that Paul was healthy and normal. The bad news was that he was unlikely to stop seeking attention.

Bobby had bought a small car, an NSU Prinz. Arriving home from work at six o'clock, he would sit outside in the car reading his evening newspaper because he knew there would be no peace inside until Paul was in bed.

World news appeared good in 1963. John F. Kennedy, the young American president, of Irish descent, had come to symbolize a new age of peace, justice and prosperity. The gap between the goodness in ordinary people's hearts and the policies of world leaders seemed narrower than ever before. In Britain, Labour leader Harold Wilson promised to end thirteen years of Conservative rule. There would be a new Britain, Wilson pledged, 'forged in the white-hot heat of technological revolution'. In anticipation of a better time to come, Britain began to swing to the sound of the Beatles, whose youth, irreverence and provincial working-class background were deemed real and therefore good. The social divisions based on class that had paralysed Britain would be no more. The new aristocracy would be talented, imaginative and, above all, open to people and ideas from all classes and educational backgrounds. The old ruling élite had had its day.

In the United States, racism was being confronted by President Kennedy and his brother Robert, the Attorney-General. The administration had declared its intention to lease power to America's 'best and brightest' men and women who would tackle injustice in the darkest corners of the world's largest democracy.

Because Kennedy was of Irish descent and Catholic, Ireland could readily identify with the global mood. There were other good reasons too for native optimism. Pope John XXIII's Second Vatican Council hinted that on matters such as birth control and ecumenism, the Roman Church might in future be more sensitive to the everyday concerns of its people. The grace of God seemed, in 1963, within reach of those to whom it mattered. The Irish government, led by Taoiseach Sean Lemass, had placed economic prosperity at the top of the national agenda. Jobs and houses for the people rather than the old Nationalist dream of a United Ireland, about which he was decidedly agnostic, were the planks upon which Lemass built his political platform. In 1963 the IRA was an anachronism. Whilst a United Ireland was still the declared aspiration of all Irish political parties, they agreed that unity would have to be achieved by peaceful means. In reality, the Irish Republican Army's *raison d'être* was not on the political agenda for the 1960s. Understanding this and acknowledging their increasing isolation from the public, north and south, many of the movement's more enlightened warriors talked of abandoning the armed struggle and entering parliamentary politics. Those who continued to believe in the gun numbered fewer than one hundred, fanatics with rusty pre-war weapons which served as relics of a lost cause. Violent revolution was a spiritual cul-de-sac down which the Irish people refused to go.

The world was an optimistic place that summer of 1963. There was reason to believe that the good guys were winning. All the solutions had yet to be found but the rhetoric was fine, the heroes convincing. As well as the Kennedys, Pope John and Harold Wilson, there were others, like Martin Luther King, Bob Dylan and Muhammad Ali, crusaders in search of truth, beauty and justice for all. In June 1963, Jack Kennedy visited Ireland, conferring on the country a glorious sense of participation in world events. The president arrived at Dublin Airport on a dull, warm June evening. His motorcade made its way into the city along the main Drumcondra Road. Tanned and handsome, with a wide and gracious smile, he was welcomed 'home' by tens of thousands. As he frequently reminded the nation in the days ahead, he was one of us. And thus we could feel our small island to be the fount of the wisdom, courage and beauty America's young president now personified.

Bobby Hewson took Norman and Paul down to the main road to see Kennedy pass by in his open-topped car. Paul at three had stopped crying all day and was now talking. He was a funny little fellow, Bobby thought. One evening that summer he watched Paul in the back garden. The boy was probing a bush, talking away to himself. When Bobby moved closer he was startled to see a bee crawling along Paul's open palm. He shouted a warning, saying he would be stung. 'No, it's all right, Dad,' Paul smiled. 'I've made friends with him.'

By the time Paul was ready to go to school the following year, Norman was ready to move on to high school, the prestigious Protestant Secondary School. Norman was a good lad, bright, conscientious academically, obedient and helpful in the house. If you asked him to run upstairs and get your hairbrush he'd be back with it in thirty seconds. If you asked Paul, he'd wander down ten minutes later. 'Where's my brush?' you'd ask. 'Brush?' Paul would enquire. 'What brush?' He seemed to live in a world of his own much of the time. When he wasn't daydreaming, he was rummaging about the house, asking questions and generally sticking his nose into Bobby and Norman's business.

Paul started school at Glasnevin National School, Botanic Avenue, Glasnevin. As he had with Norman, Bobby had decided Iris should raise Paul in the Protestant faith. Glasnevin was a Protestant primary school, a ten-minute bus ride from Cedarwood Road. Had he been Catholic, Paul would have gone to the local national school in Ballymun along with the other kids on Cedarwood. Thus, subtly, quietly, undramatically, the separating process of Irish apartheid began to work. You were a 'Proddy', somehow different, even if you lived next door.

This made no difference to Bobby and Iris. Theirs was a mixed marriage, so they had a foot in both camps. Iris's best friend, Onagh Byrne, in No. 14 Cedarwood, was Catholic. They never spoke about religion, never really thought about it. Still, it was there lying around in the background, visible only on Sunday mornings when they went to worship. Paul played in the street with Mrs Byrne's boys who were around his age. The fields behind the houses, rough and open, were a marvellous playground. There was menace and mystery among the hills and hollows, wild scrub and hedges. The local shops at the end of Cedarwood provided an alternative source of adventure.

Paul relished street life. No sooner was he home from school and fed by Iris than he would be off, not to be seen again until dusk or tea-time, whichever came first. Paul was a scamp, engrossed in the melodrama that awaited him outside the front door of No. 10 Cedarwood Road. In the house Iris was his ally and protector. Because of the almost eight-year gap between them, the Hewson brothers lived separate lives. They had different interests, different friends and different temperaments. Norman listened to Bobby, Paul didn't or at least didn't pay attention. Norman didn't lose his school-books. Norman stayed quiet while Bobby relaxed with his record-player in the evenings. Paul sang along, or otherwise intruded. Bobby was a stern father. He liked to be obeyed, and he would occasionally banish Paul from the room. Paul would linger, try to have the last word. One night Bobby lost his cool, picked the scamp up and physically removed him from the room. All went quiet. Ten minutes later Bobby left his armchair to investigate – and there just outside the living room door lay a banana skin, left by Paul, who lurked in the shadows of the hall waiting patiently for his dad to slide to defeat. At such moments Iris would plead on Paul's behalf. Bobby and Norman loved him, but he could be a bloody nuisance after a hard day working or studying. To Iris he was deeply affectionate, lovable, vulnerable on account of the trust he placed in the world at large and the zest he possessed for adventure, discovery and stimulation. Physically short and sturdy, vital and intense of spirit, Paul was, Iris felt, not unlike the man she'd met years ago on Oxmantown Road.

Each Sunday morning the family set off to worship in their separate ways. They went by car, Bobby dropping Iris and the boys outside St Canice's Church of Ireland before heading off alone to eleven o'clock mass at St Canice's Catholic Church.

When their service was over Bobby would be sitting outside waiting to take them home. Paul felt detached from the Protestant community. They were slightly posher, a little bit more reserved, somehow High, a bit more stylish than he felt himself and his family to be. He felt Catholic among Protestants, he felt a bit rougher, a bit less together than they seemed to be. Among Catholics he was similarly estranged, knowing that school and Church rendered him separate, different from the other kids on the road. The Hewson family's Sunday morning ritual gave form and substance to the vague but constant feeling of separateness Paul grew up with. Sunday prompted the questions: *What was he? Where did he belong?* That you were identified socially as well as spiritually by the church you attended served only to compound Paul's confusion.

As part of a radical housing initiative to clear some of the worst inner-city slums in Europe, the Irish government built Ballymun Flats in 1967. The site chosen was the green space behind Cedarwood Road. This attempt to find an instant solution to a problem that was many decades old was not welcomed by the existing community, who feared for the verdant character of their pleasant suburb. The government planned to create a satellite village, housing several thousand people from the worst city slums, in seven tower-block apartment buildings. The arrival of bulldozers, cranes and building workers in the fields behind Cedarwood brought a new and vastly entertaining dimension to the lives of seven-year-old Paul and his pals.

He was a popular but somewhat elusive playmate. He was as curious about people as about everything else. This led to restlessness, a tendency to flit from friend to friend, group to group. Thus he discovered the Rowens who lived around the corner, a rumbustious, unruly family of Plymouth Brethren, a Protestant sect characterized by extreme simplicity of belief. The Brethren based their faith on a literal interpretation of the Bible, and in an Irish context the Rowens constituted an alien presence.

Paul became best friends with Derek Rowen. Derek was blond, bright, sharp of feature and of mind. The bond of friendship which Paul and Derek formed owed much to their mutual feeling of not quite belonging to the conventional suburban community in which they lived. Nourished in the hardy environment of his large family – there were eleven Rowens plus mum and dad – Derek was unusually independent. If his and Paul's separateness was rooted in their religious backgrounds, it also extended to other things. They laughed at the idea of football, a consuming passion for other kids. Bare, hairy legs chasing a ball around amused Paul and Derek greatly. They discovered that they shared an interest in messing about with paints, and many a sunny summer day they would sit in Paul's garage drawing and painting. Sometimes they would head off over the fields to the flats on an adventure. Derek's older brother, Clive, often led these expeditions. Clive was renowned for his rap and organizational abilities. He was given the name 'Clive Whistling Fella' and later 'Clive Jive' by Derek.

The Rowens' house became a second home to Paul. Amid the chaos created by eleven children in a small three-up, two-down house, his own foibles went unheeded. There was always someone to talk to and to listen. On his tenth birthday Paul chose Derek to accompany him downtown to the pictures to see *Butch Cassidy and the Sundance Kid*. Cinemas were out of bounds to members of the Plymouth Brethren, but Derek's mother turned a blind eye on the strict understanding that Mr Rowen wouldn't find out. Robbie Rowen worked for Ever Ready at that time. He was a stern advocate of the Brethren's beliefs, which he was perfectly happy to explain to young Hewson, who pumped him for information. The established Churches were more interested in power and their position in the world than in God, Mr Rowen argued. Worldliness and all the other trappings of religious worship came between man and his Creator. Jesus was within all of us, accessible to all of us. The rituals, paraphernalia and interdenominational strife with which the orthodox Churches were obsessed, were man-made obstacles to real devotion. The word of God was written in the Bible, and that alone should be our guide. Mr Rowen went on to explain the politics of the Reformation and what had followed. All this blew Paul's mind. The rules and re-gulations that bound his own life, the hassle with different schools and separate churches on Sundays, the whole Catholic–Protestant thing, seemed absurd in the light of what Robbie Rowen was saying. He would air the subject at home.

When Paul tried to enlighten the folks at No. 10 he was told to get upstairs and do his homework. At home he was still the kid, at least to Bobby and to Norman, who was now working and was taken seriously by his father. The distance between Paul and his dad and older brother was too great. To them he was a kid, and the Rowens were, to put it politely, eccentric. Any discussion about God and the meaning of life would have to wait until Paul tidied himself up, got a bit more organized, and concentrated somewhat more than he had been doing on the here and now. Disdain was not the word.

Paul's increasingly unconstitutional behaviour apart, 10 Cedarwood Road was a haven of suburban contentment. Bobby and Iris were as much in love as ever after twenty-one years of marriage. Leaving Norman and Paul with Iris's sister Ruth, they still snatched an occasional holiday together. Bobby played golf on Saturday mornings. He still performed with the Musical Society and in amateur dramatics during their seasons. He had his collection of records and his painting. Onagh Byrne, from her house, could often hear Bobby singing lustily in the Hewsons' bathroom. Of his strained relationship with Paul it could be said that Bobby, like most Irish fathers of his gener-ation, felt that eleven year olds should be seen and not heard.

Iris was, similarly, in the Irish tradition of the woman as

homemaker. She understood her three men better than they understood each other. Emotionally, physically, psychologically, she was the provider of comfort and reassurance. She put herself last: Iris was a giver. What she gave was stability. She spent a lot of time with Ruth, shopping in town or gossiping about her men or just the family in general. She was in the Mothers'. Union. On summer weekends she and the family would go out to Rush on the Co. Dublin coast where the Rankins owned a beach chalet. Altogether, she was completely content with family life.

Unlike Norman and Bobby, Iris was interested in Paul, his notions, desires, ambitions. She understood his frustrations. In the summer of 1971 Paul was facing up to another crisis. He had just finished primary school in Glasnevin. After the holidays he was bound for St Patrick's Secondary School in the city. The school was set in the shadow of St Patrick's, the more austere of Dublin's two Protestant cathedrals, built in 1190 by John Comyn, the first Englishman to become Archbishop of Dublin. The history didn't impress Paul. He wanted to go to high school as Norman had done. But Norman had won a scholarship. The fees, Bobby explained, were too expensive, and anyway the High School had now moved to Dartry, a few miles further south out on the Southside. Paul would have to take two buses. St Pat's was a perfectly good school. That was that.

Paul had done well at Glasnevin National School. He'd finished second in his class. He was bright, well behaved, though untidy. After school he would hang around in Griffith Park, just along Botanic Avenue from the school, a gathering-place for Drumcondra kids. There were various little scenes involving girls, smoking, music and sport in Tolka. Paul hung out with the music gang. The one advantage of having an older brother was the musical sophistication that accrued from listening to Norman's records. Most of his contemporaries were into pop music but Paul, thanks to Norman's good taste, could talk with authority about the heavy stuff. He dropped names like Jimi Hendrix, Keith Moon and Pete Townshend. The older guys were suitable impressed.

St Patrick's had nothing to offer him – not the whiff of low-life he scented in Griffith Park nor the style and elegance of thoroughbred Protestantism that, with his perpetual feeling of being rougher, more gauche, less polished, High School had promised to bestow on him. St Patrick's was, he discerned, for not-so-posh Protestants. He resented that. At first he tried to make it work. He didn't like sport but he volunteered for football and hockey. His powerful physique made him useful on the football field. He preferred chess, which he'd persuaded Bobby to teach him. For a while he really got into chess. Beating Bobby inspired him to go on. He played for Ballymun in the Community Games. They finished second in an All-Ireland tournament. He joined a chess club and competed in a junior international competition in Wesley College, a distinctly posh educational establishment. But the problem with chess was its solitary nature. He had to travel across the city alone. It separated him from his pals. Although his accomplished playing gave Paul's confidence a much needed boost, chess, cerebral and time-consuming, wasn't really the answer. Neither was St Patrick's.

At Glasnevin Paul had been a big fish in a small pond. At St Pat's he was Hewson. Nobody took much notice of him. He started missing classes, going on the 'mitch' for the day. He would scrounge money from the American tourists who came in coaches to visit the cathedral. With a few bob in his pocket he would spend the rest of the school day wandering round the shops and coffee bars in the Grafton Street–Stephen's Green area. By sneaking days off or heading back to Griffith Park after school on the days he consented to attend, Paul maintained his links with the past. He pretended St Pat's wasn't happening. His body was there but not his mind. He did not work in class.

The lady who taught Spanish was particularly contemptuous of him, ignoring him much of the time. She would look at his work and, showing no emotion, strike lines through his copy, handing it back to him without comment, without even looking at him. At lunchtime she used to take her sandwiches to the Cathedral Park, out of bounds to the students. One day Paul, resentment smouldering, followed her. Hiding behind a bush, he threw dog-shit at his tormentor. He was caught. He wasn't expelled, but no tears were shed by the school authorities when it was learnt that he wouldn't be returning for the 1972–3 academic year.

Paul had heard about Mount Temple, and Bobby had read about it in the newspapers. Mount Temple made headlines in the summer of 1972 because it was about to open its doors as the first comprehensive, non-denomination, co-education school in Dublin. As such it was radical, exciting and, in the context of Irish education, suspect. Education in Ireland was about something more than learning. School, it was said, was a preparation for life: the kind of life *they* wanted you to lead. Thus, Catholics should receive a Catholic education. Irish speakers should receive an Irish-speaking education. Boys should be given a manly education. Girls, the kind of education that would ensure they made good wives and mothers. The middle and upper classes should be trained to lead (and, of course, serve). The rest should be given the bare minimum of education, enough to enable them to participate in the process without necessarily understanding how it worked. The Catholic Church was, not surprisingly, deeply involved in and committed to the Irish educational system. The kids were theirs. As the Jesuits were fond of boasting, 'Give me a child until it is seven and it is mine for life.' Parents really couldn't be trusted with the task of inculcating their children with sufficient quantities of the Right Stuff.

Thus, religious, cultural and social divisions in Irish society were perpetuated in the classroom. Mount Temple proposed to be different. Here distinctions would be blurred, barriers removed. Here people would receive education rather than indoctrination. Here boy would sit next to girl, the academically inclined would co-exist with those whose talents were more practical. Here the professor's son from middle-class Howth would share a book with the tradesman's daughter from the unvarnished suburb of Donnycarney. And, most critically in this educational oasis, Catholic and Protestant would learn side by side under the one roof.

At Mount Temple you would check your prejudices in at the gate each morning. Maybe you would collect them again on the way out at three o'clock, but sectarian ideas about class, sexuality and religion were not, as elsewhere in Ireland, reinforced by the Mount Temple experience.

Bobby Hewson, who knew more about bigotry than most, took little persuading that Mount Temple was the right place for his volatile younger son. Apart from its ecumenical spirit, the new school was only a couple of miles along Griffith Avenue, through the old suburbs of Whitehall and Marino on the Malahide Road. The site had been occupied by Mountjoy, a Protestant boys' public school which had been struggling to fill its classrooms for years. In De Valera's Ireland, 5 per cent of the population had been Protestant. By 1972 that figure had been reduced to somewhere between 3 and 4 per cent. There were fewer Protestants because they, unlike their Catholic neighbours, used contraceptives to regulate the size of their families. Of those Protestants who were born, many had fallen in love with Catholics and, succumbing to pressure from the *one true Church*, had abandoned their own faith to convert to Catholicism. Hence the core of Mount Temple was formed by the amalgamation of four Protestant schools: Mountjoy, Marine, Bertrand and Russell.

Not much of this registered with thirteen-year-old Paul. The all-embracing religious and social nature of the new school appealed to him. But it was the fact that he could make a fresh start at Mount Temple that mattered most. He was in many respects a happy kid, loved and healthy, popular socially. His family enjoyed a prosperity that, though relatively modest, was real in comparison to life in the Ballymun Flats that lay behind Cedarwood Road, or the vast working-class housing-estate of Finglas that sprawled away to the west of old Ballymun. Materially Paul was secure, indeed, so secure and unconcerned that he frequently forgot to ask Bobby for his pocket-money.

What bothered him was more personal, had to do with spirit and imagination rather than the quality of his life. There was a vague feeling of not belonging that in his more reflective moments, when it couldn't be camouflaged by the activity of daily life, grew quite acute. He wasn't Catholic like his dad, nor yet did he possess the cool, detached style of the Protestants he encountered when he went to church with Iris on Sundays. He remembered getting a lift to church once in the car of some Protestant friends, feeling somehow rough, uncouth – dirty almost. Socially he liked his Catholic neighbours, Mrs Byrne and her sons, enjoyed being in their house and playing with the boys. But he knew, *felt*, that in matters of the spirit there was a cut-off point somewhere, at the juncture where life became serious, personal. The same was true of the Rowens whose radical Protestantism intrigued him, but wasn't his. Spiritually Paul existed in a twilight world somewhere between the Catholicism of the Byrnes and the Protestantism of the Rowens. Not a Catholic like Bobby, nor the kind of Protestant Iris was. Even at home he was the odd man out, the kid who wouldn't conform.

Whilst in the house Paul was willing if not quite able to fight his corner; outside he kept a watching brief. He adapted to the circumstances he found himself in, to the people he was with. To the Byrnes, the Rowens, the streetwise gang in Griffith Park, he was Paul – charming, amusing, curious and, when he mimicked teachers, parents and others who didn't understand, very funny. All of this was fine, yet there was, nagging and constant, a sense of not belonging, of being the outsider spiritually and socially.

While Paul had been growing up, Ireland had experienced brutal change, so that when he entered Mount Temple in 1972, the nation was itself in turmoil. The IRA was in business again, the national question once more on the agenda. Sean Lemass was dead. Buried with him was the concept of rapprochement between Republican South and Unionist North which had briefly flourished in the previous decade when, reflecting the universal optimism of the 1960s, the two historically irreconcilable traditions had for a while found common ground. Lemass had repudiated his Republican-Nationalist rump.

The moderate face of Northern Unionism was personified by Captain Terence O'Neill, Northern Ireland's prime minister, who responded to Lemass and the spirit of the age by acknowledging the deeply sectarian nature of the province he ruled. O'Neill promised reforms which would be designed to end discrimination against Catholics in housing, employment and schooling. O'Neill further declared his intention of doing something about the gerrymandering of the electoral register, by which Nationalists were denied fair representation in the Northern Ireland Parliament at Stormont. Tragically, Terence O'Neill's promises amounted to political suicide. He couldn't deliver his Unionist Party, which was as unwilling to concede what it held as the Catholic Church was down south. O'Neill was unceremoniously deposed. But the ugly essence of Unionism had been exposed to the light. Catholics and Nationalists and many who in their hearts were neither had been reminded that Northern Ireland *was* a Protestant state. Civil rights groups took to the streets where they were brutally beaten by the Protestant police force *and* the more extreme Protestant citizens whose mandate came from the highest authority. There would be no surrender to civil rights. This message was viciously underlined by the mobs of policemen who pursued the civil-rights marchers into the Catholic ghettos of Derry, Belfast and Newry.

It was as the defender of civil rights and those who espoused them that the I R A now emerged, its ranks swollen to overflowing by young men and women outraged by Unionist brutality. The British army arrived as peacemakers and as such were, fleetingly, acclaimed. But the reality was that the army would in the final analysis defend the status quo. The status quo was Protestant Unionism, fundamentally sectarian. Evil was institutionalized, as in the south it was constitutionalized.

The injustice and oppression in the North infected the whole island. Lemass's mood of conciliation was by 1972 but a bitter memory. It was time again for those less forgiving, those who had told Ireland so, those who were truly, patriotically, indubitably Irish to reassert their claims as to what was, and was not, Irishness. Hatred of the English, their soldiers, their language, their culture and their religions was fundamental to the embittered, narrow Nationalism that was now surfacing once again in Irish life.

Nothing reflected the new mood so eloquently as a spontaneous outburst of hatred directed against the English in Dublin on 1 February 1971. The previous day in Derry, the British army's notorious Parachute Regiment had opened fire on a march marking the first anniversary of internment without trial, which allowed the indiscriminate arrest and imprisonment of hundreds of able-bodied Nationalists for no good reason other than that they were able bodied. Nationalist, in thought if not in deed, and in their homes when the 'Security Forces' arrived. Thirteen people, most of them innocent, died in the

Bogside on Bloody Sunday. The following night the British Embassy in Merrion Square, Dublin, was burnt to the ground. This act was committed not by the IRA but by several thousand ordinary Dubliners inflamed by the slaughter of the previous afternoon. The national wound was open once again, its bitter pus seeping into the nation's psyche, poisoning mind and spirit. Old rebel songs were sung again, new ones composed. North and South, old IRA men came in from the cold, and new recruits were born by the minute.

The sacking of the British Embassy was an aberration, albeit one that nourished Nationalist fantasies of the people rising to drive the English out of Ireland. Alas, in Ballymun as elsewhere in urban Ireland, including Derry and west Belfast, daily life precluded such simplistic solutions. People continued to read Fleet Street tabloids, watch British television, laugh at Jimmy Tarbuck and Benny Hill, dance to David Bowie, Mick Jagger and The Who and take vicarious pleasure, as they did in London, Birmingham and Manchester, in the goings-on behind closed doors at Buckingham Palace. If anti-Englishness was a fundamental part of being Irish, then we had an identity problem of epic proportions.

In many respects life in the part of Ireland Paul Hewson lived in remained unchanged. The people of Cedarwood, indeed the overwhelming majority of people in the Republic of Ireland, could distinguish between British government policy, which was, it was felt, callous, indolent and stupid, and the English people, who were, it was also felt, innately decent.

If socially things remained as they had been, there were nevertheless changes politically and culturally throughout Ireland as a result of the Ulster troubles. There were more armed robberies of banks and post offices, to fund the IRA's war of liberation in the North. Charles J. Haughey, the cabinet minister who had been tried and found not guilty of sanctioning arms shipments to the IRA in 1970, now began to tour the nation in search of rehabilitation. His speeches to the diehard rump of his Republican Fianna Fail Party were in code. Everyone knew where Charlie stood. The songs sung at closing time in Dublin pubs were not coded. The hymns were to the IRA and the glorious war they waged with bomb and bullet. That the IRA was a terrorist organization, that within its ranks you were as likely to find the psychopath as the idealist, the gangster as the well-meaning fool, was a point of view you did well to keep to yourself at closing time. Despite the sub-human nature of many IRA atrocities, the drilling of holes in people's legs, the 'justice' of the kangaroo courts, the bombs in department stores and railway stations, the slaughter of innocent men before watching families, despite the unspeakable evil of these crimes, the IRA was worming its way into Ireland's political process. Through Sinn Fein, its political front, it took positions on a wide range of issues from trade unionism to housing, health and education. The hideous violence of Ulster was thus cloaked in political respectability. This illusion was aided and abetted by the closing-time songs which evoked the glorious past rather than the vicious present. Wolfe Tone and the heroes of 1916, Pearse and Connolly were summoned up in pub ballads to confer legitimacy on the evil of the here and now. If most of the new generation at whom the IRA propaganda was aimed resisted its emotive appeal, many extended sympathy if not outright support to the born again cause of Irish freedom. It was virtually impossible to be young and impressionable in the 1970s and not be, to a greater or lesser extent, infected by the virus of violent Republicanism.

Was it really right to stand idly by while Nationalists in the North were discriminated against, imprisoned and tortured? What kind of Irishman were you? Where did you stand in relation to Ireland's history, culture, traditions, if you turned your back on the Republican movement? Whither the modern Irishman in relation to his country's ancient struggle for freedom? Was he, were *you*, denying the centuries of oppression, Cromwell's brutality, the Famine, the wanton terror of the Black and Tans? Were *you*, with your David Bowie music, your insatiable appetite for alien culture of all descriptions, betraying your heritage and the tens of thousands who had died that you should live? Those questions now confronted a new generation. No young man or woman of reason could avoid reflecting upon them.

Mount Temple didn't disappoint Paul. It was different, an oasis of tolerance where what God you believed in didn't matter any more than where your father worked. To be a success you needed only to be bright and attractive. You wore no school uniform, a symbolic gesture of individuality. The regime was enlightened, willing to listen as well as teach. Things were discussed, ideas promoted. Mount Temple was, in every way, a larger institution than any Paul had previously inhabited.

Emotionally and intellectually he absorbed everything he brushed against. Like human blotting paper he sucked up every idea, every nuance of religion, culture and personality that floated along the corridors of this classless village. He acquitted himself well academically. In subjects he was interested in, like history and English, he flourished. He was exceptionally good at art, a keen contributor to Albert Bradshaw's music class. Socially Paul was in his element as never before. He formed a close friendship with Reggie Manuel, a Protestant neighbour from Ballymun. Reggie was a cool cat, handsome, well dressed, smart. He possessed that Protestant poise Paul had so long admired and envied. Reggie had a girlfriend, Zandra Laing, daughter of the Rev. Laing, Vicar of St Canice's, the church Paul attended with his mum on Sundays. Zandra had long legs, wore mini-skirts and was desired by just about every boy in the school.

The corridor that ran the length of Mount Temple was known as The Mall. Here at lunch-time or between classes students promenaded, gossiping, meeting friends, glaring at enemies. Pretty girls were admired, fellas who fancied themselves projected. Paul, Reggie, Cheryl Gillard, Paul's first-year girlfriend, Mark Holmes and Shane Fogarty formed their own little clique and soon established a presence in The Mall. On this natural stage Paul was in his element. There was always a buzz when he was around. He was always making some move or other, very often in the direction of girls. Although he had Cheryl, he was more than a little interested in Zandra, his friendship with Reggie notwithstanding. He hatched a plot to draw him and Reggie's desirable girlfriend closer together. Paul proposed to open his own disco-club in the old schoolhouse at St Canice's. The Rev. Laing agreed to make the schoolhouse available. Paul christened his new venture The Web. Paul was the spider, Zandra the fly. Paul was in charge. He organized and played the music, turning in a superb impression of a trans-Atlantic D J. Very soon Reggie was yesterday's man. Zandra was Paul's first serious girlfriend.

Women had always been drawn to Paul. Long before Zandra, the mothers of Cedarwood would notice him more than other youngsters. He wasn't especially good-looking and his wiry body was anything but graceful, but there was an intensity about him that reached women, who could see beyond the cheeky smile and sense the lonely, gentle boy inside.

Maeve O'Regan arrived at Mount Temple at the beginning of Paul's second school year in September 1973. Maeve was a striking girl, tall, dark-haired, green-eyed, very beautiful. She was a Catholic sent to Mount Temple by her father who believed in the concept of non-denominational education. She was academically brilliant; she wore jeans and pretty blouses; she didn't wear a bra; she personified sophistication to the watching eyes on The Mall. Maeve noticed Paul, and didn't like him. He was loud, obvious, socially promiscuous, trying it on with every girl in sight, including her. He got nowhere. But she did note his group. They were good-looking boys, all except Paul, who resembled the amusing runt of the breed. They were obviously among the social hierarchy of their year. There was an *esprit de corps* among them that was seductive: they looked like the clique to join.

By this time Paul's affair with Zandra was running out of steam. Soon he was to lose her to Keith Darling, who was older and cooler than Paul and indifferent to the smart-ass dandies on The Mall. Paul didn't mind losing Zandra since Maeve was the object of his intensity these days, but he minded losing out to Darling, who, with the passionate Zandra on his arm, would have all the more reason to look down on Paul. It took Paul two terms to break down Maeve's resistance. To do so he employed the full range of his personal gifts. Maeve found herself laughing at his jokes. He had the great actors' gift for mimicry, capturing the vital inflection of voice or movement to lay bare the pretensions of those teachers or rivals like Keith Darling who incurred his displeasure. His use of language was deft, his images vivid. In Sophie Shirley's religious education class Paul used his superior knowledge of the subject to impress his peers, especially Maeve: it was a subject in which he was considerably advanced. Sophie Shirley was a dedicated teacher, her classroom a forum for ideas. She talked about real belief in Christian ethics, about the gap between Christ and the Churches that represented him. Paul challenged her. Articulately, passionately, knowledgeably. He was the devil's advocate. Maeve was suitably impressed. There was more to Paul than the gadfly of Mall reputation. This was confirmed in the art and music classes where his sensitivity was obvious. In the more academic subjects Paul was beginning to fall behind his brightest contemporaries, for when it came to regular schoolwork Paul was hopelessly disorganized. He turned this to his advantage with Maeve.

On Tuesday mornings they had a double art class. They

would sit together talking about life, music, art. He was always soulful yet funny, and she appreciative of the dexterity of his mind, his way with words and images. After art they would spend the fifteen-minute break together. The next class was science where Maeve was ahead of him. She would pass him the answers to Mr Fox's questions. He would write her gracious, amusing letters of thanks. Their friendship grew and deepened as the school year drew to a close. His reputation in The Mall was greatly enhanced by his 'capture', the more so for his refusal to boast about it. There was in fact little of a physical nature to boast about. The bonds between Maeve and Paul were spiritual and intellectual rather than physical. Maeve was in control of that side of things and Paul in private was too much of a gentleman, besides being too respectful, to force the issue.

His empathy with women was linked directly to his close relationship with Iris. Paul did what a boy has to do on the street, in school, in any group or circumstance he found himself in. But the tenderness that was fundamental to his nature cried out for something more than the macho posturing he managed so easily to affect. This he knew about himself, so he protected his girlfriends, never betrayed them, didn't break the confidences they shared, even while flitting elusively between them.

In the summer of 1974 Paul felt happier, more confident than ever before. If Mount Temple had not provided everything he was looking for, it had helped him come to terms with himself. If he didn't yet see clearly the road ahead, he had lost that sense of not belonging. Mount Temple was catholic in the best sense of the word, emphasizing what people had in common rather than what in terms of culture, class or religion lay between them.

That year Bobby took Iris to Rome for their summer holiday. Paul went to Criccieth in North Wales to summer camp with the 'Bee Dees'. The Boys Department was the youth section of

the Young Men's Christian Association. Occasionally Paul
went with Derek and Trevor Rowen to a Sunday Bible-study
class at the YMCA in Lower Abbey Street. This was more a
social than biblical event. Attendance qualified you for the Bee
Dees' Summer Camp, held each summer in some distant part
of the British Isles. The boys pitched tent close to the beach,
attended Bible class in the morning and spent the rest of the
day enjoying themselves. At Criccieth Paul had a passionate
holiday romance with a girl from the local village. When Paul
left to return home he promised Mandy he would be back, a
promise he was to keep three years later.

In the first week of September Iris's family gathered to
celebrate her parents' fiftieth wedding anniversary. They had a
splendid night out with dinner and dancing. The following day
her father died. He'd been in great spirits the night before, and
so his death was a particularly terrible shock. Iris was hit very
badly. He was buried at the Military Cemetery in Blackhorse
Avenue. Mourners noticed how frail Iris looked at the cemetery. She held tightly to Bobby and Ruth. As they walked
back to the cars, Iris collapsed with a brain haemorrhage.
Norman drove her to the Mater Hospital where at first the
prognosis was encouraging. As they waited for news in Ruth's
house, Paul read his Bible. God, he decided, wouldn't let his
Ma die – but she did, four days later, on 10 September 1974.
Norman, Paul and Bobby arrived back at Ruth's house from
the Mater, the two boys either side of Bobby, the three of them
supporting each other as they walked up the tiny driveway.
Their world had lurched suddenly, violently, irrevocably out
of focus.

After the funeral Paul went to his bedroom. He had lost his
champion, his refuge, the one person who believed in him.
What was soothing and gentle was gone. Onagh Byrne, downstairs with Bobby, Norman and the grieving family, heard the
sound of a guitar strumming upstairs.

Mrs Byrne was never again to hear Bobby singing in the bathroom. He reacted stoically to the loss of the woman he had loved with such commitment and courage. They could manage, he told Ruth, who, grieving herself at the double loss of father and sister, offered whatever practical help she could give. Paul echoed his father's sentiment: he and Norman would look after Dad.

Bobby drew up a system that would ensure that 10 Cedarwood Road functioned. Each of the three would take responsibility for an allocation of household chores. In this way beds would be made, the house cleaned and vacuumed, the washing and cooking done. He pinned a list of duties on the kitchen door. Paul would receive dinner money every day to buy his food after school. They would manage by sharing the burden. First they had to discover how to work the washing-machine.

Paul went back to Mount Temple. He was subdued for a while, not quite his old self, but you'd have to look closely to see it. He confided only in Maeve. He joined the Christian Union at the school. The house he went back to in the afternoons was empty and silent, with Bobby and Norman still at work. Paul would turn on the television for company. In the kitchen he'd find a saucepan, open a tin of beans, or corned beef, throw it in a dish, get the powdered potato, 'Smash', and pour boiling water onto it. The money Bobby had given him for steak he would spend on his friends down at the shops in the evening. As autumn 1974 turned to winter, Paul knew that life would never again be the same in this house. Without Iris it was empty.

Chapter Two

ADAM'S STORY

Larry Mullen got no immediate response to the note he pinned on the school notice-board in autumn 1976. Dave Evans made a polite inquiry as to what it was all about. But there was no rush, so Larry decided to push things along a bit by approaching Adam Clayton. Adam had only been in Mount Temple a couple of months but he had made an impact on students and teachers alike.

The first thing people noticed was Adam's clothes. He was a hippy. He wore caftans, a shaggy fur coat he'd picked up in Afghanistan and shades. But this was the punk era, and the gear Adam was sporting was the kind of stuff that had been fashionable five or six years previously. He seemed exotic, a bit of a card. He did very little schoolwork. He seemed to be at Mount Temple for the 'crack' – for fun. He drank coffee from a flask during lessons: just got it out, poured it and drank it. Quite openly.

'What *are* you doing, Clayton?' the teacher would bark.

'I'm having a cup of coffee, sir,' Adam would politely reply. Adam was always polite.

'Clayton, why haven't you done your homework?'

'Look sir, I'm terribly sorry but I simply don't understand

this stuff,' Adam would explain. And he would continue, 'I know this is awkward, sir, and I *am* very sorry about it but there is nothing I can do.'

Word of this audacious dissident soon got round The Mall. It was rumoured that his folks were filthy rich and that he was a bass player in a rock band.

Larry approached him somewhat reluctantly. I believe you play bass guitar. I've got some drums and I'm forming a group – would you be interested? Adam thought it sounded great. He'd seen Larry's notice but had decided that the proposed band was an official school activity and had therefore ignored it. Give me a ring sometime, he told Larry.

Adam Clayton was born on 13 March 1960 in Chinnor in Oxfordshire. His father, Brian, was a Royal Air Force pilot. His mother, Jo, a former air hostess. When Adam was five the family, mum, dad, Adam and sister Sarah Jane, known to Adam as Sindy after the Sindy dolls, moved to Dublin where Brian had joined Aer Lingus. Another boy, Sebastian, was born in Dublin.

The Claytons settled in Malahide, a beautiful town on the coast about eight miles from the city centre. Malahide is middle class, with a substantial Protestant community. Elegant and rich in history, the town pre-dates the City of Dublin as a Norse settlement. Malahide offers all that is most gracious and desirable in suburban living. Surrounded by sea and countryside yet close to the city, it has its yacht club, golf, tennis and cricket clubs, a grand hotel and a baronial castle, the seat of the Talbot family, who were raised to the peerage in 1831. The 5th Lord Baron, The Right Honourable Richard Wogan, Baron Talbot De Malahide, married Emily, great-granddaughter of James Boswell, the eighteenth-century biographer. The Boswell papers, a significant treasure of English literary manuscripts, were discovered in Malahide Castle in 1926.

There are tea-shops and boutiques in the High Street, people know each other, pass the time of day, Catholics and Protestants, living comfortably, closely and in harmony. Malahide is distinct, small-town life with a touch of grandeur, with decency, respectability and moderation in all things being more important than the church you worship at.

Brian and Jo Clayton had found the Home Counties on the east coast of Ireland. They were happy. They decided to send Adam to boarding-school when he was eight. It wasn't an easy decision. Of course they would miss him and they knew that there would be little joy in it for him. But they had to think of his future. Brian didn't know how long his attachment to Aer Lingus would last. He might find himself back in England where an Irish education would leave Adam behind his contemporaries. Prep school, followed by a good public school like Eton or Harrow, and then Oxford or Cambridge – *that* was the best you could give your son. So, reluctantly, Brian and Jo put Adam down for Castle Park, a preparatory school in Dalkey on the other side of Dublin Bay.

Castle Park stood apart from the Irish educational system. It served the children of those Irish parents working abroad who needed a place to board their sons. It served also members of the Irish middle classes deluded by the notion that a boy's character could be formed by sending him away from the comforts of home and neighbourhood. Prep school made a man of you. To this notion Castle Park catered by providing the rituals of public-school life. The boys lived in Houses which were governed by older students who were called prefects. 'Fagging' was an integral feature of prep-school living. 'Fags' were the young pupils who were assigned to serve the prefects, a practice designed to teach the young their place.

Adam hated leaving home, hated Castle Park. The Clayton household would be gloomy on Sunday afternoons as the hour approached when Adam would have to return to school. Jo would make a fine tea, cream-cakes, strawberries, anything to soften the blow of leaving. At five o'clock Brian would get the car, Adam would fetch his case, kiss Sindy and mum, and bravely head off. It was a long fifty-minute drive across the town. Brian wouldn't talk: he felt as bad about the situation as Adam. As they wound their way through the Northside suburbs across the city and out the Southside towards Dalkey, father and son would sit mutely listening to the Adams Singers on BBC Radio. For the next twenty years Adam was depressed on Sunday evenings about tea-time, the memory of those cross-town drives vivid in his mind.

Sunday nights in Castle Park down by the sea in dark Dalkey were miserable. Back. Back to the cold dormitory, the plain food and the fucking rituals. You wore brown shoes indoors, black outside. You 'fagged', although if the prefect was someone you could 'rap' with, Adam didn't mind. You weren't allowed to listen to music or watch television. Music was decadent, sport was the thing. Inter-House games were promoted to foster the right spirit. The ideal pupil was diligent, enthusiastic for sports, proud of his House and his school. Adam resisted the regime, though gently at first. He was highly intelligent, with an engaging smile and charming manners. His first term report reflected the degree to which his teachers were initially misled by his gracious persona. 'Quite good. He needs to take more care,' Adam's English teacher observed at Christmas 1968. In history, 'Adam took a lively interest in the subject.' Geography was 'Quite good.' In French he made 'A good start.' His maths teacher thought 'His knowledge of the basic rules good,' but, 'He does not always work to the best of his ability.' Under conduct at school the following was written: 'He tends to be silly at times.' Mr Carter, the headmaster, concluded that 'Adam has settled in very well and he seems to be happy. A good start with his work.'

By the summer of 1969 opinions were being revised. In

English 'His work has been disappointing.' 'He is not making much effort this term,' the geography master observed. Maths had also deteriorated to the point where 'His work was unsystematic and untidy, his multiplication tables weak.' Of his conduct in school his House-master remarked, 'Adam is rather fond of entertaining the others. He is quite a chatterbox!' In terms of the spirit to which Castle Park aspired, Adam was a likeable failure.

Phillip Thursby was Adam's closest friend at Castle Park. Phillip's parents were in Pakistan. He and Adam enjoyed birdwatching, music and art rather than the more robust pursuits that qualified you for heroism at the school. They went together to the Gramophone Society after lunch on Mondays. Adam enjoyed listening to the classical music for three-quarters of an hour. No talking was the rule, so he would drift off to dreamland, peaceful, alone, undisturbed.

Misdemeanours were punishable by beating with a gymshoe. Adam suffered his share of the shoe. As he got older the beatings stopped, since it was clear that it was simply doing no good. 'He worked well for most of the term but has adopted a cavalier attitude of late,' his science teacher wrote at Easter 1973. By then he had almost finished with Castle Park and had, ironically, come to terms with prep-school life. They weren't going to get to him, he knew that and so did they. He was something of an elder statesman now, stylish, agreeable, disdainful of the school spirit but always civilized, polite, amusing.

There were moments though when hostility broke through. In the final term of the 1975–6 school year, Adam was selected to play cricket for his House. Look, he said, I don't go for this House politics stuff, I don't want to be involved in the cricket game. You *will* play, Clayton, he was told. This was to be his final glorious act of defiance. The match began with his team fielding. He took his position and sat down until the over was bowled. Then he got up and moved to the new position for the next over and sat down again. When his House batted, Adam was out for no runs scored. Next day he was called to the headmaster's study. 'Clayton, you are an ass,' Mr Carter raged. 'You are a complete washout.'

'Look, sir, I don't want to know about silly cricket games. They are a waste of time.'

'What *are* you going to do with your life, Clayton?' Mr Carter demanded.

'I am going to be a comedian, sir, when I grow up,' Adam replied. It seemed as if Adam wouldn't be going on to Eton and Oxbridge after all.

The Claytons had settled happily in Malahide. Jo's mother and father had joined them and bought a house on the seafront. The family was putting down roots in Ireland. Yet Adam's home and his school remained quintessentially English in character: he didn't watch Irish television or read the local newspapers, and he still spoke with a Home Counties accent.

Though school had separated Adam from the other kids on Yellow Walls Road, in some respects at least it had made a man of him. He was more worldly and self-sufficient than other thirteen-year-olds. He spent much of his time in Malahide exploring the beach or the woodland around Malahide Castle. In the morning he would cycle to his grandparents for breakfast. He loved to talk, or more often listen, to his granddad. He took Longfellow's view of education that 'A single conversation across a table with a wise man is better than ten years' mere study of books.' After breakfast he would wander off along the seashore. Adam was a solitary boy but gentle rather than weak, optimistic rather than bitter and self-pitying. The sea and the wildlife on the shore nourished his spirit in a way that defied definition. The strength and vastness of the sea put man's pettiness in some kind of perspective, made a mockery of what was small, mean and narrow in human existence. Somewhere out there lay a better, bigger world than the one he was forced to inhabit, and someday he felt he would make it. Someday he would do and be what he wanted to do and be. He would, Adam often thought, turning back inland from his seashore walks, stay strong, play it his way.

Much of Adam's time at home was spent in his bedroom indulging himself in things he was denied at school. He liked to lie in, listen to his radio, play records, read *Biggles* and *Just William* books. Jo and Brian had decided to send Adam to St Columba's College, Rathfarnham, a co-educational boarding school. The rigidly sectarian nature of the Irish education system restricted the choices available to Protestant families. Catholics could agonize over the quality and accessibility of the schools they sent their children to, but Protestants could not. Getting to the best or most suitable school was, for Protestant children and their parents, often a matter of great inconvenience and expense. Given Adam's academic performance so far, and the fact that Brian Clayton was due to do a tour of duty in Singapore, St Columba's seemed a reasonable choice – but not to Adam. He knew that St Columba's wasn't Eton or Harrow. He felt it was the bottom of the barrel. The school didn't exceed his expectations of it.

St Columba's College was tucked in at the foot of the Dublin Mountains at Rathfarnham, about six miles south of the city centre. The Southside suburbs stopped just short of the gates. The college was austere, the buildings were old, there were no curtains at the windows. It was cold up there, a cold Adam would always remember. You were living not with boys but among men who were bigger, stronger, rougher than the kids at prep school. Many of Columba's pupils were sons and daughters of clergymen for whom the college offered a special deal. There were some from farming stock, horsey folk and as at Castle Park the displaced children of parents in exile. To Adam the place was as foreign as the people in it.

Adam kept quiet for the first couple of terms. He read a lot, mostly thrillers by Alistair Maclean and Desmond Bagley. He read all night sometimes, secretly in the dormitory after lights out. He read in class, hiding his Alistair Maclean beneath his Latin textbook. On sport, a big deal at Columba's, Adam was clear where he stood; if he had to have a cold shower to clean his muddy knees from rugby he wouldn't get his knees muddy. If they wanted you to get dirty, why didn't they provide hot water? He didn't like the cold.

Academically it was much the same story, only worse. Adam's first school report was a litany of condemnation: 'Altogether an unproductive term . . . He has not distinguished himself . . . Progress is slow . . . He is far too casual in his approach to work.' These remarks from the teachers were summed up by his House warden: 'Not good enough. He is always polite but his pleasant exterior disarmed me into thinking that he is not as idle as he sometimes appeared to be. Very much greater effort will be required. Next term I intend to see that this effort is forthcoming.'

Slowly Adam began to make friends, two in particular. John Lesley was from the north of Ireland. Like Adam he had no time for petty discipline or sport. John was into music, he could play guitar and through his elder brother was familiar with the more sophisticated rock bands like Cream, Grateful Dead and Crosby, Stills, Nash and Young. John smuggled in tapes which they listened to. He would play his acoustic guitar along with the music. Adam was fascinated by the real sound more than the tapes. At prep school he'd often listened to classical guitar played by a pupil there, John Spencer. He'd always secretly wanted to play and watching John Lesley now stirred those ambitions again. But he wouldn't reveal his ambition. It would have been un-cool.

Gordon Petherbridge was like John and Adam, turned off by Columba's regime. Like them he felt nothing in common with the horsey/farming set or the stiff offspring of Church of Ireland curates. Gordon was a tall, sallow-skinned Australian, a gorgeous creature much coveted by Columba's girls. He was laid-back, sensitive and utterly displaced in the foothills of the Dublin Mountains. His father was the Australian High Commissioner to Pakistan and he had been sent to school in Ireland because the family had relations in Dublin. He shared many things with Adam, but nothing more than a hatred of the cold.

A little music scene was forming at the College. A student in the third year, Stuart Dolan, had persuaded the authorities to allow him to convert one of the stables into a music room. Dolan was an electronics wizard. He built a sound-bank, acquired an amplifier and, together with a drummer and a base guitarist, formed a band. Dolan's band played Santana and an emotional version of John Lennon's 'Imagine'. Suddenly, music didn't seem beyond Adam's reach. It could be done, you *could* get your own band together as Dolan had done. After all the years at school *this* was the most important lesson Adam had learnt. He felt that this was the most exciting thing that had ever happened to him. He started picking chords on an old guitar he'd bought on the Quays for £12.

Now John Lesley put a proposition to Adam; look, Dolan is leaving next year. We can get that room of his. Why don't you get a bass guitar and we'll form our own group? I'll teach you to play. You can do it, you're good. Adam wasn't sure. He loved the music but didn't feel musical himself. He could never play the way John did. Fear of failure mingled confusingly with his excitement. Up front he remained cool, amusing, *Adam*. The mountains behind Columba's were like the sea at Malahide, a refuge and a source of strength to Adam. He went for a long walk now, and thought. Maybe this was it, the something he'd always known was out there. Music was a better way, a more positive way, of telling them to fuck off with their silly rituals and tired grey minds. A better way by far, he thought, than the classroom dissidence or the comic nihilism he'd clung to. When he came down the mountain he phoned his mother and asked her to buy him a bass guitar.

Jo Clayton was delighted. Despite appearances, they weren't filthy rich, and the £52 Adam's guitar cost made a dent in the family budget. But this was a small price to pay for the enthusiasm Adam showed. He promised to work until he had mastered his bass and vowed also to do better in class. There was immediate improvement which manifested itself in his next report: 'I am much impressed by some of his more recent work,' his English teacher commented. 'On a few occasions he has done good work,' the history master allowed. Of his maths it was now said, 'When he makes a serious effort his results are very reasonable.' In biology he had 'Certainly improved and learned a good deal.' The House warden was sceptical: 'Perhaps some slight signs of improvement but clearly not nearly enough work is being done.' His behaviour was however described as 'Excellent, pleasantly eccentric.'

Adam's new bass was beautiful to touch. When he plugged it in and played a chord a shiver ran through his body. It was as if, magically, he'd been given another limb, with new powers. He couldn't play coherently yet, but looking down at the bass, fondling it, he knew that the power was in there somewhere. And in him. He and John wrote poems and put chords to them. Their compositions were depressing, self-centred, reflecting Columba's wretched starkness and their own adolescent gloom rather than anything grand and liberating.

The moderately encouraging tone of Adam's end-of-year report in 1975 came as some relief to Jo and Brian, who were now temporarily exiled in Singapore. Adam visited them that summer. It was a pleasantly exotic break from Rathfarnham. He returned to Columba's with stories to tell and a pair of shades which he sported instead of regulation spectacles. The regime got heavy about his shades. He was sent for by the headmaster.

'Clayton, what are those things you're wearing?'

'Shades, sir.'

'Clayton, you know the rules here. You can't wear sunglasses around the school.'

'Why not, sir? I need them to protect my eyes.'

The shades had to go. The rule book was brought into play again several weeks later. Adam's parents had returned from Singapore and he was going home for the weekend. When Jo and Brian arrived at school to pick him up Adam was wearing his hippy gear: the shades, an Arab headdress his grandmother had made him a present of and a flowing caftan he'd picked up somewhere.

'Clayton, what's that you're wearing?' the housemaster pounced as he was about to climb into his parents' car. 'You know the rules, Clayton. School uniform must be worn when going out. You're incorrectly dressed. Go back and change or you're not going out today.' Fuck you, Adam thought. But back he went. He changed into his uniform, stuffed his hippy clothes into a bag and passed the master. When his adversary was otherwise occupied, he did a quick change, gave the uniform to John Lesley to take back to the dorm and dived into the car. Alas, as the getaway vehicle left the school grounds the housemaster spotted an Arab headdress showing defiantly from the back window of the car. Clayton was in trouble.

When he returned to school he was hauled before the headmaster.

'This is a serious offence, Clayton. I despair of you. What have you got to say for yourself?'

Adam thought of reasoning with him. What was wrong with wearing your own clothes when you were going home? What was the big deal? But there seemed little point.

'Nothing, sir,' he replied.

'OK, Clayton, you're gated.'

To be gated was to be restricted in your movements to certain parts of the school. You were not allowed outside the gates for any reason. Adam had reached the point of no return with St Columba's. He didn't know what the hell he wanted to be, apart from a musician, or where he was going, but by God, he knew he didn't want to be like this lot and he wasn't going to be. They were not going to break his spirit. Somehow, somewhere along the way he knew that it was important to keep his independence. He had reached the point where when he got into trouble he would own up, say fair enough, I'm guilty, what's my punishment. Sometimes he would be beaten. Sometimes fined. Sometimes he'd have to do extra chores, like getting up early and waking everyone up. They didn't understand him.

'Clayton, I can't figure you out,' his housemaster tried one day. 'Every time you get into trouble you are the most reasonable person I come across. You understand my problems, you understand your problems. Why the hell do you do it in the first place?'

'Because the rules are stupid, silly, and I'm not going to do something stupid even for the sake of appearances.'

Adam's parents had begun to have doubts about the value of keeping him at Columba's. Academically he was going nowhere. As his warden had pointed out in the latest report, 'Adam's promotion to IV Form at the end of term must not be taken for granted.' Doubt hardened to conviction with news of his gating. And it appeared things were even worse. When Jo phoned Mr Gibson to discuss removing Adam, she was informed of yet another transgression; he had been seen at the local shops and had therefore now breached the 'gating' rule. Adam had denied the offence but was not believed: he was to be suspended. Adam was able to gain a stay of execution by offering to prove that he hadn't been down to the shops. The problem he faced was that what he *had* been doing was equally offensive to the Columban regime. He'd been up the mountains with a couple of girls, smoking. Thus in one bound he was out of the frying pan and into the fire. Distressed, but determined not to throw good money after bad, the Claytons removed Adam from St Columba's. He would go to the nearest free school, Mount Temple.

Adam was bitter. His musical career was now critically interrupted. He'd been improving academically *he* felt, even getting into sports, acquitting himself quite well in cross-country and sprinting. He felt he was now being thrown to the lions.

Jo and Brian Clayton softened the blow of sending their eldest son to what he contemptuously referred to as 'the local comprehensive' by allowing him to accept an invitation to join his Columba's friend Gordon Petherbridge for a holiday in Pakistan. Adam spent a glorious month in Rawalpindi. He fell in love, smoked his first joint and, among the sons and daughters of the diplomatic community, felt free for the first time in his life. He was Adam, not 'Clayton'; the only rule observed was 'Don't get caught'. Rawalpindi put the tyranny of public school in perspective. Adam flew home reluctantly, bringing with him a suitcase full of hippy gear. He would go to Mount Temple, but the month in Pakistan had restored his determination to remain his own man. He wouldn't take shit from anyone in this new school.

Chapter Three

LARRY'S STORY

'

Larry Mullen was two years behind Paul Hewson at Mount Temple. But Paul noticed him. Paul *saw* everything. Even while entertaining his group or clocking girls on the The Mall, Paul was looking over shoulders – watching. He checked out boys, girls, passing teachers, wondering about them, what the looks on their faces meant, what they were thinking about. Paul was insatiably curious. Who was that good-looking kid? Larry Mullen was exceptionally good looking. He wore his blond hair shoulder length. His face was clear, strong, composed, his body muscular, masculine. Even though he was young, quiet, no part of any particular group, there was something about him that registered.

In class Larry's progress was satisfactory, no more, no less. Academically he wasn't especially gifted nor particularly hardworking. He did what he had to do. He was well mannered, pleasant, if slightly out of teacher's reach. Socially, he was cautious. The cool, leather-clad look he cultivated set him apart from the adolescent pseudo-sophisticates who occupied much territory in Mount Temple. Larry despised phonies, hated their glib talk, resented the peals of hollow laughter that emanated from their cliques on The Mall. Larry was nice but his niceness was somewhat exaggerated. He was tougher than the clean-cut good looks suggested.

Although he didn't play sport, was not part of Mount Temple's academic or social élite, Larry was a confident young man. He could play the drums. Long before coming to Mount Temple he had mastered drumming. This was his distinction. It set him apart, was his weapon as well as his pleasure, made posing unnecessary. He played in the Post-Office Band, and travelled the country making music. He'd played at the St Patrick's Day Parade in O'Connell Street. From this an inner core of self-esteem existed to fuel his contempt for phonies. In his head Larry Mullen was a musician. When he dreamed, it was of making music his life, of pouring everything he felt, good and bad, *all* the energy, into those drums. But Larry was practical, as wary of dreams as he was of phonies.

Larry's drumming hadn't all been satisfaction. There had been much frustration since he'd started as a nine-year-old in the School of Music. Wherever there were drums there were teachers with sheet music. You had to play *that* music, *their* music. Larry resented this as well. He wanted to play – period. He wanted to play the way he felt, naturally, without intrusion from teachers, composers, bandmasters. For much of his fifteenth year an idea had been forming in his mind; he would start his own band. When he discussed his plan with Donald Moxham, his tutor, and Colm McKenzie, one of Mount Temple's music teachers, they encouraged him to pursue it. The note he pinned on the school's notice-board was cautious. It promised nothing. Instead, Larry's note referred to 'Money wasted on a drum-kit' and posed the question: 'Were there others out there' who, perhaps, had done the same on guitars? Nobody replied.

Larry's home was just a mile up the Malahide Road from Mount Temple, in Artane. The Mullens, Larry, older sister Cecilia, younger sister Mary, father Larry Sr and mother

Maureen, lived on Rosemount Avenue. Rosemount had formerly been Harmonstown Avenue but the residents had demanded that the name be changed to distinguish their semi-detached privately owned homes from the local authority dwellings on the Harmonstown Estate built by Dublin Corporation in the 1960s. So the decent citizens of the Avenue, wishing to make their decency clear and prevent a drop in the value of their houses, petitioned the corporation for the right to become Rosemount. (Coincidentally, around the same time, Ballymun Avenue, close to Cedarwood, became Glasnevin Avenue.)

Artane was not just another suburb. It had an identity that was distinct and exclusive to the Northside suburbs of Raheny, Killester, Donnycarney and Marino. This was Charles J. Haughey's community and in his earthy, streetwise, roguish persona these Northsiders saw themselves. He liked a drink but still he went to mass. He was Republican but probably not violently so. He loved horses, and through his association with St Vincent's GAA Club he reflected community pride in the parish's renowned sporting achievements. To the citizens of Artane, Killester, Raheny, Donnycarney and Marino, Charlie was, whatever *they* said about him, 'One of our own'. What *they*, the Southside-based political intelligentsia, said was that Haughey had a 'flawed pedigree'. He was nevertheless sent back to Dail Eireann after each election with the largest majority in the country.

There was little reason for Charlie's constituents to seek radical change. Artane and the adjoining communities enjoyed the best that suburban life could offer. The sea was close at hand. There were parks, shops, pubs, churches and schools in abundance. St Vincent's provided sport for the best young footballers and hurlers, inspiration for those who merely stood and cheered. 'Vincent's' home in Parnell Park lay between Larry Mullen's Artane and Mount Temple. Clontarf Golf Club r offered sport of a more leisurely nature. Thus he grew up; five minutes from the sea, ten minutes from the city, behind him the countryside and the beaches of Portmarnock and Malahide.

Larry Mullen Sr was born and reared on the Northside. One of a family of seven, he grew up in Marino. His father was a carter for Johnson, Mooney and O'Brien, one of Dublin's two great bakeries. The carter drove the horse-drawn vehicle that delivered bread and cakes around the city. As a child, Larry Sr often rode proudly with his dad. He was a diligent, popular student at St Joseph's Christian Brothers School in Marino. (Charlie Haughey attended 'Joey's' around the same time.) Larry achieved some distinction by playing football and hurling for 'Vincent's'.

In his early teens Larry Sr began to consider the priesthood. The Brothers encouraged him to seek a vocation. Today the Catholic Church has to advertise in newspapers to attract young men to the priesthood. Pre-war it was a great honour to be chosen to serve God. In 1939, aged sixteen, Larry entered a seminary in Ballinafad, Co. Mayo, to begin the long preparation for ordination. His vocation was the source of immense family pride. He was the first of his stock to study for the priesthood. Life in the seminary was tough, indeed brutal in many ways. The community was exclusively male, and comfort was not a priority. Would-be priests slept on hard beds in bare dormitories. The showers were cold, the food frugal, the baths made of tin. Larry moved on to Cork and then to university in Galway.

Larry Sr fulfilled the promise of his early years. He was popular, a little shy, emotional at times, but a regular guy, not, as some were, pious, forbidding, older than his years and holier than anybody had a right to be. His academic diligence earned him a good degree, but as the final, irrevocable step of ordination drew closer, he began to experience misgivings. Yes, there was a heroic aspect to the priesthood, especially to missionary work. It was this that had appealed at the beginning. Now he wasn't sure that he could endure the loneliness, wasn't sure that he could supply the measures of selfless dedication required of a good priest. When Larry sought guidance from his superiors he was treated sympathetically. The Order sent him home on a one year sabbatical that he might reflect before deciding what course to follow.

Going home was tough, too. To the extent to which your vocation was an honour, the losing of it was a source of disappointment tinged with shame. These things you now brought upon your family as surely as initially honour had been bestowed upon them. Larry's mother felt deeply disappointed. He, himself, was lost, in some kind of limbo, neither a priest nor not-a-priest. This year of reflection proved to be the most traumatic time of his life thus far. In 1948, aged twenty-five, Larry Mullen decided against joining the priesthood. He had chosen the tougher option, the one that very few young men faced with the choice would have had the courage to take.

Uncertain of his bearing in a world that had experienced a war while he'd been away, Larry drifted for a while. Most of his friends were priests. His contemporaries in neighbourhood and school were gone, married with young families and bedded down in good jobs. Larry was well educated, alone and bearing the marks of failure. He took a course for health officers run by Dublin Corporation in conjunction with the Eastern Health Board. He finished first in the subsequent exam. His diligence hadn't deserted him. He became a civil servant in the Department of Health and Environment.

Larry met Maureen O'Rourke in the summer of 1954 in Ballymoney on the Wexford coast. He'd gone to Ballymoney on holiday with Larry Skelly, a friend from his seminary days. Skelly was studying for his MA at Cambridge before setting off for Ghana on his missionary work. Maureen was staying with friends who ran the boarding house.

Maureen O'Rourke came from Leitrim in the West of Ireland. Leitrim is a beautiful county, the lakes and rich green woodland providing an idyllic setting for tourists passing through. But life was grim then for the natives of this lovely place. There was no indigenous industry, no good farming land. Unemployment was high. Leitrim was, and remains, a place that people left. They went to Dublin, London, New York, in search of work.

Maureen was born in 1922 in Anna, a townland on the Leitrim-Roscommon border. Her mother died giving birth to her. She was reared by her maternal grandmother in Leitrim Village. In 1932, when Maureen was ten, the desperate poverty in the area moved a local man, Jim Gralton, to begin agitating for land reform. Gralton had been to America where he saved some dollars to return home to buy a small farm. Inspired by American radicals like Joe Hill he returned to Leitrim a communist. Gralton used his savings to build the Pearse-Connolly Community Hall in the village of Drumsna, a few miles down the road from Maureen's home. In this small hall named in honour of two of the heroes of the 1916 rising, Jim Gralton hoped to establish a forum where dissident voices could be heard. Radical pamphlets and other socialist literature would be distributed and discussed. This modest attempt at reform enraged the Church and local politicians, and Gralton was denounced from the pulpit at Sunday masses. Persuaded that he was promoting atheistic ideas, a group of locals burnt down the Pearse-Connolly Hall. De Valera's Fianna Fail Government took matters even further. Jim Gralton was deported to America. He is the only Irishman to be thus banished from his homeland since the state was founded. He arrived back in the United States penniless, with no possessions other than the clothes on his back, and he died without ever seeing lovely Leitrim again.

The following year Maureen O'Rourke left Leitrim. Her guardians had decided to send her to Dublin to complete her education and perhaps, afterwards, find a decent job. She would stay with her mother's two spinster sisters in their Georgian house on Leeson Street in the elegant, fashionable Southside of the city centre. Nothing was too good for Maureen. She attended the Sacred Heart convent school before going on to Alexandra College. She took piano lessons, becoming good enough to win medals at music festivals. Despite her difficult, unsettled childhood, Maureen grew up to be a cheerful young woman who made light of the burdens fate had imposed upon her. Leeson Street was elegant but there weren't many other kids around and it could be lonely. The maiden aunts were loving but stern. In so many things the gulf between the young woman and the adults was unbridgeable.

Maureen started work as a typist in Bowmakers, the credit finance house on Stephen's Green. She liked to dance at weekends. Dancing was no simple matter of entertainment in the Ireland of the early fifties. A new, exciting era had dawned with the opening of ballrooms around the city and the arrival of showbands to fill them. These bands were eight- to ten-men ensembles with a featured vocalist. They wore smartly tailored outfits and played American and British popular music. Dancing was by then big business. De Valera's Public Dance Hall Act of 1935 had sought to regulate dancing by making it necessary to obtain a licence to put on dances. The Ireland De Valera 'dreamed of' might be threatened by impromptu dances held at rural crossroads or in private clubs or homes. Contact between the sexes was the problem. Dancing stimulated desires forbidden by Catholicism, created the 'occasion of sin'. Licensing made the dance-hall more amenable to supervision by state and clergy. Those who received these licences would be men of good character, Catholics and supporters of De Valera's Fianna Fail party. In the popular mind, at least that belonging to the older generation that Maureen's maiden aunts were part of, these new dance-halls were bad news. Things dark and forbidden happened in them.

The showband explosion in the early 1950s became a source of friction or worse between the generations. The dances in places like the Four Provinces Ballroom (the 4 Pees), the Crystal and the Metropole didn't end until two a.m. Many curfews were imposed only to be broken by sons and daughters who danced gaily, until the clock began to bear in on them later on, just when a glance had been exchanged, an interesting conversation struck up. The pleasure of the last waltz was, for many young men and women, overshadowed by fear of the consequences of dwelling too long in the presence of sin.

Maureen's maiden aunts took a dim view of her activities, and continued to do so long after she was twenty-one. She moved to lodgings, taking rooms in Harcourt Street and other places around the city before eventually settling with a family in Dartry in the Southside suburbs.

Like Larry, her life had been blighted, if for different reasons. Together they found the contentment that had eluded each alone. On their first date Larry and Maureen went to see Gary Cooper in *High Noon*. They married in 1956, and set up home in Harmonstown Avenue where within a year Cecilia was born. Larry Jr followed four years later, on 31 October 1961. Another girl, Mary, was born three years later, but died in 1973.

Larry Jr was a good child. He liked plenty of attention, which he got from Maureen and Cecilia. To make sure he knew what was happening he managed to tear two peepholes in his pram out of which he would gaze happily upon household life. When he was four he smashed a plate-glass window with his head in Killester Shopping Centre. His head remained unsmashed.

After spending one year in the local national school, Larry was enrolled in Scoil Colmcille, Marlborough Street. Scoil

Colmcille was *the* Irish school, all subjects being taught through the first language. Without honours in Irish you couldn't go to university or gain a place in the civil service, so Larry Sr reasoned that it would be easier for his son to master it early on. There was the added advantage of small classes, with no more than fifteen pupils in each.

Larry travelled to town each morning by train with his dad. Then they would walk the few hundred yards to school. Each afternoon Maureen would travel in to collect young Larry. Once when he was seven Maureen was delayed. Uncertain what to do but determined to do something, Larry set out accompanied by his best friend Basil King to walk the four miles to Artane. For several hours they were listed as missing. The police were called and Larry Sr hauled from the department. To the relief of the two distressed families, Larry and Basil showed up at six o'clock.

Maureen Mullen had found happiness of a kind she'd never known. This was her first real home. She was a loving, attentive mother, taking no interest in things outside her home. Having spent her life in other people's houses, she had no desire to wander far from Harmonstown Avenue. Later, when Larry Jr joined the scouts, Maureen would become a Cub Leader. Mother and son were especially close. He loved to be with her. They were friends, companions, as well as parent and child. Sometimes she would play the piano Larry Sr had bought for Cecilia. She didn't play impromptu but would get sheet music out and play the old songs.

Cecilia was taking piano lessons at the School of Music, Chatham Row. When he was eight Larry Jr decided he too would like to learn to play. He stuck it for a year, but was a poor pupil. He attacked the piano vigorously but he wouldn't do the exercises he was asked to do at home. At the end of his first year his piano teacher suggested ever so politely to Maureen that her money was being wasted.

As they walked down the hall on the way out of the school Larry heard a drum-kit being played. *That*, he told Maureen, was what he would like to do next. OK, Maureen agreed, but she and Larry Sr decided that he would have to pay the fee for his first term himself. Young Larry promised to do household chores to the value of the £9 his parents were spending.

Larry joined Joe Bonnie's drum class in the autumn of 1971. Joe Bonnie was Ireland's best-known drummer. He had played in the old music-halls, as a session drummer and in showbands. If you wanted a drummer you sent for Joe. Larry was as loath as ever to go by the book, preferring to establish his own personal relationship with his instrument. At first he enjoyed the novelty of the military-style drumming Bonnie taught but boredom soon set in. Joe warned him that he wouldn't make it unless he mastered the basic techniques that the class was designed to teach. If over the next couple of years Larry's reluctance to follow the classroom rules frustrated Joe the teacher, the youngster's energy and feeling for the drums endeared him to Joe the musician. Music, Joe knew, was either in your soul or not. No amount of musical theory could compensate for the absence of passion or a sense of rhythm.

Joe gave Larry a rubber pad to take home to do his exercises on. Larry used his pad to follow the pop drummers on *Top of the Pops*. He tuned in every Thursday night to watch groups like Sweet, the Glitter Band and Slade, watching closely every move the drummers made. After the programme he would fly upstairs to work out on his pad. He dreamed of a drum-kit of his own and broached the subject with his dad. A girlfriend of Cecilia's had a brother who was selling his drum-kit, price £17, quite a bit of money in 1973. One evening when Larry was at the scouts, Cecilia bought him his drums. When he came home they were laid out in the box-room upstairs. He was speechless with excitement. From then on every penny of his pocket-money went towards adding to the basic Hohner kit. He bought more drums, cymbals and drumsticks. Every day after school he went to the tiny box-room to experiment. At last he could do it his way, make his own mistakes, create his own beat and sound. He flung open the window and the sound drifted down the street, attracting the neighbourhood kids who would come and sit on the garden wall shouting approval and special requests.

Larry loved it. He loved the sound and the attention he got. His taste in music was determined by Cecilia's record collection. She was into the Stones, Bowie, the Eagles and David Essex, one of whose LPs, *Rock On*, was a particular favourite of Larry's. *Space Oddity* was the first record he bought, Bowie and Roxy Music proving to be enduring passions of his young musical life. He was trying to understand pop and rock drumming, feeling his way into the music, constantly measuring the distance between the drummers on the record and himself.

Joe Bonnie died in 1974. Despite Larry's determined individuality they had been good friends. Joe, who had a soft spot for the quirky kid, had taken Larry with him as a special treat on a prestigious engagement at Christchurch Cathedral, allowing the proud youngster to turn the sheet music for him. After Joe's death his daughter Monica took charge of the class. Larry and Monica were quickly at odds with each other. Monica liked things done properly. Larry's days at Chatham Row were numbered.

Larry was by now at Mount Temple. The decision to send him there was more a matter of convenience than conviction since Larry Sr had no strong feelings one way or the other about non-denominational education. Larry was academically average. Mount Temple offered subjects like business organization and accountancy, music, typing, applied maths and art: a wider range of possibilities to those not distinguished in the three Rs. In any case, Larry was passionate about very little apart from his music. It occurred to Larry Sr more than once that his son might well be heading for a career as a professional musician. With this in mind he broached the question of a stint in the army with Larry. Why not sign for seven years, join the army band and learn to play all the percussion instruments? Why not do it properly, get a complete musical education, Larry Sr reasoned. Larry Jr decided that he didn't fancy seven years away from mum's cooking and his friends, though in truth he had never been a great one for going out to play in the neighbourhood. He had friends around the Avenue, Paul Phillips who was known as Beezer, Sean Sodon (Bread) and Chopper Fagan, but going to the Irish school in town and his interest in music had created a gap, made him less dependent than his mates on aimless play. Larry liked to *do* things: aimlessness was not his thing. He collected stamps and coins, even in his friendships he tended to be intense, making one exclusive friend at a time, going to his house or inviting him home.

After leaving Monica Bonnie, Larry settled on the Artane Boys' Band for his next musical step. Alas, membership of the band, renowned for its playing on All-Ireland Day at Croke Park, depended on wearing your hair at a suitable length. At Larry's first rehearsal the bandmaster quietly drew him aside to point out that his lovely locks would have to be tidied up. Larry agreed. When he went back the following week, having had his haircut, Larry was told that more would have to come off. He agreed, but this time he didn't go back. He was finished with the Artane Boys' Band.

Larry Sr pulled a few strings to get his son a place in the Post-Office-Workers' Union Band. The next two years were the happiest of Larry's life. The Post-Office Band played all kinds of music, from Irish airs to popular hits at small festivals and country fairs like the horse fair at Ballinasloe. The highlight of the year was their participation in Dublin's St Patrick's Day Parade, and on 17 March 1975 the Mullen family went to the parade to see Larry make his debut. His trousers didn't fit, his drummer's hat perched precariously on his head, but he was having fun. He and his pal and fellow-drummer Martin Levins would dispense with the sheet music and improvise. Nobody seemed to notice or care. 'That was great drumming, lads,' the band's veterans would praise them afterwards. Musically, Larry learnt a great deal doing his own thing quietly. Socially he loved the band's unpretentious informality. And the girls who formed the band's colour guard were a welcome distraction. The drummer with the long blond hair was much admired by the colour guard.

Larry travelled Ireland with the Post-Office Band. They would set off from Dublin in the early morning, have sandwiches on the coach, play the gig, then have dinner and a few pints. On the long coach journey home spontaneous sessions would take place. Band members would do their own thing, singing and playing uninhibitedly in the best Irish tradition.

Those were long, happy days. Larry sensed the comradeship that was a part of 'being on the road'. It made him more determined than ever to find a career in music, to turn a hobby into a way of life. As a drummer he felt he had grown up, matured, broken free of the sterile world of teachers and formulas. He felt the gap between him and the drummers on *Top of the Pops* had narrowed to the point where it was bridgeable. All he needed now was a group to play with. He resolved to do something about it.

Chapter Four

EDGE'S STORY

When Albert Bradshaw heard that young Mullen in fourth year was starting a band he immediately thought of Dave Evans. Evans was the sort of boy who made teaching worthwhile. Dave was quiet, intelligent, interested, he had a good ear for music and was diligent without being priggish or a pest. He hadn't seen Larry's ad. When Albert told him about the note Dave's face lit up and he went off in search of Larry.

Dave Evans was born in Barking Maternity Hospital, East London, on 8 August 1961. His family moved to Dublin a year later. Garvin and Gwenda Evans were born in Llanelli, a Welsh town famous for its rugby players and choirs. This is coalmining country, rich in tradition, melancholy, stark, the landscape blotched by the pit-head coal mountains. The people here work hard, know poverty and tragedy, too, for mining folklore is trimmed in black in memory of those who died when things went wrong down the pit. The menfolk play a brutal game of rugby and sing in the Male Welsh Voice Choirs. There is not, as might be the case elsewhere, any contradiction here. Welshmen have nothing to prove in terms of masculinity, their courage is vouched for every morning when they step into the cage that takes them down to the bowels of the earth to mine Britain's coal.

Chapel is as important as rugby and song to the people of the valleys. God, his blessings and his wrath, is no abstract figure but a living presence in the mining communities, his relevance to daily life reflected in the bond that exists between Christianity and Welsh politics. The British Labour Party's ideological backbone was formed around the values of the gospels. Chapel socialism given voice with evangelistic fervour has down the decades transported the great orators of British politics from the valleys to the seat of Her Majesty's Government in Westminster. There, passionately, lyrically, men like 'Nye' Bevan, Michael Foot and Neil Kinnock have advocated the values of decency, compassion and justice which might constitute the theme of a Chapel sermon on any Sunday evening in the valleys.

Garvin Evans and Gwenda Richards were born into Llanelli's middle class. Both came from church-going family backgrounds, the Evanses being Presbyterian, the Richards Baptist. Both moved away with their parents, he to London with his father, who was a pharmacist, she to the mining village of Blaegwynfi where her father had a grocer's shop. During the Second World War Garvin was evacuated back to his grandparents in Llanelli, where he went to secondary school. There he met Gwenda. They both studied at University College London in the early 1950s and married after they graduated. Garvin had qualified in engineering, Gwenda as a teacher. Faced with two years' National Service in the Fleet Air Arm, Garvin asked for a posting in Wales. To his dismay he was sent to Eglinton in Northern Ireland. To their surprise, the Evanses enjoyed their stay, so much so that when his National Service was completed and his employers, Plessey Engineering, offered him the choice between moving to Wigan in the north of England or Dublin, he chose to cross the Irish Sea. His boss suggested they settle in Malahide, which had an active Protestant community. Dave was one year old, his brother Dick three, their sister Gill was born in Dublin.

It was Dave, *not* David. The Evanses were unpretentious. Almost thirty years on they still live in the same comfortable suburban house half a mile from Malahide town centre. They are still distinctly Welsh in voice and values, warm, decent, hospitable people, popular among their neighbours. Garvin is now in business for himself as a consulting engineer, working from an extension he has built onto his home, a vibrant man who pursues with relish a variety of seemingly irreconcilable passions. He is an Elder of the Presbyterian Church, an enthusiastic club golfer, the lead tenor and a founder member of the Dublin Male Welsh Voice Choir and a dedicated follower of the Welsh Rugby Union team. Gwenda is a member and active participant in the Malahide Musical Society. Music is very much a part of their backgrounds. Both their families provided members for the local choirs in the valleys. Gwenda's mother played the piano. Garvin was a competent piano player and he and Gwenda, who was only a beginner, played for their children at home when they were growing up.

Dave's was a happy, conventional, suburban childhood. He attended St Andrew's Church of Ireland school in Malahide Village where he briefly encountered Adam Clayton before Adam went off to Castle Park. St Andrew's was a tiny school, cosy and intimate. Dave sailed through the work. On first meeting, the quietly spoken, watchful boy gave the impression that he was timid. In fact he was clever, amusing, with a sense of humour tending towards sarcasm, very tough-minded. Any inhibition he felt had to do with his accent, which was distinctly Anglo-Irish in tone. Out of school Dave played happily in the streets around his home in St Margaret's Park. The seashore and Malahide Castle were minutes away, and by negotiating some scrub and a steep bank round the corner from the house he and his pals could escape from the adult world onto a disused railway line complete with old carriages and steam engines. All in all Dave enjoyed as good a deal as childhood had to offer.

Mount Temple was tougher going. Shane Fogarty, Dave's best friend at St Andrew's, had gone to Mount Temple the year before. The word back was that the bigger school was fun. There was this chatty character there called Paul Hewson who caused explosions in class. But Dave found Mount Temple rowdy, frantic and much too brash for his liking. He was slight for his age and tended to be ignored. Girls were a big problem. Dave was shy and didn't possess the glib patter you needed to connect on The Mall. He wasn't callow enough to make this scene so, pride wounded, he opted to withdraw and concentrate on his studies.

For his first two years at Mount Temple Dave was a loner. These were hard times, for he was at heart a lively fun-loving lad. He was intellectually sophisticated and a good conversationalist, gifts that were sadly superfluous in those early teenage years. He had slightly outgrown his street gang but found nothing to replace it. Music offered some relief from his adolescent anguish. He learnt the basics of Spanish guitar and started piano lessons. He acquired a small repertoire of classical piano pieces which he could play by ear. Dave's brother Dick also played guitar, and together they started knocking out old Beatles songs. At the local convent sale of work their mother found an old white acoustic guitar without any strings which she bought for £1. She took it to a shop in the village and had some strings put on before giving it to Dick.

Dick had inherited his father's gift for making things. He was a contributor to *Everyday Electronics*, a magazine for do-it-yourself buffs. Responding to the mood of the time one issue of *Everyday Electronics* featured a handsome electric guitar on its cover with, inside, instructions on how to build it. Dick and his friend Barry O'Connell decided to have a go. Dave watched them construct it in the shed at the bottom of the Evans's garden. The more he got involved with the instrument the more the idea of joining a band took root in his mind.

Larry Mullen approached Dave at just the right time. Yes, he would be interested in a meeting. He would bring his brother Dick with him. The home-made electric guitar was ready. It looked beautiful, yellow and cleanly designed in the shape of a swan in flight. The only trouble was the sound. Something in there wasn't quite working as it should.

Dave and Dick met Adam Clayton at the bus-stop in Artane village. Adam was wearing his shades. His bass was slung insouciantly over his shoulder. Under the other arm he carried an amp. Adam looked the part; he clearly meant business. As the three of them walked up to Larry's house Adam spoke knowledgeably about the rock 'n' roll business, dropping words like 'gigging' and 'jamming' to establish his *bona fides*. By the time they reached 60 Rosemount Avenue Dave and Dick were suitably impressed. The scene inside was somewhat confused. Larry's note had sought guitarists, and he now found himself with five. Paul Hewson had turned up with another Mount Temple pupil, Neil McCormick, who, like everyone else present except Larry, fancied being lead guitarist in the new group. Nobody wanted to be the vocalist.

Although they attended the same school and were vaguely aware of each other, the six protagonists weren't friends. They barely knew each other. There was much jockeying for position as they settled in Larry's front room to discuss their project. None of them was especially into rock music as such, nobody owned an enviable record collection or had a declared allegiance to any particular star or group. Their tastes were eclectic. They all liked Bowie and the Stones, Larry liked David Essex and the Sweet, Paul was into 1960s rock 'n' roll, was just discovering Elvis and of course the punks. Dave liked Rory Gallagher and Taste, the Beatles and Yes. Adam broadly shared those tastes with a dash of San Francisco thrown in. Neither Neil nor Dick expressed any contrary preferences. The question of what the as-yet-unnamed band should play was therefore left open. First the logistics of accommodating a six-piece band in the Mullens' modest semi-detached house had to be decided upon. The kitchen was chosen as the only suitable stage. With the back door open and Larry's drum-kit set up in the garden the five competing guitarists could just squeeze in between the fridge and the bread bin. They belted out a couple of grim-sounding Rolling Stones classics, 'Brown Sugar' and 'Satisfaction', which quickly attracted an audience of curious teenage neighbours. Larry told them to clear off but the sound was intoxicating and the back-garden drummer was forced to turn the hose on his admirers before the show was over.

This first meeting revealed important truths. Larry and Dave could play. Paul and Adam were less accomplished. Dick could play but his lovely electronic guitar couldn't quite make it. Ivan decided to bale out. Dave was still the quiet man but a spectacular two-minute solo rendition of 'Blister on the Moon', a Taste classic, earned him respect and an unchallengeable claim to the role of lead guitarist. Larry was as proficient as expected. If not as musically gifted as their accomplices, Paul and Adam had other, no less important, assets to bestow on the group they now proposed forming. Paul had conviction. They could do it. And he had ideas about how they should proceed. They would ask the school for permission to use a classroom to rehearse in. There were lots of places on the Northside where they could get gigs once they had a basic act together. He had broader visions too about what rock 'n' roll could achieve, about how it could provide them with a voice in the world, at least the world around Mount Temple. Paul was infinitely more convincing talking than he was playing guitar. With his thick young labourer's fingers it was, Dick idly thought whilst listening to him, a miracle that Paul could play guitar at all.

Adam nodded agreement as Paul outlined the plan of action. A cigarette poised at his lips, his well-modulated public-school voice effortlessly commanding the attention Paul had to gyrate to get, Adam projected worldliness and confidence. They would get gigs, he would get them himself. He knew a few people in town, he confided. Thus Paul and Adam repaid in ambition and confidence the optimism they had drawn from Larry and Dave's music. A reasonable bargain was struck. They would call themselves Feedback, a wry reference to the sound that emerged from Adam's amp. Dick could stay aboard provided he got a guitar that worked.

For Larry, Feedback was a logical progression in his musical career. For Dave, the guitar was a means of self-expression, the band a way of coming out from behind his shy persona, of proving that he was no weed. For Paul and Adam, Feedback was more, much more than it should have been. Behind the resourcefulness they both undoubtedly possessed there lay a different, sadder story. Both were refugees from home and school, from the very culture that they nominally belonged to. They were both of them intelligent, imaginative – and lonely. Paul and Adam were going nowhere, had nothing to lose. They both needed a cause they could believe in, an institution over whose values and ambitions they could exert some influence. Feedback was that cause, that institution.

Chapter Five

THE PUNK

Punk was honest, brutally and indiscriminately honest. It raged and mocked *everything*, it rejected everything and in the process scrawled the final chapter of a rock 'n' roll era. Led by Johnny Rotten and Sid Vicious, the punks emerged in 1976 to say fuck off. The punks were angry. They had a right to be. They'd been born into post-war prosperity, had grown up in the optimistic 1960s, when poverty, racism and injustice appeared to be on the point of being eliminated. They had grown up listening to the rhetoric of freedom, to Kennedy, Harold Wilson, Bob Dylan, the Beatles and the flower-power people from San Francisco. Now, in their early twenties, the leaders of the punk movement could see that nothing had changed. Things had got worse. Racism in Britain was as rampant as it had ever been. Unemployment was rising sharply. This, despite the fact that Labour, the party of liberation, had been governing Britain for nine of the previous twelve years. Harold Wilson, Britain's Kennedy *circa* 1964, left politics in 1976. He had survived allegations linking him to corrupt land-speculation deals in the early 1970s. Now on his departure from 10 Downing Street he caused more controversy by publishing an honours list that ennobled many whose only distinction appeared to the watching nation to be their willingness to serve the interests of Wilson and his entourage. The promises of the 1960s, put to music by the Beatles, had not been kept. There was no greater equality of opportunity, no freedom, no beauty.

There *was* a new aristocracy in the Britain Harold Wilson left behind. Its members were not the best and the brightest, but the shrewdest and the most opportunistic: the property speculator, the land developer and the builder. Alongside them, still spouting the rhetoric of socialism, stood the powerful trades union barons seeking ever more money for ever less work, seeking, seeking, seeking, for *their* members. The punks lived in the new socialist Britain that the speculators and their friends the builders had built. In a frenzied spasm of socialist-directed activity, old communities had been swept away to be replaced by tower-block apartment complexes and flat, featureless housing estates. Those who used to live on city streets which they knew, understood and identified with, found themselves transported to an ugly maze of fly-overs and underpasses. Tradition was bulldozed, neighbourhoods vanished overnight, the people, men, women and children, the old and the young, drifted now on a sea of concrete, cut off from friend and foe, school and church, pub and shop. Your new world would have everything, except a sense of place, of who you were and what you came from, everything except your identity. Life in these urban ghettos was cold and bleak, as cold and bleak as the landscape. Thus, in the mid-1970s, the great British cities of London and Glasgow, Birmingham and Manchester, Liverpool and Newcastle, stood as monuments to a dream betrayed. It was out of this that the punks, bitter, cynical, spewing hatred as indiscriminately as the hippies had spewed love, burst in 1976.

Johnny Rotten and Sid Vicious belonged to a band called the Sex Pistols, the name a satire on the phoney peace-and-love retailed by the generation that went before them. They claimed to hate everyone: politicians, sociologists, social workers, journalists, *all* those who had conspired to fuck them up, but it was for the rock 'n' roll business and its idols that the punks reserved their most withering contempt. Rock 'n' roll was the greatest betrayal of all. Rock was supposed to be the music of the dispossessed, yet its working-class heroes were multi-millionaires. The flower children who had eschewed money, jobs and possessions now lived in mansions and travelled like medieval princes. Where once there had been anger there was now Rod Stewart. Where Elvis had begged us not to step on his blue suede shoes, the new breed of rock 'n' rollers were more concerned with protecting their Rolls Royce Corniches, and employed armies of 'minders' to do so. Where there had been anger there now was decadence. Where before, with three guitars and drums, young men had articulated pain, anguish, frustration and despair, there was now a vast array of technology with which bloated idols indulged their personal conceits. Rock 'n' roll had gone corporate, put on a collar and tie and turned its back on the mean streets and even meaner tower-blocks where it belonged. Good Golly Miss Molly! Punk was a disgusting, disgusted, reminder. It's not music, they said, and they were right. Punk was performance art, a tuneless, anarchic kick in the balls for all those who didn't live on Concrete Way. Punk wasn't music but it carried a powerful message for the music business: Fuck off, we've had enough. This is our music, *anyone* can play it. The Sex Pistols didn't hide the fact that they couldn't play their instruments: they *gloried* in it. Nor did they cultivate their audience. Acclaimed by a generation who, whether they came from urban deserts or not, knew what the punks were on about, Rotten and Vicious spat on those who would idolize *them*. It was this idolatry that had caused the problem in the first place. Fuck off and find your own answers said the gospel according to the new anti-heroes.

Punk happened as Paul Hewson began his final year at

Mount Temple. He understood it immediately. He loved the energy, the raw basic sound. He saw through the vulgarity to the anger and despair that lay beneath. And he understood and was excited by punk's first law: that anybody could use rock 'n' roll to do their thing, have their say, express their own ideas. You didn't have to be a virtuoso or handsome or a millionaire. Paul was the first punk on The Mall. He turned up one day in autumn 1976 with a spiky haircut, tight purple straights, pointed boots, a sixties jacket, wearing a chain that stretched from his nose to his ear. He wanted to identify himself with the punks, he wanted to say fuck off. Deep down a Paul who rarely if ever appeared on The Mall wanted much more than the nihilism punk had to offer.

Although he continued to shine socially, the two years since his mother's death had been pretty desperate for Paul. Iris's soothing presence had never been replaced at 10 Cedarwood Road. It was a house not a home, a place he shared with two men with whom he had little in common. He was permanently behind the eight ball; he would lose his housekey; he would forget, or simply not bother, to do his share of the household chores; he'd sleep for weeks in an unmade bed. Food was cornflakes, instant potatoes, anything quick and convenient.

Paul had made some new friends in the neighbourhood. They formed a group which called itself The Village. They prided themselves on being smarter, more hip than their peers around Ballymun and Finglas. The Village congregated in Paul's house during the day, when Bobby and Norman were at work. The place would be a mess when Norman got home, dirty cups and dishes, cigarette smoke, the sound of insolent laughter. This was something more than Norman could take after a hard day's work. Life was tough enough for him and his father without this lot invading the house. He and Paul would fight, sometimes physically. One evening's hostility ended dramatically when a knife thrown by Paul lodged in the framework of the kitchen door inches from Norman's head.

Maeve O'Regan saw the other side of Paul. She was, at sixteen, taller, more beautiful, more confident and more desired than ever. There was a physical dimension to their relationship, but that was not the most important thing for either of them. Theirs was friendship, one that deepened after Iris's death. Alone with her, the raunchy social animal of Mall renown cast off his armour to reveal the sensitive young man within. They would talk about art, literature, music and religion. At lunchtime she would take him home to Clontarf where her mother, seeing all too clearly his waif-like vulnerability, would feed him. He was a nice, well-mannered boy. Why, Maeve would chide him, was he always trying to prove himself? Why that fire in the classroom with the rivets he'd stolen from the workmen's hut exploding round the room? Why the punk gear? Why all the girls? How could one Paul be reconciled with the other?

This was his last year in school, his Leaving Cert. Exam loomed, he was not up to scratch academically. The serious business of life lay ahead, and among his peers on The Mall Paul lagged behind. Maeve was an honours student. Reggie Manuel, Mark Holmes and Ken Trimble were similarly gifted. Mark and Ken planned to go to medical school. They all knew when the messing had to stop, they all knew when to switch off, when the studying had to start. They were all achievers. Paul was the odd man out, the fool, the mystic, the ladies' man. Soon he knew they would no longer be laughing with him but at him. There was a hint of desperation now about the chameleon; he'd tried to start an acting group but that had died a death. He'd flirted with the rugby team but soon grew bored. The Web, his disco-club, had closed with the passing of Zandra Laing. Two constants remained, music and religion. Paul had joined Mount Temple's Christian Union after his mother's death. He attended the Saturday-morning prayer meetings and persuaded Maeve to join him.

If you were young (or indeed not so young), idealistic and spiritually alive, the world could be a bleak, unresponsive place in the mid-1970s. In those post-Watergate years it was hard to believe in anything. There were no heroes, no great causes, there was no sense of the world becoming a better place. Indeed, with western economies in disarray as a result of the quadrupling of oil prices in 1973, the opposite was the case. Life became a matter of survival. It wasn't about heroes and causes anymore but about jobs and money. Spirituality was a luxury few could afford. America elected Christian Jimmy Carter, in a noble attempt to atone for Nixon. But the old democracies in Europe knew better and were turning right-wards in search of leaders who might restore prosperity.

Detached, insensitive, concerned more with their own internal politics than their pastoral responsibilities, the Established Churches hardly filled the spiritual vacuum that now existed. Thus, it was left to freelance evangelists, Christian sects, new and old, and pseudo-religious cults like the Moonies and Scientologists to minister to those, especially the young, in need of spiritual comfort. The more spiritually awake you were the greater your need. Paul Hewson was wide awake, acutely in need of some solace. Since his mother's death he had stopped mocking Sophie Shirley, Mount Temple's religious teacher, and started listening to Christ's Gospels. In them he found logic, coherence, truth. He could relate to their idealism. There were no snags, there was nothing sly or misleading in the Christian message. It made sense in a way that nothing, not home, school, culture or Christ's established representatives on earth did. The Gospel was real and true. Paul and Maeve weren't alone in believing this. As the world outside Mount Temple became ever more selfish, a growing number of students began to take an interest in the Christian movement.

Music was another source of refuge from the hard world. Music was an integral part of the school curriculum, with a wide range of tastes, from renaissance choral works to Spanish guitar, being catered for. Even those not especially into music found themselves inspired to try by Albert Bradshaw, Mount Temple's dedicated music teacher. Paul was a member of Bradshaw's choir. Even at his lowest ebb he found music soothing.

The real world, outside Sophie Shirley's prayer meetings and Albert Bradshaw's music room, continued to frustrate Paul. Maeve had taken up with a tall, handsome American basketball player called Lloyd. Unfaithful though he remained throughout their friendship, Paul was loath to make way for this older boy who was eighteen and, because he knew the lyrics of Bob Dylan's songs, rumoured to be an intellectual. Apart from being jealous, Paul was intrigued for a while by his rival, whose books, records and opinions he devoured. In the end he retreated gracefully, remaining close to Maeve whose romantic preference he understood and accepted.

Paul didn't see Larry Mullen's note, but he'd heard something about a group being formed. Yes, he told Larry when the handsome blond kid broached the subject, he could play guitar. Larry was delighted. The band would need a frontman, someone with a bit of cheek to introduce numbers and chat up the audience. This guy looked right for the role, looked like the kind of guy who should be in a rock band.

Norman had taught Paul how to play the C chords on an old guitar they had around the house. Paul had occasionally picked the instrument up and fooled around. He had done likewise during music lessons at school. To say he *played* guitar was fanciful. As he walked up Rosemount Avenue to Larry's house, Paul took with him lots of gifts, but musical ability — at least in so far as it applied to the guitar under his arm — was not one of them. He couldn't play, nor could he sing. What he brought with him to that first meeting was presence. Paul was an accomplished actor. He could veer from nice guy to heavy in the time it took to walk to Mount Temple from Maeve O'Regan's home close by. Depending on the company he was keeping he could be a sexy, streetwise kid or lonely little-boy-lost. He could be as vulgar as anyone on the rugby team and as spiritual as anyone in Sophie Shirley's prayer meetings. Paul's problem was that he wasn't acting; he was all of those people and more. He was as sensitive as a poet and as aggressive as a streetfighter. He was tolerant and intolerant. He was Bobby, Catholic, robust, courageous, a 'Dub' in his heart. And he was Iris, gentle, serene, Protestant. Sometimes his head ached with the conflict. As a baby he'd cried all day, restless, tormented, trying to reconcile the conflicting voices in his head, the competing demons in his soul. He didn't cry anymore. But the conflict raged on in his vast spirit. In the bland suburban world around him Paul felt clumsy, lost and very often alone. He still hadn't found an identity large enough, deep enough, universal enough, to house the spirit within him.

The punks had made rock 'n' roll accessible again to kids like Paul, kids who couldn't find a niche for themselves in the real world. 'Anyone can do it,' Paul remembered as he made his way to Larry's house. It was the best news he'd heard for ages.

Chapter Six

THE VILLAGE

On the last day of 1976 Graham Dougan, a fifteen-month-old baby boy, was buried in Belfast. He'd been killed in crossfire between IRA terrorists and a British army unit. Photographs of Graham's grieving parents were prominent in Irish newspapers on New Year's Day 1977. Alongside them on the front pages was the tragic story of Monica McAvera, a buyer from Macey's, a large department store in Dublin. Monica had been in Belfast to visit friends in the Republican Markets area of the city. In an operation designed to kill British soldiers, the IRA booby-trapped Monica's car, choosing the wrong vehicle. When Monica opened her car door the explosives meant for the soldiers blew both her legs away. A week later nobody in Ireland would remember Monica McAvera's name. She had given her legs for The Cause. The Troubles Up There might have been a million miles away from Dublin for all that they impinged upon the consciousness of Dubliners. Stories like those of Graham and Monica were read with detachment and forgotten within minutes.

Dr Garret Fitzgerald was Minister for Foreign Affairs in the ailing coalition government at the beginning of 1977. He and some other liberal activists in the Republic had been making noises about the need for social change. The Republic, these people argued, might show the bigots in the North by enacting some reforms in the areas of contraception, divorce and education, to allow the Protestant minority in the state to practise their beliefs unencumbered. Ecumenism was abroad in the early days of the new year. Church Unity Week was an attempt by liberals on both sides of the Catholic–Protestant divide to move forward from entrenched positions. Church Unity Week opened with a speech from the Most Reverend Jeremiah Newman, Bishop of Limerick, one of the most influential members of the Catholic hierarchy. He reflected upon what he described as 'recent utterances' by 'people in high political places who seem to think that all would be well if only the Roman Catholic Church were to be less unbending as regards the question of divorce, the availability of contraceptives, mixed marriage and undenominational education'. Warming to his theme, Bishop Newman went on: 'It is not all that easy. Some of these matters were germane to the entire issue of the well being of civilization.' Among these matters was the question of Catholic education which was, the bishop claimed, *at the beginning of Church Unity Week*, 'Basic to the consecration of The Faith'. Rigidly, dogmatically and uncompromisingly the Roman Catholic position had been stated, as it was, as it had been and it seemed would remain. Stunned by the Catholic Church's opening onslaught, Bishop Walton Empey spoke the following day of the Church of Ireland's 'dismay'. 'At a time such as this in our history,' the Protestant bishop pleaded, 'it [Church Unity Week] ought to be surely a week in which we thank God for all we have in common. Sentiments such as yours,' Empey wrote to Newman, 'make it very difficult for those engaged in the work of reconciliation.' On day three of Unity Week, Newman expressed 'regret' at 'causing pain' to his fellow Christians. He was, he vouched, *'Quite* ecumenical'. Five years after opening its doors, Mount Temple, the non-denominational school, remained an affront to Catholic teaching.

With the help of a sympathetic teacher, Donald Moxham, Feedback had acquired a rehearsal room in the school. The non-denominational rock band agreed to practise three times a week. Inspired by David Bowie, the Rolling Stones, the Sex Pistols and Elvis, Paul, Adam, Dave, Larry and Dick were, in their wanton disregard for things Irish, Gaelic, Nationalist and Catholic, examples, sad examples, of what happened to young people in the age of television and ecumenism. The formation of the band did not radically alter their lives. Adam still wore his shades and hippy gear, was more than ever at odds with the school regime. He had Mount Temple sussed. The thing to do, he decided, was to get in with the smokers. You were allowed to smoke in certain parts of the school. Most of Mount Temple's dodgy characters smoked. Adam started hanging out with them. They went to gigs and wine bars in town in the evenings. There was a groovy Northside scene which floated between Moran's Hotel, Hijack's Wine Bar in O'Connell Street and the Crescent and Spinning Wheel Coffee Bars in Mary Street. Every downtown area in the world has such places, dark, cosmopolitan, loose, not quite respectable. There was smoke, drink, girls who might (but in Dublin usually *didn't*), the odd bit of dope. The music playing incessantly in the background was rock 'n' roll. Here for a few darkly illicit hours, young people, alienated from much that was respectable, felt happy. Adam would catch the last bus home at 11.30, often throwing up the ale he'd drunk on the final walk up Yellow Walls Road. School the next day was just something that had to be got through.

Dave, Larry and Dick belonged in the system, while Paul's spirit functioned on many different levels. Characteristically, he was keeping his options open. He was in his last year at Mount Temple with his Leaving Certificate Exam to face in

June. He fancied going to university but in order to do so he needed to work at the subjects he was good at, like English, history, art and music. He was making an effort. Most of the time. In his final academic year Paul was a part-time rebel. He was close, if only platonically, to Maeve and trying very hard to get close to Alison Stewart, who was in fifth year with Adam and Dave. Ali was a lovely girl. Lovely to look at, with perfect, light-brown skin, a gorgeous figure and long, shiny black hair; and lovely of disposition, calm with a warm, humorous smile which was all the more attractive to Paul for the barest hint of mockery it contained. She was smart, too. Paul had tried it on with her the day she arrived at Mount Temple but she'd brushed him away. In the years since, he'd engaged in guerrilla warfare, trying to win her attention by using humour as his weapon, and he'd been more successful than he knew. Ali, despite her self-protective instincts, liked him. In truth, few women, young or old, wise or foolish, were left unmoved by the intriguing character Paul Hewson had become as he approached his seventeenth birthday. He was the hooligan who read Patrick Kavanagh, the Believer who tried it on with girls, the budding rock 'n' roll star who played football, the comic whose face in repose revealed a touching sadness. On top of her more obvious virtues Ali was a sensible girl, no prude, but no victim either. She wasn't going to become 'just another one of Paul's girls'. Their relationship moved slowly, at her pace.

Whenever Bobby Hewson raised the subject of his younger son's future he failed to get a clear-cut answer. Paul claimed he'd like to go to university but Bobby couldn't see the academic basis for such an aspiration. All he saw were weird-looking youngsters in his front room. Ten Cedarwood Road had become a club for Paul and his mates. After school, when Bobby and Norman were out, or late at night when they'd gone to bed, The Village would meet to chew the fat.

A number of new faces had joined Paul, Derek Rowen, 'Strongman' and Reggie Manuel to form an alliance that was something more than a street gang. Indeed the word gang is singularly inappropriate in relation to The Village. They were more sophisticated than that, much more.

Fionán Hanvey lived in the cul-de-sac at the top of Cedarwood Road. They called it 'Handbag Country' because of Fionán. Everyone in the neighbourhood knew him. He was 'The Hippy'. He was a roguishly good-looking young buck, pretty rather than handsome, yet muscular and unafraid. He was a T. Rex and David Bowie fan, affecting his idol's sexual ambivalence in dress and gait. He carried his possessions in a shoulder-bag. In the King's Road in London's Chelsea Fionán wouldn't have attracted more than a second glance. In Dublin his persona was daring beyond belief. To walk around Cedarwood as he did required the kind of courage that earns men V Cs.

When Fionán walked down Cedarwood past Paul and his mates he could feel them sniggering. He kept cool, kept walking. It wasn't always that easy. Elsewhere in Ballymun and Finglas he faced something worse than mockery; he was frequently beaten up by local youngsters who didn't like 'nancy boys', as gays were unfondly known in Dublin. Fionán wasn't gay, as it happens, indeed, he was an inveterate ladies' man. But the louts never stopped to discuss his preferences. He fascinated Paul. And Paul knew how to get to know anyone who fascinated him. 'I see you like Bowie,' he ventured one day as Fionán was ambling by. Paul pointed to the David Bowie badge decorating Fionán's shoulder-bag. 'Yeh,' the hippy replied. A discussion ensued about the relative merits of punk and Bowie and a new partnership was formed.

The Village had no acknowledged leader, its members were too smart, too independent for that, but when it came to music Fionán and Paul were its most influential characters.

Membership of The Village was exclusive. Derek Rowen qualified, so did Strongman and Reggie Manuel. There was Skello, David Watson and his brother Niggles. David Watson had contracted meningitis when he was a child. The illness left him physically incapacitated, affecting his movement and responses, and he looked mildly disturbed. In fact he was very bright, with a rich sense of humour. Rumour that David had a great record collection drew The Village to him. The vivid personality that lay behind his handicap ensured a lasting friendship. Anthony Murphy, a big strong teenager who lived next door to the Rowens, was also in. Most were friends of Paul and Derek, some like David and Niggles, old pals of Fionán's.

As they got to know each other in the Ireland of 1977, the bond between these witty, energetic, imaginative boys grew stronger. The Ireland of bombs and bullets, craven clerics, of public houses and cheap American television programmes, of pork-barrel politicians so obviously on the make that they were regarded as a joke rather than the obscenity they *really* were, the Ireland they lived in had no use for them or they for it. If the official Ireland, the Gaelic, Nationalist, Roman Catholic Ireland, was no longer quite the oppressive force it had been in the lives of their parents, the new Ireland, rendered somnolent by pub and telly, was to be resisted with equal vigour. The Village was a resistance movement, something to identify with, a substitute for the country that ought to have been there, but wasn't. Unable to identify with the culture around them, The Village people invented their own world. Sitting in Paul's house late at night they would reflect on life as it presented itself to them in semi-detached suburbia. Their reflections would be condescending, but oh, so very true; look at those arseholes down the road, eating the chips, drinking the cider, married at twenty-one, four kids at twenty-five, a beer-belly in their early thirties. Go to mass, eye the secretary or the office-girl, work for your boss, kiss his ass for fifty years. Then get a portable telly, a night on the piss and fucking die. *That* was the prospect, *that* was what school was about, conform, conform, conform, to *their* fucking way. Say your prayers and vote for Charlie or Garret. Be a good citizen.

Fionán was into confrontation rather than assimilation. He went to the local Christian Brothers school. It was sport, Irish and get your hair cut. And clips behind the ear (and worse) from the Brothers, some of whom were fascist bastards. He was reading Oscar Wilde, who wasn't on the school syllabus. Barney Rock and John Kearns, two of Ireland's best Gaelic footballers who played for Dublin, were the school heroes. Fionán hated sport. It was part of the chips and cider syndrome. The Brothers *worried* about Fionán, when they weren't beating the shit out of him. What kind of boy *was* he?

The Village's response was humour, contempt rather than overtly expressed anger. The Village was a state of mind, subconscious as well as conscious rejection of the stereotypes of young Irish manhood on offer. Having rejected their cultural identity, they proceeded to adjust their personal identities as well. They invented names for each other, names that would be truer to their real personalities than the names their parents had given them.

Fionán Hanvey became Gavin Friday. Given his feelings about Catholic-Irish manhood the Gaelic name Fionán seemed like a perverse joke. He looked like a Gavin, smooth, daring, cool. Gavin was nicely trans-Atlantic. A singular sight around Cedarwood, Gavin was often referred to as 'yer man with the handbag'. Man – Man Friday – Gavin Friday.

Derek Rowen was also a bit of a stand-out in the neighbourhood. He was into bikes, wore leather jackets with silver studs everywhere, had long unkempt blond hair and sported a pair of stiletto-heeled, thigh-length boots. He was a brilliant oil painter. His Village name was, however, a reference to something more substantial in his character than the way he dressed.

Derek was Guggi because of his lower lip. There was an indefinable something, a hint of vanity that needed constant assuaging, in Guggi's face. Gug, Gug, Gug ... Gug-gi ... There was something warm and sloppy about the sound of G-U-G-G-I if you said it slowly. It was like warm honey, dripping out of a tap.

Guggi christened Paul. The Village were walking down O'Connell Street one day when they saw a sign on a shop-front opposite the Gresham Hotel: Bonovox. They were baffled, intrigued, amused by the name. What did it mean? The place turned out to be a hearing-aid shop. Paul became Bonovox of O'Connell Street, Bono for short. There was a strength about the sound of Bono. It didn't suggest a skinny, matchstick character, it was round, deep, resonant: Bon-Oh. Bono. What did it mean? What did he mean? What was he? Bono of the many personalities. Bono the Elusive was as baffling as the original sign that suggested his name.

Trevor Rowen suffered from asthma, thus he became 'Strongman'. People thought David Watson was a fool. They talked s-l-o-w-l-y, patronizingly, to him. They called him Day-Vid. He knew what they were doing, he wasn't daft. So he began to call himself Day-Vid and to declare his daftness. 'I'm Day-Vid, I'm mad,' he would smile crazily, relishing the confusion this would arouse in the listener. 'Yes, yes,' they would stutter, 'I'm sure you're not ... er ... mad.'

'I am, I am,' Day-Vid would insist. 'Quite mad.'

Anthony Murphy was an idealist, an honest, up-front, fortune-favours-the brave idealist. They nicknamed him Pod after some character Gavin had read about in English fiction: Sir Poddington, the Bravest Knight of All. Like his fictional clone, Pod was a warrior, a fighter with hot blood and no time for phonies. Pod was impatient. Reggie Manuel had been tagged 'Cocker Spaniel' by Bono at Mount Temple. This was now revised. Handsome, wickedly handsome, cool,

High Protestant, ladykiller, Reggie was from now on Bad Dog.

As well as names, The Villagers assumed roles that were allotted to them by their peers. Bono was The Judge, albeit a judge who could be told to go stuff himself if his pronouncements didn't meet with popular approval. Gavin was in charge of being in charge. Guggi was the principal giver of names. Pod was in charge of morale, Strongman in charge of ignorance. Not everyone *got* a role, Strongman would be told when he complained about his.

The Village visited Mount Temple to watch Feedback rehearse. They met Adam, Dave, Dick and Larry and started to socialize with the Mount Temple set. Cedarwood Road flanked by Ballymun Flats and Finglas Housing Estate promised much less than the new world they now discovered. A short ride in Guggi's car or on the moped bikes they owned took them across the Northside through flatland in Drumcondra, out past Marino's semi-detached slumber to the richer pastures of Clontarf and Howth. Here looking out on the sea a world awaited to be explored, a world that if not *entirely* or even essentially different from Cedarwood, was to seventeen-year-olds seeking stimulation, somewhat more inviting. Such adventures usually began, when, as an antidote to Ballymun boredom, someone would suggest going to see the 'Howth Pigs'. This wasn't meant to be vicious. It was just that Howth conjured up images of middle-classness that were impossible to define. There was about Howth and Clontarf a vastness, a fatness, a certain plumpness that, together with the area's aura of smugness and comfort, reminded The Villagers of – pigs! Mark Holmes was also known as Pompous Holmes. 'Let's go out and visit Pompous Holmes,' The Village would cry, making poor Mark sound like a new, up-market housing estate.

Behind the humour lay something close to despair. Most of them were in their last years at school. The man with the weekly pay cheque and the portable telly was waiting – if you were lucky; the dole queue if you were not. Guggi had left school and was working for his dad who now had a family business. He had a small car, an NSU Prinz, like the one Bono's dad once owned. For the price of a gallon of petrol the little car would take them anywhere. One night in spring 1977, broke and bored, they filled the tank and headed out towards Howth. Just to see what might happen. *Something* might, Gavin, Bono and Guggi thought.

They were driving through Fairview's inner-city bustle about to join the coast road. Guggi stopped at the traffic lights. Bono hopped out of the car. They thought he was going to the shops for sweets, so they pulled over to wait. Suddenly there was a great commotion behind them, buses and cars honking their horns, people stopped on the pavement pointing aghast. Bono was standing in the middle of the road with his trousers and underpants down round his ankles. Mooning it was called. He'd done it before in town. Never told anyone, just dropped 'em. Bang. Commotion. Now Fairview was in turmoil as he stood there, jumper clenched between his teeth. 'Pooh, Pooh, Georgie Higgins,' he muttered to himself. Two Dublin 'ole wans' stood pointing at his body. 'Jaysus, look at the size of it,' one exclaimed to the other. Bono waddled across the road towards them. 'Excuse me, could you tell me where Georgie Higgins lives?' Then he was back in the car and they fled in the direction of Pompous Holmes.

Bono did surprisingly well in his Leaving Cert. Exam, scraping together enough points in his strong subjects to apply for a university place. His father was dubious about sending him to University College Dublin. Bobby had seen plenty of fellas dossing around UCD for five years, playing student and wasting the hefty fees their parents coughed up. Knowing his own son's capacity for dreaming, he feared university might be the worst thing for Paul. But he couldn't deny him the opportunity. They made a deal: Bobby would pay the fees for the first year. If Paul worked and got good results he could stay and complete his courses. If not, if there was any messing about, he'd be out looking for a job.

Bono entered UCD in September 1977. Two weeks later Bobby received a letter from the university bursar demanding a meeting. Oh my God, he thought, what now? Challenged as to his behaviour, Bono proclaimed his innocence. After a sleepless night Bobby travelled out to Belfield to meet the Bursar. It was better – and worse – than he feared. I'm very sorry, Mr Hewson, he was told, but Paul will have to be removed. We didn't realize when we accepted him that he'd failed Irish in his Leaving Cert. Bobby was furious. How could they accept his son, and the fees, without checking Paul's credentials? This would have a devastating effect on the boy. Surely there was something that could be done? Sorry, Mr Hewson, this is a cast-iron rule, there is nothing we can do, Bobby was told. If Paul went back to Mount Temple for another year and passed his Irish Exam next time then he could be guaranteed a place in 1978. Bobby received a letter confirming this arrangement. Reflecting, years later, on the cruel rejection (command of Irish was not essential for the arts degree Paul proposed taking) Bobby and his son agreed that this incident more than any other determined the course his life would subsequently take.

With nothing to do at Mount Temple except study Irish, and little interest in doing that, Bono devoted more time to Feedback. The school had decided to organize a talent contest for the pupils. The news galvanized the new group. During the months of practice a bond had developed between them, based on acceptance of each other's strengths and weaknesses. Larry was experienced as a musician and a public performer. Dave could play the guitar sufficiently well to 'cover' the mixture of rock classics and current hits that formed their repertoire. He could also deliver the odd impressive sounding guitar solo. Bono's guitar playing was unexceptional to the point of being superfluous. His singing was loud, rough and tuneless. But he possessed the courage of the truly desperate. He wasn't afraid to fail and the importance of this asset to the band was understood and acknowledged by the others. Bono had balls. He was prepared to stand up front and present a target for the derision that might otherwise be aimed at them. Bono was larger than life, big enough to hide behind. He also had ideas about how they should deploy their talents and the conviction that, if they set about it the right way, Feedback could amount to something. Adam was even more convinced of this than Bono, if that was possible. Adam had seen the English punk band the Clash play at Trinity that summer. He knew that Feedback could make it. And he knew *how* they should proceed. Even before their first gig Adam was a rock musician in his head. He talked about getting a 'record deal', about the need for 'good management', and when the four of them had finished with this school bullshit, 'going on the road'. He was as desperate as Bono but cooler, giving the others an impression of nervelessness that, when it wasn't amusing, was reassuring. Destiny beckoned, according to Adam. They would take in the talent show along the way.

Feedback were due to go on second last. They would have ten minutes. Most of the other students treated the contest as a lark. Everyone who could do something did it. There were singers, dancers, comedy acts doing impressions of famous people and teachers. Performers and audience swapped insults. Bono smiled reassuringly at his friends as they waited to go on. Larry needed little reassurance, he'd been here before. Dave was very nervous, he didn't like to be exposed, he wasn't a natural performer. This was traumatic. The part of Adam that wasn't quivering with nerves didn't give a fuck. He felt numb and couldn't distinguish one feeling from the other. They'd prepared a set consisting of Peter Frampton's 'Show Me The Way', a parody of the Bay City Rollers and a climactic medley of Beach Boys' hits. Bono was determined not to smile. He hated his smile, which seemed grim and somehow false when he flashed it at himself in the mirror. But in the end he couldn't help himself. The applause was loud and enthusiastic. People stamped and whistled for more. Feedback's intensity had seemed funny at first, then touching and had finally earned the audience's respect. It was their willingness to give themselves, Bono's in particular, which separated them from the other performers. The teachers who sat as judges didn't give the band the prize; that would have been inappropriate, not to mention an affront to the teacher who walked out in disgust during the set. But everyone left Mount Temple that night talking about the four lads. They themselves were proud and relieved. From that night on Dave Evans felt more confident. People, especially girls, now knew he existed. He was anonymous no longer, he was a guitarist in a rock 'n' roll band. Larry had proved that he could play the drums the way he'd always wanted to, make his own rules and, despite Monica Bonnie and the Artane Boys' Band, be a musician. Adam glowed with an unprecedented feeling of achievement. Unconditional approval such as the audience had displayed had never shone on him before. It was cool, a justification of *everything*. He wanted more and he wanted it soon.

Walking home with Alison, Bono felt elated. His joy had to do with something more profound than vanity. In their beautiful song of teenage alienation, 'She's Leaving Home', the Beatles had a line that came very close to summarizing Bono's life to date. Like Lennon and McCartney's anonymous heroine, Bono felt 'something inside that was always denied'. Like her he didn't know what that 'something' was. In the song she's 'leaving home after being alone for so very long'. He hadn't left home, at least not physically, but despite his enviable success as a social animal Bono had been alone for so very long, isolated by his spirit which lay rumbling like a volcano beneath the raunchy, streetwise persona. That massive sensitivity to the world and everything and everybody in it was the 'something' inside Bono that was 'always denied'. He'd sought relief in his faith, in the tenderness of his girlfriends, among his comrades in The Village. He'd taken some comfort from each of these experiences, but it was never enough to suppress the frustration lodged deep within him.

Bono had always been cautious about rebellion, had, unlike Adam, always tried to stay in the fold. But recently the conflicts and confusions within him had caused severe physical and psychological distress. He'd begun to have nosebleeds and had blacked out on a couple of occasions. Once, in a spasm of unprovoked rage, he'd overturned a desk and stormed out of the classroom. Gossip on The Mall attributed this behaviour to Bono the 'character', but others like Maeve and Ali who were close to him knew better. They encouraged him to talk to Jack Heaslip, a teacher who was regarded as a bit of a rebel himself and known to be sympathetic to Mount Temple's students. Heaslip was, like the youngster he found himself counselling, a spiritual man who would eventually leave teaching to become a Protestant minister. He understood how spirituality could distance you from the Ireland of the 1970s. He empathized with this suburban youngster who saw beyond the cider, chips and babies syndrome, who felt there was more to life than semi-detached, saloon-car suburbia had to offer. Heaslip understood as well what it was to be Irish and not feel Nationalist or Gaelic, to be Dublin and not belong to the mythical city created by Joyce and O'Casey. These were identity problems common to the generation Bono belonged to, doomed to fight their grandfathers' battles, obliged by the myth of Irishness that served as history to pay lip-service to a cause, The Cause, that, ironically, most of their grandfathers had rejected. Whatever confusion was caused by the difference between what Bono's generation felt and what they were supposed to feel was in his case exacerbated by his religious identity. As well as not being truly Irish and failing to conform to the stereotype Dubliner, Bono was neither Catholic nor Protestant, but lost somewhere between the two. Of the many traditions competing for his soul, there wasn't one with which he could align himself. It was no wonder that, as he himself would recall years later, he was 'fucked-up'.

Thus he sought refuge in his Mount Temple role of 'character', a part with which he now felt increasingly ill at ease. Jack Heaslip offered support if not relief. 'Mooning' offered relief but no escape. The Village was an alternative world, one whose people and values he understood, a world he and his friends had created for themselves. But The Village was narrow, claustrophobic, insular. They laughed at the world, mocked it, claimed that they were different, better. Bono wanted to prove it. He wanted to find others who felt the same as they did, to create a community much larger than The Village. He was into subversion but on a scale much grander than his friends envisaged.

That idea and the possibility that it might be realized through the medium of Feedback, that it could be realized through rock 'n' roll, lay behind Bono's elation as he walked home after their first gig. He had offered himself, passionate, in all his fucked-up desperation, to the audience and they'd responded. He hadn't given them a piece of himself, he'd given everything; the 'character', the raunchy lover, the evangelist, the Catholic *and* the Protestant. He'd gone for broke on the notion that they felt as he did, that *their* spirits were as alive as his was, that they too had 'something inside that was always denied', 'something' that was beyond Church and state, myth and legend. For him the triumph of this first night was not feeling as alone as he had for so very long. Yes, the band would need to write new songs, songs that would give voice and substance to the 'something within', and when they did he knew after tonight that he could deliver to an audience much larger than the one in his front room. At last he knew what he was, who he was and where he wanted to go.

Word of mouth around the Northside ensured a good crowd for their second gig in St Fintan's School Hall in Sutton. The talk was of a new band that was going places. The singer was however said to be a real pratt who threw himself around all over the place. At a policy meeting after their debut the band had decided on a change of name. Feedback, a joke against themselves, would become the Hype, a comment on the music business. Sutton was a nice middle-class suburb. The audience in St Fintan's small hall was made up of kids much like the band themselves. This was their Saturday disco, an occasion for dancing rather than standing around listening to a band. Bono wanted their attention. He wasn't content to play background music. The Village was out in force to support its friends, standing front of stage to offer encouragement and protection if that became necessary.

The band had added some Rolling Stones and a Boomtown Rats number to their successful Mount Temple set. Bono didn't try to imitate any contemporary rock 'n' roll hero. Where Bob Geldof and Phil Lynott projected mean, moody sexuality, seemed detached and (at least until the gig was over) inaccessible, Bono oozed sincerity. Instead of seeking to put enough distance to lend enchantment between himself and the audience, Bono craved contact. He talked about the band's beginnings, its dreams and its desire to be with them, the audience, who were he told them the ones that really mattered. He *was* a 'fuckin' eejit' some of the young men thought, why didn't he play some fucking music. Down in the hall Ali found it hard to reconcile this gauche, desperately eager-to-please puppy with the bright, passionate, funny boy she was fond of. Behind him the band waited patiently for the talking to stop, Larry hunched dreamily handsome over his drums, Adam ever so slightly amused, Dave as still as the guitar held lightly in his hands. As he talked in this suburban church hall about his desire to create some kind of bond between band and audience, it seemed ridiculous. Yet when he sang and the three boys behind him played, the convictions so awkwardly expressed by the vocalist began to make a kind of sense. The intensity of the sound moved even those who had shuffled uncomfortably during Bono's homily. The bleeding passion in his voice was real, and rarely heard around comfortable Sutton. He was weird, strangely compelling, more than a pratt, even the hardest heart was forced to concede before the evening was over. They'd had all kinds of bands at St Fintan's, but never one like the Hype.

Alone in bed that night, Bono felt better. The headaches and nosebleeds had stopped. Performing had a cathartic effect, freeing his spirit, quieting the rage against the lie that life was. Now he wanted more than mere relief. He'd never been a happy rebel, had always tried for positives rather than negatives. It wasn't enough to rage against the lie, you had to offer truth in its place. That's what the band should be about. That was what the talk was about, an attempt to establish a *real* relationship with the audience. The punk idea was fine as far as it went, but it didn't go far enough. Punk wasn't an idea, it didn't offer anything in place of the conceit and deception it raged against. The Village argued about this. Bono felt the new music should strive for truth and honesty, should reflect what was really in people's hearts. Gavin saw it differently. Music should confront and offend those who spread the lies, music should be shocking, not good.

But the music in Bono's head was good. He was unhappy with the songs the Hype were playing, other people's music carrying other people's notions. This he knew was the bum note in the Hype's performance. Where before there had been frustration he now felt chords and words echoing in his head. They had learnt how to play and how to perform, now they would write their own songs. That would be the ultimate truth.

Inspired by the Hype's emergence The Village began to think of forming an alternative group. Gavin, Guggi and Pod approached Dick Evans, who'd dropped out of the Hype. He agreed to provide the music. Nobody could sing, but that didn't matter because what they proposed to do was more performance art than music. Their band would be called the Virgin Prunes. Gavin would be the front man. After years spent challenging Ballymun's ideas about masculinity, taking his act onto the boards would be no great hassle. Pod, game as ever, promised to learn how to play the drums. Guggi would be Gavin's straight-man up front. Day-Vid would also appear, as himself. Reggie would be the Prunes' manager. The Virgin Prunes first appeared in public at a party in Glasnevin given by James and Isobel Mahon, two old National school friends of Bono's. Backed by Dick's guitar, Gavin held centre stage in the Mahons' back garden. He'd written a song called Art Fuck, a punk diatribe, which attacked the cider and chips syndrome, Spanish holidays, the Beatles and anything else he could identify as central to the tacky culture they inhabited. *He* wanted to get up people's noses. Bono, who listened and laughed with the rest, wanted more. *He* wanted the Hype to uplift its audience, to help them rise above the things in life that beat them down.

The difference of opinion that followed from these points of view were left for late-night debate in Bono's, Pod's or Gavin's front rooms. Parties such as the Mahons' were for socializing, having fun, pulling girls. Being in The Village helped. They'd had badges made with The Village printed on them. They had established themselves as a force in Northside society from Glasnevin to the grander suburbs out by the sea around

Pompous Holmes. Adam, Dave and Dick often travelled with The Village; Larry, being younger, had his own friends and was thus less frequently around. Dick was adopted as an honorary member through his association with the Prunes. Adam thought he was a member, but he wasn't. They liked him, admired his brio, but he belonged to the vastness, fatness, smugness and comfort of prosperous Dublin. He was coming at life from a different angle. So was Dave. They gave him a Village name, but not membership. Bono christened Dave Edge. This had to do with the shape of his head which was, like his mind, sharp. It had to do also with his presence, which was watchful. Edge was never at the centre of things, but always on the fringe, observing.

The advent of punk and the British chart successes of the Boomtown Rats and Thin Lizzy had inspired many young Dubliners to form garage bands. There were other Northside groups like the Hype (although *none* like the Prunes), all of them hustling to get the few gigs that were going. Adam worked hard to honour his promise to provide gigs. He was working on Lloyd McIntyre, a mate who had influence in the Nucleus Disco, which was run in a church hall in Raheny by a committee of youngsters. Lloyd arranged for Adam and Bono to meet with them to argue the Hype's claims on the gig. After much persuasion the committee was divided, but willing to travel to Edge's house in Malahide to audition the band. Gwenda Evans, now known as Mrs Edge, laid on some lavish Welsh hospitality and the Hype were set for their next gig. The gig turned out to be a bit of a disaster. They planned to open with 'Jumpin' Jack Flash', at least Edge did. Dick planned to open with another Rolling Stones number, 'Brown Sugar'. The innovation they'd hit on was that each instrument would come in separately starting with Edge's guitar and climaxing with Bono's vocal. They went down the road to the Green Dolphin public house to take some courage. When they were announced on stage they burst on, ran to the instruments they had carefully put in place before going to the pub and Edge began to play. There were only two problems: they'd forgotten to tune up and Edge and Dave were playing different songs. As each member joined in, the initial problems were compounded. By the time it was Bono's turn the music was unrecognizable. The committee sat impassively, realizing too late that they'd engaged the wrong band.

Neither band could get a gig for the October Bank Holiday weekend. It loomed bleakly ahead for The Village. Bono and Guggi proposed an adventure; they would go camping in Wales for the weekend. The others, somewhat dubiously, agreed. Wales could be cold in late October. Wales could be cold in July! Someone organized a tent. They cadged money from all the usual sources. Frank Mangan, a friend of Gavin's who was working and therefore had money, was made an associate member of The Village for the weekend. They bought a primus stove for cooking and rucksacks to carry food and clothes. On board the Dublin–Holyhead ferry on Friday night Bono and Guggi recalled their happy times in North Wales with the Boys' Department. Bono talked fondly about Mandy, his Welsh sweetheart of three years ago. Yes, he remembered, she was gorgeous in that black bathing-suit. As they reminisced, the others slowly grasped the point of this weekend adventure. They had been conned, but as the ship steamed into Holyhead they realized there was nothing to be done except head for Criccieth. They made camp on the beach. It was Saturday. They discovered that the shops in Wales stayed shut on Sundays, so before searching for Mandy they stocked up with bread and ham and cheese to make sandwiches for Sunday lunch. A tin of mint potatoes was the luxury they allowed themselves. A pact was struck; nobody would touch the food until Sunday lunch-time.

When they found Mandy in the village that night she'd

changed. She had a boyfriend and didn't care for Bono anymore. The Village was greatly amused at his discomfort. As
they trudged back to camp the Irish punks drew puzzled
glances from the citizens of Criccieth. Strongman had bought
an airgun in Dublin before the trip and now it nestled
menacingly on the crook of his arm. It was raining, and a gale-
force wind swept along the North Wales coast. The tent was
down when they got back. You put the tent up, I'll cook some
food, Bono ordered. No food until tomorrow he was told.
Every time they fixed the tent, it collapsed. In the end they
slept with it on top of them.

As dawn broke a noise outside the tent woke The Village.
Bono was standing outside in his underpants bent over the
primus stove, heating the precious tin of mint potatoes. The
bastard, Strongman thought, as he reached for the airgun. He
aimed at the thief's arse. Bono's screams echoed along the
beach. He rushed Strongman, and the others had to pull them
apart. Later that morning Strongman suffered an asthma attack.
They took him to the doctor in the village, who recommended
a warm bed. Frank Mangan coughed up for a room in the local
hotel. The sandwiches were all soggy, inedible; even Bono
couldn't look at them. The weekend had turned into a disaster,
but a kind of hysteria had now taken hold of The Villagers;
things were so bad they were funny. The rest of Sunday was
spent taunting the natives, 'vibeing them out', as Gavin put it.
Bono's clothes were drenched, so he wore his yellow mac over
his underpants. He covered his head from the still-pouring
rain with a fox's head he'd bought the previous day. The rest
huddled in a ladies' toilet, using the hand dryer to blow warm
air on their wet feet as they waited for evening and the train
back to Holyhead. The police were looking for them now,
interested in the gun which villagers had, in their description
of the wild Irish gang, identified as a rifle. The local Bobby
advised them to get out of town, out of Wales, something they

were glad to do once they had collected Strongman from his sickbed.

Wet, broke and hungry, The Village returned to Dublin in triumph. To some the weekend may have looked like a disaster but they saw it differently. Their spirit remained unbroken, they had survived the worst that North Wales in October could throw at them. They had won. And it *really was* lovely to be home. What more could you ask of a Bank-Holiday weekend!

Chapter Seven

THE SCENE

A streaker was spotted in The Mall sometime in late February 1978. Nobody was caught by the school authorities but the word in the Staff Common Room was that the boy Clayton had now taken to running naked through Mount Temple's corridors. Clayton was a pleasant boy, but exasperating. Even Donald Moxham, his sympathetic form tutor, had given up hope that the school could make something of Adam. His report at the end of the previous term was, according to Moxham, 'disturbing'. The tutor sent for Jo and Brian. The news was grim. Unless there was a radical change of attitude Adam had no chance of sitting his Leaving Cert., much less of passing. Socially, Moxham recorded, he was a delightful boy, when he wasn't being silly, but he had done no academic work in the eighteen months he'd been at Mount Temple. Perhaps Jo and Brian should consider taking Adam away from school, which Moxham kindly speculated their son might have 'outgrown'.

Relations between Adam and his parents had been strained since his departure from Columba's. He seemed to think of nothing but his music. He remained polite but distanced from Jo and Brian. The streaking episode sealed his fate at Mount

Temple. The school would give him a decent reference, there would be no question of expulsion. Getting wind that discussions about his future were taking place in the principal, Mr Medlycott's, study, Adam hid in a bush outside the window to eavesdrop. He was apprehended and thus left the Irish education system as he had spent most of his nine years in it, under a cloud. In the circumstances, Mr Medlycott's valedictory letter was generous, not to mention discreet:

To All Whom it May Concern

Adam Clayton, born 13.3.1960, was a pupil of this school from September 1976 to March 1978. He has worked well when stimulated. He has shown considerable initiative and organizing ability, especially in relation to his music 'group', which has had considerable success.

He is a pleasant, cheerful person, was popular and took part in the social life of the school. Because of his late arrival, he has not held a position of responsibility in the school but I have found him to be a generally mature person. I believe him to be honest, truthful and reliable, and am sure that in a suitable position he will be both conscientious and committed.

Signed, J. T. Medlycott
Principal.

Jo Clayton was a strong-minded, capable woman. She'd had to be with her husband away flying for much of their married life. Now she promised to impose some discipline on her errant eldest son. He wasn't going to get away with this. Jo drew up a list of jobs that needed doing: her car would be washed once a week; her mother's garden needed digging; her own garden needed mowing; the glassware needed cleaning. Adam complied. He had no choice, since Jo was his only source of finance.

Freed of the burden of school Adam now assumed the role

of band manager while Larry, Edge and Bono studied at Mount Temple. The Hype had by now conquered the Northside circuit of church halls and youth clubs. They were, at least in their own minds, ready for town and the big time. Larry spotted a notice in the *Evening Press* announcing the *Evening Press*–Harp Lager Talent Contest for new groups to be held in Limerick on 18 March as part of the city's Civic Week. The first prize was £500 and a chance to audition for CBS record company. Adam was assigned the task of entering the contest and organizing the trip south. A few gigs in town would be the ideal preparation for Limerick, the band decided. Adam promised to secure the work. With his bus pass, which could be used during school hours, and the money for a few vital cups of coffee, the manager set off to suss out The Scene in town.

Dubliners were feeling mildly optimistic about 1978. A new Fianna Fail government led by the avuncular Jack Lynch was promising better times ahead. The Irish economy, stagnant since the oil crisis of 1973, would now it seemed expand as it always did under Fianna Fail. Household rates and motor taxation were abolished, leaving people with more money in their pockets. Generous government subsidies to first-time house purchasers created jobs in the building industry and placed the dream of owning a semi-detached home within reach of tens of thousands of newly married people. After years of gloom and doom the message from Fianna Fail was that everything was going to be all right.

The city's rock 'n' roll community had its own reasons for feeling optimistic. The seventies had proved that Dublin rock bands could make it in the British charts. The success of Bob Geldof and the Boomtown Rats and Phil Lynott and Thin Lizzy drew London and Dublin closer together, made Grafton Street and its rock 'n' roll environs seem somehow more relevant, less a provincial outpost than they had been up to now. Suddenly, dramatically, tantalizingly, the dream of making it seemed less outrageous. Seeing the Rats and Lizzy on *Top of the Pops* nourished the hopes of guys who only weeks before had shared amplifiers, cigarettes and groupies with Geldof and 'Philo'. When they measured themselves against the new rock 'n' roll heroes, local bands like Revolver, the Vipers, Berlin, Fit Kilkenny and the Remoulds, the Radiators and Atrix, U2 knew something that they had never been certain of before: there was no mystery ingredient for making it that *they* lacked.

Geldof was a hustler from the Southside, a Blackrock College boy, brazen, imaginative, a showman – and a ruthless bastard – but where it mattered, musically, Geldof was fuck all. If he could make it, we could, we *can*. Philo had been around. He was a protégé of Brush Sheils, who'd sacked him from Skid Row. Brush was an old legend on the Dublin scene. He was still around with Skid Row playing every Thursday in the Baggot. If Geldof inspired his peers by making it despite his musical inadequacies, Brush had the opposite effect. Brush was a brilliant bass player and double smart, yet he hadn't made it. This was an uncomfortable thought. Way back in the early 1970s Skid Row had got a record deal with CBS. They'd gone to London and seemed all set. But the whole thing had collapsed acrimoniously, with Brush claiming he'd been ripped off. He'd returned defeated and bitter to the local scene. His experience had taught him that in rock 'n' roll being good wasn't enough, indeed, hardly mattered. It was about hype, image, being in the right place at the right time and being sufficiently clueless and artificial to allow record companies and managements to mould you to the fashion of the time. He had failed, Brush would wryly acknowledge, but because he was too good, too smart. He had tried to wise-up Philo, but the wild kid from Crumlin's working-class Southside hadn't listened. Rock 'n' roll stardom made Brush laugh. He would settle for being the best.

With Geldof and Lynott departed to the big time there was a

sense among those who remained in Dublin in the spring of 1978 of battling for the vacant crown, the title of best band in the city which in the wake of their success promised more than it ever had before. In this struggle for supremacy no quarter was asked or given. Town was full of good bands. There were only a few gigs that mattered: the Baggot Inn, McGonagles, Moran's Hotel, the Project Arts Centre. The Celebrity Club was low rent but acceptable when nothing else was going. Dirty tricks, many of them allegedly patented by Geldof, were ruthlessly deployed. A rival band had a gig at the Baggot Inn, you had a free night. So you rang up Charlie McGettigan who ran the Baggot, pretending to represent your rivals; very sorry but we can't make it tomorrow night, the lead guitar-player's sick. Half an hour later you dropped in on Charlie to see how things were going. There's no chance you'd be available tomorrow night, he would plead? Well, I suppose we *could* get it together, you would respond, flipping anxiously through your diary. Whatever happened the following night as a result of the confusion you had caused could only be to your benefit – and would inevitably cast a cloud over your rivals' gig, not to mention their reputation for reliability.

Another popular ruse was the phone call to the gig promoter purporting to come from a major UK record company. Hello, we're coming to Dublin next Friday to see – here you inserted the name of your band. We understand yours is the best venue in town. Could you put them on for us on Friday? Faced with the choice of honouring his original deal with your rivals or promoting a Historic Occasion the gig organizer would invariably opt for his place in history. When the UK record company never showed it would be put down to such organizations' legendary contempt for the local scene. There were other less sophisticated ways of wrecking other bands' plans. You could simply pour a pint of ale over their amps or cause an affray in the audience in the middle of their set.

These diabolical schemes were probably more talked about than practised, but their prominence in the folklore of the time conveys something of the atmosphere around the claustrophobic Dublin rock scene. The idea that rock 'n' roll success was a matter of hustle and hype rather than musical accomplishment was Bob Geldof's legacy to the city he'd now left behind. Brush Sheils was on hand to confirm this if anyone was in doubt.

The rock scene occupied a square mile of the city with Grafton Street at its heart. Dublin's most fashionable boulevard was the place to head for when you left your suburban home in search of rock 'n' roll fame. In 1978 the punks occupied The Street, which was a pedestrian walkway. Their leader was Brummie, a Dubliner in his early twenties who'd lived in Birmingham for a while and sported a Midlands twang. He and his acolytes, Little Reb, Dustin, Garret and Aengus, sneered at everyone who wasn't working class and punk. That some of them were middle class was beside the point. They constituted a presence on The Street, provided seasoning and colour as they forced shoppers to detour round them on the way to smart stores like Switzers and Brown Thomas's. Brummie and his mates provided cover for rockers who stalked the vicinity. However out of place, however inhibited you felt, nobody was going to pay too much attention to you while the punks were on display. Afternoons were spent around the Dandelion Market in Gaiety Green at the top of The Street. The market gave off fashionable vibes, allowed loitering without intent, provided a setting for casual encounters. Advance Records in Gaiety Green was the place to browse if rarely to buy. When it was time for coffee you strolled down to Bewleys or across to The Coffee Inn in St Anne Street.

There was a small amount of dope around the scene and a few girls who did. But mostly the decadence was only on the surface. Days were passed gossiping about gigs and speculating about your 'deal'. Gigs were what town was about, but Getting A Deal was what it was *really* about. A record deal was the way out, the key to fame and fortune and all the other things you'd gone into rock 'n' roll for in the first place. After Geldof and Philo had proved it could be done, Deal Fever swept Dublin for a while. Every band either had a deal, was about to get one or had turned down a deal that 'wasn't right'. Your deal was your vindication and the day you stopped believing that your deal was imminent was the day you started looking for a proper job. The really bad days were the ones when news of some other band's deal spread like bushfire through The Street. The proud possessors of the contract would hold court that night in Davy Byrne's pub in Duke Street, the Bailey or Larry Tobin's. No pint of Smithwicks would ever taste so sweet as the one you supped the night you got Your Deal. The night would end on a high at one of the gigs close by in McGonagles, the Baggot or Toner's pub next door.

As far as official Ireland (Dublin branch) was concerned, none of this was happening. Like foreign games and religions other than Catholicism, rock 'n' roll was alien to the Irish people and as such not to be encouraged. The established monopoly broadcasting system, Radio Telefis Eireann, ignored rock 'n' roll. Those who wanted to listen to rock or pop music bought themselves a decent radio and tuned in to the BBC or Radio Luxemburg. Irish newspapers mentioned rock 'n' roll only to chronicle the excesses of its wilder sons and daughters, whose often tragic stories were offered as testimony to the evil of the music.

If you wanted to read about rock 'n' roll heroes you bought the *New Musical Express* or *Melody Maker*. If you were really sick you scouted the shops in town for a copy of *Rolling Stone*. None of these periodicals covered the Irish rock scene. The BBC and Radio Luxemburg didn't play records cut by Irish bands who'd got their deal. Making rock music in Ireland was a lonely, sad, self-contained existence. There was no infrastructure to sustain and nourish its heroes, no means of communication between them and the hundreds of thousands of youngsters throughout Gaelic Ireland who might have inspired and encouraged Brush Sheils, and men like him.

Through the Swinging Sixties of Beatles, Stones and Dylan, down the years of excess and self-indulgence of hippydom, supergroups, Bowie, Rod Stewart and Elton John, those Irish who subscribed to an alien culture and dared to emulate its heroes marched alone, unheard on airwaves, unwritten about in newspapers, ignored at best, despised at worst. Then in Jack Lynch's expanding Ireland something remarkably subversive began to stir. Ireland's first serious rock music magazine, *Hot Press*, appeared on the news-stands in the late summer of 1977. Simultaneously, a crazy guy called 'the Captain' started a pirate commercial radio station in a terraced house on the Southside. The world around Grafton Street would never seem so small again.

Niall and Dermot Stokes were brothers, past pupils of Synge Street CBS, failed rockers who'd played in a group called Eyeless in the singer-songwriter era *circa* 1973. In 1976 they'd started a magazine called *Scene* which had flourished briefly. This venture had foundered on the indifference of the publishing group who'd sponsored it but whose main interest and source of revenue were the trade magazines that formed the bulk of its output. Pissed off at the lack of support Niall and Dermot left *Scene* to launch *Hot Press* in 1977. Bill Graham, who'd laboured alongside the Stokes brothers on *Scene*, went with them. *Hot Press* took the music scene seriously. Gigs and records were intelligently reviewed. Ideas were discussed, the Grafton Street world given shape and identity for the first time. What *was* a record deal? Who had one, and who was spoofing? Which were the best Irish bands? What music was popular and why? Where were the gigs? How much did they cost? Now the questions could be asked and answered – authoritatively. *Hot Press* made Irish rock 'n' roll legitimate, gave Grafton Street a sense of itself, provided this twilight world with a hint of grandeur. It created heroes. Irish heroes. Phillip Byrne, Revolver's handsome blond singer, who lounged provocatively in the back room of the Berni Inn with all the best-looking girls, was somehow more real for being celebrated in *Hot Press*. Paul Boyle of the Vipers had shocked the crowd in Moran's one night by telling them to 'fuck off' when they growled impatiently as the band tuned up. *Hot Press* spread the legend, created interest in and a market for these local heroes.

Bill Graham wrote intelligent, well-informed essays about rock. Bill approved of punk – indeed he may have been the only journalist in Ireland who understood the New Wave, what it was about and why the revolution it heralded in rock music was necessary. Graham had been at Blackrock College a year ahead of Geldof and had graduated from Trinity before becoming the country's first rock journalist. Like all the best specialist writers, Graham loved his subject.

Dave Fanning had also gone to Blackrock College. Like Bill Graham he loved rock 'n' roll. He was Southside middle class, like the Stokes brothers. When Niall and Dermot broke away from *Scene* magazine, Fanning moved into the editor's chair in Terenure. He was sitting in his office one morning in September 1977 checking a special issue of the magazine commemorating Elvis, who had died the previous month, when the Captain burst in. 'I'm Eamonn Cooke, Captain Eamonn Cooke,' Fanning's visitor announced. He went on to claim that he ran Radio Dublin and was interested in swapping ads on his radio station for ads in *Scene*. Fanning explained that he was in the business of chasing ads not giving them away. And anyway, what was Radio Dublin? The Captain assured him that his station existed, transmitting pop music all night at the weekends. Half believing this guy to be crazy, Fanning agreed to come and visit Radio Dublin to see for himself.

The Irish Broadcasting Act was explicit; radio and television belonged to the state. That was it. There was no commercial radio and nobody would be daft enough to try to breach the act in a city the size of Dublin, where detection was inevitable. Nobody with any sense, that is. The radio station Fanning found when he visited the terraced house in Inchicore the next day consisted of a transmitter and a small record collection spread out in Captain Cooke's front room. Claiming to be an electronics wizard, the Captain produced the brief-case he'd been carrying in Fanning's office the previous day.

'Listen to this,' he ordered his bemused guest.

This was a recording of their conversation the day before. The Captain was thinking of expanding his operation to midweek broadcasting. He offered Dave the Wednesday night slot from eleven p.m. till two a.m., in exchange for ads in *Scene*. Fanning agreed.

The Captain didn't believe in paying his staff. When the subject of wages arose he would point out that there were 'a million little fuckers out there' who'd love to be doing what you were doing. In December a couple of Radio Dublin staffers left to set up A R D, a rival station. Radio Dublin was raided by the police who were accompanied by the national press. Next evening Radio Dublin and Captain Cooke formed the lead story in the Irish papers. Everyone tuned in that night.

Within a month there were pirate radio stations all the way along the Irish wavebands. The Captain had broken the mould in Irish broadcasting, although he never benefited himself. His tiny house was full of electronic equipment and he was an easy target for the authorities. Others were more elusive, moving from house to house, keeping several steps ahead of the Department of Posts and Telegraphs. In March 1978 James Dillon, a former associate of the Captain – who was by now embroiled in lawsuits – started Big D, the most professional pirate set-up to date. Fanning went to work for Dillon.

By now Dave Fanning was committed to broadcasting. He'd persuaded the Captain to let him broadcast all-night shows on Radio Dublin. He loved playing the music he liked and doing it the way he liked to do it. Disc-jockeys on the BBC and Radio Luxemburg were notoriously plastic with their mid-Atlantic accents and coy little hey-look-at-me personas. They got between the music and the listener, or rather, their egos did. Fanning did it differently. His flat Dublin accent was real, he never used ten words where one would suffice, the humour was spontaneous, not scripted. Dave was a natural. On Big D he formulated a policy for his all-night radio show. First, he told James Dillon to keep out of the studio. You sell the ads, James, let me run the music. You won't be sorry. Fanning wanted to play records made by Irish bands as well as those in the great big Hit Parades in the UK and the States. He brought new Dublin bands into the studio, interviewed them and played the demo discs. Soon his show was compulsive listening for those who'd had to tune in to foreign stations before Big D. When the *Hot Press* DJ Poll was published in the spring of 1978, Dave Fanning came second to the BBC's John Peel. Even though the wages on Big D were no better than the Captain's, Fanning was a made man.

Out in Malahide Adam listened to the Dave Fanning Show and put the DJ's name on his list of People To Contact. Adam's afternoons began with the No. 42 bus into town. The policy was to spread the band's name around the city among those who mattered on the pub gig circuit, and to make anyone else who might be useful aware of the Hype. Before he set off from home Adam would make his phone-calls. These calls were part of the Plan. They usually began as follows: 'Hi, I'm Adam Clayton, I play bass with a new band called the Hype. We're just starting off and we wondered if you could give us some advice.' The idea was that as well as getting advice, this would spread the message about the band.

Gerry Cott was the Boomtown Rats lead guitarist. He was on Adam's list. Cott's home number was the problem. Adam knew a guy who knew Cott's sister. Told of the plan, Adam's friend refused to give the sister's telephone number. Then the Rats came to play in Dublin and Adam scrounged two tickets for the gig. His friend wanted to go but had no tickets. Adam supplied them, in exchange for the secret telephone number.

'Hi, I'm from CBS Records in London,' Adam lied. 'I believe Gerry is having dinner with you this evening, and I was trying to contact him. It's urgent.'

'Gerry's not here,' the sister replied, 'Why don't you try him at home?'

'I haven't got his number handy,' Adam ventured.

'Hold on,' the sister commanded.

Next day Gerry Cott learnt about the Hype. Adam reported back to Bono, Edge and Larry that night. He'd been talking to Gerry Cott from the Rats. Gerry had said this – and that – and wished them all the best. The exercise was good for morale.

Getting gigs meant catching the 42. As the bus sped past Mount Temple on its route into town, Adam would allow himself a smile. What lay ahead wouldn't necessarily be fun but he was free of the Irish educational system. First stop in town was Moran's Hotel in Talbot Street. Adam had ingratiated himself with the manager in Moran's, where the Rats had done some legendary gigs.

Adam's pitch was the soft sell. What bands were due to play? Could he get in free to see Friday's gig – and bring a couple of friends? He was a pleasant, curious, personable young man. With his nice manners and nice accent he seemed to the manager to be a cut above the 'hard chaws' who usually hung about Moran's. Young people weren't all bad. Adam began to talk about his own band. They had just started and weren't ready for Moran's, he admitted, but who knows, maybe someday . . .

The Project Arts Centre in Essex Street down by the South Quays was a fifteen-minute ramble across town from Moran's. The Project was the fashionable alternative to Dublin's established theatre. It was run by Jim and Peter Sheridan, two talented Northsiders who wrote and produced their own and other people's plays. The complex housed a pub, coffee bar and art gallery. Rock music was an occasional moneyspinner. The Project served the arts in much the same way that *Hot Press* and pirate radio served rock 'n' roll. It drew original minds, the talented, angry and those who were simply crazy. There was a buzz down there, a sense of something different happening – or about to happen.

Adam hung around, sipping his coffee, smoking, being cool. He got to know Caragh Coote, who was in charge of booking bands. Her heart went out to this nice kid who could never afford a second cup of coffee. They became friends, conspirators. He told her about his band and begged a gig. She promised that she would see what she could do. Look, he pleaded, we're playing in this talent contest in Limerick the day after Patrick's Day, it would really help if we could play here before we went. Caragh promised to think about it. Meanwhile she talked about Phil Lynott who she knew from the old days. Thin Lizzy were playing in town and she was going to the gig as Philo's guest. Adam was more interested in getting his phone number. Caragh told him that Lynott always stayed in hotels these days. Which one? Adam pressed. The Clarence.

Phoning Phil Lynott was pushing it a bit, Adam reflected, as he sat at home the day after the Lizzy concert. It was 9.30. He'd just be getting up now, Adam thought, he'll be in good form. (Years later when he learned more about Philo's lifestyle, Adam recalled ruefully that his target was probably getting *into* bed, not out of it!) Before he called the Clarence he made himself another cup of coffee and lit a fag. Then taking a deep breath he dialed.

'Hi, I'm Adam Clayton . . .'

Lynott's advice was succinct, but not ungenerous in the circumstances; get a good demo disc, send it to all the record companies in London – and get a manager. Adam went back to the lads and told them that he'd been chatting to Phil Lynott. Bono was getting impatient. Adam was talking to lots of people but the Hype weren't getting the gigs. A certain tension existed between bass player-manager and vocalist. Adam went back to Caragh and laid it on the line. He needed that gig. Faced by sheer desperation she booked the Hype for St Patrick's night.

Steve Rapid was the vocalist with the Radiators. He got a phone call from Adam. 'Hi, I'm Adam Clayton, I went to school with your brother. I'm in a band. I wonder if we could rap about the business.' By day Steve Averill worked in Arrow, one of Dublin's leading advertising agencies. He was a talented designer and by reputation one of the smartest heads on the rock scene. Adam asked all the usual questions, but seemed particularly concerned about his band's name. Steve agreed that he was right to be concerned. The Hype sounded too blatant, wasn't subtle, suggested a certain contempt for the rock 'n' roll business. Adam thought they needed a name that would be slightly mysterious, wouldn't pin them down to anything or place in particular. He loved X T C, which was the name of one of the bands around. Steve thought about it for a few days before coming up with U2. The name rang a bell with Adam. Something to do with spying? he ventured. Yes, Steve confirmed, there had been an American spy plane called the U2. There was also a U2 submarine and one of Ever Ready's biggest selling batteries was also called U2. Nobody knew what it *meant*, but the name stuck in your brain. There was a pun in there as well; *you too* or even *you two*. Adam liked it.

When he put it to the band, the others were less than bowled over. Bono especially was sceptical about U2 and Adam's Important Contacts. Adam stuck by his guns and won a compromise. Their next gig was at Howth Community Hall. They played the first half as a five-piece with Dick on additional guitar, calling themselves the Hype, and the second set minus Dick as U2.

In between sets Adam, Edge and Larry backed the Virgin Prunes, who were also on the community hall bill. The Prunes act had more to do with theatre than rock 'n' roll. They opened with a dark, empty stage and some taped sound effects playing in the background. Gavin came on in drag, smoking a cigarette. He stood staring brazenly at the audience which was entirely composed of Howth Pigs. His look and his clothes said fuck *you*.

'Art. Fuck,' Gav spoke the words with feeling. Then he minced off. Day-Vid followed to recite his monologue about everything and nothing. Then Gav and Guggi strode on as two Dames and Dick, Adam, Edge and Larry appeared as musical conspirators behind. Where Bono and U2 wanted to convince, be accepted and move the audience, the Virgin Prunes led by Gavin wanted to shock the Howth pigs out of their complacency, their sureness about *every fucking thing*.

The Village travelled *en masse* to Limerick for the *Evening Press*–Harp Lager Talent Contest. There were over thirty acts who would run off in heats before the final six were chosen for the evening show in front of an audience. The first thing Adam did on arrival was change the band's name from The Hype, which they'd entered as, to U2. Then they had a look at the opposition. They noticed that all the other acts were using the four mikes allowed to mike up voices and guitars. U2 decided to mike up the bass drum and snare through the PA system, thus achieving a louder effect. As the morning heats progressed, Jackie Hayden of CBS, whose record company was giving the winners a chance to cut a demo disc, and Billy Wall of Radio Telefis Eireann, the two most influential judges, remarked on how poor the standards were. Only the East Coast Angels, a Gary-Glitter-style pop group, and U2 showed any promise at all. Bono's voice was 'shot' from the Project gig the night before. He had been unable to hold back, to take it easy despite the importance of the talent competition. But even hoarse he had presence, a commanding intensity that the band around him matched, and this set against the inhibited what-are-we-doing-here coyness of the competition won U2 the respect of the judges. Attitude won the day. That night, adrenalin flowing in front of an audience, U2 turned a potentially embarrassing talent contest into a celebration of their own engaging enthusiasm. They took £500 and the promise of an evening in the CBS studios back home with them. At least they brought home the promise. The cheque they gave for safe-keeping to Adam's father who'd come across from Shannon Airport to lend support.

Adam hustled a support gig at McGonagles on the strength of Limerick. Playing support at the bottom of the bill was tough going. The place was just filling up, and people were more interested in getting a drink and sussing the place out than listening to the first band on. There were about thirty or forty people there, drinking and chatting at the back of the room. The Village constituted U2's only audience, clapping noisily in front of the stage.

Terry O'Neill had been around the Dublin rock scene for years. He'd managed various bands including Brush Sheils' Skid Row when Phil Lynott was lead singer. He'd been there when Brush sacked Philo because he couldn't sing. And he'd been around when Lynott and Thin Lizzy had topped the English charts with 'Whiskey in the Jar' and listened to Brush insisting that he'd been right about Philo. Terry smiled a lot, it was the only way to stay sane. Now he was about to start a new job as manager of McGonagles. Bill Fuller owned the place.

Fuller was a legend round Dublin and further afield. He owned the Fillmore West Ballroom in San Francisco where many of rock's great names had performed for the legendary American promoter Bill Graham. Fuller was droll. He did business with a handshake, which made it difficult to sue him when later on he told you to 'Fuck off, boy, and don't annoy me.' Tonight Fuller was showing Terry O'Neill around McGonagles. Business was bad. Fuller had bought it when it was the Crystal Ballroom in the days when Bobby and Iris Hewson and Larry and Maureen Mullen had danced there to the showbands. It had subsequently been the Nashville Rooms before its latest re-birth as McGonagles. When O'Neill outlined his plans to create a first-class rock 'n' roll club, Fuller cut him short, 'Do whatever you want with it. It's yours.'

Looking towards the stage, Terry was surprised at the youth of the band. They looked like schoolkids and, in their earnestness, played that way too. After their set the four band members knocked on O'Neill's door. 'We've come for our money,' Adam opened. 'How much do you want?' O'Neill asked. There was a pause, while Adam, Edge, Larry and Bono scrutinized each other's faces, looking for a clue. 'Do you mind if we go outside and discuss it?' Adam pleaded. When they returned a couple of minutes later they asked for £7. 'Twenty-five,' O'Neill smiled. 'Everybody gets £25 for opening.' Embarrassed, they took the money and made an undignified exit.

This incident underlined their need for a manager. Taking stock after Limerick, they had reached a number of decisions. They would use their own material on the demo disc for CBS. They would contact Bill Graham of *Hot Press*, who seemed to be the most serious journalist around, to make him aware of them *and* to ask his advice about how best to tackle the Grafton Street scene. Dave Fanning on Big D was another target. Bono had been reading *NME*, *Melody Maker* and *Hot Press*, and realized the value of little mentions in their columns with if possible a photograph of the band. Publicity got you gigs, he understood, *not* the other way round. They also had to control their work in recording studios. They wouldn't be rushed into churning out the first take. The most important decision U2 took at this time was to work even harder developing their own songs and sound. Bono, Larry and Edge were due to leave Mount Temple in a few weeks. They would lose their rehearsal room and much more if they didn't take care, for Larry was due to start work in the summer, Edge to go on to technical college and Bono back to UCD if Bobby Hewson had his way. This was make or break time for U2.

Adam rang Bill Graham and invited him to come to one of their Saturday-afternoon rehearsals at the school. Afterwards Adam suggested they could rap together. They needed some advice. Graham agreed to come.

Bill was twenty-seven, ten years older than the band he now gave up his Saturday afternoon to go and listen to. He was a beautiful guy in the hard city world of music and journalism. Had any of his peers seen him slip onto the No. 33 bus just off O'Connell Street that Saturday afternoon and asked him where he was off to they would have sneered at the answer, 'Off to the suburbs to find a great band!' 'All the best, Bill.' He was an enthusiast for people and music. That both constantly let him down didn't corrode his spirit, never would. Bill was a large, jolly, slightly untogether man, still after all the years a believer in the 'something inside that was always denied', the something called soul, as dirty a word in journalism as it was in music, politics or the Church.

As he listened to U2 that day, Bill ached a little bit. They were nice kids, different, younger, fresher than the bands in town. But musically, U2 had a mountain to climb. Nevertheless, they excited him in a curious way. They were serious about the thing he loved. After their rehearsal they went to a public house to have a chat. The Village accompanied them. They wanted to know about a record deal, gigs, money, other bands. They declared their ignorance but also their determination to make it. He suggested they forget about a record deal for the moment. He told them a couple of horror stories about £½ million deals that had left the bands concerned *owing* money. It worked like this he explained; U2 sign a £½ million deal. Your record is a hit. Now the record company does its sums. So much for studio time, so much for promotion and marketing of your hit. Then there's the cost of a studio for your follow-up record. That £½ million is a purely notional figure. Forget it. You're young, take your time, develop as musicians, wait until you can control a studio situation.

Bill could see that they were listening, that his advice was registering. So many young bands bluffed, pretended they knew it all and ended up broken years later. So many were in the music game for sex or booze, so many had dabbled in the drugs that were freely available in town, so many weren't prepared to work at their music. Most of the people Bill Graham encountered around Grafton Street made him feel tired and sad. These kids sent him back to town feeling better. He left them with one piece of advice more important than any other; get yourselves a manager. He gave them a name, Paul McGuinness.

Chapter Eight

BABY BAND

A son, Paul, was born to Flight-Lieutenant Philip 'Mac' McGuinness and his wife Sheila on 16 June 1951. Philip and Sheila had been married eighteen months previously in Mac's home-town, Liverpool. Paul, their first child, was born in Rinteln near Hanover, West Germany, where Philip was stationed at the Royal Air Force base.

Philip McGuinness had worked as a clerk for the Mersey Docks and Harbour Board at the outbreak of World War Two. He volunteered for the Royal Air Force a number of times before he was old enough to join. He was eventually accepted during the desperate days of the Battle of Britain, the darkest hour of Britain's six-year war with Hitler's Germany. The RAF won respect as the most courageous of Britain's services, one in every three of its aircrews meeting their death defending their country. Philip was well aware of the odds but was a cheerful, lively officer in the RAF's renowned, 'dashing' tradition. He was awarded the Distinguished Flying Cross, the flyers' highest honour, at the end of the war.

In peacetime Mac decided to make a career in the airforce. He joined the Communication Squadron whose task was to liaise between the various RAF outposts around the world. It was a damn sight more invigorating than clerking for the Docks and Harbour Board.

Although his family were three generations removed from Ireland, Philip McGuinness still regarded himself as Irish. He loved to visit 'home', especially west Cork, where he fished and boated with friends whenever he had leave. It was in Cork in 1947 that he met Sheila Lyne, who was born on the Kerry side of the Cork–Kerry border. Sheila's family bore a famous Kerry name. The Lynes could trace their roots back to 1485. Sheila's great-great-grandmother was the sister of Daniel O'Connell, the radical nineteenth-century political leader known as the Liberator, after whom Dublin's O'Connell Street is named. Sheila was studying to be a teacher when she met Phillip and an officer friend in a Cork hotel. It was love at first sight between the dashing, handsome young war hero and quiet, intelligent Sheila from Kerry. She followed him to England where she taught in the Holy Child Convent in Liverpool before they were married in 1949.

It would be a service life, home would be an airforce base, a different one every three years or so. After Rinteln in West Germany the McGuinnesses moved back to England, to Thorney Island in Hampshire. Paul was a healthy boy who played happily with the other officers' children. His private passion was reading. From the age of three Paul was a prodigious reader of anything that he got his hands on. Sitting reading a fairy tale, he would squeal with delight as good triumphed over evil, wanting always to share the news with mum and dad.

After a spell at Cosford near Wolverhampton, Malta was the next stop on Mac's tour of duty. He was an efficient, popular officer who seemed destined for the Royal Air Force's top commissions. Sheila loved service life, especially the sun of Malta. Occasionally she travelled with Mac on a two-day trip to Paris, Rome or London. In between she used her teaching skills to supplement the less than satisfactory schooling arrangements service life imposed upon its kids.

In Malta, when he was seven, an outline of Paul's character began to form. One of its features was self-sufficiency. The family could enjoy life as an extended beach holiday for most of the Maltese year. There were however about three months in winter when it was too cold to swim, although walking on the beach was very pleasant. Paul decided to create a museum to keep him occupied during the winter months. His dad's working week entailed travelling for a day or two to other RAF stations around Europe. Paul asked for museum pieces from those trips. He explored the beach and the famous Hypogeum, Malta's prehistoric caves, to gather his own material. Soon he had a stone from the Forum, a similar item from the Appian Way, bones from Malta's beaches and artefacts from the Colosseum. What seemed so unusual to Philip and Sheila was the boy's meticulousness in showcasing his collection. Every piece was labelled and dated and the seven-year-old curator took great pleasure in showing his museum to friends and visiting relations. Everything was skilfully presented, even the most banal piece was enhanced for being the object of Paul's devoted attention.

He had a highly developed sense of what looked right and this, together with a facility with words, led his tutor in Malta, Miss France, to report to the McGuinnesses: 'I can see Paul having a career in writing or television.' His meticulousness extended to the presents he bought for his mum and dad and younger brother Niall, who was lately arrived. Gifts from Paul were always useful, appropriate and beautifully wrapped.

News that the family's next posting was to be Poole in Dorset was greeted stoically by Paul. Although well able to fend for himself, he was a popular boy, one of the lads rather than the solitary swot his museum-keeping suggested. Yet leave-taking didn't appear to upset him unduly. When the time for moving came he busied himself gathering books, toys and artefacts together for transportation to the next destination.

Paul's education was beginning to exercise Philip and Sheila. Thus far she had availed of her own teaching experience, but her pupil was rapidly outgrowing front-room lessons. Searching for a word for an essay he was writing one day Paul approached his mother. She thought for a moment and provided what seemed like a reasonable answer.

'No, Mum, that's not right,' her eleven-year-old son insisted.

'Well, it will do,' she fobbed him off.

'No, Mum, I heard you using the word I'm looking for last week,' he badgered.

The nuance and the context had to be right. It *mattered*. Even his educated, reasonable and literate mother couldn't escape the rigour of the child's mind. They consulted the Oxford English Dictionary. He was proved correct.

When Paul was ten, in 1961, his parents sent him to Clongowes Wood College, one of the best boarding schools in Ireland. Clongowes, run by the Jesuits, educated Ireland's middle classes, usually for the professions. The school always enjoyed a reputation for first-class rugby teams. It was set in Kildare, some twenty-odd miles from Dublin. The Jesuits are less intellectually narrow than other Catholic Orders, or so tradition has it, and the arts and debate were encouraged at Clongowes.

The six years he spent at Clongowes had the most profound influence on Paul. This was the longest period he had spent anywhere. Clongowes felt more like home than any of the RAF bases he had lived on. It had what they signally lacked, a sense of identity, a sense of place. He visited his parents, with whom he enjoyed a loving, trusting relationship, in places as diverse as Aden and Lincoln, yet returning to college was never the sorrow for him that it was for many other boarders.

The friendships Paul made in school remained firm over twenty years later. Donnell Deeny, son of a Northern Ireland doctor, was his closest friend. Donnell would later become a leading Queen's Counsel at the Northern Ireland Bar. As Paul's year grew up and began to establish a presence in college, it became clear that they were an unusual intake. They didn't like sport very much and concentrated their extra-curricular energies on the school's magazine and drama group. Much interest was also taken in the debating society.

Paul McGuinness was bright, a first-class mind, the Jesuits thought, but not a Desperately Serious Young Man. He acquired power and influence nevertheless. He edited the college magazine, directed two plays and in his final year won the gold medal as Clongowes' star debater. All of this was achieved with an easy charm that only rarely turned to baleful arrogance. He was as rigorously tough-minded with others as with himself. What was craven, sloppy, pretentious or merely average could draw from McGuinness a contemptuous comment or stare. This determination to get things right rather than any interest in the status conferred prompted him to seek the positions of influence he gained on the magazine and in the drama group. Après show or magazine issue Paul was as gregarious with the chancers and wasters as with those like himself who pursued excellence. He was an office-hours élitist.

While at Clongowes, Paul developed an interest in art. On one visit to his parents, now in Lincoln, he set out to buy his mother a Van Gogh print he'd seen in the city. The airbase was seven miles outside Lincoln, with an infrequent bus service. Upon missing the bus on the day appointed for his purchase Paul walked the seven miles into town to get the print. He was thirteen at the time. A couple of years later, when the family were stationed in Penhill, Dorset, Paul spotted some Old Masters postcards in the village post office. He asked his mother to send him one a week for the the rest of the year. He would appreciate them more that way rather than receiving them all at once. His reading habits now changed from books to newspapers, which he devoured daily for news of the world outside Clongowes Wood. He was fascinated by politics and current affairs, indeed by almost everything in the papers. He admired good newspaper writing and thought that he might eventually try for a job in journalism. Television and the theatre were other possibilities. But first he wanted to go to Trinity College, Dublin, an aspiration shared by the best and the brightest of his Clongowes peers. The academic requirements for this were carefully calculated by a young man whose school experience had taught him that there was more to success than academic distinction, which was at the end of the day only a means to an end. That end was operating efficiently and successfully in the real world for which he felt the interminable exam system was something less than the ideal preparation. Entry to Trinity did however require displaying some measurable promise, so Paul acquired honours in three Leaving Certificate subjects, English, Latin and French. That was sufficient.

In the centuries between Trinity's foundation and 1971, when reluctantly and not without resistance The Hierarchy deemed it no longer necessary for Catholics to receive a special dispensation to study there, the university changed more than the nation it educated. Trinity in modern times was a bastion of another kind, its ambience perhaps best described by Jeremy Lewis, a student of the early to mid-sixties who later wrote of 'loving Trinity not only for its kindliness and its ambivalence, its lack of commitment, its tolerant cynicism, for its being in so many ways neither a part of England nor of Ireland'. Alas, by 1968 when Paul arrived at college the revolutionary fervour of Paris, Berlin, London and Chicago had reached Dublin. The flavour was, however, distinctly Trinity. Student democracy aroused passions at Trinity as elsewhere, but in this too the college exhibited its penchant for eccentricity. Whilst students worldwide agitated against America's involvement in Vietnam, Trinity's most memorably violent riot focused on Belgian Imperialism. When the King and Queen of Belgium visited Dublin in 1969, the Maoist-led demonstrations they provoked at Trinity were described as the worst student disturbances in the college's history. Present on that occasion, Paul Tansey and Shane Ross, two of McGuinness's closest Trinity friends, were prominent student activists. Tansey was later to become one of Ireland's foremost economists, whilst Ross, a Wildean figure, went on to combine stockbroking with radical politics, which he practised as the Independent Senator for Trinity.

Paul McGuinness was sympathetic to the Trinity revolution but it wasn't something he felt compelled to lead nor was he likely to be found among the mob following those, like Tansey and Ross, who issued the rhetoric. He had come up to read philosophy and psychology with more interest in the latter, which was a new subject on Trinity's curriculum, than the former. Indeed, he only read philosophy because it was mandatory for those taking psychology. He spent his first year at college in digs in Drumcondra, taking the No. 11 or 16 bus to College Green. He discovered girls, many of the loveliest and most liberated of whom went to Trinity – or, alternatively, were interested in the Old Clongownians who were attending Trinity. A measure of sexual liberation had reached Dublin. Girls frequently did. Or at least could reasonably be assumed to be interested in doing what their mothers had rejected out of hand. With the advent of the pill, fear of pregnancy was no longer an acceptable excuse. Fear of God was even less believable. Paul soon became active in Players, Trinity's famous theatrical group and, as at Clongowes, got involved in the college magazine. The philosophy course was disappointing. But the company of bright sophisticated young men like Shane

Ross, with whom he shared rooms in his second year, Donnell
Deeny, who'd joined him at Trinity, Paul Tansey, Mike Colgan,
a contemporary in Players, later to become Ireland's leading
theatrical administrator-director, and the young Chris de
Burgh, stimulated the social animal that lay beneath
McGuinness's dry, somewhat spiky exterior.

Michael Deeny, Donnell's older brother, who'd been up at
Oxford, was now living in Dublin with a good job as financial
director of Kennedy's Bakeries, and he introduced Paul and
Donnell to a group that was neither political nor intellectual
but more business and pleasure orientated. Among them was
found John Kelleher, a legendary wit and ladies' man, who
later became controller of programmes for RTE Television,
Sidney Minch, who was to become managing director of
Securicor, and David Coyle, an accountant who achieved fame
as the piano player in Daddy Cool and the Lollipops. This was
a smart set around which intensity, a desire to change the
world, was passé. They were gregarious, more interested in
making money, in being successful (whilst having a good time)
than in matters theological or philosophical. Between the
swingers, Players, the magazine and Tansey and Ross, who
shared his tastes across the board, Paul moved quite comfortably.

In 1969 Paul spotted Kathy Gilfillan, who was in her second
year in college. Kathy was from Eglinton, about eight miles
from Derry. She was one of five children of a Protestant
farming family, and had been educated at grammar school in
Limavady, Co. Derry. Kathy was poised, cool and slightly
detached, characteristics that to most Catholic eyes would
immediately identify her as Protestant. Closely observed, her
confidence was enthralling, her face handsome, with bright
intelligent eyes. Kathy was a woman rather than a girl, capable
and attractive, neither in need of nor susceptible to male pat-
ronization. Paul fancied her madly. Clear-mindedness, self-

sufficiency, virtues he possessed himself, were irresistible in this woman. At first he simply hung around when she appeared on the Players' scene. As Kathy would later remember, 'he kept popping up'. He used to draw strange pictures which later in the evening he would give to her, without saying a word. She had no idea who he was. Gradually she came to like him. He was great fun, very knowledgeable, you could never be bored by him. She was flattered by his single-minded pursuit of her, the stoic, undemanding, slightly gallant gestures, the sense that he was strong rather than weak, strong enough not to try a macho number on her. They became close friends, falling in love at a later stage, when circumstances forced them apart.

As a third-year student Paul was appointed editor of the college magazine. He had lost interest in philosophy and psychology. He used his time to explore the worlds of journalism and drama as possible sources of a career. He started contributing the occasional piece to Dublin newspapers and began to formulate a strategy that might ultimately enable him to direct films. He directed two Players productions, showing some promise. If university was a means of discovering yourself and making contacts that would be of use when you entered the real world, Paul was the classic beneficiary. He had seen the established middle-class world in microcosm, and if not yet quite sure what role there was for him in it, Paul had some pretty clear ideas about what was *not* for him. He would not, it was clear, become a professional man, a doctor, accountant or barrister. He was no time-server. He was interested in ideas rather than money or security. Despite his talents, a first-class mind, a rigorous approach to studies, a natural air of authority and a vivid imagination, he still hadn't found what he was looking for.

Kennedy's Bakeries were closing down, which left Michael Deeny without employment. He decided to open a mobile

discothèque. John Kelleher, Sidney Minch and David Coyle
were invited to be partners in the venture. Paul, now a third-
year student, was offered the job of disc-jockey. They played
all around Dublin or anywhere within driving distance of the
city. The experiment failed pretty miserably and soon the
partners were looking for a buyer for the expensive disco
equipment they'd invested in. A hotel in Kerry expressed an
interest, so they hauled their van down south. Alas, the cute
'hoor' who owned the hotel wanted the stuff for next to
nothing. They hauled it back up to Dublin again. On the way
Paul had an idea. Donovan, the English folk-pop singer, had
moved to Ireland to 'get his head together – man', and was
living in a mansion in Kilcullen just outside Dublin.
McGuinness stopped the mobile disco and knocked on
Donovan's door. He claimed that he and some associates were
concert promoters and that they planned a series of major
concerts in the Royal Dublin Society (RDS), Dublin's most
prestigious venue. Fortunately, Donovan didn't look around
the corner where the associates had hidden their means of
transportation. Instead he listened to the beautifully modulated
public-school voice, observed his visitors' agreeable manner
and agreed to perform at the RDS. From being failed mobile-
disco operators, McGuinness and Deeny drove off as concert,
major concert, promoters.

The profit from this exercise Paul used to embark on an
overland trip to Florence to indulge his passion in art. Back at
Trinity, trouble awaited. A piece Paul had run in the college
magazine written by Merily Harpur, later to become a famous
cartoonist in England, was deemed to be libellous by the junior
dean, the then young and subsequently distinguished Irish poet,
Brendan Kennelly. The libel was contained in an innocuous
article about the politics of Trinity's choral society. Kennelly
imposed a fine of £50 on McGuinness, who as editor bore
overall responsibility. Paul appealed, employing Shane Ross as

his advocate. The disciplinary committee found in favour of Paul, ruling that Kennelly had no power to impose the fine. However, it was also established that the board of Trinity College could overturn the disciplinary committee's finding, which in fact it did. This minor College sensation was resolved when the company that published the magazine liquidated itself. No fine was paid. But a certain stigma attached itself to McGuinness's reputation among the despised Establishment. When it emerged weeks later that Paul hadn't attended enough lectures to sit his third-year exams, he was sent down, the first philosophy student in living memory to be so dismissed. His grant was gone and thus his means of staying at College.

It was a bitter disappointment he carried home to his parents in Dorset. His father, now Squadron-Leader McGuinness, was not amused. His eldest son stood in disgrace before the family of which a girl, Katy, was the newest addition. Paul's parents refused to return him to Trinity at their own expense, decreeing instead that he enrol at the University of Southampton close by. After Trinity, Southampton was provincial to an unacceptable degree. Paul lasted two weeks before deciding to go to London to earn the money to go back to Dublin.

He got a job driving a mini-cab around Earls Court and Chelsea, bedsit land, where he dossed down as best he could. It was a black period in his life, dislocation again after almost ten years of stability in Ireland. He worked in a book warehouse to supplement his taxi driving. Then, realizing that living in London, even modestly as he did, was too expensive, Paul applied for a job as a tour guide on package holidays. The job he sought was with an English tour operator in Dubrovnik in Yugoslavia. Upon discovering that he was Irish his new employers had a better idea: Lourdes.

Lourdes was the scene of a miraculous appearance of Our Lady. The waters there were said to have healing properties which drew thousands of Irish pilgrims every year, many sick

ABOVE Iris Rankin.   TOP RIGHT Bobby Hewson.

ABOVE RIGHT Lovers defying Church, families and the culture around them.

BELOW Bobby and Iris take tea in a Dublin cafe, 1948.

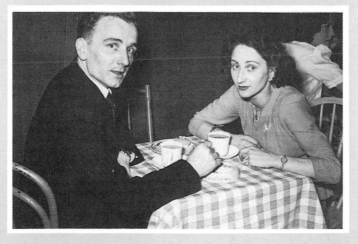

Adam with his dad.

Adam, off to Castle Park, with 'Sindy'.

Jo Clayton

Garvin and Gwenda at a Dublin North Rotary Club Annual dinner. Garvin was a founder member and past President.

Dick (left) and Dave.

Larry Sr and Maureen with Larry Jr,
Cecilia and Mary.

Larry with mother and best friend,
Maureen.

An early performance in the front
bedroom at Rosemount Avenue.

Adam on a good day at Castle Park.

Paul McGuinness in Malta.

Bobby and Iris on holiday with Norman and Paul,
who is determined not to smile.

ABOVE Early days at Mount Temple. Left to right: Paul Hewson, Dave Evans, Larry Mullen and Frank Kearns.

BELOW The Virgin Prunes. Standing, left to right: Dick Evans, Strongman (Trevor) Rowen, 'Mary' (occasional member). Sitting: Guggi and Gavin. Front: Day-vid. (*Ursula Steiger*)

'Art fuck'; Gavin vibes out an early audience, with Guggi in the background.
(*Patrick Brocklebank*)

Paul McGuinness (centre) meets U2 for the first time, at the Project, on 18 September 1978. *Seated, left to right:* Adam, Edge, Paul, Bono, Rachel O'Sullivan (Aislinn Evans' sister) and Larry (drinking orange juice). *(Patrick Brocklebank)*

Paul McGuinness on the road with his baby band. (*Colm Henry*)

The first rose of summer, '78. (*Phil Sheghy*)

Dublin, 1982. Bono out front, with very little behind him. (*Christine Bond*)

Bono sings while Edge and Adam look for clues. (*Christine Bond*)

In studio for the *Boy* album.

Steve Lillywhite, producer of *Boy*, *October* and *War*. (*Colm Henry*)

or dying and desperate for divine intervention. Paul spent three months meeting such people off their planes and guiding them through their week of pilgrimage. One of the aspects of Lourdes he found most intriguing was the liveliness of the bars which were dotted in between the various shrines. Irish people who might have experienced Calvinist pangs of guilt on a holiday in the Costa del Sol felt holier in Our Lady's Lourdes and therefore drank all the more enthusiastically after dark.

Lourdes provided Paul with enough money to re-enter Trinity to repeat his third year. It was Dublin and Trinity he wanted to come back to rather than philosophy and psychology. But things had changed. Michael Deeny was now managing the folk-rock band Horslips. Donnell was taking his finals in law. Ross was at the stock exchange and Tansey with the *Irish Times*. Most depressingly, Kathy, whom he'd missed terribly during his 'lost year', had gone to London to take a position as a picture researcher for Blackman Harvey, a noted art-broking house. There was less of a buzz about the Trinity of 1972. On the look-out still for opportunities in the world of entertainment Paul met Seamus Byrne, a film production manager who had an idea about producing a free-distribution five-channel TV guide to service the suburban housing estates which were now being cabled up for multi-channel reception. The free sheet would be supported by advertising. Paul would supply the editorial copy and have a share of the profits which seemed likely on paper to be considerable. It was a neat idea, but there was a snag. Investigating with his usual thoroughness, Paul discovered that the copyright to programme schedules was owned exclusively by the television companies: BBC, RTE and ITV. They each produced their own magazines which had as the major attraction listings of programmes for the week ahead. The possibility that these organizations would waive their copyright to facilitate a competing free sheet was in Paul's estimation non-existent. Seamus Byrne was more of an optimist and, despite the fact that Paul declined to become involved, he pushed ahead. Byrne produced one issue of his schedules before Paul's opinion was validated. He lost money but appreciated the advice that he'd been offered and the charming manner McGuinness displayed. It was on Byrne's recommendation that the Trinity student got the job of location manager on *Zardoz*, a film directed by John Boorman, starring Sean Connery. Paul now faced a choice; filming ran from March to August, right through the period designated for his third-year exams. He decided in favour of filming. He would take his chances in life without a degree.

He worked on in film production after *Zardoz*. Michael Deeny's Horslips were a growing force on the music scene. Donnell was practising law on the northern circuit. Paul had ambitious plans in relation to the film business. He would like to direct and felt capable of doing so given the money that governed all such ambitions. He and Michael Deeny were also interested in how money for films was raised, and there was a germ of an idea to get involved in that.

In 1975 Kathy Gilfillan in London faced a choice of her own. She missed Paul, parting *had* made the heart grow fonder, on both sides. But he loved Dublin and wouldn't now move. The problem was resolved when she came back to the city, her departure from England hastened by the memory of the blackouts and cold three-day working weeks her adopted country had endured during the miners' strike.

Most of Paul's work was as assistant director on commercials. He was seeking his director's ticket, but to get it you had to direct three commercials. In order to shoot a commercial you needed a ticket, agencies being reluctant to trust ambitious but inexperienced young men. Ambitious young men in the role of assistant were left to grapple with problems such as one that confronted Paul in early 1976.

Certain countries offered tax breaks to businessmen who

invested in films. Canada was one such country. A consortium of Canadian dentists had decided to dispense some tax-free patronage. Their film was awful, but it was to be shot in Dublin and therefore meant employment for local technicians, actors and assistant directors. Paul was on the Canadian dentists' job. For the tax break to work filming had to be completed by a certain date, which was rapidly approaching when they came to a big stunt involving a crash on Stephen's Green on New Year's Day. The safety procedures on films were of the utmost importance and were the assistant director's responsibility. The Canadian dentists weren't keen to spend the money required on safety. Instead they asked the actors and crew to sign something called a 'blood chit' which, in return for £10 a day, indemnified the producers from any responsibility for injury or death. McGuinness refused to be party to this expedient. He lived and worked with these people and he wasn't going to collude in any exploitation of them. The Canadian dentists would find a more accommodating assistant director next time.

Soon after this Paul was approached by an old Trinity friend, Don Knox, who was a member of a well-known local folk group, Spud. Inspired by Horslips success, Spud had extended their line-up to include a drummer and electric guitar. They were now in the folk-rock idiom and had just been dropped by Polydor, their Irish record company. Don Knox asked Paul if he would manage them. Paul agreed to do it for one year with a get-out clause on either side.

Spud had been playing on the club cabaret circuit even though they carried all the overheads of a dance-hall group. The dance-halls paid much better and McGuinness started booking them into venues that had been opened up to folk-rock by Horslips. Income increased dramatically. Spud had a once-a-year residency in Sweden. Paul took a new single record they'd released in Ireland and did a deal with Sonet Records, one of the major Scandinavian companies, who also had an office in London. They signed to make an album for Sonet and did a lucrative publishing deal. With the money earned they invested with Paul's encouragement in a new truck and a sophisticated P A system. Realizing the value of publicity, Paul contacted Bill Graham, another friend from Trinity, who was writing for *Scene* magazine. He took Bill on a trip with Spud and the resulting publicity was impressive. Success outside Ireland made people at home sit up and take notice. Spud was beginning to 'happen'.

Among themselves the band were beginning to squabble. At issue was the music – how much should be folk, how much rock – and money. Some of them had mortgages and families and wanted to take their share of the spoils as they materialized. Others agreed with Paul that they should invest their short-term profits for long-term gain: much better to do a loss-making tour of Germany or the U K and gain fans than be restricted to their present market. This argument failed to win the day. With no hard feelings, for Paul understood the need to feed families and pay mortgages, he opted out when his one-year stint was over. Insofar as it had been applied, the Horslips-Deeny strategy had worked for Spud and Paul McGuinness. He returned to film-making bloodied but unbowed by his experience in the music biz. Occasionally during his year on the road, Paul shared a late night bottle of wine on Leeson Street with Bill Graham. They'd go to Samantha's or Maxwell Plum's unlicensed disco-wine bars, the only après-pub activity in town. There in the small hours he and Bill would theorize about how an Irish band could make it given sufficient talent – of which there seemed to be no shortage – and intelligent management. Horslips had almost proved the point; not necessarily with their music, for folk-rock was proving a notoriously difficult idiom to master, but with the strategic attack Deeny's band had launched in the States and the U K.

Their fate was contrasted with that of Phil Lynott who, despite the legend that had grown around his 1973 British chart success, 'Whiskey In The Jar', and the fact that he could pack any rock club in Dublin, was really going nowhere in any real sense.

Paul's parents came to live in Ireland in 1976, bringing Katy, now thirteen, and Niall with them. Paul and Kathy Gilfillan were married in 1977 and moved into a flat in Waterloo Road, Ballsbridge. The punk-rock explosion of that year repelled Paul McGuinness. He was intrigued by Bill Graham's embrace of this brutality and ugliness. Graham was writing in the new magazine *Hot Press*. During their late-night debates Paul had confided in Graham a desire to one day find his own 'baby band' and with them apply to rock 'n' roll the lessons Deeny had applied to folk-rock with Horslips. You could, Paul had argued passionately in Samantha's, bypass the local scene with its petty jealousies and limited horizons. What did headlining in McGonagles or the Baggot amount to anyway, or, if it came to that, a brief flirtation with glory on *Top of the Pops*? With a baby band who were committed enough, game enough and without domestic encumbrances such as mortgages and families, he was sure it could be done. In America, the UK and Europe. But you'd have to *go there* – they wouldn't come to McGonagles! Bill Graham saw the logic. All they needed was the baby band.

Chapter Nine

TRIAL

Adam rang Paul McGuinness the Monday after the band's meeting with Bill Graham. McGuinness was non-committal. Spud was still being wrapped up. He was talking to a talented American singer-songwriter, Thom Moore. He didn't like New Wave music or punk, as he called it. Wouldn't he come and see them play and perhaps they could talk? Adam persisted. Yes, McGuinness agreed, he would, but he was busy shooting a Smithwicks commercial at the moment, so maybe Adam would contact him again in a week or two.

It was May 1978, the school year was coming to an end, indeed for Bono, Edge and Larry school itself was at an end. Adam was now full-time musician-manager, with little business cards printed announcing: Adam Clayton, Bass Player, U2. Everyone who was anyone on the scene had an Adam Clayton card. Everyone who was in town whether they were *anybody* or not had the card. The mystery was where he got them printed, for he had no money. Not even enough for his bus-fare in from Malahide. Everyone in Dublin knew that if you got stuck on a bus without money you were allowed by CIE regulations to give the bus conductor your name and address. CIE would then send you a bill. You would occasionally see an embarrassed passenger fumbling desperately in pocket or purse for the necessary, realizing that he was short and writing out his name and address. Adam's variation on the manoeuvre greatly amused his friends and infuriated the city's bus conductors; he came on board prepared. No embarrassed fumbling, no fulsome apology, just a matter-of-fact submission of the note, with relevant details, written *before* leaving the house that morning. If, as frequently happened, the bus conductor became a bit edgy, Adam would smile sweetly and refer the fellow to the city's bye-laws reciting the relevant subsection. Adam's decision was long made; it was rock 'n' roll or die.

Edge was in a dilemma. He was due to start third-level education at Kevin Street Technical College in the autumn. Unless something happened with the band. Something like getting a manager and/or a record deal. He needed something of substance to take to Garvin and Gwenda Evans if they were to allow him to become a full-time musician. Edge had recently met Aislinn O'Sullivan, a very pretty, raven-haired girl whose extrovert character provided a delightful counterpoint to his own droll intelligence. Despite his Welsh blood, he was no great chat-up merchant. He first saw Aislinn at a U2 gig, but it was weeks before he plucked up courage to talk to her when both were attending a gig headlined by the Buzzcocks, from Manchester.

Bobby Hewson now despaired of Bono. His son was out all hours of the night with The Village. Pod, Bobby didn't mind. Young Murphy seemed decent enough. But Fionán, or Gavin as he called himself these days, was a bloody drop-out and young Derek Rowen, the 'Guggi' fella, was as weird as the rest of his lot. One night the two of them called at the door for Paul, or Bono as they called his own son now. The Gavin chap had eye make-up on and Guggi was wearing high-heeled shoes. Bobby barely restrained himself. The university idea was out of the window. His son wanted to be a full-time musician. He said he'd started writing songs though he couldn't sing to save his bleeding life. Bobby had got him an interview with an insurance company but Bono hadn't turned up. So Bobby said, bugger that, I'm not subsidizing some bloody punk band. Bono would get no money from him. He'd no bloody regard for money anyway. Bobby had lent him £25 to go to one of his mates' wedding in Cork the previous year. When Bono came back he told his dad he'd had a marvellous stroke of luck. Somebody at the wedding had had a tip for a horse and Bono had put £10 on it. The horse had won at fourteen to one. Great, Bobby said, where's the money? 'I gave it to the fella who was getting married.' Paul was in a world of his own, Bobby concluded. Secretly, he was deeply disturbed. He knew a little bit about music and singing, so he knew the distance Paul would have to travel before anyone would pay to hear him sing. But you couldn't talk to the young fella.

Larry was exercising his option to leave school after his Intermediate Exam. He had the choice between staying to do his Leaving Cert. in two years' time or getting a job now. The idea of becoming a full-time member of U2 never really appealed to him. He wanted security, a few bob in his pocket, a chance to suss out the real world. Cecilia had got him a job as a messenger with Seiscom Delta, an oil exploration company where she was an accounts clerk. Larry liked the band and the lads but he wasn't quite sure where it was all heading. He was the only one who could really play and he knew that lots of other bands around were interested in getting him. He was still waiting for the others to catch up to him. Looking to the future, Larry was aware that there were older, more accomplished bands around town who'd been banging their heads against brick walls for years, bands like Revolver, Berlin, Atrix, all of whom seemed as far away from *Top of the Pops* as U2. For the others the thrill of performing live in recent months had represented real progress, had proved that things were happening. For Larry, who had been doing live gigs for years, the buzz was somewhat muted. Unlike the others, he felt the disappointments keenly.

Two particular incidents stuck in his mind. They'd been booked into McGonagles as a support act a few weeks previously. Adam and Edge had called in to Terry O'Neill to confirm the date. 'Sorry, lads,' Terry had informed them. 'It's off.'

'Why?' Adam asked.

'I'm putting on the Boy Scoutz this time,' O'Neill told them.

'The who?' Edge asked incredulously.

'The Boy Scoutz, they're an all-girl rock group with a big following of their own,' O'Neill explained.

'But you promised us that spot. You can't do this,' Adam insisted.

'Sorry lads. See you another time,' O'Neill closed the conversation.

This bitter taste of the rock world underlined their vulnerability without a proper manager. Victory in talent competitions meant nothing around Grafton Street. In some ways Larry's other recent memory was even worse. They were playing in Howth and Bono was doing his thing with the audience. Two girls were trying to dance front of stage. They weren't watching Bono, who liked to feel that he was reaching everyone, making contact emotionally. In between numbers he spoke to one of the girls. 'What's your name?' he tried. She blushed and didn't quite know how to respond to the microphone she now found thrust under her nose. But her friend did. 'Fuck off, dickhead, get on with the bleeding music, who do you think you are anyway, David Bowie?' Those around the stage smirked. Bono shrank back into the shadows, wounded.

Bill Graham called McGuinness. He thought he'd found

that baby band Paul was looking for. U2 were younger, by six or seven years, brighter and more committed than any other band around. The drummer was first class and the singer called Bono had something.

'What?' McGuinness bluntly inquired.

'Go and see them,' Graham urged. 'They're what you need if you're serious about "breaking" a young band.'

Paul consulted Kathy. Bill Graham wanted him to see this young punk band from the Northside. What did she think? Kathy knew Bill and liked him. He'd been her campaign manager when she ran for president of the students' union at Trinity (she'd lost to Eugene Murray who went on to produce *Today*, *Tonight*, Ireland's leading current affairs television programme). Kathy advised Paul to have a look. She'd come with him.

When Adam rang again Paul was more positive. Yes, he'd come next week and talk to them. They made a date to meet in the same pub Graham had met them in in Artane. McGuinness had to cancel at the last minute. He'd go to the Phibsboro Festival where U2 were playing one Sunday in May. Again he cancelled. Spud was winding down and he wanted to make sure that everything ended smoothly. He was making the Smithwick's commercial. And in his heart he hated punk, which had to be negative and destructive, no matter what Bill claimed for its cleansing properties.

The lads were pissed off. Adam approached Steve Averill, the friendliest face on a hostile scene. Would *he* manage the band? Sorry, he wouldn't, but he would help them all he could. They told him about McGuinness and about some songs they'd started writing. Steve gave them one piece of advice which he said was crucial. He'd seen too many bands break up over money, who wrote what, and why the writers should get a bigger share of the money. Split *everything* you get four ways, Averill advised, that way you're less likely to fall out.

McGuinness finally kept his appointment on Thursday 25 May 1978. U2 were supporting the Gamblers at the Project (thanks to Caragh Coote). The Virgin Prunes were to open the show. McGuinness took Kathy and a friend, Tom Saunders, along. Besides seeing U2, Paul was on a retrieving mission for his fifteen-year-old sister Katy and her friend Paula Flynn, who jointly managed the Gamblers, but could never get paid their 20 per cent. It wouldn't be a wasted evening.

Paul had been working hard for Smithwicks all day. He had his *Irish Times*, unread, with him. When he arrived in the Project a stripped-down Prunes line-up with Gav and Guggi in drag were on stage backed by Adam, Edge and Larry. This most definitely wasn't McGuinness's scene. He opened his *Irish Times* and started to catch up with world events. Pod, still not proficient enough to make his stage debut on drums, sat sceptically in the shadows. So this was the Great Manager. Bit of an asshole, wasn't he, reading his fucking paper while the lads were on stage? Bono urged him to be quiet.

The Village waited anxiously for U2. McGuinness affected lack of interest in the whole scene. But he noticed when U2 hit the stage running. Visually they looked interesting. The drummer was very handsome, tough, blond, innocent. And he could play his drums. The bass player was elegant, good looking in an indolent way. The lead guitarist was fascinating. For one thing he was playing solo *notes*, unlike other punk guitarists McGuinness had seen. That you only strummed the guitar was an article of faith, at least punk faith, as he had understood it. The guitar was a flash job, a Gibson Explorer, angular shaped, all corners. Any guitarist who had the arrogance to carry a Gibson must have something more than the dark little guy seemed to have on the surface. There was a trace of real guitar playing in the U2 music, Paul thought, evoking for a moment in this punk stronghold the legendary Duane Eddy. The singer was extraordinary. He couldn't sing, but

Paul knew his theatre, knew stage presence when he saw it and Bono *had it*. He stalked the tiny stage, making no fashionable pretence at 'cool'. It was the thing in punk to ignore the audience, to look out beyond them or at your mates on stage, as if you were sharing some private joke at the expense of these sticks who'd been stupid enough to pay to see you play. Bono made eye contact with those in front of him, drawing them into his act, making everyone in the room react in some way to the sounds and happenings on the stage. As far as Paul could tell the music was original, with a couple of songs by Television, one of the better punk groups, thrown in. He was interested. They were fresh, young, different. He wasn't sure what he could do with them. Kathy and Tom Sanders were up dancing, the place was alive. They looked right. Paul considered the snags; the route he envisaged taking his baby band was long and tough. It would take three, maybe four years to get there. Would they have the commitment, the patience? Would he? What about money? He had very little; the few thousand pounds he'd made with Spud had gone on his wedding. The long road would require finance. How would he live? How would they? U2 were very visual, very 'live', but would these assets work on a record? Being good to look at and having stage presence was great – if you were prepared to tour, which was a slog, a poorly rewarded slog, before it got to be fun. If it ever did.

After the gig McGuinness took the band next door to the Granary pub to tell them all this. He had it in mind to say, 'Look lads, this is a tough business you're getting into.' What came out was slightly different: 'Look lads, this is a tough business *we're* getting into . . .' There was an impulsive streak in Paul for all he tried to disguise it. When he was moved, he was moved very deeply. There was a freshness, a kind of beauty about these kids – and that was all they were. They listened to Paul. They responded intelligently. Yes, they knew it would be hard and long. Yes, they were committed. No, they didn't want overnight fame and *Top of the Pops*. They had written their own songs, they'd go on the road. They wanted to make it, to be the best rock 'n' roll band in the world, however long it took. Adam did most of the talking, asking most of the questions. Bono had a nice urchin grin. Larry was curious, shy, patently decent. Edge was intelligent, quietly spoken, wiry and Welsh. U2 was the baby band all right, McGuinness felt after talking to them. He promised to draw up a contract and organize a proper demo session. They needed a good demo. Kathy loved them and on the way home to Waterloo Road told Paul he was right.

U2 were euphoric as they headed out into the early summer night. They had their manager and he looked and sounded the part. Gavin, Pod and Guggi hung around for Bono.

'Is that asshole going to manage you?' they choroused.

Bono confirmed their fears.

The demo session was the first real pressure imposed from outside on the group. They had to deliver on the claims they'd made in the Granary. They had to be as good as their aspiration to be the best rock 'n' roll band in the world. Live they always improvised, following the mood Bono created. He'd ad-lib words to the couple of songs they had written, and Edge, Adam and Larry would wing it with him. Words were the problem. They didn't write words, they composed sounds around images. Words came spontaneously. Bono had written a song, or to be more correct, *imagined* one on his eighteenth birthday, a few days before meeting McGuinness for the first time.

He always remembered Iris on his birthdays, indeed on every so-called special day of which, since her death almost four years before, there had been few. The void she'd left had not been filled. Now on the morning he woke up eighteen he was aware of emptiness in the small front bedroom of 10

Cedarwood Road. Norman was married now. Bono shared the house with Bobby. Bobby was at work. Being eighteen was nothing special. No home really, no job, not great looking, not well educated; there was Ali, The Village and the band. But nothing right now to hug, nothing here in this house to draw solace from. Death. He had never got over the suddenness of her death. The uncontrollable grief he, Norman and his dad had felt that day coming back from the Mater Hospital lay somewhere within ... within him, within the house, within the world. Out of control. The image grew, *'Out of Control'*, and the emotions around it. He heard the chord in his head, the opening chord, then another and another. He spent the morning playing and replaying, feeling again and again the pain and the joy of Iris. He took his guitar and picked the chords. He had a song. But not the lyrics. He had the emotions, a musical sequence, a sound that was ethereal but that he couldn't reproduce. The sound was in his head, the emotions in his heart, the images before his eyes. He went to the others to explain to them.

He'd done the same with 'Street Mission', the first song he'd written. They sat around listening to him explain, play the basic chords, tell them what it was about, what he could *see*. Yes, he saw the songs as much as heard them. 'Shadows and Tall Trees', 'The Fool', 'Cartoon World', they were all images to be given life by the appropriate sound. The words were incidental. But not in a recording studio, where you paid by the hour and hardened pros hovered impatiently by the dials waiting for your music – your prepared, packaged, three-minute song, with catch-line and chorus. You only created sound in a studio when you had the money to pay for it. Creating sounds other than guitar and drums took time. The CBS demo after Limerick had been a disaster. Jackie Hayden was sympathetic but was working for CBS. A demo tape should be your best eight songs put down bang, bang, bang.

U2 had managed three before Larry's dad arrived to take him home. Larry was in the middle of preparing for his Inter. Exam and in Larry Sr's mind *that* came first. More to the point, Larry had taken Frank Kearns with him to the studio and Mrs Kearns had been on the phone to the Mullens wanting to know where her son was at eleven o'clock at night.

Fearing another disaster, the band spent the summer working on their songs for the demo session McGuinness had promised in the autumn. They had all left Mount Temple now, so they had nowhere to rehearse. Edge suggested the shed in the Evans's back garden in St Margaret's Park. It was tiny, eight foot by four. They could hardly get themselves in, never mind the equipment. But every day through June, July and August, Bono, Adam and Edge worked from mid-morning till late at night. Larry would join them after his day's work as Sciscom. They worked on composition. Bono or Edge would come in with an image or, in Edge's case, a series of chords. The three of them would play around with the idea. Adam was great. Never sceptical or jealous, always willing to give it a go. 'Let's try it and see,' was his attitude. In the evening when Larry came he would improvise the drum lines, weaving into the song they were on the ideas he'd spent his day at Seiscom Delta working out.

It was during this process that the band's character formed. They weren't friends in the conventional, palsy-walsy sense of the word. They had different tastes, friends and interests outside of the band. Adam still liked the low-life and a good piss-up. Bono's life outside U2 was a complex mix of Village and girls, of which Ali was the most important. Edge was an associate member of The Village through his blood relationship with Dick, who was in because of his position in the Prunes line-up. Larry worked and knocked around with Frank Kearns and from his position behind the drums retained a healthy scepticism about U2 and its music. What they shared was a desire to make the U2 concept work and an understanding of the band's ethos. They were in it together. The music served the band, not any individual member of it. Here intelligence and the trust they had in each other served them well. They shared ideas, money, ambition, and what they possessed was invested in each other, in U2. During the long days spent working in the summer of 1978, the bond that had formed between them in the preceding year grew thick and strong. Each had strengths, musical, emotional, psychological, and all of those assets were at the disposal of the thing called U2. Between Adam, Edge and Bono a healthy competitiveness existed. Who could master this song first? Who would get the lead guitar? The politics of the group were still evolving. Bono and Adam had been the dominant voices for different reasons thus far. Now, as the quality of the sound became paramount, Edge asserted himself. Bono would come with an image, a sound in his head. Edge would make it happen, transform a theory into a song. What do fear, death, innocence, the mystery of adolescence *sound* like? Edge knew and could deliver. He had been the quietest, the least assertive, the Man on the Edge. Now he became the Man – the man who best understood the sound U2 were striving for. And thus they became a group at last. Each had led at some stage: Larry in the beginning and, technically, much longer. Bono up-front when there was nothing behind, the provider of ideas, the point of emotional contact between band and sceptical audience, Adam the hustling manager sustaining them through the period when U2 might have been aborted. Now in the summer of 1978 each had proved himself to himself and to the others. Lives that were purposeless and unappreciated were no longer so, thanks to U2. Gwenda Evans supplied sandwiches, drinks and meals to her son and his friends down in the shed. She was kind and supportive, never hinting at the doubts she felt inside. Bono often had to walk the eight miles home to Cedarwood or half that distance to Ali in Clontarf after his day in the shed. He had hardly any money and was too proud to beg from Bobby, whose doubts about U 2 were loudly and clearly on record.

U 2 broke cover to play McGonagles on the last day of July. The word on the Grafton Street scene was that the young band had acquired a mystery backer, a posh Englishman with lots of money. Although Trinity College stood at the bottom of Grafton Street, the gap between the world of Dublin rock 'n' roll and that hitherto inhabited by McGuinness was wide and virtually unbridgeable. Paul might have come from Mars when he appeared with the band in McGonagles that night. He appeared confident, self-assured, proprietorial. In fact he hadn't a clue about the rock circuit. He had no money either. And that was a real problem in relation to the strategy he'd mapped out for U 2.

There was no point, he considered, in becoming a big band around Grafton Street. After a record deal, a residency at McGonagles, the Baggot or Moran's was the next most desirable status symbol for local bands. But *then* what? McGuinness asked. If people could see you every Thursday in the Baggot, and someplace else at the weekend, they'd soon get fed up with you. This was guaranteed hero-worship, for a while. There was no challenge for the band and after a while no sense of occasion in the audience. On the credit side regular appearances provided money: £600 or £700 a week. If they didn't earn wages playing a residency where would U 2 money come from? Paul had none. Yet his master plan precluded residencies, indeed involved playing very little on the scene. In the end he figured rock 'n' roll success was about longevity, not a one-off hit single, a brief encounter with fame. Real success was built from the foundations upwards. It wasn't a question of getting a record deal, any old record deal, that merely allowed the major record companies to stick your record in the slot-machine of popular taste hoping for a jackpot. The record deal he wanted for U2 would be a long-term arrangement which allowed the band to develop, touring the UK and the States, establishing a relationship with rock fans *and* learning to play at the same time. The relationship he envisaged was like that between a young author and a publishing house in which the latter nourishes the former while a craft is learned. Glory (and money) quickly gained usually evaporated pretty quickly as well. And there was the *Realpolitik* of the music business: once you had a solid, long-term perspective in which the record company was partner and patron, it was harder for a major company to drop you. The fans you wooed along the way assured you of decent record sales and insured you against summary dismissal.

In the context of this strategy Dublin mattered only in terms of building a reputation. Doing that required of you that *every* gig you played was special, eagerly looked forward to, well reviewed, an occasion. Then you made your demo and went knocking on doors in London. *There* rather than Dublin the real battleground existed – it was London and the States you had to win. Dublin was the Phoney War, fought by local heroes who would soon be toppled by others. When Paul outlined his strategy to the band, they approved it. They also accepted the financial proposition he put to them; whatever they earned would be invested in equipment, their own sound-system and a van for touring. He would give them a subsistence allowance of £25 a week and reimburse them for any expenses they incurred. If and when they needed to finance a tour of the UK he would find the money. If and when they started making money he would take 20 per cent – off the top. It was a tough deal but absolutely up-front. They were kids on an adventure, he was a twenty-seven-year-old married man proposing to put his career in film-making on the line.

Revolver, the band U2 were supporting in McGonagles that night, were living proof of the McGuinness theory. Revolver were a good band. They'd got their deal, made their record, failed to make the charts and, having peaked thus, were now back headlining in McGonagles. There was nowhere to go from here. Phillip Byrne, their vocalist, looked like Sting, but his fame was strictly local, its boundaries set by the Berni Inn on Nassau Street, the Baggot on Baggot Street, the Gaiety Green and Bewley's Coffee Shop on Grafton Street. There was a world outside this square mile, harsh and real. Ultimately the only dream worth having lay beyond the Dublin scene.

Dave Fanning earned his money Dee Jaying in McGonagles. He watched U2 play a vivid, confident set that night. This was fury rather than passion, but Fanning's unerring instinct told him that this band projected qualities that he hadn't seen before in Dublin. The sound and the singer were unique. Whether that was good or not Fanning couldn't decide. Afterwards Adam and Bono hustled him for an interview on Big D. The Village also introduced themselves. Day-Vid fawned on Fanning, who was by now the voice of Irish rock 'n' roll.

'Oh Dave, I think you're fabby,' Day-Vid crooned. 'I wish I was a bottle of tomato ketchup so I could pour myself *all over you*,' the blond, starry-eyed youngster gushed.

Pod, Gavin, Bono and Guggi looked on, betraying no amusement.

'Are you for real?' Fanning laughed.

'Oh, I'm real all right, Davie, very *real*,' Day-Vid smiled. 'Don't you think I'm real, Davie?'

'Yes, yes of course I do,' Fanning assured his fan.

Out of the corner of his eye he caught Bono and the lads laughing. He agreed to put them on radio the next night.

'Does this mean I'll be a star, Dave?' Day-Vid inquired, deadpan now. There was no answer to that, Fanning decided before retreating to the tranquillity of his mixing booth.

Paul McGuinness received a phone call from Jo Clayton the following week. She understood he would be managing her son's, er, career, Mrs Clayton began. There was, Paul thought, a hint of disdain in the Home Counties voice at the other end of the line. 'Yes.' Well, she would like to have a chat about things, would he mind coming to see her. It sounded more like a command than a request. 'Of course,' he replied, 'I'll bring my wife Kathy.' 'Oh! you're married, are you? Well, come for dinner then.' Jo was a little taken aback by the self-possession she sensed on the other end. When the two Trinity people came to dinner she was delighted that Adam appeared to have found a better class of person to consort with. Jo thought the whole thing was crazy, but her fears were largely assuaged by Paul and Kathy's obvious intelligence and good sense.

Paul took Adam to Wembley where Horslips and Thin Lizzy were playing at the Arena on a special Irish double-bill. He had decided to ask Barry Devlin to make the U2 demo. Devlin was a good-natured northerner who sang and played bass guitar with Horslips. McGuinness and Devlin had struck up a friendship through Michael Deeny. Devlin was smart and had absorbed the lessons of eight years' touring and recording with Deeny's band. He'd never produced but knew his way around a recording studio. He would be a guide rather than The Producer for U2. He was also honest enough to give an unvarnished verdict on the baby band. Adam loved the Wembley atmosphere, the backstage buzz and the opportunity to meet his 'old friend' Phil Lynott in the flesh.

U2 had their own big gig supporting the Stranglers, one of the top punk groups, in the Top Hat Ballroom, Dun Laoghaire, in September. They arrived at the Top Hat all fired up, only to find that the Stranglers had occupied both dressing rooms. As they changed in the corridor, Bono's temper rose with the sounds coming from the stars' dressing room(s). Punk was supposed to be anti-star. The Stranglers' latest album had been called *No More Heroes*. What were these guys playing at? Finally, Bono burst in the door of dressing room No. 1. There, sprawled around drinking wine and generally having a ball, sat the enemies of excess.

'Fuck you,' Bono raged, 'I thought it was about no fucking heroes.'

'What's the problem, man, help yourself,' a mocking Strangler offered.

'Stick it up your arse,' Bono raged as he banged the door behind him.

U2 went out to try to blow the bastards off the stage. But that's not the way things worked out. A punk gang front of stage jeered and spat throughout the set. Bono fought back, but it was a losing battle. The big gig turned out to be a bitter lesson. The Top Hat was the real world and good intentions weren't enough. Afterwards they didn't hang around any longer than it took Bono to slip into the heroes' dressing room to liberate two bottles of wine.

Playing the Arcadia, Cork, the following month they noticed how good the sound-system was and how professionally their needs were serviced by the local crew. U2 were supporting another Dublin band, D. C. Nien. All bands hired sound-systems or used those at the venues they played. In U2's case, their sound being so distinct, the system was always the greatest threat to the gig. The Arcadia was a revelation in that regard. It was a great night. The Cork audience loved U2 who were the antithesis of the cool-Dublin-band-down-to-show-the-locals-how-it's-done that they were used to. McGuinness, curious as always to learn about the dynamics of the rock business, noticed the improved sound here and the crew, which was led by a short, stocky guy called O'Herlihy. Joe O'Herlihy was foreman and managing director of Stage Sound Systems, the company the Arcadia hired its sound-system from. McGuinness introduced himself and complimented Joe on the sound.

The band went into Keystone Studios in Harcourt Street on 1 November to make their demo. They'd decided to record three songs: 'Street Mission', 'Shadows and Tall Trees' and 'The Fool'. Devlin was impressed by the originality of the material. The songs were neither lyrically or in terms of sound derivative of any existing rock 'n' roll. There were shades of New Wave, Devlin thought, but this music was distinguished by its freshness and verve.

The Beatles had sung of Wanting to Hold Your Hand, a metaphor for screwing, the Stones of getting No Satisfaction, a lament for sexual frustration, Bowie was Fantastical, Elvis had raged against his Hound Dog, Bill Haley had simply wanted to Rock Around The Clock, another plea for sexual freedom. Much of pop music was simply harmless, amusing sonnets featuring idealized lovers who won or lost the game of love. U2's songs referred to none of these concerns but rather to life as they'd experienced it, life in a suburban world that was supposed to be real. 'Shadows and Tall Trees' was the most lyrically complete composition.

The images of Shadows – 'restless streets at night', 'walls of white protest', 'a gravestone' – depict the lyricist as the lonely outsider. 'Do you feel in me anything redeeming, any worthwhile feeling?' he asks. 'Is Love like a tightrope, hanging on my ceiling?'

> Life through a window, a discoloured pain
> Mrs Brown's washing is always the same.
> I walk the sweet rain tragicomedy
> I'll walk home again to the street melody.

Edge's task was to give the pain, confusion and loneliness of those images a sound. Halfway through the session Devlin, who was more guide than director of the operation, made a suggestion to Edge about a chorus line. It was politely rejected and as he walked back to the control desk Devlin glimpsed a look of incredulity pass between the kids behind him. These lads know where they're going, he thought to himself.

Paul McGuinness sat stony-faced, watching. He was tense, curious, helpless in these circumstances.

'What do you think?' he anxiously inquired of Devlin when the lads had left. Devlin, who had told him at the outset that he was 'mad' to get involved, thought carefully about his reply.

'They are self-assured, intelligent and funny. You will certainly have a major British success with them. It's about chemistry, Paul, and they have it.'

Two weeks later Maureen Mullen was tragically killed in a road accident in Raheny.

Chapter Ten

HARD TIMES BEHIND HYPE

Paul McGuinness took the Devlin demo tape to London. He had few contacts in the music business. He got the Yellow Pages and started calling the record companies. Nobody was very interested, and few offered to see him or hear the demo in his presence. Most told him to put it in the post, they'd give it a listen. CBS looked the best bet. They knew of U2 through their Dublin rep, Jackie Hayden, but they hadn't been impressed by the last U2 tape they'd heard. This one was better but not quite what they were looking for right now. McGuinness came home dejected. He would travel back and forth to London several times in the next few months. Always with the same result.

Meanwhile other elements in the strategy were working. U2 appearances were rare and special. They played the Dark Space Festival at the Project in early February 1979. This was a twenty-four-hour rock 'n' roll extravaganza headlined by the Mekons, an English band from Sheffield. Paul Rambali, a top rock journalist from the *New Musical Express*, attended. U2 were still a baby band and their 3.30 a.m. slot on the Dark Space bill proved it. They played superbly, Dave Fanning thought, and said so in the next issue of *Hot Press*. The next edition of the *NME* was eagerly awaited by McGuinness and the band. Sadly, Rambali ignored them. The *Hot Press* polls were published later in the month. U2 and the Virgin Prunes both figured as honourable also-rans in the Most Promising category, which was won by the Bogey Boys. Bill Graham profiled U2 for the March issue of the magazine, an important first public airing of their story. In a sympathetic and brilliantly perceptive article Graham captured the endearing honesty and the scepticism they felt even then about rock 'n' roll's tradition: 'U2 aren't interested in gang-bangs, New York pimps, whips and furs, high-fashion queens or indeed the imminent British counter revolution. Bono's testimony is that after acne comes anguish, songs about back-seat lovemaking at sixteen which is substituted at eighteen by wider spiritual insecurities.' Graham concluded: 'U2 are unmarked by sin, exuberant because they retain innocence.'

None of this helped with the record deal. In March McGuinness was forced to return to Jackie Hayden at CBS Ireland to accept a deal Adam and Bono had turned down after Limerick (on Bill Graham's advice). Strictly speaking the deal now proposed *was* crucially different. It would be for Ireland only, leaving the band free to pursue an international arrangement elsewhere. Hayden was enthusiastic. Chas de Whalley came from London to produce three songs which would form a single record with an A side and two B tracks, and McGuinness and Ian Wilson devised a clever promotional scheme for the release of this, their first single. The idea behind McGuinness's compromise was to have an Irish hit single to boost his sales pitch in London. The sale of 1,000 records would achieve the desired hit. The state had at last recognized the popularity of rock 'n' pop music and a second radio network, RTE 2, solely devoted to hit-parade material, was now in transmission. Dave Fanning was now legit., the grooviest civil servant in the land with his own programme on the new station. Wilson was his producer. Wilson and Fanning agreed to cooperate with McGuinness in a novel marketing plan. Only 1,000 numbered records would be pressed. Bono and Edge would come into the Dave Fanning Show, play the three tracks, 'Out of Control, 'Boy-Girl', and 'Stories For Boys', and Fanning's listeners could choose which song should be the A side of the limited edition disc. This daring and imaginative ploy worked brilliantly. It was to be characteristic of U2 strategy in the years ahead in combining clever marketing with the identification of fan and band. It involved the fans in a decision right at the core of the music business, made them feel they were participating, which indeed they were, and appreciated and respected, which was also true. The Fanning interview took place in June. U2 were playing another of their 'special' events: Xmas in June, The Jingle Balls, at McGonagles. Edge arrived in the studio wearing a Father Christmas outfit and eating an ice-pop.

All the hype and pre-publicity created intense interest and a keen sense of anticipation for a record that wasn't due out until October. In the Bailey, the Berni Inn and other watering holes around Grafton Street, Dublin's rock 'n' roll cognoscenti muttered into their Campari and sodas about the manipulative powers of the rich English bastard who managed U2. It was mistakenly assumed that McGuinness managed the Prunes as well, and maliciously rumoured by the more envious that he was sleeping with one or all of them.

The truth was rather different. Paul was under pressure on all fronts. At one band meeting, a formal U2 ritual that existed from day one, progress was discussed. Or rather the lack of progress towards the real rock 'n' roll world to which McGuinness had promised to lead them. Why was he failing with the record companies in London? Why not accept the international deal CBS seemed ready to offer? What about money? It was all very well playing 'special' events but they paid very little. Other bands were earning £600–£700 a week playing residences, headlining at McGonagles, the Baggot and Moran's. They were averaging £300 a fortnight – if they were lucky. Edge's parents had given him a year to make it after the Devlin demo and that year would soon be up. Larry had given up work. Paul was still working on his films. Bono was the spokesman. He wanted action, not hype.

Paul was reassuring, but firm. Look, we went into this with principles about a record deal, which we've compromised on, and residencies. The CBS international deal is no good for you. They want to release your single in the UK and it's not good enough. They are offering no backup money for touring and they won't take original material unseen for an album. You'll be just like a thousand other bands, here today, gone tomorrow. Bono persisted on the question of headlining at McGonagles. He wanted that spot. And then what? McGuinness countered. Well, where are we *now*? Bono argued. The heavy summer rain fell outside McGuinness's flat in Waterloo Road as the argument continued through the afternoon. At six o'clock they broke up, matters unresolved. Paul drove them to O'Connell Street to catch their buses home. He and Bono had a fierce row in the rain beside the Finglas bus-stop outside the Carlton Cinema. Office workers heading home looked aghast at this odd couple tearing into each other in the pouring rain.

Bono's simmering resentment, stirred by The Village, was directly related to McGuinness's occasionally off-hand manner. The boys were permanently broke. Bono would sometimes wander into Paul's flat-cum-office in Waterloo Road looking for a chat or perhaps a few quid. Paul might be reading the *Irish Times* with his feet up on the desk. Engrossed in what he was reading he sometimes failed to acknowledge Bono's presence, a slight that cut deeply into the singer's soul. This hurt was compounded by the sight of Paul's cash-jar on the mantelpiece, into which he tossed whatever loose change was in his pocket. U2 bus fares regularly came from the jar, which in bitter moments was seen as a rich man's indulgence.

Adam was as reasonable as Bono was unreasonable. He and Paul got on well together, almost like older and younger brother. They spoke the same language, in the same accent. Adam was as happy as he'd ever been. Sure, it wasn't 'happening' as quickly as they'd hoped but fuck it, he was having fun. He was a handsome young guy, the embryo of the rock star he'd always wanted to be. He was free, the pressures were manageable. He and Paul would have morning coffee and play around with tactics for the band. They enjoyed each other's company.

Dissatisfied with almost everything, Bono decided on direct action. He went to London with Ali and the demo and visited every music paper and rock journalist in the city. They travelled by boat from Dublin to Holyhead and on by train to Euston. His open, naïve approach appealed to the Londoners he met, who were more used to jaded, elderly teenagers whose desperation kept breaking out from its 'cool' cover. Bono was desperate too, but his desperation was naked. He got some promises that his contacts would look out for U2 when they came to London and some reassurance that the tape was a good debut effort.

Pod and Guggi were sitting in McDonald's one afternoon having coffee and a Big Mac when a row broke out at the next table. A man with a rolled-up brolly was shouting at a quiet guy who was sitting down, apparently minding his own business. Brolly was standing over him pointing accusingly at what appeared to be a Bible on the quiet man's table. Words like God, evil and rubbish were being screamed by Brolly. The staff moved in and removed the attacker. Guggi inquired if the quiet man was OK. Pod and Guggi joined the owner of the Bible, and they began to talk. He introduced himself as Dennis

Sheedy, a preacher. He asked them if they knew the Lord. Pod, a Catholic, had never heard this kind of talk before but Guggi knew the score. With his Plymouth Brethren background he knew the Bible in a way that Catholics never did. Mass was abstract devotion; Bible-reading was a literal understanding of God's story. Guggi evinced scepticism when Dennis talked about the need to be born again. He quoted Scripture to back up his claim. Guggi was a back-slider, he scolded.

'What's that?' Pod, fascinated, intervened. This was a foreign language to him. Pod had stopped going to mass when he was thirteen because the Catholic Church didn't have what he needed. Dennis wouldn't explain his reference to back-sliding but he invited the lads to come to his prayer meeting. He gave them an address on the North Circular Road.

Dublin, particularly the fashionable area around Grafton Street, was full of minority religions and sects in 1979. And young people were gravitating towards them in numbers sufficient to worry the Catholic Church, which had set up its own monitoring unit to observe the phenomenon, and parents whose children got involved. The Hare Krishna group featured prominently on the streets, while others, like Scientologists, the Moonies and the Church of God, a Californian sect, were more discreetly active. The Charismatic Christian movement evangelized on the fringes of Protestantism and on the streets as well. These groups offered spirituality in a world whose culture, politics and established religions were all bound together in a mutually supportive web of cynicism, decadence and corruption. Political idealism had died with the Kennedys and Martin Luther King. Harold Wilson's Labour Party had seen it off in Britain. Thatcher and the soon-to-be elected Reagan were the least worst options for a generation seeking success and material protection, in a world devoid of spiritual grace. In Ireland the promised Fianna Fail economic boom of '77 was now being exposed as the last desperate throw of the political dice it had always been. Soon the Pope would visit and condemn the killings up the road in Northern Ireland. The youth of Ireland flocked to him; he was a media star with a moral purpose. Alas, when he returned to Rome his words echoed bitterly for those sensitive and intelligent enough to see the reality behind the rhetoric. Priests continued to make things easy for the killers, offering more, much more, than a decent burial to IRA men. They still had their flag-draped coffins, their glorious graveside orations and the ritual defiance of a volley of rifle shots fired over the departed hero's grave. All of these things and more that was equally despairing sent the young, the sensitive, the spiritual in search of a simple message, a God that was understandable and, unlike those on earth who had hijacked his name, decent.

Dennis Sheedy was a leader of the Shalom group of Charismatic Christians. Pod and Guggi went to a prayer meeting, feeling curious. There were some young people there, plain, middle-class youngsters, serious looking. There was a quiet guy in his thirties, a genteel couple in their sixties, a widow, sad in black, and a military-looking type, middle-aged, erect. The group prayed and sang together. Dennis read an American Standard Bible. The word of God was simple and true, spoke about fairness and justice. God was goodness, God was in everyone, God was alive, caring for us, caring how we lived. The atmosphere was calm. The weight of confusion, doubt, fear and anxiety lifted from Pod's heart as he listened. They sang a beautiful Christian hymn to finish the meeting. Guggi and Pod had gone in smirking. They left feeling good, more certain of their spiritual bearings, at peace.

On the way home they called on Bono. They told him about the meeting and the feeling they'd got from it. He nodded as he listened, yes, he knew that feeling, from Sophie Shirley's meetings in Mount Temple. It was good. Did he want to come next time? Pod ventured. No, not for now, Bono replied.

Maybe some other time. Pod and Guggi continued to attend the Shalom group. After a few weeks Bono came, to protect them, he joked; these things can get out of hand, he asserted, remembering the bigotry that had consumed Mount Temple after a while. The Village joined the group. Bono persuaded Larry and Edge to come along. Larry had grown closer to Bono since his mother's death, which had devastated him. Bono had been through that experience and knew better than anyone the pain Larry felt. Edge's family came from the evangelical tradition in the Welsh valleys. He was curious to explore Christianity. Adam passed on this one – it wasn't his scene.

John Fisher owned a badge stall in the Dandelion Market off Stephen's Green at the top of Grafton Street. There was a big storage shed at the back of this trendy covered market. Fisher, son of an RTE producer and brother of Caroline, later to make her name as a journalist and broadcaster, started running gigs in the shed on Saturday and Sunday afternoons. Bono approached him to see if U2 could play some Saturday dates. Many of U2's most fervent fans were too young to attend pub gigs at the Baggot or McGonagles, where liquor was served. The Dandelion Green was ideal for a U2 audience. The band only played four or five gigs at the Dandelion Green, but a legend built up around the most successful of their special events. Kids, many of whom had never seen a live band before, came from all over the city.

Paul McGuinness meanwhile announced that U2 would shortly undertake a London tour playing some of the English capital's most prestigious venues. The London trip was publicized as the culmination of a successful year, during which the band had 'broken through' with their first single, radio and television appearances plus the coveted spot on the cover of *Hot Press* magazine. McGuinness hinted at an international recording deal which was 'imminent'. He also went to see Mr Kilmurray, manager of the Bank of Ireland in Leeson Street, to arrange to increase his overdraft facility to £10,000. Mr Kilmurray was benign. He liked this charming young man who always kept his promises and never appeared reckless in any way. Paul had kept the Spud account in the black and promised his benefactor that this arrangement, which was in his own name, would work out all right in the end.

More good news arrived in the shape of Gary Bookasta, who introduced himself after a gig in McGonagles. Gary claimed he was from K R O Q, a major west-coast radio station in the United States. He was in Europe looking for bands to bring to the west coast to play the clubs there. He *loved* U2. He was staying at the Shelbourne, why didn't the band drop by the following day and they could talk? Bono was delighted, they all were. Paul was privately cautious. The Village watched the scene and were duly impressed by the flash-looking American. The next evening, a wet Sunday, they all turned up at the Shelbourne, the band, McGuinness, the Prunes and Bill Graham, who was a curious observer in search of a possible scoop. Bookasta was staying in one of the Shelbourne's luxurious and expensive suites. Pictures adorned the wall featuring Gary alongside numerous celebrities, among them Elton John and Richard Nixon. The former president of the USA was now disgraced, but clearly hadn't been when photographed with Gary against a White House backdrop. Room service arrived with drinks and light refreshment. Then they kicked around some ideas. Gary was well connected in the music business, he'd helped 'break' some big bands on the west coast. It was a tough business, especially for bands from this side of the Pond. But not to worry, Gary *loved* U2, they were *original*. He'd be glad to help when that deal they were signing happened. There was no doubt he was for real, they decided, as they filed out in the wet Irish night, dreaming of California. Even the loo-book was class, somebody remarked. 'What was it?' Larry asked. 'Dante's *Inferno*, the Penguin edition.'

McGuinness set to work next morning checking out Bookasta. Meanwhile Gavin devised a scheme of his own. Gary hadn't really majored on the Virgin Prunes. It was U2 this and U2 that, Bono doing most of the talking and that arrogant arsehole McGuinness. He talked to Guggi and Dick Evans. Look, Gavin said, let's go back and see if he's interested in the Prunes. He could come and see us play, we'd blow his mind away. The others were dubious. What about Bono and U2? They won't know, will they? Gavin assured them. Anyway if they find out we can say we met Gary on Grafton Street. Look, Gavin insisted, this is the music business, it's work and we need a break as badly as U2. The Virgin Prunes kicked some more ideas around with Gary Bookasta that afternoon. McGuinness was having less luck. Nobody in the States had heard of him, although the radio station he claimed to be representing *was* real. However, when McGuinness rang the Shelbourne for more information the next day he learned that Bookasta had left. Bono found out about Gavin, and called a crisis meeting of The Village at 10 Cedarwood Road. He forgave Gavin, Guggi and Dick, but not before fucking them from a height for the dirtiest trick imaginable.

U2 played their last concert before going to London at the Dandelion Green. It was an event, a real one. There were about 600 people packed in to an old car park. It was a fusion of all the rock 'n' roll constituencies: those that already liked the band, kids who had thought them too precious, others who didn't like their post-punk music, even those on the scene who hated Bono's pratting around and the 'Little House on the Prairie' lyrics. They all came, following the scent of success, wanting to see for themselves the legends of Dandelion

Green. It was a glorious concert, a climax to a wonderful year. Everyone knew they were getting an international deal. Except that nobody knew where it was coming from, least of all U2.

Clever marketing and pre-publicity ensured the success of U2's first single, released in late September 1979. The Fanning show audience had chosen 'Out of Control' as the A side with 'Boy-Girl' and 'Stories For Boys' forming a double B side. The 1,000 numbered copies were quickly sold and the band had an instant chart success. Sandy Harsch produced a favourable review in *Hot Press*, although it was suggested that 'Stories' was the best track and therefore ought to have been the A side.

Paul McGuinness took the evidence to London to have another go, this time at Tom Nolan, EMI's A-and-R man, who was sympathetic to U2's cause. Nolan persuaded two senior EMI executives to travel to Dublin to have another look at the band. McGuinness was ecstatic. On their home ground, with the confidence of a hit single behind them, he was certain U2's live show would convince anyone. News that London was coming to town always created a buzz. More was inevitably made of such visits than was often justified. The band were tense, but word was out that *this* was *it*. They chose to play their make or break gig in the Baggot. The place stank of sweat and urine, the toilets being just beside the entrance to the club. It had a low roof and held only about 200 people. The Baggot was rough but atmospheric, stage and audience separated by a narrow strip through which only one person could walk at a time. Ali, Ann, Larry's girlfriend, The Village and Paul and Kathy McGuinness all piled in to lend support. Dave Fanning and Bill Graham were on hand to see a little piece of history made. The house was full long before the 8.30 p.m. starting time. The VIPs eased their way to their reserved table.

The band backstage (the toilets) told each other to 'go for it'. They hit the stage running, blazing through a set that contained all the sure audience grabbers, 'Out of Control', 'Shadows', 'Concentration Cramp', 'In Your Hand', 'The Fool'. It was powerful, original rock 'n' roll and it drew a wild response from the crowded room.

Halfway through, Chris Briggs and Ben Edmunds, the EMI men, slipped out. Sorry, they whispered to McGuinness, we want to see the Specials on the *Old Grey Whistle Test*. Paul was speechless. Nobody else had noticed the visitors' departure from their back-row seats. The band played on, oblivious to their fate. Paul wandered along the lane connecting the club with Baggot Street. He was hurt, as wounded as he'd ever been in his life. He was worried too: he had virtually ceased film-making to devote his time to the band, they were living off the money Kathy earned as a copywriter in an advertising agency – and now this. They hadn't been able to keep the A-and-R men at the gig, much less convince them that U2 was, potentially, an international act. All of this ran through McGuinness's mind, but nothing bugged him as much as the sheer bad manners of the EMI people. They were staying in Jury's Hotel. Paul got in his car and drove the two miles to Jury's. In the middle of *Whistle Test* he burst in on Briggs and Edmunds and told them precisely what he thought of them. Then he went out and had a drink.

Back at the Baggot U2 played a couple of encores, Bono searching anxiously for the EMI executives. He assumed they had left with Paul to negotiate a deal, convinced by the opening half of the gig that U2 were good enough. Kathy broke the news to the band when they came off. She'd no idea where Paul was, he'd said nothing to her. This was the lowest moment in the band's life, a sense of failure, embarrassment and doubt welling up inside each of them and no Paul around to rationalize and reassure. The fans' excitement as they begged autographs and told the boys how great the gig was only compounded the sickness in their guts.

Kathy walked home alone to Waterloo Road. She was a tough, spirited lady but she was saddened to the point of despair by what had happened, and so sorry for Paul, who she knew to be emotional beneath the formal exterior and more committed to the U2 ideal, to the spirit of the band, its honesty, openness, decency, than was wise for a twenty-eight-year-old sophisticate whose Trinity contemporaries were now making their way in the world, carving niches for themselves in a society far removed from the sweaty squalor of the Baggot Inn. Kathy felt for Paul.

Larry went home to Artane on the bus with Ann. They were a beautiful young couple, she as prettily blond as he was dashingly, brazenly handsome. But they were nice rather than brash or posing, nice, decent, bright kids, sick now that the dream appeared to be dissolving into disappointment. Larry Mullen Sr was more sympathetic to U2 now than he had been at the beginning. The boys had rallied round Larry Jr after Maureen's death, been real friends, especially young Hewson. The striving ambition had kept Larry Jr occupied, helped deflect his grief at his mother's passing. When Larry had asked for a year off to try to 'make it' his dad, encouraged by Cecilia, had consented. Maureen's death had put many suburban preoccupations, particularly those concerning security, in perspective. Really, there was no security. Larry Sr often reflected on his time in the seminary, on the different course his life might have taken if he'd joined the priesthood. He'd found the Department of Environment frustrating, a joke really, demanding that you leave your energy and imagination at home when you went to work, for such things were inimical to the pushing around of paper that was the business of the civil servant. Larry Jr now felt shattered, and wondered seriously about the point of being in a band.

Bono and Pod waited for a taxi home from the rank on Stephen's Green. Taxis were never there when you wanted them. They sat on the kerb. It was cold, damp and dark. Bono had his stage clothes in his little red bag slung over his shoulder.

'I think I'll give it up,' he laughed at Pod.

'You're right,' Sir Poddington, the knight who never surrendered, agreed.

But Bono was smiling, grimly, to himself. The smile suggested to Pod that Bono would never give it up. Arriving at 10 Cedarwood, Bono found he had forgotten his key – again. Whilst Pod waited below he began to effect entry by the usual route, up the drainpipe to the bathroom window, slipping the catch and hauling his awkward body through the tiny opening. Bobby was in bed. He heard the noise.

'Is that you, Paul?'

'Yes,' said Bono, still hanging from the drainpipe twenty-feet up.

'What are you doing?'

'Just cleaning my teeth, Da.'

'Make sure all the lights arc off.'

'OK.'

He let Pod in through the front door and they talked until dawn about London.

At a band meeting the next day McGuinness betrayed none of his inner despair. He was confident they'd get a deal in London. Ian Wilson, their London agent had booked prestigious venues like the Hope and Anchor, the Bridge House in Camden Town and the Moonlight Club. There was a possibility of an opening slot with Talking Heads to climax the ten-day tour. Playing live was their great strength, he'd make sure the record companies and press were there. They were still on course, Paul assured them.

The London trip involving Paul, the band and a three-man

crew would cost £3,000. The money was available through a publishing deal McGuinness had agreed with Bryan Morrison, an English music publisher. The deal was £3,000 now and £3,000 when they signed to a major international label. Three days before they were due to leave for London, Morrison rang Paul to say that he'd had second thoughts. He was prepared to pay only the first three grand. He gave Paul twenty-four hours to think about it. Paul was now in a large hole, but he rang back twenty minutes later to tell Morrison the terms were unacceptable. Then he called the band in. He could raise some money, he wasn't sure how much, but if they could get £100 each off their parents, the London trip was still on. Tiernan McBride and Seamus Byrne, two old friends of Paul's, advanced a substantial amount of the £3,000 required. Larry Mullen Sr chipped in his £100. 'I'll pay you back Dad if it takes me one year or ten,' his eighteen-year-old son promised. The Evanses also came through, as did Bobby Hewson, happy at least that Bono was committed to *something*. Jo Clayton refused to give Adam any money. Brian was away on secondment to some airline or other. Jo believed in youngsters *earning* money, not getting handouts. She did what she thought was best for a son she still regarded as fundamentally irresponsible. Adam felt some shame and humiliation that *he* couldn't come through in a crisis. Paul and the others quickly reassured him on that score. But worse was to follow for Adam. The day before they were due to leave, Jo lent him the new family saloon car to drive himself and Edge to rehearsals. Denying him the £100 had been tough, so now she recanted over the car. Just outside Malahide the car hit a wet patch on the road and crashed into a truck. Edge was not wearing his seat-belt and pushed his hand through the window to save himself. Bono and Larry were waiting at rehearsal. Adam stayed behind to clear up the car mess, urging Edge to bus it into the city to tell the lads what had happened. Blood pouring from his wound, Edge made it.

The band came first, the hand second. Stitches weren't necessary but a bulky strapping was placed – too tightly – around the injured tendons. The boat trip from Rosslare to Fishguard the following night was agony for U2's lead guitarist, and he would still have the problem of *playing* to face when they arrived.

The London audiences were indifferent. Bono assaulted them, talked to them, sat among them, climbed on and knocked over the amps, bled, to communicate the passion and spirituality of the music. At the Moonlight and the Rock Garden he won in the end. The Hope and Anchor, before an audience of nine, was a disaster. Edge, playing at half-pace anyway with his swollen hand, broke a string midway through the set. He ran off the stage to try a repair job. The others, knowing he was struggling with his hand, ran after him. Paul was standing in the room with the A-and-R man from Chrysallis, the record company that he felt offered their best hope of the kind of deal he was looking for. Embarrassed, McGuinness rushed to the dressing room. What the hell's going on he pleaded? Hell was going on.

They were staying at some short-stay apartments in Covent Garden. They returned dispirited to the small bar in their lodgings after the show. Adam and Paul had gone elsewhere. Larry, Edge and Bono drank with the crew and a pretty girl from Ian Wilson's PR company. The girl fancied Larry strongly. This was *Time Out* London, feminism was the thing, especially among a certain type of middle-class girl who imagined emancipation had arrived. If *you* wanted to go to bed with a fellow you propositioned *him*. Why not? (Why not indeed?) The signals were sent but Larry wasn't up for it. He had a girlfriend, Ann, in Dublin and he was going to bed. This *was* unbelievably coy and strange behaviour for a rock 'n' roll star. Deciding it was a new kind of Irish come-on, the girl headed upstairs after Laurence, who had sussed the possibility out and tipped the wink to Bono and Edge to get him out of this embarrassing situation. After a few minutes Bono went to investigate. He found Larry explaining to the girl that he really wasn't into this. Bono took her downstairs.

'Why didn't you mind your own business?' demanded Niall Shortall, the sound man, a veteran of the Dublin scene. He challenged Bono, displaying open contempt for what he characterized as 'all that Bible crap'. An ugly row ensued, and it became clear that a new sound set-up would be needed.

Next day Paul McGuinness rang Joe O'Herlihy, the little guy with the good sound in Cork, and asked him to come and do the Talking Heads gigs. Joe had his own business to run and had already declined to work for U2 because they couldn't pay anything like the going rate, but he agreed to help out in the emergency. The Talking Heads gigs went well. But when their van headed back to Fishguard for the return journey to Dublin U2 still had no recording deal. It looked as if McGuinness's strategy had failed. Sitting in line to board the ship in Wales they twiddled the knob on the van's radio to catch the Dave Fanning show on Radio Two. Fanning was interviewing Jake Burns, leader of Stiff Little Fingers, a ranking Belfast band. Burns bemoaned the lack of sparkle on the music scene; nothing was happening. Nothing? Fanning queried. Well, Burns reflected, there *is* one band that I think could be the greatest rock band of all time. U2. That raised a cheer in the little van at the end of a long queue in Fishguard.

Chapter Eleven

THE END OF THE
ROAD TO NOWHERE

The following month, January 1980, U2 won five categories in the *Hot Press* readers' poll. This was wonderful as far as it went. But it didn't go far enough. The truth was that band and manager were in despair, their strategy for conquering the rock world in ruins. Without a major international recording contract U2 were going nowhere except back to the Baggot and McGonagles. They were in the traditional trap, familiar to Irish rock bands. They had reached the end of the road to nowhere.

At a band meeting early in the new year they reflected on their dilemma. Money was the basic problem. Without money they couldn't tour the UK and Europe, much less the United States which in McGuinness's mind remained the ultimate objective. No touring, no fans, no record sales, those were the realities. An international recording deal of the kind they'd been seeking would solve the problem. The right deal would provide what was known in the business as 'tour support money', £50,000 or so to cover a small crew and expenses, but the only deals on offer were the wrong ones, cutting a succession of singles with the Hit Parade in mind, with a quickie tour to follow if you made the charts.

On the optimistic side of things the band were perceived to be on the up and up by the Irish public. They should capitalize on that, McGuinness decided. It was all they *could* capitalize on. Rather than own up to being broke the band pretended they were big time and booked a major Irish tour that would climax with a gig at the Stadium. The National Boxing Stadium on the South Circular Road housed over 2,000 people. It was used for concerts by the top Irish folk groups like the Dubliners and the Wolfe Tones, and visiting UK and American stars with reputations big enough to sell it out. No unsigned Irish rock band had ever risked the humiliation of playing to its open spaces. Headlining there was an enormous bluff, hardly justified by five *Hot Press* awards and one successful single in the Irish charts. The tour would start in February and run for a month, ending audaciously on the South Circular Road. A new single, 'Another Day', would be released in February to coincide with the tour.

McGuinness was now at the stage of waiting for *something* to turn up. He had been managing the band for eighteen months, gradually shedding other interests and responsibilities, but the day of reckoning was coming and privately he was pessimistic about the future. They were running out of record companies. Island Records, a small independent label run by Chris Blackwell, was next on Paul's list. Rob Partridge, Island's publicist, was a U2 fan and was working hard on Bill Stewart, the company's A-and-R man, on the band's behalf.

While all this was going on McGuinness had a little local problem to take care of. A fanzine called *Heat* had carried a gossipy item alleging that McGuinness had played a dirty trick to pinch a Trinity College gig from Rocky De Valera and the Gravediggers, another Dublin band. Somebody – probably Paul McGuinness, *Heat* suggested – had rung the Trinity promoter and asked that U2 be allowed to replace the Gravediggers on the grounds that A and M Records were sending someone to Dublin to 'scout' the band with a view to signing a major deal. Tradition demanded that such a request be acceded to. As it was, on this occasion Rocky De Valera, alias Ferdia MacAnna, the streetwise son of one of Ireland's leading theatrical personalities, went mad when the news was conveyed to him that his band had lost the gig. He suggested someone check with A and M Records in London. A and M denied any knowledge of an imminent trip to Dublin or any major deal with U2. *Heat* put two and two together and hit the newsstands with a story that McGuinness believed was both libellous and malicious. *Heat* was run by Pete Price and Jude Carr. Carr's brother Eamonn had been a member of Horslips which by now had broken up, acrimoniously, after ten years on the road. Carr led one ex-Horslips faction, Michael Deeny supported by Barry Devlin, the other. McGuinness saw himself as a victim of this feud. He was furious, and a solicitor's letter arrived at the Carrs. McGuinness was prepared to settle for the magazine to be withdrawn from sale. The Carrs accepted this proposal, but the following week McGuinness saw the magazine on sale in Easons and flipped. This time he would sue. This minor scandal around Grafton Street ended with *Heat* going into liquidation. Nobody ever did find out who made the phone call to Trinity.

By the time the Irish tour reached Queen's University, Belfast, Paul had got things moving again in London. Chris Blackwell owned his own music publishing company called Blue Mountain Music, separate from Island Records but obviously close to the record company's heart. Paul figured that a publishing deal with Blue Mountain could be the way to interest Blackwell personally in U2 and might lead to a recording contract. Three of the Blue Mountain's executives flew to Belfast to see the band perform. Island's A-and-R man, Bill Stewart, was due to watch them at the Stadium in Dublin the following week. In a very real sense *this* was Paul's last throw of the dice.

The tour had gone well. They'd hired Joe O'Herlihy to do the sound, and the audiences, primed by the good publicity vibes about U2, had responded. U2 gigs were always a battle, always viewed as such by the band. The music was original, no instant hits, no catchy tunes. The music was personal and success in concert depended on establishing a rapport with the audience at the beginning. Bono was the point of personal contact. Sometimes at the Dandelion Green, the Baggot or McGonagles, the battle was won before it began. Fans knew the band, knew the music, the buzz of compatibility was instant. Sometimes Bono had to work. He'd look early on for a vote of confidence from the audience; he'd ask them to clap and if they did he was rolling. Or he'd make a statement about music, the world they lived in, the town or hall they were in that night. If the hall responded the band's confidence grew. If not, things could get desperate. Occasionally people stood back in the well of the hall or round the sides, watching, waiting for the magic to come off the stage. This gutted Bono. 'Come on, come on up, we're up here,' he would beckon insistently. If only two or three sloped forward he – they – were in trouble.

Belfast was like that, only worse. Bono could be confrontational, staring out at the audiences, challenging them to ignore *him*. He'd seen Iggy Pop in London and been heavily influenced by the rock showman's stagecraft. Iggy was physical, launching himself at the audience, offering not just music but his body, attempting to reach people on all levels, breaching the barrier between performer and people, between art and life, between what was real and unreal. Iggy Pop was a genius of performance art, a seminal influence on Bowie and on the desperate young Irishman dying now upstairs at Queen's University. Behind Bono, Edge felt that sick, sinking feeling that came like a wave when things went wrong. But things had never been as wrong as this. It was the tail end of punk and the Queen's student union now began to abuse the band in the spirit of the times. 'Play this, play that,' they started screaming. 'Stop fucking preaching and play; you can't fucking play,' someone screamed. Bono, angry and hurt, struck back. It was going to be a long night, Adam thought.

McGuinness was devastated; his three guests from London, embarrassed. Queen's was a black, agonizing night when the future seemed utterly without hope. Home was the only place left to go.

Tickets for the Stadium were going slowly. Less than 500 tickets had been sold when they reached Dublin. A massive guest list was compiled for the 'celebration' concert. All the parents would come including ex-Squadron-Leader Philip McGuinness and his wife Sheila. The Village and friends of The Village, *Hot Press* staff and friends, old school friends and their friends. Everyone in Dublin soon seemed to be going to what was now *The Gig*. On the day the Stadium seating was rearranged to hide the gaps. Joe O'Herlihy was asked to turn the sound up a few kilowatts. Adam was having a hard time persuading Jo and Brian to come to the show. In the end, he left the tickets on the kitchen table. They came, along with Bill Stewart from Island and about 1,000 other people, most of whom were 'guests' of the band. It was a brilliant night. From the opening song the audience were with the band, every response was right and Bono rode the waves of affection and *understanding*, of him, the music, the band, the night that was in it. The show climaxed with thirty or forty people on stage in celebration. Bill Stewart was won over.

Afterwards he offered U2 a deal – on the spot, in the Stadium dressing room. They'd talk about it tomorrow, they agreed. For now the place was overflowing with relief. Paul stayed cool, for a man who knew that he and his band had achieved a miracle of nerve and guts. U2 were out of the hole and into the real world of rock 'n' roll.

The deal Bill Stewart offered was long term, for four albums using the band's original material which Island would accept unseen. There was also crucial tour support money for the UK, Europe and America. Island was an outsider in the corporate world of rock music, its wealth and reputation founded on the legendary Jamaican reggae music of Bob Marley and the Wailers. It was said that Chris Blackwell *was* Island Records and, insofar as that company had an ethos and an identity that extended beyond the corporate values of the major powers in the record industry, this was true.

Blackwell was born in England, his father Anglo-Irish, his mother from Costa Rica of a Portuguese-Jewish family. Chris grew up in Jamaica, where his father was in the army and his mother's family was in the rum, banana and coconut business. His childhood was spent in the company of Jamaicans, servants of his family, the black gardener being a particular friend and guru. Blackwell came to school in England when he was ten, to Harrow School. He left without qualifications, returning to Jamaica in his early twenties after failing to settle in the London business world.

After working as an aide-de-camp to Sir Hugh Foot, the British High Commissioner, Blackwell set up in business renting cars to tourists, and started a successful water-skiing school at a local hotel. He loved one of the local bands playing at the hotel and decided to record them, and, as a consequence, got interested in the business. Also, he loved the low-life, the easy company of musicians. There was no popular music in Jamaica, except calypso, so Blackwell started going to New York, to export records, which were heavily in demand, to the island. He was the first. He created a market and competitors. Soon he started travelling to England, taking Jamaican music, now popular, home-produced reggae, to outlets in Brixton and Lewisham in south London where large immigrant communities existed. Blackwell's cottage industry changed character when a Jamaican recording by a girl called Millie topped the English pop charts. 'My Boy Lollipop' was a classic pop song. It provided Blackwell with the money and credibility to create Island Records.

Bob Marley and the Wailers walked in off the London streets one day, looking to make a record. They were one of the top Jamaican bands and cult figures in Britain's black ghettos, but held to be unreliable by the major record companies. The truth was, as Blackwell understood, that Marley was a strong man, an artist with too much pride to put up with the overtly racist attitudes he encountered in the music business. Blackwell felt that reggae music's time had come, that the mainstream market was ready to accept it as the great music it was. Marley wanted to cut a single. Blackwell suggested an album. How much would it cost? he asked Marley. When Chris was told £3,000–£4,000, he offered the higher figure. If the rumours of Marley's unreliability were true, Chris knew his money was gone. But he believed in trusting strong people, it *was* people you backed. His sense of Marley was correct. In the process of becoming rock 'n' roll legends, Bob Marley and the Wailers secured the future of Blackwell's independent label.

Although Blackwell himself hadn't heard U2 before they signed to his label, the deal reflected Island's governing ethos; you backed people, looked for commitment, took the long view and were prepared to work. Rob Partridge and Bill Stewart were the Island executives primarily responsible for the U2 deal. The financial benefits to the band were minimal, £50,000 up front, most of which would be absorbed in recording costs. There was also that critical tour support money, amounting to another £50,000. For Island's part the hope was that with the label's support U2 would go out and win the fans, develop as musicians and writers and in time fulfil their potential with albums that sold in millions. It was the conviction with which U2 vowed to do this that attracted Stewart and Partridge. In the age of super groups, talented individual musicians drawn together to form best-of-everything bands, there was something appealing about an old-fashioned unit, a group that stood or fell together, where four hearts really did beat as one. CBS Ireland would continue to distribute U2's records in Ireland. But with the Island deal the U2 battle had moved onto a different plane.

They had three months before beginning to record their debut album in Windmill Lane, Dublin. Meanwhile they set out on a long tour of Britain to establish a market for their album and to promote '11 O'Clock, Tick Tock', their first Island single, in the UK.

Niall Shortall was off the team after the London incident. Paul tried to persuade Joe O'Herlihy to tour the UK with them, but the price wasn't right for the Corkman and an English sound crew was hired. Around Grafton Street, Shortall was retailing his version of the London row. Larry, he claimed, had clicked for this gorgeous chick. Bono and Edge, carrying their Bibles, had gone upstairs, kicked the bedroom door down and dragged Laurence and the girl out of bed. They read the Bible all the time and were a pain in the hole according to the disaffected sound engineer. McGuinness got to hear of this rumour, and threatened to sue Shortall if lies about the band's religious beliefs or sex lives were spread around Town.

The Shalom group had become increasingly important in the lives of Larry, Edge and Bono. Pod, Gavin and Guggi, Ali, Aislinn, Maeve O'Regan and Rene, Gavin's girlfriend, were also members of Shalom. They accepted the biblical stricture that 'Unless you be born again by water and the spirit you shall not see the Kingdom of Heaven.' Bono and Edge had been baptised, in the Holy Spirit by immersion in the sea. The prayer meetings had now moved to an old house in Templeogue. The group met twice a week, each meeting lasted two or three hours. They began with songs, beautiful gospel songs, then people would discuss the values expressed in the Bible. There was no fire-and-brimstone preaching, no symbolic paraphernalia at these Meetings. Shalom gatherings were, in relation to the ceremonies of established Churches, real. There was a spirit of humility, a sense of God in the form of goodness being present. Within this simple suburban front room people of all kinds, from all walks of life, many of them weakened by the harsh, Godless world outside, found strength and protection in the grace, or spirit, of God. His word came to the meeting through the Bible and sometimes in the form of speaking in tongues, a stream-of-consciousness outpouring of the human spirit's most deeply felt angsts and desires. Speaking in tongues dated back to the Apostles who it was said spoke thus to each other to communicate God's word.

For the ostensibly strong and together young men and women who came to Templeogue, the Meetings conferred a feeling of spiritual wellbeing greater than anything available in the world outside. This was essentially the feeling devout Catholic and Protestant men and women got from real devotion where it existed. Hindus, Buddhists, indeed anyone in any religious grouping reflecting contemplatively on a God who was good, just and fair, would have achieved the spiritual state those who attended Shalom gatherings experienced. For strong young people, fortunate in so many worldly respects, the prayer meeting allowed a feeling of humility that was cleansing. Ego was sacrificed, and strength, worldly strength, shared with those who needed it. There was a wonderful egalitarianism of the spirit. You didn't laugh at those less well-equipped for the battle outside, but empathized and offered support and understanding. The Meeting would end by people joining hands and singing, hugging, breaking down the barriers between them. Peace was the final dividend.

There were many radical Christian groups in the city, to which a number of the brightest, most sensitive young people were drawn. In a world where family life was breaking down, which was preoccupied by the make of car you drove, the type of Spanish holiday you went on, a world of hi-fi, portable colour TV, where sexual fidelity was a joke, Christianity was a balm for the more sensitive spirit. Outside, this brand of Christianity was scorned as freakish. Inside, it seemed like a quest for the values of fairness, decency, justice and humility that Christ had proclaimed in the Bible. That these aspirations were considered daft by the community at large showed only how damaged society was by the conduct of the established Churches, whose conniving and expediency with politicians and businessmen had rendered *them* incredible as God's representatives, and much more seriously, had placed the Christian ethos itself in contempt. Thus the challenge for Christians in the Shalom group: don't be ashamed, proclaim your values and your faith, read your Bible if you want to, whenever, wherever.

This seemed a reasonable proposition to Bono and the others. Bibles were nothing new in Edge's home. The Evanses came from the valleys in Wales where evangelistic Christianity was a living tradition. Some of Gwenda and Garvin's relatives were evangelists. Despite the home influences, Edge, a highly intelligent, rational, young man, was deeply sceptical about organized religion of any kind. As a ten-year-old he would skip off down to the shops with his mates on Sunday mornings to avoid attending church. He was aware of the sectarian nature of Catholicism, but had no illusions about his own Presbyterian Church's ecumenism. One incident from his childhood remained with him, feeding his doubt about religions in general, his own in particular. A local Catholic lady called Chrissie helped Gwenda Evans at home, sometimes baby-sitting when she and Garvin were away. When Edge's grandfather died, a service was held in Malahide's Presbyterian Church. The Evanses invited Chrissie. During communion the family friend was publicly and embarrassingly snubbed by one of the church elders. Edge felt deeply ashamed. His initial attachment to Shalom derived from curiosity rather than any great conviction. Aislinn had come to the meeting with him and it was only after she made her commitment to Christianity that Edge responded positively to the spiritual awakening he increasingly felt.

Bono was subdued and reflective at the Meetings. Prayer meetings were not new to him, but this second time around he understood better why he needed the Spirit of God. Christianity moderated his raging, questing ego, provided a focus for his massive reservoir of spirituality. All his objections to the religious institutions of his childhood, whose dogma had separated his family every Sunday, were resolved by this simple concept of people meeting God in a suburban front room. 'Where two or three are gathered together in my name I am present,' Christ had vouched. *That* you would never believe looking at the divisions among the established Churches.

Larry found peace after Maureen's tragic death. He found also great joy in the community feeling generated at the prayer meetings. He hated ego, flashness, conceit, in himself as much as in others. In Shalom that stuff was out. Larry was Larry, not the handsome sex object behind the drum-kit. Larry Mullen Sr first noticed a change when Larry Jr stopped going to mass and started reading the Bible at home. He was worried. Dublin was full of extreme sects, the newspapers regularly carried stories about children leaving home to follow some cult or other. But Shalom was not that kind of thing, Larry Jr reassured his dad. 'I'm staying at Rosemount Avenue,' he laughed. 'You're not getting rid of me that easily.'

The Village, Edge and Larry still laughed and joked, didn't change character and become Holy Joes. But morally and spiritually they had found a refuge. Bono had stopped mooning and chasing pretty girls. He and Ali were committed to each other now, she, as beautiful as she was bright and sensible, looked after him, guiding him through the real world of food, house-keys, money, clothes and things that he hadn't a clue about. Bono did the business on stage and in his fertile imagination which was on permanent overload with ideas and images of music and song. Edge and Aislinn's friendship had deepened. They were in love, committed to one another. Larry and Ann remained sweethearts. Not all that much was changed. They felt as they always had. They were decent lads who knew now why it was important to be so. And what the odds against remaining so were.

These spiritual developments ran parallel with the U2 cause. They brought their Bibles on the UK tour, reading during the day and holding prayer meetings in their hotel rooms. There was a responsibility to infuse your working life with Christian values. It wasn't for you to evangelize or proclaim too loudly, but neither was your faith to be denied, hidden away from those with whom you came into contact. They were twenty years old, the same age or sometimes much younger than their rock 'n' roll constituency. Their values were not considered normal in rock music. Young men recently famous, with money in their pockets, had traditionally and quite understandably availed themselves of the pleasures of the flesh which abounded around rock 'n' roll heroes. Sometimes nobody got hurt. Sometimes girls were savagely abused or taken advantage of. Sometimes, more than was commonly perceived, it was the rock idol who was destroyed by indulgence and excess. 'It didn't make you happy' might have been the epitaph for sex-, alcohol- and drug-sated heroes who'd got lost amid the carnal delights of Being A Rock Star. Nobody laughed at them. Nobody who knew U2 laughed either. Many who heard second-hand about their Christianity did mock the notion of spiritual rockers playing spiritual rock 'n' roll. But around the band the reality was known; Edge, Bono and Larry hadn't changed and were still respected for what they were – musicians. Their faith was their own business.

Adam had gone to a couple of meetings but it wasn't for him. He was an elegant young man with an easy, sympathetic manner off stage. His tastes in après-concert diversion were more traditional than those of his U2 colleagues. Adam and Paul were close and would look for bars and clubs to have a few drinks after the show. Adam liked girls and had a ball. He usually slept late the next day, sometimes waking up in his own bed. He knew the others disapproved, but there was no real hassle going on and no problems as far as their work went. Everyone's private life was his own.

Paul McGuinness had learned many lessons during his two years in the rock 'n' roll business. The most important was about people. He had been ripped off by music publishers, record companies, promoters and crew, the idea behind the sharp practice always being that *you had to do it that way to get on*. He had found that offensive, to him and his band, and despairing. But the Island people had been more reassuring. There were people with ethics, applying them to rock 'n' roll business. There *was* honour and a commitment to long-term objectives in a business that offered seductive alternatives. During Paul's first meeting with Chris Blackwell *each* was reassured by the other's professionalism and basic lack of bullshit when it came to talking rock 'n' roll business. They shared a similar background – service life and public school – as well as an aversion to spivery and a respect for the artists committed to them. In every business there were *good* people, McGuinness reflected, often somewhere near the top, no longer taking cheap shots, smart enough, tough enough, to see that ultimately the trick wasn't the treat. It was called class. Sometimes that too was laughed at.

McGuinness was thinking now about America, the ultimate proving ground for U2. Blackwell suggested that Paul talk to

Frank Barsalona who ran Premier Talent in New York. Premier wasn't the biggest agency booking live shows in the States, but with its small, select clientèle, Barsalona's was among the most prestigious. The Who and Bruce Springsteen were Premier acts. Blackwell was a neighbour of Barsalona's in Nassau in the Bahamas, where both had homes. He'd send Frank a U2 tape, he promised Paul. The rest was down to him. Paul flew to New York, rang Barsalona and arranged to come and see him. It was 10 August 1980. That night Philip McGuinness died of a heart attack. Shocked, for there had been no ill-health, and grieving, Paul flew back to Dublin without meeting Barsalona.

Steve Lillywhite had come to Dublin to produce U2's debut album. Steve was a twenty-five-year-old with a growing reputation in London. He'd worked for Island Records as a staff producer before going freelance. He'd had minor chart successes with Ultravox, Eddie and the Hot Rods and Siouxsie and the Banshees. He thought U2 were great: not great *players*, but there was a pleasing rawness about them and the sound was good. For the first time in his life, Steve Lillywhite was the oldest person on a project, an amiable older brother. They agreed to do a single, 'A Day Without Me', to see how things went in the studio. If all went well, Lillywhite would produce their first album. 'A Day Without Me' dealt with suicide, a poignant reminder of the circumstances that had led to Lillywhite's presence in Windmill. Martin Hannett, who'd produced '11 O'Clock, Tick Tock', had been due to produce their album but had withdrawn when the lead singer of Joy Division, a band with whom he'd made many records, committed suicide.

U2 and Lillywhite worked well together. He hated the single, but loved the band for its appetite for and attitude to work. Bono was the pusher, as hard on everyone else as on himself. Yet he was vulnerable, agonizing over lyrics which Lillywhite was amazed to find were not yet written. All Bono had were themes, images, sounds and bits of paper with jumbled lines scrawled upon them. Edge was the musical driving force, Steve decided. Intense and self-confident, Edge would spend hours fiddling with sounds and, once he found what he was looking for, five minutes playing it. He was, Lillywhite thought, 20 per cent guitarist, 80 per cent brilliant engineer. Larry was imaginative and determined to do his own thing. There were better technicians, but he was right for U2, playing to the music, his drumming as distinctive as the band's overall sound. Adam was the most musically innocent. Confidence was his problem. He could be technically accomplished but very bad if his confidence went. On *Boy*, which the album was now called, Lillywhite nurtured Adam, encouraging the bass player's self-belief. They did lots of over-dubs on the album, producing extraordinary sounds that, Lillywhite felt, worked really well. Adam and Steve, chipped from the same, clever, amusing, self-deprecating block, became close friends during the making of the album.

Working with a young, unranked band on their first album, Steve could have indulged himself at their expense by going for a Steve Lillywhite sound. Instead he was generous and perceptive, identifying their strengths, veiling their weaknesses. The result was a superb debut album full of ideas, sounds and images unique to these four people, true and real in a way that rock 'n' roll had rarely been before. The dangerous and ultimately futile business of interpreting rock 'n' roll, with its abstract blend of image, sound and performance art, is made easier here when you understand where the four young men who made *Boy* came from. The feelings and emotions given expression on *Boy* reflect the passions and adolescent confusion of these young men and others of their generation who grew up in Dublin between 1960 and 1980. On 'Twilight', Bono deals with the fear, wonder and confusion of adolescent sexuality:

My body grows and grows,
It frightens me, you know.
An old man tried to walk me home,
I thought he should have known.

Twilight ... I lost my way,
Twilight ... Can't find my way.

(In the shadows Boy meets man.)

and later,

I'm running in the rain,
I'm caught in a late night play.
It's all, it's everything,
I'm soaking to the skin.

This strange, sad song which seems to be about a sexual encounter between a boy and an older man appeared on the B side of U2's second single, 'Another Day', and keeps its place on the *Boy* album. 'Out of Control' and 'A Day Without Me' reflect on death, in the case of 'A Day Without Me', suicide.

'I Will Follow' was selected as the single release off *Boy*. The lyric of this inspiring rock 'n' roll song can be taken as a declaration of the writer's intention to follow his spiritual inclinations or, perhaps more accurately in this case, as an expression of regret for time wasted when Iris Hewson was alive. *She* had followed him by giving her love unconditionally, his preoccupation with life outside the home notwithstanding.

A boy tries hard to be a man,
His mother takes him by the hand.
If he stops to think
He starts to cry. Oh why?
If you walk away, walk away, I will follow.
If you walk away, walk away, I will follow.

When he had walked away from Iris she had followed. God's love was also unconditional. The closing lines speak of regret,

I was blind I could not see,

and optimism,

I was lost, I am found.

The hope that Christianity might provide the tranquillity lost when his mother died and a vow that this new source of peace would *not* be taken for granted, shines through when Bono's lyric is matched to his experience.

The optimism is most scintillatingly expressed in the music Edge created to give expression to the images. The collaboration between Bono, the poet-painter-image-inventor and Edge, who could find a sound that would give musical expression to the ideas Bono brought to the studio, lay at the core of U2's rock 'n' roll. Bono would arrive at rehearsal at the Little Gingerbread House with ideas, images and half-completed songs colliding in his head. The house they christened the Gingerbread House was a run-down gate-lodge on the edge of Balgriffin cemetery where Iris Hewson is buried.

Working long hard days in the Gingerbread House, U2 discovered and defined themselves as a unique rock 'n' roll band. Although on another level U2 public relations and marketing worked superbly, when it came to the music and live performance of it the goal was to communicate to those who listened a sense of the experiences *they* had had. The Boy was Paul Hewson, but not exclusively him, for Bono was too much the artist, the communicator, the chameleon, to confine the story to his own incomplete personal life. Boy was everybody – male or female – who wondered, feared, was confused or alienated, and wanted to share the emotions involved. They were wide-ranging and deeply-felt emotions, rather than political ideas or social comment or rock 'n' roll's other traditional common denominator, sexual frustration, that U2 played to. The Boy was also Adam, the charming schoolboy rebel, Dave Evans, the inhibited, determined, intelligent fourteen-year-old anxious to make a mark at Mount Temple. The Boy in *Boy* was also Larry, single-minded, bent on doing things his way, nice, innocent but smart, with a radar system designed to detect phonies beneath the Handsome-Youth exterior. Bobby and Iris, Maeve and Ali, The Village, Castle Park and St Columba's, Albert Bradshaw's Renaissance choral class at Mount Temple, The Mall, Maureen Mullen's death, the failures, successes and half-realized fears and dreams of four twenty-year-old Dubliners from the Northside suburbs – all were on the *Boy* album. It took twenty years to make.

Producing U2 was hard work for Steve Lillywhite. This was a long way from the superficiality of the London studios he had worked in so far. Bono in particular could never make his mind up about the finished product. As a unit U2 totally underestimated their own ability. They missed what Lillywhite could see, U2's freshness of manner and the originality of the material they brought to Windmill Lane. They had nothing to measure themselves by and they had a long way to go before becoming a great rock band. But U2 was a unit, with a unique blend of personal and musical gifts and a hunger for knowledge and perfection which was rare in the producer's experience. Not a man to bang the big drum, Steve Lillywhite none the less thought U2 could become an important band in the 1980s.

Critical reaction to *Boy* was amazing. In London *Melody Maker* raved: 'U2's live performances have raised their audiences' expectations to what must have seemed like an impossible height, but not only have they reached that peak with their first album, they've risen above it.' Given that even the band themselves realized that the impact their music made live was impossible to capture on record, this from *Melody Maker* was praise indeed. Other respected rock critics compared *Boy* to the best debut albums of all time, from artists like Patti Smith, Roxy Music and the Velvet Underground. This latter comparison was especially pleasing because Lou Reed, Velvet Underground's singer, was one of Bono's few rock 'n' roll heroes. The only negative reaction to *Boy* had nothing to do with the music or the band but revealed much about the world they were breaking into in late 1980. Steve Averill, their old mentor from Grafton Street days, was chosen to design the album cover. The band wanted to portray innocence and together with Averill chose Guggi's younger brother Peter Rowen as the symbol they wanted. Peter, or Radar as he was known to The Village, was a beautiful boy of about seven. The *Boy* front cover showed him alone, naked from the chest up, looking poignantly at the camera. There was no mention of U2 or the album's title, *Boy*. This was a huge marketing gamble for a band making its album debut, undertaken in a determined effort to communicate *Boy*'s essential meaning. The back cover carried the slogan U2 in reduced type on the top corner over four moody photographs of Bono, Adam, Edge and Larry. Peter again dominates on this side in a pose depicting wonder. Some reactions in America suggested that U2 were pandering to paedophiles, the new rage in sexual deviancy in the States. Claims that the album broke in gay clubs in San Francisco when it was released in America in early 1981 added to the controversy. The fact was that Peter had appeared on the cover of the U2 *Three* EP a year earlier, and caused no stir when it was released by CBS Ireland. 'We put him on the cover because he's a pretty smart kid. And sometimes I wonder what his future will be like – and I wonder about *ours*,' Bono explained when faced with the paedophile theory. Nevertheless, Warner Brothers, licensed by Island to release *Boy* in the United States, changed the artwork on the cover for their market.

Frank Barsalona had met many rock-band managers. Most

of them were a problem. Some had their egos inflated by their band's success. They had reached the big time and were now 'calling the shots'. Others were ripping off their bands. Quite a few tried to rip off Barsalona. The British were often the worst. They came to America with a chip on their shoulder, reeking of the snobbery that characterized British attitudes to the New World. They didn't want to learn about the rock 'n' roll business in the States, which was vastly different and infinitely more complex than in England. America was the money machine and they'd come for their share.

Barsalona was smart and tough and saw them coming a mile off. He'd fought through the 1960s madness, the excesses of the 1970s, he'd worked successfully with the best, and the walls of his New York office at the top of a skyscraper on Third Avenue were lined with gold discs and signed photographs from appreciative legends like The Who, Springsteen and the Rolling Stones. If you were smart you didn't mess with Frank. Most rock 'n' roll managers only thought they were smart. There were a thousand ways to blow it in American rock 'n' roll and Frank Barsalona knew them all, had seen it all a thousand times. In most cases it was to do with the belief that there was quick, easy money to be made and greedy impatience to get as many dollars in the manager's pocket as quickly as possible.

Barsalona liked Paul McGuinness when they eventually met in autumn 1980. Paul declared his ignorance of the American scene *and* his willingness to learn about it. He talked constantly about what was right for U2 artistically, rather than financially. They were, he told Barsalona, willing to work as long as it took to gain an American audience. U2 would start wherever Barsalona suggested. *Boy* was due out in the States in the new year. Why not a short, ten-day introductory tour in December and then a major three-month assault in the spring, Frank proposed. It was agreed.

U2 were a small band for Barsalona's agency to book but, like Blackwell, Frank was secure enough and experienced enough to back people, and these Irish kids with their smart, civilized manager looked like the Right Stuff. After twenty-odd years in the business Frank was tired of drugheads, ego-maniacs and poseurs. He was a regular guy, liked the ball games, liked to have dinner with friends in New York's good restaurants, he didn't need that psychedelic shit anymore. The times had changed. The 1980s would be a time of sanity, he hoped.

With Premier Talent's support, U2 had moved within a matter of months from the Baggot-McGonagles circuit to the toughest rock 'n' roll challenge in the world. Barsalona wasn't going to make them, he was simply giving them a chance to make themselves. They would be starting at the bottom, the Penny Arcade in Rochester, New York. The Penny Arcade was about as far as you could get from Madison Square Garden.

Paul McGuinness and the band had never forgotten Joe O'Herlihy, the stocky little guy from the Arcadia in Cork, with the good sound and the professional approach. He'd worked for them on and off since, always on the basis that they hired him *and* his sound-system. Joe was in business for himself now. The sound-system was the business: where it went, he went. Now McGuinness put the proposal to Joe that he should come to America and do the sound for U2. McGuinness understood the value of pros who got the job done and explained the problems *afterwards*. Paul recognized the quality in Joe O'Herlihy, a tough, no bullshit guy who didn't work for sentiment.

Joe O'Herlihy was twenty-four, young to have seen the world of rock 'n' roll from the inside. But he had. He was no provincial rock businessman making a few bob with his sound-system. He had travelled the road U2 were now setting out on.

He knew about the States and every other territory where rock was played live. He knew the strokes, the hassles, the dangers of life on the road. He knew what the prizes were and what they cost you.

Joe was born in April 1954 in St Anne's Park, Montenotte. He went to school in St Joseph's at the Mardyke and from there to the North Mall secondary school. He was a good hurler but interested in music as well. Rory Gallagher was the local hero who inspired Cork kids to pick up guitars and start forming groups in the late sixties and early seventies. He symbolized rock 'n' roll as a Way Out.

After playing the Isle of Wight rock festival along with Jimi Hendrix and the Doors, Rory Gallagher and his band, Taste, broke up. Gallagher then formed the Rory Gallagher Band and successfully toured the world. Every Christmas Rory would come home to play a string of dates across Ireland. Rather than bring Third Division bands from the UK, Gallagher always gave the support slot on his Irish shows to local bands. The Cork band, Sleepy Hollow, were chosen for this honour for four years from 1970 to 1974.

Joe O'Herlihy, now just leaving his teens, was Sleepy Hollow's roadie. He was happy. He listened to the stories Rory's roadies told about playing the mega-gigs with 50,000 people in this, that or the other foreign land. It was another world, but Joe felt connected. He'd been forced to work for six months in Roches Stores in Cork as a messenger boy, and had started hanging around Crowley's music shop on Merchant's Quay. He had no money, he was just curious, obsessed by the instruments, guitars, drums and keyboards that were showcased tantalizingly there. He called by every day, driving the owner, Michael Crowley, crazy asking for demonstrations and explanations of the latest guitar or drum-kit. When Crowley's moved to McCurtain Street, Michael Crowley offered Joe a job helping out in a general way. Joe just loved to touch the new guitars, hold them, feel the vibes coming off this inanimate object. Imagine himself having one of them slung over *his* hip in Madison Square Garden (or even the Crystal). He learnt to tune a bass guitar, and something about keyboards and other rock 'n' roll instruments at Crowleys. He was a much better roadie for the experience, which he applied enthusiastically to his night-time duties. He married Marion, his childhood sweetheart, when he was eighteen and an itinerant roadie with a dream inspired by Rory Gallagher.

Gallagher thought so much of Sleepy Hollow that he took them to England with him to make a demo record, and support him over four nights at the Marquee Club on Easter weekend 1973. After that he had a college tour lined up for them. It was decision time for newly married Joe. Michael Crowley had been good to the long-haired youngster but he couldn't hold Joe's job open for a couple of months while he toured the English colleges. Joe chose Sleepy Hollow and the tour supporting Rory. One of Gallagher's roadies burst his appendix, leaving a place on his team for a return date at the Marquee. Joe, the busy, conscientious little Sleepy Hollow roadie, was offered the gig with Gallagher. He thought about it – for ten seconds. He saw opportunity staring him in the face. He gave it one thousand per cent. If someone said lick arse, he licked, and smiled while he was doing it. And asked if there was anything else he could do. Joe thrived and survived. He worked on a major Rory Gallagher tour, four nights in the Stadium in Dublin, three in Galway, three in the City Hall in Cork, finishing off with four nights in Belfast's Ulster Hall. Joe went home to Marion for the happiest Christmas of his life. All his old friends in Cork patted him on the back, and gazed enviously at the arse pocket of his Levis, where the wages he'd earned with Rory formed a proud little lump.

On 5 January, Donal Gallagher, Rory's brother and manager, called in at Joe's house to tell him that there was a chance for him with the Gallagher organization. Joe could do the 'back-line', Donal proposed. Doing the back-line meant setting up the band's instruments – guitars, drums and piano – on stage before they came on. You tuned them up, made sure they were ready when the band hit the stage. You also packed them away afterwards and they were your responsibility until the next night. Joe was in. He got his passport, kissed Marion and Mark, the baby boy they now had, good-bye, and within days was on the road to the UK, Europe, America, Australia, New Zealand and Japan. From 1974 to 1978 Joe toured the world with the Rory Gallagher Band.

Gallagher ran a professional organization. Himself, his brother Donal and the crew of five had a good time. They often had a few beers and a bit of a hoolie after good shows. But there was no rock 'n' roll excess, no going around out of your head day and night, no sex orgies. You were on the road to work. If there was any fucking about, Rory was the man up front, the one who suffered at the end of the day. Joe was a can-do man. He solved problems first, told Rory or Donal the might-have-been afterwards. He was extra smart, with a good grasp of what was going on around him. He worked forty-eight-hour days, fourteen days a week. For Rory Gallagher you couldn't put a price on Joe. Within two years Joe had been promoted to monitor engineer. Rock was acquiring new technology all the time. The new sound-systems were sophisticated, powerful, but useless in the wrong hands. Gallagher was conservative in his attitudes. He was a brilliant guitarist, he'd been doing it for almost fifteen years, and he wasn't sure he needed the stuff that kept arriving with the plastic wrappers still on. Each new piece of equipment arrived with a minder from the company retailing it. Joe would use his considerable Cork wit to chat the man up. Within a day or two he had it and had explained the new equipment's advantages to Rory. By 1977 Joe had the job he really wanted, front of house engineer controlling Rory's sound. He'd come a long way quickly from Cork. At twenty-three he was a rock 'n' roll pro, responsible, efficient, ambitious, a man infinitely different from the feckless roadie of rock tradition. As FOH engineer he was responsible for just about everything to do with performance. Each venue was different, had its own quirks that affected Joe's job. The promoter's people didn't give a damn about Joe, Rory Gallagher or the man in the moon. Here's your desk, go to work. If you wanted to change something or adjust it to suit your man, they would freak. Nobody else has ever wanted it *that* way, you'd be told, we've *always* done it this way. Joe would have to persuade, sometimes bully, to get his way. He could do both.

The novelty of life on the road began to pall after two or three years. The longer Joe was 'out', the more he missed Marion and the two boys they now had. He'd see them for three months a year, a month here and there in between tours. It was too little. All those years on the road Joe had been formulating a plan in his mind. There were bands starting up in Cork all the time, with nothing except guitars, drums and a basic amp. His idea was to provide sound-systems for such bands, hiring out microphones, monitors, speakers and PA stacks of the very best quality. All the time he was on tour Joe kept his eyes open for bits and pieces. A mike that cost £120 at home, if you could get it at all, could be found for £20 in a pawn shop in San Francisco. He'd buy it. After a couple of years he had two top-quality sound-systems at home in Cork. He was ready to quit the touring scene.

In September 1978 Joe came home for good. He set up in business straight away with enough equipment to service two bands at a time, and employed two friends from the Cork scene to help him, Tim Buckley and Tom Mullally. The students' union of University College, Cork, ran gigs in the Arcadia Ballroom. There would be five bands on the bill. Most bands didn't know their arse from their elbow or, as Joe would put it, 'a jack-plug from a tin of St Bruno'. Nevertheless, Joe's training with Rory Gallagher had instilled in him values that he could not ignore now. For himself, Timmy, Tom and others like Sammy O'Sullivan and John O'Sullivan, the O'Herlihy ethos was spelt out: it doesn't matter how big a pain in the arse this little band is, do your best for them. They hired our stuff, they are paying our wages. Punk rock was the rage and there were some shocking sights on stage, but fuck it, this is the business we're in.

When Joe first met Paul McGuinness he saw a smart guy out of his depth. This was 1978, McGuinness was learning, knowing U2 had something but not exactly sure what it was. Joe thought punk was garbage, drivel, he couldn't believe it. He'd been brought up on the blues, which was authentic music. Anything outside the blues was trash, shit, whatever you wanted to call it – anything except music. Joe thought he knew it all, a notion confirmed by the punk stars he was now servicing. U2 were different. Most of the bands who knew nothing didn't want to know anything. *They* did. They wanted to know everything. Why this, why that, can't you try this, that, or the other? U2 also cared about the Cork audience, really cared. But it was Edge who fascinated Joe. After touring with Rory, guitars were Joe's thing. Edge was experimenting with echoes. The sound was something Joe had never come across before. How could he use it in the context of what he had been taught? The way rock 'n' roll worked as Joe knew it, the way he learned to do sound for a band, consisted of setting up the drums and bass guitar – the muscle of the band – first, then colouring in the lead guitar and vocals. You couldn't do that with U2. Edge's guitar *was* the basic sound. Joe had to work hard to understand what was going on. This was a 'kick up the arse', as he put it, but something new always triggered the Go button in him, so he grafted. There was something incredible here, a development in guitar sound as revolutionary as Hank Marvin of the Shadows' first use of echoes or the experiments of Dave Gilmore of Pink Floyd. Gilmore would use his experiment with echoes on one song in four. Edge used it on every song. It wasn't an experiment. It was the U2 sound. It was trial and error, Joe thought, but there was no doubt in his mind that some new and dramatic advance in sound was taking place. Edge was not a virtuoso player, but a technological wizard. He would play one note and, because of the way he'd set the boxes up, six notes would reverberate. Joe's task was to integrate this new sound into his old systems. He worked hard, with much head scratching on all sides.

Joe worked for U2, or, rather, hired them his system, on and off for the next couple of years. They knew he was the best but they couldn't afford him full time until the Island deal and the release of *Boy*. Paul McGuinness put it straight to Joe. He outlined the strategy, promised it would be tough for a few years and offered Joe the job of front of house engineer, beginning December 1980 with a short ten-day tour of the United States. O'Herlihy accepted. He was excited by U2, respected the way they worked and, what the hell, he would keep Sound Systems Ltd in Cork with Timmy Buckley in charge.

As the plane circled low over New York, the images, myths and legends of America rushed up to meet them. Elvis, the Kennedys, Muhammad Ali, Martin Luther King, Hollywood, Sinatra, John Wayne, Buddy Holly, Nixon, New York cops, Mickey Mouse, death, tragedy and glory on a scale unimaginable if not unimagined by the four young men from Dublin on board the Aer Lingus jet. America was a film running in the imagination of all, everywhere. A fantasy, a nightmare, a dream, a place about whose culture, myth, legend, politics and people you knew or felt you knew better – much better – than your own. Their stomachs lurched, flesh grew cold, they felt excited and afraid. Cruising in towards Kennedy, looking down you knew that on those streets, visible clearly now, Mailer and Woody Allen lived, walked, dined out in those Italian restaurants and Jewish delis. You knew the jokes, the nuances of Brooklyn, the Bronx and Greenwich Village, where Andy Warhol hung out in the Factory, where Lou Reed and the Velvet Underground got it together. As you hit the runway, you took a deep breath, composed yourself and smiled to your companion: 'Well, this is it.'

US Immigration disabused you of romantic notions.

The Ritz was a ballroom in New York City. Frank Barsalona had leant a little on the owner to put U2 in there on Friday night. Friday was dancing night, it wouldn't be a U2 audience. People expected a band they could dance to on Fridays. 'But if you need it, Frank, you've got it.' Barsalona took a small party with him to see Premier's new act. Barbara Skydel, Frank's deputy at Premier, accompanied him along with some people from Warner Brothers. When they took their VIP places on the balcony, the hall was three-parts empty.

Backstage the lads were high, and nervous about their New York city debut. Joe was on the sound desk, Paul, grim, upstairs with Barsalona. Joe O'Herlihy needed all his resourcefulness on this important evening. The Ritz sound was iffy, more suited to disco dancing than live music. Bigger and better equipped bands than U2 had struggled with the cavernous acoustics in this room.

It was apparent straight away that this was going to be another battle. The Ritz had filled up with New Yorkers waiting for the dancing bands to come on later. U2 were *opening*. The crowd wasn't hostile, they just didn't react at all as Bono worked the stage. He made his statements, guff about being in America and all that. Nothing. McGuinness thought of Queen's University, Belfast. Jesus. Bono had stopped the band. 'We're up here,' he yelled down the hall where the crowd had gathered indifferently. Turning to the record company fat cats on the balcony, he roared, 'We've come to play for you. Get up off your fat arses and dance if you want to dance.' The band went for it, hitting them with everything, Joe giving them max power. 'I Will Follow' was the centrepiece of the set, a great rock song delivered with absolute conviction. Looking down from the balcony, Barsalona noticed it happening. Slowly, layer after layer of this New York Friday-night dancing crowd, there to groove and get laid, edged forward towards the stage. Frank looked at Barbara and the Warner's people and grinned like he'd been afraid, in danger; it reminded him of things in his own past. Frank loved sport. He'd been the owner of a soccer club, the Philadelphia Furies, he loved to go to the ball games, the Giants or the Jets, *see* the winning and losing, watch guys slug it out. Frank knew what guts were. Now below him the Ritz was on its feet screaming for U2, looking for more as they closed the set with 'Out of Control', the song of death composed in 10 Cedarwood Road on Bono's eighteenth birthday. Barsalona, Barbara Skydel, the Warner's people, the whole place had gone crazy. Paul felt tears welling up inside, forced them back. Joe felt a glow he'd *never* experienced with Rory.

Frank Barsalona, one of the most powerful men in American rock music, then did the dumbest thing he'd ever done; he ran – *ran* – to the dressing room. He'd never met U2, but now he grabbed them and pushed them into a corner, McGuinness hovering on the edge. 'I've got to tell you something,' Barsalona began. 'I know you've had a difficult time getting airplay for your singles and you will have it tough when your album comes out. But I give you my word, you are going to happen in this country.'

All weekend Barsalona figured out ways that he could help. This is it, he decided. After all these years I'm going to start calling in some chits. He'd done favours with tickets for big shows down the years. *Never* asked for anything in return.

Now he was going to call all those programme directors on all those radio stations he had obliged down the years and tell them about U2. Radio was the key to 'breaking' in the USA. Frank Barsalona had found a cause. Soon people were calling U2 Barsalona's act. That mattered.

On Monday 8 December, three days after U2's New York debut, John Lennon was murdered outside the Dakota apartment building in the city. Out in California Ronald Reagan was preparing to come to Washington. Jimmy Carter, America's Christian president, having been refused a second term, Reagan was about to begin his occupation of the oval office. That would matter too.

Chapter Twelve

OCTOBER

U2 topped the *Hot Press* poll in nine categories in January 1981. The band spent most of the first couple of months of 1981 touring the UK ending with a sell-out concert at the Lyceum Ballroom in London in February. They toured Britain in their small van, Paul driving, the four lads along with Joe O'Herlihy, Pod, who was now their roadie, and their equipment in the back. Money was tight. They stayed in small hotels, allowing themselves one major indulgence at Paul's suggestion: good food, eaten in restaurants chosen from *The Good Food Guide* which lay on the front seat beside the manager-driver. When the van developed mechanical trouble there were enough bodies on hand to get out and push. *Boy* had not rushed the charts in the UK, nor indeed had any of their single records released over the previous year. Reaction on the road was, however, encouraging. Live, U2 were brilliant, the critical relationship between O'Herlihy and Edge adding a stunning new sound dimension to Bono's dramatic stage persona. U2 gave themselves in performance the way no other rock 'n' roll band did, challenging the received wisdom that British audiences would reject the passionate embrace deemed to be more suitable for American fans. At the tour's end in the Lyceum,

700 fans were locked out. The band had found its constituency, a committed audience that in time would buy U2 albums to reflect nostalgically on the night they played in their town.

The strategy was working. But elsewhere the news was grim. The Village was splitting. The reason was the Shalom group, which had increasingly come to dominate the private lives of those members of Village and U2 who continued to attend the Meetings. Guggi had dropped out, claiming to be getting evil vibes off the Meetings, which were tending more and more to focus on members' mode of living, less and less on the Scriptures. In particular the Shalom group began to question rock 'n' roll and its relationship to God. U2 and the Virgin Prunes found themselves under pressure on account of their lifestyle. One of the tenets of Shalom's Christianity was the surrender of ego so that you might be filled with the Spirit of God. U2 were a big band in Ireland now, Bono in particular its public face. How could he reconcile that with his love of God? Most of those at the Meetings lived ordinary lives. Their days were dull, some particularly sad and lonely. Life was not as exciting as it was for U2 and the Prunes. Gavin was singled out for special attention. Why did he wear earrings? What about his stage show where he dressed in women's clothing and said things like 'Art . . . Fuck'? And his hair was too long, his clothes reeked of bohemian decadence. Gradually it was implied that a choice would have to be made between rock 'n' roll and God.

Gavin reacted. Bitterly, and without deleting the expletives. He wasn't going to be manipulated. The Shalom group could fuck off, he declared angrily as he stormed out of his last Meeting, his girlfriend Rene by his side. What particularly incensed Gavin was the fact that his and U2's presence at the Meetings had drawn a number of youngsters, mostly girls, to the Shalom group. Dublin is a small place and Bono's involvement was well advertised in and around Christian circles.

Shalom was prepared to accept the positive side of Gavin, Bono, Larry and Edge's commitment, but not the music and culture that went with it. They were being used, Gavin decided, and he was getting out.

The Virgin Prunes had established a cult following in Dublin and some recognition further afield in Europe. Pod, now on drums, Strongman, Dick Evans, Guggi and Gavin were the group's backbone. Day-Vid did his stream-of-consciousness on an ad-hoc basis. If U2's music was to lift the spirit, to inspire belief (and of course primarily to be rock 'n' roll) the Prunes attacked their audiences from a different angle. When Gavin looked out he saw smugness, complacency, a world that was brutal and insensitive. His stage show (and the ideas came mostly from him) set out to shock. He'd come on stage with a pig's head, a real one, impaled on a stick and laugh as the audience drew back in horror. Gavin had long been into shocking people, confronting them, vibeing them out. The pig's head was a variation of the shoulder-bag, feminine gait and eyeshadow of other days. Life isn't as simple as you think it is, was the essential theme. Gavin had worked for a year for Dublin Meat Packers, a slaughter-house down by the Royal Canal. *He'd* seen pig's heads before, he was familiar with the process, ugly, bloody, often inhumane, that ended with bacon and cabbage, the much loved staple of Irish families, on the table. This is it, folks, he would suggest, holding up the bloody pig's head.

When Gavin and Guggi left the Shalom group, Pod urged that they be kicked out of the Prunes. Sir Poddington, the bravest knight of all time, was the Villager most inspired by Charismatic Christianity. He was a good, straight, honest lad, incorruptable, intense, who felt at last that the Spirit of God and the feeling of goodness that it imbued in him was the most important discovery of his life. He gladly surrendered his body and soul to God.

Bono was passive through most of this, neither condemning, as Pod did, nor supporting Gavin's allegations of manipulation. Bono was deeply disturbed and confused. He had always been a chameleon, his spirit too large, his curiosity too intense, his imagination too vivid, his lust for experience too constant to be confined to the strait-jacket of being a type of person. At root his life was a search for identity; was he a lover or a fighter, a man of peace or a warrior, humble or egocentric? Was he the clown of The Mall or the sensitive young man so gentle and emotional with Maeve and Ali? Was he Catholic rough or Protestant cool? That question had never been resolved. Now almost twenty-one, with fame and some influence, the questions became harder to answer. Was he a man of intellect or the spirit? Was he performer or composer? And, most pressing and disturbing of all the questions he had ever faced, the one that he reflected on now after Shalom meetings; was he Bono the rock 'n' roll star or Bono the Christian, committed to God and life as prescribed in the Bible? Would *he* surrender? Did his ego need the celebration of Bono the rock 'n' roll singer? Being celebrated was confusing, embarrassing, wrong. Yet a high public profile, an image, the creation of some kind of artificially heroic persona, was part of the rock 'n' roll deal. Fame may not be the spur, but it was the inevitable consequence of being in U2.

Bono was tormented by the conflict raging within him. He would often go out to Templeogue where the Meetings were now held in the home of a Christian couple who had befriended the young men. Chris and Lillian had two children. They had given their lives to God. Chris had no job. When money was needed he'd go odd-jobbing. Theirs was true humility. There was a curiously poignant link between their lives and Bono's dilemma. In the film *Chariots of Fire*, the hero, Eric Liddell, is torn between his athletic ambitions and radical Christianity, which demands the subjugation of ego. His sister begs him to forsake his Olympic ambitions, but he argues that he loves to run and feels that God is with him when he's on the track. Liddell realizes his dream of an Olympic gold medal before declaring for God and spending the remainder of his life as a missionary in China. One of his fellow missionaries was Chris's father. Bono was struck by the parallels between his life and Liddell's. Also by the parable of the Talents in the Bible.

Edge and Larry faced the same fundamental question of reconciling rock 'n' roll fame with their radical Christianity, but in much less acute personal and professional circumstances. Edge was a more self-contained character than Bono. He had no identity problem. He could rationalize his beliefs, intelligently and convincingly. Nevertheless, he saw the conflict between rock and religion as indeed he saw the potential for manipulation within Shalom. Those were almost side issues. Edge's relationship was with God and the spiritual rewards of *that* relationship outweighed all other considerations.

Larry's attitude was for the moment much like Edge's. He loved the sense of goodness and the spiritual calm he felt at and after meetings. He felt strengthened and renewed by the community that prayed, sang and talked together. He had known nothing of the Bible, now he found its stories inspiring, fascinating as stories where moral values prevail against the odds. Ego was no problem for Larry. He hated posing and all the other forms of pretentiousness that seemed to be the norm in the music business. Although he lent himself grudgingly to the photographic sessions that were essential to the marketing and image-making of U2, he drew the line right there. He didn't do press or magazine interviews nor did he wish to cultivate the personality of Larry Rock-Star in any other way. Larry was a musician, a drummer, *not*, repeat, *not* a teen idol. The public perception of good old nice-guy Larry that consequently existed was an illusion. Larry was a nice guy but from the recording studio to the dressing room, at the formal band meetings and in the general everyday life of U2, the drummer-musician had plenty to say and a singular point of view, which he expressed in no uncertain terms.

Unlike Edge and Larry, Bono couldn't bide his time resolving the growing conflict between membership of Shalom and membership of U2. A new album was required, songs, music, images had to be provided and at the embryonic stage of creation Bono was the primary source. U2's music had all been about their lives, experiences, personal concerns, fears, doubts and passions. How could the spirituality that now consumed them be translated into rock 'n' roll music? How could Bono convey an image true and real when he was himself riddled with doubt? Not just about who he was, not simply about the songs for the new album *but*, more fundamentally, doubt about whether there should be an album at all!

The nature of these problems remained secret, shielded from the public at large by the aura of success U2 now wore. Of course there were rumours on the Grafton Street scene and elsewhere in the large village that was Dublin, but the agonizing was done in private. Publicly, U2 were preparing for their major US tour in April to support *Boy*, which had been released in the States in March. The band's public stance on their Christianity was outlined in a *Hot Press* profile written by Neil McCormick, their old school friend who had attended the initial band meeting in Larry's house four years before. Dealing delicately with this sensitive subject, Neil, an agnostic who believed in the best rock 'n' roll tradition that 'the devil had all the best music', drew Bono out on the conflict between his God and his music: 'It's very important that we don't want to be the band that talks about God. I do not want to talk about it in terms of music. Anything that has to be said on that personal level is in the music or on stage and I don't want to go through the media. I don't want to talk to the world about it because we will face a situation where people will see us with a banner over our heads. That's not the way U2 is going to work. If there is anything in what we have to say it will be seen in our lives, in our music, in our performance.'

Although to the general *Hot Press* reader this declaration was neither particularly striking nor revealing as it stood, seen in the context of U2's private agonies it does point to the compromise between Christianity and rock 'n' roll that Bono, Larry and Edge were discussing among themselves. 'In our lives, in our music, in our performance' was the key phrase. If a reconciliation of public and private lives *was* possible, it demanded they challenge the conventional behaviour of rock 'n' roll heroes. The exploitation and self-indulgence that was the fruit of fame would in U2's case be denied, forbidden. No sex, no drugs, no groupies and no orgies. Their band, their organization, would lead a revolution against the old tradition. And on all fronts; audiences would be respected, not abused by bulky minders. U2 shows would give value for money. U2 T-shirts would be made from best cotton, not some cheap substitute. There would be no excess, no decadence, nothing cheap or degrading. U2 would take on the idiom of rock 'n' roll which quintessentially lent itself to negatives, to simple declarations of protest, alienation or simplistic pleas for 'Satisfaction'. The love U2 wrote and sang about would be spiritual as well as carnal. Thus, their lives, their music, their band, would bridge the gap between the rock 'n' roll they loved and the Christian ethos they were committed to.

U2 began their first major US tour on 3 March 1981, with two shows at the Bayou Club in Washington, DC. It was to be a tough three-month grind. They all travelled by coach: band, crew, manager and Ellen Darst, who was doing marketing and promotion for Warner Brothers. They were on a tight budget, staying at cheap-to-medium-priced hotels and occasionally sleeping on the bus between gigs. Darst, an astute young businesswoman, had been assigned by Warner's to check on U2

during their ten-day visit the previous December. On the basis
of her report the record company would decide how much it
would invest in marketing and promoting the band. Things
were tightening up financially in the American music business.
Old indulgences no longer applied. You backed quality,
winners, you helped bands that were prepared to help themselves. Ellen Darst reported favourably on U2. She was a 1960s
idealist saddened now at what had happened to those ideals,
how little relevance they had to America and to the music
business. Artist development was her specialization, which frequently meant introducing new British bands to the States.
Echo and the Bunnymen had been her previous assignment.
U2 were different. They were, off stage as on, energetic, enthusiastic, curious about America, how the rock business worked
there. They were naïve but that was wonderful after the blasé
cynicism of so many other trans-Atlantic acts. U2 knew they
weren't a big band yet, and appreciated the work that lay ahead
if they were to become The Next Big Thing, a tag they were
beginning to acquire, one that had proved to be the kiss of
death for so many others.

Paul McGuinness typified the U2 attitude to America. Most
visiting managers would try to con Ellen into believing that
they knew more than they did. Afraid to be found out, they
usually left the States knowing little more than when they
arrived. McGuinness asked questions. Absorbed the answers.
And went to work making an academic study of American
rock 'n' roll. Radio was the key medium. It was regional and
specialized, each station playing its own kind of rock music.
There was college radio, blues radio, heavy metal stations,
rock stations, MOR stations. You name the music and somewhere across this vast continent it was played – exclusively –
on some radio station. There was no one-off breakthrough on
a network television show like *Top of the Pops*. There was no
RTE radio, no Dave Fanning, but ten thousand guys with

shows like his influencing *their* audience, promoting *their* personal taste. U2 would have to break through layer by layer. It was a huge, complex, long-term challenge. The press was regional too, no *Hot Press* here, although *Rolling Stone*, the blue-blooded magazine mixture of rock and politics, would be the natural target of any intelligent press campaign. But ultimately U2's potential would be measured by their live performances and the personal qualities they possessed, their youthful zest for dialogue, their American-style openness, their rare, in a European context, willingness to expose themselves as people and talk about their lives and their music without pretence or pretentiousness. Fresh and real was how they seemed to the Americans they encountered.

They played colleges, ballrooms and rock clubs, the Third Division circuit, from Washington, D C through San José State University. They hit the south, Ole Man Rivers in Avondale, Louisiana, and, in Canada, the Ryerson Theatre, Toronto. In California they played the Santa Monica Civic Center and the California Hall, San Francisco.

The American audiences loved them, loved the music, loved their spirit, their guts. This was no laconic, laid-back rock band but four desperate lads reaching out to embrace their audience, talking to them about their lives, playing music that was spiritual, personal *and* great rock 'n' roll. Here was a European band that *wasn't* condescending, as desperate to be loved and accepted as the audience, in the first year of Ronald Reagan, was to see and feel something real, not plastic, something human and uncontrived. Bono and U2 were it. Just over a year ago the band had died in the urine stench of the Baggot. It was a year since Belfast and the Stadium scam. U2 remembered, every night before they went on. There to bear personal witness to this, their first US tour, was Bill Graham, who understood better than anyone where they had come from, what the odds against getting out had been. Reporting as perceptively as

ever, Bill dispatched news of a triumph at Harpo's, a club on
the outskirts of Detroit:

> U2 persuaded the Motor City audience to three encores, sym-
> metrically finishing as they do all sets with '11 O'Clock, Tick
> Tock' and 'The Ocean'. The largest crowd with the least pre-
> publicity, the strongest response, it has been the most profit-
> able date I have seen.
>
> In the dressing room the pressure had finally fallen on Bono
> and he quits to a private corner when the business well-wishers
> arrive. His voice has become huskier each day since Chicago,
> but that affliction is welcome for someone who tonight can't
> handle another round of ritual handshaking. The other three
> represent the band, but they're happier talking with the few
> fans who slip through the security cordon. In any other country
> this concert would be accounted a triumph, yet U2 could still
> be on the outside, their record company still pleading for air-
> play. Bono retires. He needs to breathe deep, very, very, deep.

The following day Graham interviewed Bono. U2's singer-
songwriter-catalyst was as usual passionately verbose, sharing
with Graham and his *Hot Press* readers the conflicting emotions
and images of his American journey. Apart from fantastic
audience reaction to the band, Bono urged readers to celebrate
something else; the birth of a baby daughter to Joe and Marian
O'Herlihy. Five days later Bono, Ali, Edge, Aislinn, Larry,
Ann, Paul, Kathy, Pod, Adam and Steve Lillywhite flew to
Nassau in the Bahamas for a ten-day break. Lillywhite was
there to discuss their next album, which they were due to start
recording in six weeks' time.

Bono had been losing things all his life: keys, money,
cheques, phone numbers, addresses, socks, underwear, indeed
everything and anything that wasn't attached to his awkward
body. People wondered jokingly how he found his way to
work in the mornings. But this time the loss was no joke. Six
weeks before going into Windmill to record what would

become the *October* album, Bono had no lyrics, images, notes or musical ideas. He'd lost them all, plus money ($300), passport – the lot – when his briefcase was stolen somewhere between Portland and Seattle in March on the first leg of the tour. Walking in downtown San Francisco earlier in the week with 'Sir Poddington', Bono had spotted a neat briefcase in a shop window. He was always losing things, so why not get the case and get organized? U2 loved to fraternize with their American fans. The band were as curious about the people who came to see them play as the fans were about these intensely original Irish rockers. Fans were in the dressing room, on the bus and in the hotels. No bullshit, no barriers, no artificial distance between performer and audience. It was policy. The briefcase was stolen either in the dressing room at the Fog Horn, Portland, or on the bus to Seattle. It was missed during the journey. Bono was devastated. It wasn't the money, the passport, the personal knick-knacks. It was the words he had written. And the breach of trust. Was that worse than the loss of the seed material for the album? It varied from mood to mood. Bono was unapproachable for a few days. The album was always going to be tough, more than tough, attempting as it had to, to reconcile the acute inner conflicts of this time. Now the task seemed impossible and the fear of that failure blended with the sense of outraged betrayal to produce a mood of despair that touched everyone aboard the U2 tour bus.

That mood had been uneasy to begin with. They were a small group spending long, claustrophobic days on freeways dissecting this strange, vast country: the band, Paul and Ellen, Joe, John Kennedy, the tour manager, and Pod acting as general roadie. Although the bus wasn't rigidly divided, for much of the day, it seemed to be. Bono, Larry, Edge and Pod occupied the back lounge. There they read their Bibles and, occasionally, sang a gospel song. It was the atmosphere rather than the behaviour that was strange. Further down the bus the other tourists lived, conscious of the *Christianity* behind. In the beginning the boys at the back would come down and mingle, pretend things were normal – but they weren't. There was tension, unspoken rebuke, suppressed resentment. Adam was isolated most distressingly.

Adam had always been vaguely spiritually aware. He'd been confirmed. He'd always respected religion. In school when other kids were chucking Bibles at each other across the classroom or just generally fooling around with them he felt it was wrong, and didn't participate. He just didn't like church, would sit there neither praying nor singing – because he didn't believe in it. He had been aware of Bono's interest in the Bible from way back at Mount Temple. It didn't bother him. Bono seemed a fine guy and Adam respected his personal convictions. When Larry and Edge got involved, Adam's only fear was that their beliefs might interfere with the band. He felt the same way about girls and courtship. For Adam U2 was the thing, U2 *was* life, the best most satisfying thing in life. The most *spiritual* thing in his life. U2 was, although he would never openly depict it as such, his home, his lover, his spiritual resting place. If at the beginning all four agreed that U2 was to be an ideal they would work for and serve, the band the very essence of their identity, nobody meant it, felt it or needed it more than Adam, the seemingly insouciant youth who played ropy bass guitar.

Now Adam, hair bleached blond, shades in place, casual-chic clothes hanging elegantly, epitomized the rock star having it all. But there was more to Adam than that. He had experienced the harshest times carving a path through the hostile jungle that was his childhood and adolescence. He had known loneliness and despair at Castle Park and St Columba's. He had been a real rebel, always charming, courteous and reasonable, but equally determined to fight against the minor tyrannies of his young world. Adam was a very brave young man, a man for whom Hemingway might have written his definition of courage: 'grace under pressure'.

Now Adam was under pressure, all the more insidious for being unspoken (mostly) and in many ways not malicious in intent. He was living the life of a rock star, wildly but not insanely. After the show he'd go looking for action, a drink, a girl, a good rap with the local groovers. He was twenty-one, single and free, perhaps for the first time. He had a few dollars in his pocket and a direct line to the prettiest girls in town. This was a way of life directly in conflict with the one now being celebrated in the lounge at the back of the bus.

Was U2, Adam wondered, now a Christian band? That *hadn't* been part of the deal when they'd started out. Although he operated with all his old style, Adam was feeling very vulnerable as they arrived in Nassau for their ten-day rest. Musically he was the least accomplished. But surely U2 was about something besides, indeed utterly different from, musical virtuosity? Yes, it was, Paul McGuinness assured Adam when they went out together after shows. Paul felt sorry and angry about Adam's isolation. When Bono, Larry and Edge had come to him to explain their convictions, Paul had observed that while he was sympathetic to their personal beliefs, he had his own. Now what had been personal was becoming an intrusion into the working life of U2. Like Adam, Paul was committed to the U2 concept. Like Adam, he knew that that meant commitment to fair dealing, hard work, honest music, no exploitation, no self-indulgence. The idea that these values, relating to professional integrity but linked inevitably to personal behaviour, were exclusive to Christianity, a notion implicit in much of the activity on the back of the bus, was ludicrous, and personally offensive to Adam and to Paul. So was the possibility that Adam would be dropped – on *any grounds*. U2 was about the strength of the unit. It was a group, not a collection of virtuosos. Yes, Bono brought passion, poetry, vivid images and his unique, instinctive, musical imagination. And yes, he was the catalyst for ideas, emotions and the wonderful rock 'n' roll that flowed from both. In performance on the big nights, the not so big nights, *every* night, Bono's heart was the heart exposed, the soul offered, on U2's behalf, to the audience. Bono was the thing that made U2 different, at least when you saw them live. But on his own, what *would* he have been, except a dumb, inarticulate evangelist for the music in his head?

Edge possessed other qualities; more than his technological genius, more than his glorious ear, his visionary deployment of the weapons of rock 'n' roll war. He had redefined the idiom, yes. But all of that *alone* might have amounted to a puff of wind in different circumstances among people other than those he now shared the bus with. Edge was calm, rational, extremely intelligent, tough, wiry-Welsh and self-assured. Now. But not always. Not before he'd met his band-mates at Mount Temple. Like Bono, Edge was indispensable to U2. Like Bono, Edge was *made* by U2.

Larry was now a good drummer. He had a distinctive style. He played the drums the way Larry Mullen Jr *felt* they should be played. Larry was a nice guy – and an awkward bollox. He had no real public image, didn't 'do' press, except for a specialist drumming magazine to whose reporter he talked freely for hours. Larry had sown the first seed for U2 with his notice on the school board. But that didn't matter, was an old, stale cliché trotted out in desperation by writers with space to fill and only *pictures* of Larry to fill it with. If those writers had glimpsed behind the studio or dressing-room door, Larry Mullen would be portrayed as someone other than the handsome drummer. Larry fought his corner for drums. Larry insisted on organization: if we're leaving by 2.30, let's be there by 2.30. Right.

Larry was Dublin suburban youth personified, and given

musical ability, smartness, and the courage or – as it often
manifested itself – obstinacy to say no. He was U2's conscience,
the one who looked askance as Bono indulged in flights of
fancy with visiting writers or other dignitaries. That harsh, flat
Artane voice would evoke the past, the reality, identifying him
and them, U2, as a group of fellas from the Northside who
worked hard at rock 'n' roll. Larry enforced other values: no
sexual exploitation of the girls around the stage door, for
example. There *were* no groupies. There were U2 fans there
because of the music, and anyone who wanted to take advantage of that and get laid had better do so out of Larry's sight.
Yes, Larry was shy all right, and he felt unsophisticated some
of the time, most of the public time. Larry was twenty. He'd
lose the shyness, develop the veneer of sophistication, acquire
taste. In his own time. He wouldn't fake it, and for now he
didn't need to. Like Bono and Edge, Larry was indispensable
to U2. Like them he was *made* by U2.

Adam brought his worldliness and charm to the cause from
the beginning. He also brought his courage, his unyielding
determination to be his own man, qualities that had enabled
him to survive Castle Park and Columba's, qualities that had
been from the first day quintessential to U2, the band who
would be their own men, create their own separate identity in
their business and even more profoundly, in their own country
and culture. Adam didn't invent the qualities that served U2
from day one, but he was the first of the lads to try them out in
public, alone and unsupported. He went to town, explored the
scene, hussled the gigs, found Bill Graham, who found Paul
McGuinness, who married Kathy, who supported him – and
them – through the awful, sweaty, ignoble stage of being U2.
Adam always worked hard. He'd play hard too but always *after*
the biz was done. Adam was a sympathetic listener when Bono
came to the Evans's shed with his images, unformed, uncertain,
unfulfilled. Another stylish bass player might have laughed,

questioned originality, knocked down what he didn't understand. Not Adam. 'Come on, we'll give it a try.' Tolerant, reasonable, unbegrudging Adam. He was good with the crew, asking questions, listening when sometimes Bono wouldn't, reasoning out whatever the problem was. He was great with the business people, record companies, marketing and PR. Adam knew how much an album cost to make, where the money was spent, how it could be wasted. His rapport with Steve Lillywhite was critical to the production of *Boy*, his rap with Paul a decisive influence when band and manager first embarked on the U2 journey. Adam had grasped the essentials of American rock 'n' roll, the stuff about radio stations, television and press. Adam was tolerance, charm and intelligence. Adam was indispensable to U2. Like Bono, Edge and Larry, Adam was made whole by U2.

Sadly, none of this appeared clear to the party who flew into Nassau for a brief rest on the evening of 22 April 1981.

Chapter Thirteen

DECISION

Bono walked along the empty beach. It was autumn. Portrane, out past Malahide and Portmarnock, was bleak. An east wind swept up the shore causing him to hunch up against the cold. Nassau was almost six months back. They had been unhappy months, public acclaim rubbing traumatically against private misery. U2 had recorded 'Fire', a new single, with Steve Lillywhite, at Compass Point Studios in Nassau. When it was released in June 1981 it had provided the band with their first British chart success. Lillywhite was beginning to understand the band and define his role accordingly. The lyrics and images were powerful and personal. He had to balance the emotion with sharp, clean sound, shed light into the darkest corners of the songs.

In 'Fire' the imagery bore testimony to the angst consuming Bono and to the fact that he had been reading the Book of Revelations.

> *Calling, Calling, the sun is burning black,*
> *Calling, Calling, it's beating on my back.*
> *With a fire, fire,*
> *With a fire, fire.*

The song opens with these pained words. Later the singer cries:

> *There's a fire inside, even when I'm falling over.*

Later still:

> *The stars are falling down,*
> *They knock me to the ground.*

In the end Bono confesses:

> *I built a fire, fire, but I'm going home,*
> *Calling, Calling, Calling, Calling.*

His two Christian friends were around somewhere as he walked the cold beach at Portrane, reflecting on the recent past and more tantalizingly on the future. The compromise he, Larry and Edge had agreed to which would enable them to continue in rock 'n' roll *and* fulfil their obligation to their faith had not worked. It was impossible to isolate themselves at the back of the tour bus and not alienate their travelling companions. Adam was intimidated by the arrangement. A gap was beginning to open between Adam and Paul and the Christian members of U2. Was it now a Christian band? *October*, their new album recorded at Windmill Lane during the summer, was overwhelmingly an expression of the conflict alluded to in 'Fire', between the original U2 concept and the path now chosen by Bono, Edge and Larry. Compromise was impossible.

The three of them were here in Portrane with their Christian friends, living a simple, contemplative life in the service of God. They came here to join the others whenever they could. Shalom had some mobile homes scattered along Portrane's isolated beach where they lived on retreat from the city ten miles away. Back from the rock 'n' roll circus Bono, Edge and Larry now observed a radically different daily routine. They rose at six a.m., prayed and studied the scriptures for an hour, then had a simple breakfast. Out here among their fellow-Christians they felt close to nature and to God. If they had to go to town during the day the three returned in the evening to read their Bibles, talk and sing with the others around the campfire on the beach. Although this way of living sounds grim and joyless, nothing could be further from the truth. The evenings were joyous, there was laughter, song and camaraderie between people who had found peace and purpose through the Spirit of God. From here the perspectives were different. The insanity of materialism, of religions cluttered with icons and symbols of the established Churches who waged war on each other like politicians, could be seen for what it was: the Spirit of God made perverse and corrupt by the weaknesses of man, by ego, by man's refusal to surrender his spirit to God. That was the world. The world of U2 and rock 'n' roll. From the peaceful perspective of Portrane, where God was truly, simply and wonderfully present, rock 'n' roll seemed a worldly distraction in conflict with the spirituality man must seek for his salvation.

It was against this background, with increasing pressure falling on them to make a choice between the spirit and the flesh, between God and ego, that Bono, Edge and Larry entered Windmill in June 1981 to make the *October* album. The American tour had ended spectacularly with two sell-out concerts at the Palladium in New York City and the Fast Lane, Asbury Park, New Jersey. Now U2 needed an album to fulfil the promise of *Boy*, something that would enable them to build on the passionate support their live performances in America, the UK and Europe had inspired. That was what the strategy demanded. Alas, when it came to the music U2 couldn't conform to strategy, however rational and necessary to their professional ambitions. U2 music was personal, the seeds of creativity existing in their experiences and emotions. The rock 'n' roll the band played had to conform to something more profound than the strategy. It had to be about the lives of the four men who created it, and Steve Lillywhite's sense of those lives, his respect for their preoccupations, his technical ability to build a musical bridge between spirituality and rock 'n' roll. Making *October* was very tough. They came to Steve with sounds, richer, more confident than before. Edge was achieving greater mastery of guitar technology all the time. He had also learnt to play keyboards, a dividend from the piano lessons Gwenda had sent him to back in the pre-Mount Temple days. The effect achieved by his guitar and keyboard mix added a plaintively evocative dimension to the U2 sound.

Adam also shone on *October*. Lillywhite, his friend, understood his lonely place in the order of things and created a potent role for Adam's melodic bass on the album. Steve's sensitivity and special feel for drums inspired Larry's contribution to the album, which was uninhibitedly passionate, distinctive and joined seamlessly to the music.

October's lyrics were written by a desperate man and tell more about the conflict gnawing away at the band's existence than is suggested by the accomplished playing. 'Gloria', the rock-hymn that became the single off the album, was not about a girl. Trapped without lyrics, consumed by the impossibility of reconciling Windmill Lane with Portrane, Bono was writing on the run. Night merged meaninglessly with day. While Lillywhite and the rest of the band watched from the control room, he composed the lyrics standing at the microphone in the studio. Bono, always the courageous optimist, claimed that the virtue of recording under stress was that the adrenalin triggered by fear was invigorating, helped him to get the core of his being, swept away pretence and superficiality. The stuff at the front of your brain was a lot of rubbish, things you only *thought* you were concerned about. The real concerns lay deeper down and, he reassured the others, were coming up fast. Edge thought the process was a nightmare. Adam resented the capacity of things Christian to distract Bono and U2 from the business they should be getting on with: making rock 'n' roll.

Bono had been studying a book of Gregorian chants. Now, using stream-of-consciousness, as believers did at the prayer meetings, he created a lyric that gave voice to the torture within:

> *I try to sing this song.*
> *I, I try to stand up, but I can't find my feet.*
> *I try, I try to speak up, but only in you I am complete.*

Thus, the indecision, the feeling of helplessness was given expression in U2 music. 'Only in you I am complete.' 'Gloria' continues with the plea,

> *loosen my lips,*

and ends:

> *Oh my Lord, if I had anything, anything at all,*
> *I'd give it to you,*
> *I'd give it to you.*

There is confusion in the lyric, no coherent line is followed, rather a ragged path veering between passivity and activism, between promises and pleas, between rock 'n' roll and Christianity:

> *I try to sing this song,*
> *I, I try to get in, but I can't find the door.*
> *The door is open, you're standing there, you let me in.*

The confusion tormenting Bono, Edge and Larry focused on this fundamental question: did God require, as their Christian group seemed to be implying, that they give up U2 and rock 'n' roll?

> *Oh, Lord, if I had anything, anything at all,*
> *I'd give it to you,*
> *I'd give it to you.*

But *would* they? And was it necessary?

The personal uncertainty expressed in those lyrics is, on *October*, coloured by powerful surging rock 'n' roll music driven by guitar, bass and drums. *October* can be viewed with hindsight as an astonishingly gallant attempt to express, through an idiom more used to dealing with fantasy, the complex personal dilemmas of the four young friends who created it.

In the song 'Rejoice', Bono flirts with one solution:

> *I can't change the world,*
> *But I can change the world in me.*

This refutes the notion central to the compromise between U2 and God: that he/they can use rock 'n' roll and their fame and influence to evangelize for Christianity. The line, 'I can change the world in me', argues that this, the saving of one's own soul, *can* be achieved but only, it seems, by making a choice between ego and God. *October* closes with 'Is That All?', Bono the optimist asking,

> *Is that all You want from me?*

Here, maybe God understands and approves the compromise; is *that* all you want from me?

In their less optimistic moments, Bono, Edge and Larry wrestled with a less palatable truth: that Christianity did require them to surrender ego, and maybe they were unable to find within themselves the humility to do so.

Despite the personal and creative crises preoccupying those principally concerned with the making of *October*, the atmosphere in the Windmill Lane Studio was lightened from time to time by the sound of laughter. There was a great deal at stake for all of them; they would have to bear the brunt of critical analyses, explain *October* and live with it on the road for the next phase of their touring career. Steve Lillywhite's reputation was also on the line. Since *Boy* he had produced major recording artists like Joan Armatrading and Peter Gabriel. Producing had been revolutionized since the old 'white coat' days at Phonogram Records in Marble Arch. Record producers were now identified with and acknowledged for their work. They were stars in their own right and as such subject to criticism as harsh as any meted out to the artists they produced. Like most top producers Lillywhite had his own agent-manager who negotiated production deals every bit as complex as those elsewhere in the music business. Lillywhite could no more afford a duff album than U2.

Adam gained most from his friend Steve's presence. Lillywhite defined a role for Adam's bass guitar and lent support in other less tangible ways. The feeling was growing in Adam that his indifference to Christianity combined with his vulnerability on bass, the latter not entirely unconnected to the isolation created by the former, might now lead to him being dropped by the others. No amount of reassurance from Paul, Steve and Joe O'Herlihy could replace the confidence Adam had lost in the previous six months. It was lonely on stage and off, and although he used his well-practised nonchalance as a shield, for much of the time life was pretty miserable.

Often over those few months Adam had found himself partying the night away. The post-concert euphoria would sustain him through the witching hours but, as dawn crept slowly across the horizon and he rode home alone in a taxi, he would reflect on the emptiness that lay beyond euphoria and wonder despairingly what was happening to U2. From outside looking in, Adam appeared to be having a ball. But it didn't feel like that from the inside.

Paul McGuinness didn't hang around Windmill Lane.

Instead he suffered like a pregnant father, as Lillywhite teasingly put it, waiting for news of the new arrival. It would be his task to take the album to Island and Warner's. Despite the underlying tensions, a residue of respect, affection and the kind of love only those who have travelled a hard road together can share, kept bitterness and resentment at bay. Bono, tortured and under pressure creatively, was still a good companion, if a different one from hour to hour. He was, as on The Mall at Mount Temple, the wicked mimic, 'doing' everyone from Elvis to Brush Sheils to Paul McGuinness and B. P. Fallon, the eclectically gifted Irish rock eccentric, in between agonizing over lyrics and sounds. His fetish for mooning was still occasionally indulged. Steve and the band would often relieve the pressure by getting mildly pissed in the Dockers, a rough-and-ready public house on the Quays. Christian beliefs did not preclude humour or a mild bout of hedonism. But always passion was focused on the work to a degree that Lillywhite found quite extraordinary. There could, he thought, have been few bands in rock 'n' roll history so irrevocably committed to studio work. Most albums contained some throw-away songs, the tired, expedient fillers offered to the producer with eyes downcast in the hope that *he* could magically transform them into something. U2 wanted every track to mean something, *every* track. There were no fillers. Mistakes, unrealized ambitions and downright bummers, yes. But as much blood was shed on the last song as the first.

In August, as they waited anxiously for *October*'s autumn release, U2 played a major Irish concert at Slane Castle, co-headlining with Thin Lizzy. The castle was the home of Lord Henry Mountcharles, a smart young Anglo-Irish peer. The Anglo-Irish aristocracy was renowned for its endearing eccentricities, many of its more prominent elders conveying the impression to the population at large that they were quite mad. Henry was not of that ilk. Through television appearances and political activity he projected an image that was an attractive blend of style – he wore odd socks – and substance – his views on the governance of Ireland being fashionably progressive. His was the civilized and graciously acceptable face of a dying and nowadays impoverished breed. In order to restore his beautiful ancestral home, Henry joined forces with Jim Aiken, Ireland's most ambitious concert entrepreneur, to promote extravagant shows in the castle's natural amphitheatre. Lured by money and the idea of performing in such a unique setting, the world's biggest acts came to Slane, among them the Rolling Stones, Bob Dylan, David Bowie and Bruce Springsteen.

Slane was the kind of challenge U2 usually responded to. That Lynott and Lizzy were sharing the billing with them added a vital competitive edge to the gig. They opened their set with *October*'s most evocative song, 'Tomorrow'. Although there are references in it to Jesus coming and the love of the Lamb of God, 'Tomorrow', with its opening lines,

> *Won't you come back tomorrow?*
> *Won't you come back tomorrow?*
> *Can I sleep tonight?*

is a lament for Iris Hewson. In the second verse, Bono relives the dreadful morning of her funeral:

> *Outside, somebody's outside,*
> *Somebody's knocking at the door.*
> *There's a black car parked at the side of the road.*
> *Don't go to the door, don't go to the door,*
> *I'm going out. I'm going outside,*
> *Mother I'm going out there.*

'Tomorrow' goes on to refer to his own violent reaction to Iris's death and to ask who will 'heal the wounds' and 'scars' now that she's gone.

Steve Iredale, a young man from Kiltimagh, Co. Mayo, had

joined the U2 camp as general roadie and back-line operative during the summer. Steve at twenty-one was a veteran, having spent three years on the road with Horslips. Slane was his first U2 gig and it soon began to go badly wrong. Every time he handed Edge a guitar it was thrust impatiently back. While the crowd in the amphitheatre below cheered the previous number, Steve checked the tuning. The guitars seemed OK to him. But back they came after every song. He asked someone else to check, one of Lizzy's roadies, who assured him he was right. The problem was that the band had forgotten to tell him that in concert they tuned their guitars a semi-tone down to facilitate Bono's singing. Typically, U2 battled through the crisis. Adversity was an old friend.

The presence of Phil Lynott at Slane Castle that August day in 1981 was very significant in the context of U2's inner conflicts. Philo was a good guy, they liked him, respected his work. Yet they couldn't help but notice the price their fellow-Dubliner was paying for his rock 'n' roll fame. Lynott came from the working-class Southside suburb of Crumlin. His father, a black sea-farer, had never been around during his childhood. As Fintan O'Toole was to write in a brilliant essay after Philo's death in 1986,

> The music never completely filled the gap left by his father. Philip looked for heroes, in books and in the cinema. At the Roxy and the Stella he acquired a taste for stand-up saviours, lone men pitted against the world. In his songs he would again and again return to the figure of the hero of the Wild West or of Celtic mythology. Thinking of himself as an orphan, he had himself adopted by the heroic loners of his dream world. He called one of his first bands the Orphanage, and wrote songs like 'Shades of a Blue Orphanage';

> *The Roxy and Stella,*
> *Where film stars starred,*

> *That's where me and Hopalong Cassidy,*
> *Roy Rogers got drunk and jarred.*
> *And we might have been*
> *The Saviours of men,*
> *The captured captain in the devil's demon den.*

Thus, O'Toole observes, Philip acquired

> The peculiar mixture of an arty romanticism and macho hard-man strutting that would become his image for stardom.

This persona was fleshed out in lyrics he wrote, none so uncompromising as those for his song, 'The Rocker':

> *I am your main man, if you're looking for trouble,*
> *I'll take no lip 'cause no one's tougher than me.*
> *If I kicked your face, you'd be seeing double,*
> *Hey, little girl, keep your hands off me.*

Philo hit the big time when 'Whiskey in the Jar', a rock 'n' roll version of an old Irish folk-song, made the British charts in 1973. He made money only three years later when the single, 'The Boys are Back in Town', reached the Top Ten in Britain and the USA, taking his album *Jailbreak* along in its wake. With money and fame came sex and drugs, old pleasures, available now in the kind of quantity that could soothe *forever* the pain and emotional insecurity that lay beneath the macho image. Philo, ten years older than U2, could be seen around town, the rock star as hero *and* victim, having it all and yet sadly wasting, the tired, haunted eyes giving lie to the funky laugh, the smiling face. He was rock 'n' roll and this was the world U2 were into now. The world of tragic children, where fame was but a fleeting moment between adolescent pain and lonely drug-created death. Rock 'n' roll was Janis Joplin, Keith Moon, Brian Jones, Keith Richards hanging on, but with desperation etched in every crevice of his ravaged face.

U2 noticed. Early autumn in Portrane was a time for talking among themselves, and with their friends. Christianity could not be reconciled with a culture that dealt in death, abuse and exploitation. Perhaps *October* was as close as you could come. Maybe now was the time to surrender to God, to choose to walk away from rock 'n' roll as their friends had walked away from their worldly preoccupations.

October received a measure of critical acclaim when it was released. Although the album was never to reach the American charts, it entered the British equivalent at No. 11 the week it was released. 'Gloria', the single, also entered the charts, albeit a long way off the Top Ten. These modest achievements showed the value of touring. Once seen live, U2 was never forgotten. Strangely, for reasons that weren't all that dissimilar, the UK critics wrote favourable reviews of the new album. Personal acquaintance with the band was a refreshing change for writers more used to the posturings of the tyros of the rock 'n' roll community. Where other bands boasted about their rather threadbare talents, U2 talked honestly about their limitations. Where rival bands issued press kits in which the members were depicted as supermen or objects of sexual fantasy, U2 came in person to talk about their music, their hopes and their struggles. They represented reality in a rock 'n' roll world populated by platoons of posing youths, each as unbelievable as the clone you met last week. U2 were not cultivating an image. They were trying to sell *themselves*. The words 'real' and 'refreshing' would constantly be associated with the Dublin band. To English writers in search of a good story, reality was news. It was to write about something real, someone you understood, someone you could actually respect. This feeling about U2 was copper-fastened by Paul McGuinness, their educated, straight-talking manager who engaged journalists on a level far removed from that aspired to by the spiv hyping the next big thing that hacks more usually dealt with in the line of duty. Virtue being more than its own reward, *October* was sympathetically reviewed by writers who had first met U2 on their disastrous trip to London eighteen months previously:

> 'Their whole musical sensibility is shaped by a strong emotional bond to their homeland,' Adam Sweeting wrote in *Melody Maker*. 'It gives them a completely different frame of reference from most groups,' Sweeting went on, 'and on *October* it's given them the strength to assimilate a barrage of disorientation and to turn that into a cohesive body of music.'

Melody Maker was a powerful friend. Dave McCullough of *Sounds Magazine* was another U2 convert:

> There's a classicism about U2 that's best relayed by their covers. You can imagine *Boy* or now *October* perched in a record shop in the middle of nowhere in ten years' time having more to do with Grainy Old Mayall, Them or Yardbird sleeves than the moderns of the time. U2 will endure. *October* hits that home magnificently.

McCullough went on to claim that *October* pointed U2 in a more interesting direction, 'of restrained reflection, more poise, less beef. This *October* will last forever.' Another English critic, Ian Cranna in *Smash Hits*, vouched that *October* left *Boy* standing. 'If that album [*Boy*] was magic, this one [*October*] is sorcery.'

Hot Press also provided a rave review, penned by Neil McCormick, who knew more about the background to this story than most:

> It's a Christian L P that avoids the pedantic puritanism associated with most Christian rock, avoids the old-world, emotional fascism of organized religion and the crusading preaching of someone like born-again Bob Dylan. It is fortunate that the main spiritual issues dealt with can be related to a wider frame of reference than Christianity; man's struggle to know and control himself and his own nature is something that comes to everyone in some guise.

Bono, Edge and Larry arrived unannounced at Paul's flat in Waterloo Road one afternoon in early November. They wanted to talk. They had, they told him, decided not to tour the *October* album. They weren't certain yet, but they felt that they were finished with rock 'n' roll. They simply couldn't reconcile the way of life with their religious beliefs. It looked as if the band would be touring America, the U K and Europe for the next twelve months and Bono, who was spokesman, said that they simply couldn't make the commitment required. McGuinness was stunned, but reacted sympathetically. Could they give him a couple of hours to think about what they'd just told him and come back and talk to him then? They agreed to do so.

Paul had always respected Bono, Edge and Larry's Christian convictions. From the moment he'd met them in the Project he had felt that they were unusually decent and intelligent young men, all of them, Adam included. It was those personal qualities *more* than the music that convinced Paul to get involved. Musical ability could be acquired, learnt. Decency, intelligence and integrity, the stuff that you needed to take on challenges in this world, you could *not* acquire. It was either present or absent, in a face, a pair of eyes, the line of someone's mouth. He had liked the cut of their jib. It was simple once you knew the code. His faith in them had wavered, but only his faith in them as performers, never his belief in them as people. In Belfast at Queen's, that awful night, he'd doubted U2's ability to win over audiences. But that doubt had subsequently been erased a dozen times, at the Stadium, the Ritz and in rock clubs anonymous and uninspiring the length and breadth of Britain and the United States. Even now with *October*, the wrong album for marketing purposes, Paul's faith remained strong. He could live with *October* because it was true to the band's experience, wrong for the market place, but morally, spiritually and artistically faithful. O K. Wasn't that what U2 claimed they

were about? The Charismatic Christianity was something Paul
felt the three lads would grow out of. That wasn't meant to be
patronizing, rather a reflection on his own youth at Trinity
when men he now knew as stockbrokers, barristers and account-
ants, pillars of the Irish establishment, had espoused Maoism,
calling for the overthrow of an Irish government whose leading
politicians were 'the running dogs of Capitalism'. Bono, Edge
and Larry were twenty-one. They were entitled to their passions. But whenever he thought about it McGuinness believed
that at the end of the day they would be guided by their basic
intelligence and instincts which he knew to be honourable and
decent.

When they filed back into his office-flat it was to their sense
of honour that Paul addressed himself. He accepted the
commitment they'd made to Christianity. But he had entered
into commitments, legally as well as morally binding, on U2's
behalf. In two weeks they were due to play at J. B. Scott's in
Albany, New York. There were twenty other dates booked by
Frank Barsalona on that month-long tour. Then they were due
back in the US in February and March before touring the UK
and Europe for the rest of 1982. Promoters were committed, as
was their own crew, people like Joe O'Herlihy who'd bound
himself to them at the expense of family and business, and
Steve Iredale. There was Chris Blackwell and Island. Frank
Barsalona, Ellen Darst and Barbara Skydel. Paul left himself
and Adam out of it, their position didn't need to be spelt out.
There were an awful lot of people committed to U2. The band
had majored on its integrity. How could they possibly renege
on their obligations now? Paul couldn't see how those who
were encouraging Bono, Larry and Edge to walk away from
these obligations could square such an act with Christianity.
He reminded them, among other things, of Bob Regehr, the
Warner Brothers executive who'd come through with $100,000

to support the *Boy* tour. The deal between Island and Warner's was a multi-million-dollar loser for the Americans, yet Regehr had responded to Paul's pleas and was set to do so again with another $100,000 for the coming tour. The reasoning was undeniable. If they wanted to quit rock 'n' roll it could be done, but it should be done properly. U2 could be phased out, the band couldn't simply drop out. To do so would be to deny everything they stood for.

It would be a long time yet before Bono, Larry and Edge resolved the problems they faced as outlined by McGuinness that November afternoon but the argument he put to them seemed undeniable. They resisted the Shalom group pressure and renewed their commitment to U2.

Contact with their audiences on the first US leg of the *October* tour helped heal the wounds of the past six months. McGuinness was supportive of his band when he presented Warner Brothers in New York with the *October* album. He was candid. He understood that *October* wasn't exactly what they were hoping for and would be a hard album to sell, but it had to be made, he explained. The conviction it expressed, or perhaps more accurately, the torment it reflected, was genuine. It wasn't self-indulgence, Paul assured Warners. Stick with us and we'll make it work on the road.

Confirmation that a major crisis had passed came when the band wrote 'A Celebration', their next single, due to be released in spring 1982. Bono opens,

> *I believe in a celebration.*
> *I believe you set me free.*
> *I believe you can lose these chains,*
> *I believe you can dance with me.*

'A Celebration' goes on to declare the writer's belief in the real world, of atomic bombs, Mountjoy Prison, the city's children and the powers that be;

But they won't overpower me.

The band returned to London to play two concerts at the Lyceum Ballroom on 20 and 21 December. They sold out both nights. Opening their set with 'Gloria', U2 played with new confidence and the old conviction.

Gill Pringle in *Record Mirror* described U2 at the Lyceum as 'the gig of 1981':

> Words fail me. Everyone is hugging each other as they stumble outside . . . the night air is ringing with snatches of the songs.

Karen Swayne of *Sounds* wrote:

> We were overwhelmed by their music and lifted by their feeling and the world outside seemed a million miles away as we were carried into a world of passion and beauty.

English music critics were, like English people, slow to embrace something or someone new. Thus the Lyceum was an unusually gratifying triumph.

A remarkable incident midway through U2's set on the opening night underlined the band's genuine concern for those who came to watch them. One of the minders holding back the audience slapped a youngster who was getting a bit carried away by the occasion. As the row escalated the slaps became punches: the kid was being beaten up. Larry stopped playing his drums, ran off stage and jumped the minder. Bono piled in behind Larry and they hauled the heavy off. Bono jumped back on stage, grabbed the mike and called for the Lyceum management. He spoke calmly, in measured tones, but *clearly*, so that everyone in the packed room should know.

'I want this guy out of here,' he called, pointing to the heavy. '*Now, before we sing another song.*' It was an extraordinary demand from a young band playing such a prestigious venue. His demand was acceded to by the management who, with 2,000 people looking on, would have been hard-pressed to refuse.

In January U2 toured Ireland, ending a series of wildly successful concerts with a big show at the RDS, attended by 5,000 people. The second half of their American tour began in New Orleans in February. Barbara Skydel of Premier Talent had put a proposition to Paul McGuinness at the end of the first leg of the *October* tour. The J. Geils Band, one of Premier's leading acts, would be touring during U2's return trip to the States. The J. Geils Band had had a string of No. 1 hits and were currently at their peak. They were playing arenas, 10,000–15,000 seaters, a different league to the clubs and colleges U2 had played. Barbara offered U2 the support slot for ten of the J. Geils dates.

The band were looking forward to breaking their schedule to play in the New York St Patrick's Day Parade. Alas, when they discovered that the Grand Marshal due to lead the parade had links with the 'Armed Struggle' at home they decided not to lend the U2 name to the cause.

Paul had learned a great deal about the American music industry in the previous eighteen months. Now sitting opposite Barbara Skydel, the New York skyline serving as an intimidating backdrop, he understood that what she was proposing amounted to the biggest musical challenge U2 had ever faced. Premier liked the band, were charming people, but it wasn't who you knew that mattered in the United States, but what you could do. If people like Frank Barsalona and Barbara Skydel really liked you they didn't give you presents – they offered you an opportunity to prove yourself. In this instance there were huge risks. American concerts were about the stars. Support acts played as the auditorium filled up with popcorn-chewing, coke-swigging fans who were looking for their seats and their friends across the arena. The J. Geils Band were big just now and they would be playing to J. Geils audiences.

There would be no residual U2 fervour, just huge arenas, larger, noisier and less attentive than any Paul's band had played before. It was a gamble on U2's ability, Barbara and Paul agreed. If they *had* potential here was the chance to prove it. *October* probably wouldn't make it in the States, there was nothing on it suitable for the radio stations that made albums. It was impossible to classify and therefore a problem. Accepting the J. Geils challenge was a way out of that particular hole and the money would be good in any case.

Joe O'Herlihy smiled grimly to himself when he heard the news about J. Geils. If Paul knew it was a gamble, Joe knew precisely what the odds were. This was the big league and he had been there before with Rory Gallagher. Joe knew coming from the same Premier stable as J. Geils wouldn't mean a thing. They'd be all smiles and nice to meet you but, like any other major band, J. Geils wouldn't want their show climaxing while they were in the dressing room. Their crew would do the best they could to ensure this didn't happen. The sound check would be the key. Great rock 'n' roll performances began in the afternoon. You got to the venue, set up your gear and worked out the sound as best you could. Each sound problem had a solution, but first you had to find the problem. That was what the check was for. If the support band was promising, likely to blow you off the stage, your crew knew how to deal with that. You sound-checked as long and as late as possible. The support band would wait anxiously for their turn. Before they knew it the doors were open and the people were sitting down ready for the show.

Joe was right about J. Geils. They were charming. And their road crew knew their stuff. U2 counted for nothing here, they were the support band. Every night they barely got their gear on stage before the doors opened. Joe didn't react. He figured out how to do the best he could for his band. People remembered Joe. He was short, chunky, he wore a beard now.

He was good-humoured. His lyrical Cork brogue and pale, smiling face distinguished him from the regular road crew types who affected a weary, disenchanted, seen-it-all-before worldliness. Joe was alive and enjoying what he did. He'd loved Rory and loved U2 even more. They were game as fucking pebbles. They meant everything they said. They were hard to work for, always asking questions, never convinced by his answers until he *proved* the point. There were times when this exasperated Joe, but mostly he was exhilarated by the challenge. And he knew that Bono, who could be a pain in the arse, was hardest of all on himself.

The greatest challenge to Joe, the sound engineer, was working with Edge. It was also the richest pleasure of his working life. Edge was a genius, Joe now thought, still learning, always playing with his boxes, keeping Joe on his toes, but the result was sounds Joe had never imagined coming out of a guitar. He was proud of U2, proud of the sound and the values that underpinned everything they did. There was no partition on the tour bus this time, things were looser than they'd been. But Joe had sometimes wandered back to Bono, Pod, Edge and Larry on the *Boy* tour and prayed with them. He was a Catholic, but he respected their type of Christianity and shared its fundamental decency.

The first night on the J. Geils job Joe worked it out. Clair Brothers were doing the sound for Geils. Joe had used them for a show at a New York gig a week or two before. Now he introduced himself to Frank Darrion, J. Geils' front of house engineer. Soon they were old buddies. Mike Stall, Clair Brothers' man on the spot, was another old pal of Joe's. Mike was minding the millions of dollars' worth of sound equipment hired to the J. Geils Band. Joe was looking for a small favour. He had a little echo machine for Bono's voice. Would it be cool to plug it into the million-dollar equipment? Sure, Mike agreed. How could he refuse this nice little Irish guy? That favour, slyly purchased, made a difference to the show. Elsewhere Steve Iredale was also stroking against the odds. Every little victory counted. But what counted most was U2.

Faced by a challenge infinitely greater than any they had taken on before, Bono, Adam, Edge and Larry went for the J. Geils audience like animals. Before the first-night show, the promoter came to visit U2 in their dressing room. He had come to apologize – *in advance*. It's like this, fellas, he began. If this audience doesn't like you, they may boo you. We're in Fort Myers, Florida, this is a hockey arena and occasionally acts have had bottles thrown at them. Only last month, the promoter continued, somebody got a bottle on the head. There are 15,000 people out there. Good luck. Had the J. Geils Band sent *him* in, the lads laughed nervously as the promoter left the room?

When Paul had agreed to accept Barbara Skydel's offer, what he'd meant was that he would put it to the band. He never made major decisions unilaterally. They were his clients. He worked for them. Band meetings were formal occasions, with Paul acting as chairman. Agreements in principle were worked out elsewhere, decisions were taken here. So U2 knew the stakes they were playing for on the J. Geils gamble, the rewards if they won and the price of failure. They worked out a thirty-minute set consisting of what Edge liked to call 'the cherries' of their albums. No spiel, no folksy intro, just out and hit 'em with 'Gloria', 'Out of Control', 'I Will Follow'. The staging helped. The J. Geils Band had a huge banner hung atop the set announcing the J. Geils presence. U2 walked out – under the banner – said nothing, just played. Who are they? What are they? Before the questions formed, the music, the U2 sound had got the J. Geils crowd. Bono was magnificent, his friends thought. Raunchy, brave, wild and unbelievably powerful, he found the animal charisma to fill the larger space that now yawned in front of them. If anybody talked, rustled popcorn bags or sucked too loudly on their coke straws Bono saw it, felt it and focused on the culprit. 'We're up here, not in your coke,' he bellowed, seeking mastery of every spirit in the place. Night after night he fought and won. There were encores everywhere except where the J. Geils people managed to pull the plug before Bono reached the mike. But it didn't matter. The gamble had paid off.

Chapter Fourteen

WAR

U2 spent the summer playing festivals around Europe. They made one visit to England, to Gateshead in the north-east, to support the Police. The J. Geils experience had bounced the band closer to the First Division. They still had a lot of work to do, especially in the studio, where the next album would be crucial, but the second half of the *October* tour had proved that with the right music U2 could play anywhere. Premier Talent was convinced. So was the band itself. All thoughts now focused on the coming album, due to be made at Windmill in the autumn.

Paul McGuinness had other things to think about. The U2 organization was lean, to say the least. Paul's home was still the office. He had no secretary. On the road, Joe O'Herlihy and Steve Iredale were the permanent crew. Tim Nicholson, their previous tour manager, had retired owing to ill-health. For the *October* tour they'd hired some crew from England. Pod had helped out. If U2 were to take the next big step they would need expertise on the road. They had winged it on the J. Geils job, but the need for a tour manager and someone to oversee the production of their live show was also underlined by their taste of the big time.

Such considerations inevitably raised the question of money in Paul's mind. U2 had no money. They were stars in Ireland; adored in the UK and in the States; *Rolling Stone* magazine had written of them as the next big thing. Still, the four lads all lived at home with their parents, drove small, second-hand cars and didn't dare look their bank managers in the eye. When there was money it was ploughed back into the business. Touring, equipment, crew, photographs and studio time to make records all devoured the money that came in from just two sources: tour-support money from Island and the odd big gig where several thousand pounds could be made in one strike. But by and large everything was invested in the strategy. Profit would come from a hit album and the major arena tours that would automatically follow a successful record. The next touring phase would be vital to consolidate the gains of the last two years and with luck capitalize on the album they would be taking on the road.

Paul had made inquiries about experienced tour managers who might be available and willing to take on a rising young band. An old friend, Robbie McGrath, was sound man tour manager for the Boomtown Rats. He recommended Dennis Sheehan to McGuinness. Sheehan was the best around, McGrath claimed, he'd been on the road with Led Zeppelin for nearly ten years and had also worked for Maggie Bell, Iggy Pop and Patti Smith. And, Robbie added as a clincher, 'He's Irish.' Paul arranged to meet Sheehan who lived in Bristol, at London's Portobello Hotel. Dennis was visiting his accountant in London that day and was dressed accordingly in black shoes, grey flannels, neat jacket and tie and white shirt.

'You don't look like a tour manager,' McGuinness exclaimed when he opened his hotel room door to find Sheehan outside. Dennis Sheehan *didn't* look like a tour manager, even when he wasn't visiting his accountant. He was medium height, with short, fair hair, muscular, with a serious, slightly careworn look about him. The persona was cautiously, watchfully, pleasant. He was not effusive. Dennis was the antithesis of rock 'n' roll flash; he was, in a word, dour. He was thirty-five years old and had never worked outside the world of rock 'n' roll. He was reared in Dungarven, Co. Waterford, on the sunny south-east coast of Ireland. His parents went to England for work during the war and Dennis was raised by his grandparents and educated by nuns and Christian Brothers. When he was in his early teens he went to London to join his parents. At Cardinal Manning, one of London's first comprehensive schools, he started picking a guitar and ended up in a group that was the pupils' pride and joy. At seventeen, the Cardinals, as they called themselves, were playing London clubs and American airforce bases in England and France. They played blues, Little Richard and other stuff, heavily influenced by imported American records. 'The House of the Rising Sun', later to be made famous by Eric Burden and the Animals, was the Cardinals' *pièce de résistance*. They would play it four or five times a night for the Americans who's respond by chucking money on the stage. The Cardinals played three or four nights a week, sometimes in support of top-class bands like Georgie Fame and the Blue Flames. When, inevitably, the Cardinals split, the others heading off for the real world, Dennis was nineteen and bent on staying in the music biz.

He got a job as tour manager with Jimmy James and the Vagabonds, a ranking black soul band. James was Britain's Otis Redding, a brilliant singer whose eight-piece band put on a real show. Dennis was diligent, responsible and hard-working. Behind the dour countenance he was a warm guy who loved soul music and the delightfully loose black musicians who played. James and the Vagabonds played the working-men's cabaret clubs all over Britain, mainly in the north and north-east of England, places like Sunderland, Stockton, Newcastle. It was tough, seven-night-a-week work. After a while that circuit was like living in a revolving door. The novelty wore off, you became aware of the drudgery. Dennis stepped out to take a similar job with Cartonne, managed by two well-known record-industry figures, Mark London, who wrote the score for the film, *To Sir with Love*, and Don Black, a prominent pop-music arranger. The band were going to play some dates in America after a couple of years off the road. Dennis travelled as tour manager. The first gig in New York was a disaster. Nerves were blamed. The manager decided to bale out. Have a good week in New York, he smiled, as he headed for Kennedy Airport and London. The four band members were shattered. Dennis contacted the booking agency. He was assured the dates were still booked and, explaining the disappearance of Mark London, Dennis offered to fulfil the planned schedule. He drew up a budget, talked the band round and spent the next month making ends meet. When they boarded their plane back to London, Dennis had £1,000 profit in his wallet. He handed it over to Mark London, who was amazed and grateful. Sheehan was a rare bird in the rock business; competent *and* honest. The perfect can-do man. This was 1969, Dennis was twenty-two, earning £25 a week: it wasn't good money. Mark London and Peter Grant, who managed Led Zeppelin, were jointly looking after Maggie Bell, a talented singer on the verge of international acclaim. Dennis was offered the job of tour manager with Maggie and her band, Stone the Crows. Les Harvey, brother of the famous blues musician, Alex, was their lead guitarist. They were playing a club in Swansea one night when a drunk wandered into the sound-mixing area and started yanking wires out of their sockets. Dennis was alerted and ran back to the mixing desk to clear the drunk out of it. As he surveyed the mess, Les Harvey and the band made ready to play. Harvey put one hand on his guitar strings, the other on the mike. He was killed instantly. Dennis rode with the body to the hospital. When people commented on Sheehan's uncompromising perfectionism in the years ahead, when his grim unblinking working face turned icily on liggers having fun backstage, the personal hostility didn't bother him. He knew the cost of complacency. He knew that rock 'n' roll parties ended up at someone's graveside.

Peter Grant got Dennis the job advancing for Led Zeppelin. The band, managed by Richard Cole, were breaking new touring ground. Nobody had played the enormous outdoor venues before, well, the Beatles and the Rolling Stones, maybe, but without moving their lips or playing their instruments. Those were freak shows. Zeppelin were serious. They sold 120,000 tickets, week in, week out, in Europe, the States and Britain. And anywhere else they wanted.

Advancing was different, more responsible in many ways. Dennis organized the travel, tons of equipment, scores of people. These were the days of rock 'n' roll excess. Nobody had seen so much money before. Costs almost didn't matter. Led Zeppelin stayed in the best hotels, travelled first class. Dennis booked the suites – six of them usually – decided who slept close to whom, which band members to keep on different floors, which to house in adjoining suites. Security was a factor, so were personal likes and dislikes. Zeppelin were usually a party of eighteen. They would base themselves in, say, Chicago for three weeks and fly the few hundred miles to the gig and home to the hotel afterwards. Dennis's job was to create a home from home in anonymous hotels; flowers would be waiting in every suite, laundry and dry-cleaning had to be taken care of *every* day. The whole operation was a bubble barely penetrated by the outside world. The band, Robert Plant, John Bonham the drummer, nicknamed 'Bonzo', John Paul Jones and Jimmy Page were superstars. Outside the bubble there were *people*; people who wanted to talk, to tell them how wonderful they were, how the music had changed their lives, how really great it was to meet them after all those years watching Led Zeppelin and playing the records. It *was* a thrill. There had been a time when it was a thrill for Robert, Bonzo, Jimmy and John Paul. But no longer. Now people were a pain. Even the nice people who you knew meant everything they said, and they were the majority. There were others, the brazen, the weirdos, the sad and sick and those whose imaginations were inflamed by all the hype who thought that inside the bubble life was one long glamorous ball, some kind of life-long party with wall-to-wall girls and champagne on tap. And dope, smack and coke in bottomless bags. This was the 1970s and that's what they said.

Some of it was true. But the bit that was left out when the rock 'n' roll dream was vicariously imagined was the most important bit of all. Nobody referred to the boredom of having it all. The awful, awful emptiness you felt, when you could fuck any chick, or any combination of human beings, drink as much as you wanted, eat from the à la carte and get Dennis to make sure your underpants and blue jeans were clean, could only be experienced. It couldn't be explained. This was a world where compliments were meaningless, where one-to-one love was virtually impossible, where there were no children, where there was no place for mum and dad, where man's capacity for self-destruction was tested daily. For almost ten years Dennis Sheehan lived in a bubble of his own. He was a manservant to madness, but he slipped the service under the door, remaining outside, remaining sane.

Bonzo died in 1979. Richard Cole, the smart manager who guided Zeppelin to the summit of rock 'n' roll ambition, indulged as heartily as anyone the fruits of this success. He sold his story later to the newspapers. Dennis Sheehan didn't sell. He had nothing to sell. He liked the guys, liked and admired Richard Cole, saw the great times of those years, decent people you met, wonderful gigs when the music that lay at the centre of the madness, the music that ironically underwrote that madness, cleansed the spirit of the despair that swirled around inside the bubble. Dennis protected his memories, treasured them and wondered why it had to be like that.

Through it all Dennis stayed straight. He got his buzz on his boat, a little cruiser he took out of Bristol when he wasn't working. He liked to play Sunday football for the music-biz team. Most of all Dennis liked getting his job done. After ten years with Zeppelin he knew all there was to know, but still stayed alert for the trick he had yet to learn. He knew about money, how to spend it and how it was wasted. Freight, airplanes, hotels, getting into town and getting out unscathed, these were the things that Dennis knew. Zeppelin had really died with Bonzo. Robert Plant had tragically lost his young son around the same time. Dennis was close to Robert, who wanted him to come to work on the Midlands farm the singer had retired to. Dennis chose instead to stay on the road freelancing as tour manager for various rock 'n' roll acts.

He hadn't worked for four or five months when he called to see McGuinness. He was getting a little choosy. They had a glass of wine while Paul told his story. U2 were going to be a big band. But the challenges, the really tough ones, lay ahead. Three of the band were Christians, but the other guy makes up for them, Paul joked. Dennis agreed to take the job. He'd do the short tour of the UK planned for December to promote the new album. Then he and Paul could talk longer term.

Dennis met the band for the first time at London Airport. They were very young, very pleasant. There was feeling in their handshakes, respect in their eyes. Dennis hadn't experienced these things for a long time.

Paul Hewson and Alison Stewart were married on 21 August 1982 at the old Guinness Church of Ireland Church in Raheny. Thirty-two years earlier Bobby Hewson had married Iris Rankin in a similar church in Drumcondra, three miles diagonally across the north city suburbs. In 1950 the bride had been dark-haired, sallow-skinned, serene and beautiful, the bride-groom passionate, wilful, a romantic who loved to perform, who saw beyond the frigid mores of his time, who knew the value of love and was courageously prepared to pay the price of marrying his Iris. Ali was beautiful, at twenty-two a woman of substance, seeing in her man, as Iris had in Bobby, the vulnerability that lay at the core of his ebullience. The marriage of Ali and Paul joined the two young people who'd flirted on The Mall at Mount Temple. There were no rock-star vibes. There were no rock stars present. All the U2 people were there, and Bobby, Granny Rankin, Iris's mother, Norman; the Evanses, the Claytons, the Mullens, Larry Sr and Cecilia; Paul and Kathy McGuinness; Onagh Byrne, Iris's friend from No. 14 Cedarwood Road. Jack Heaslip, Mount Temple's laid-back guidance teacher who'd counselled Paul through the worst of his adolescent agony, had converted to the Church of Ireland Ministry. He conducted the marriage ceremony. The Village were there, all differences forgotten today, as Gavin, Guggi, Skello, Pod, Strongman, Reggie, Bad Dog and Day-Vid paid their respects to the happy couple. The Virgin Prunes were doing well. Their performance art-rock band had a cult fol-lowing, especially in Europe. They were still hoping to break through by the alternative route.

Bono had asked Adam to be best man. It was a generous gesture of reconciliation, a public declaration of friendship and respect, a *mea culpa*, perhaps, for the intolerance Adam had been the victim of for the past eighteen months. U2 *was* the most important thing in their lives and Adam was a loved and indispensable member of the band. His presence on the altar was balanced by the prominent part Shalom played in the service. Loyal to his friends from the group, Bono now shared his greatest day with them. The Christian guests formed a circle round the altar, singing their songs and generally cele-brating in their own inimitable way. Jack Heaslip was patient,

Bobby Hewson distressed. That young fella of his was some tulip. Granny Rankin strained to catch a glimpse of the service. The guests from Shalom didn't notice her.

At the centre of this day stood Bono, the shy, passionate man-child. Everyone there had a singular relationship with him. All had felt his compassion and his anger and frustration. All loved him. All felt protective of him. All in different ways were dependent upon him, to give voice to their secret hopes, fears and dreams. In him, so open, so exposed, sometimes strong, sometimes weak, sometimes foolish, often intuitively wise, as physically clumsy as a late-night lush, as agile and poised as Nureyev, articulate and yet painfully inarticulate, wickedly funny, embarrassingly fulsome; in this performing genius, this great soul singer, everyone could see *themselves*, the part of themselves they were loath to expose to a brutal world. Bono, loving everyone, looking after everyone and yet being looked after *by* everyone.

The wedding reception at Sutton Castle was boisterous, families and close friends being joined by colleagues and acquaintances from the Dublin music scene. Here amid the hail-fellow-well-met drink-inspired ambience the band and those closest to them forgot the stresses, professional and personal, of the past eighteen months. U2 had arrived as a force in the rock 'n' roll world. They were a big little band that everyone now predicted would go all the way. Everyone was sure of that; everyone except the band. For they faced the question of how they might get there. The new album was due. It would, they felt, be a make-or-break record. There was also the unresolved problem of rock 'n' roll's relationship with Christianity. The honour bestowed on Adam that day was a rational decision. But the spiritual unrest existed still, particularly in Bono and Edge.

Larry had decided to leave Shalom. It had, he felt, got out of hand. He was becoming a bigot, judging his friends, slowly drifting apart from those he loved. He understood the goodness and sense of spiritual commitment that was fundamental to Shalom, but its demands were too extreme, the solutions it proposed requiring not simply that you live decently but apart from the world around you. Larry felt that there was a reasonable compromise between being a musician – which is how he thought of himself, rather than a rock idol – and being a Christian. Compassion and charity were the things that mattered to him, and he wasn't going down any road otherwise signposted. For those who would now, and in the future, wish to understand the difference between the Larry of U2 mythology – the simple blond bombshell, Bono's little brother who went along with things – and Larry Mullen as he really was, a tough, smart, independent-minded man, this unilateral decision to practise Christianity in his own way, taken now, was the best clue.

Maeve O'Regan, now a Christian activist, attended Bono and Ali's wedding reception. She and Bono talked about the conflict within him still. She had made her decision. He was still searching for a compromise. And so was Edge.

The question of who should produce the next album had exercised U2 for several months. The subject was complicated by an uncomfortable musical reality; they had still not defined a rock 'n' roll identity for themselves. They knew what they were not, but not yet who they were, what U2 would become. Even the question of what they should aim for was clouded by uncertainty. Knowing you don't want to sound like anyone else is one thing, a start, but artistic fulfilment could only begin to be achieved when the objective was clear, or at least clear in outline.

The U2 sound was established in its basic form. The personal and spiritual concerns of U2 images had thus far been vividly expressed by the music. Now with the advent of this new album the visual, emotional and intellectual content would be more complex, the broad simplistic claims of youth fertilized by the experiences of adulthood. U2 worked from the gut, Bono *and* Edge, whose genius as a sound engineer flowed from the depths of his dark Welsh soul. Working like that was risky, spontaneous, informal and never amenable to arriving in studio with a package for the producer. U2 were coming from nowhere in terms of rock 'n' roll tradition. They didn't know precisely where they were going and needed a producer sympathetic to the notion of the mystery of creation.

During 1982 they worked experimentally with Sandy Pearlman, a distinguished American who had produced the Clash and many other ranking bands. The experience was enjoyable and fruitful; Pearlman was artistically imaginative and big enough for the job. In the end, however, they called Steve Lillywhite, for reasons that had as much to do with his personality as his brilliance on the sound desk. Steve *understood*. He *knew* how vulnerable U2 were and what their greatest gifts were. He felt that he could do a real job with them this time and welcomed the chance to have another go.

While Bono went off on his honeymoon to Jamaica, most of which was spent working on the album, Edge stayed in Malahide struggling with something even more important. Of them all Edge had the toughest, brightest, clearest mind. He was a realist, rigorous most of all with himself. He was deeply disturbed by the compromise achieved between Christianity and rock 'n' roll. It was himself that he was questioning. He admired Larry's decisiveness. Larry had made the right decision —for himself. Now Edge felt he must make a choice. It wasn't a matter of emotion, it was a question he must resolve intellectually, rationally, without lying to himself. Was there a *logical* solution rather than an expedient one? Had he tried to have his cake and eat it?

Edge decided that his professed beliefs must be followed through all the way. The rational, logical conclusion was to get out of rock 'n' roll *now*. When Bono came back, Edge told him of his decision. For a week the new crisis lingered, no one quite believing what they heard or daring to disbelieve too much. Edge had faced himself. The confrontation lasted several days. Finally his intellect and emotions were reconciled. He picked up his guitar, played around with his boxes and in an afternoon poured everything into some of the finest rock 'n' roll ever composed. 'Sunday Bloody Sunday' was Edge's music. Bono provided words and Adam and Larry their own contributions. Like all U2 music this song was to a degree a band composition. But in essence 'Sunday Bloody Sunday' was a tough, bold, declaratory statement issued by a man who had discovered something about himself. About himself yes, but more profoundly, through his own prolonged anguish, Edge had discovered, figured out, *reasoned*, a philosophical proposition: that you couldn't detach the mind from the spirit. That Christianity without life was as empty as life without Christianity. That those who sought to force a choice, who demanded you sacrifice one for the other, were wrong. You could surrender your spirit without losing your mind. Fanaticism, religious and political, demanded that you surrendered one or the other. Part of this was 'Sunday Bloody Sunday's' declaration, to Bono, Adam and Larry, to Paul, to the Fellowship, to the world. Edge had defined *his* Christianity. 'Religion Bloody Religion' was the result.

'Sunday Bloody Sunday' can be interpreted as a reference to other incidents in Irish history; Croke Park in 1920 when, during a hurling match, the British Black and Tans (from the land of Edge's and Adam's birth) slaughtered innocent people in retaliation for war crimes committed that morning by the IRA, who provoked the vengeance by murdering British officers in their beds. There was a Bloody Sunday in Derry in 1971 when thirteen innocent civilians were shot dead by the British army's Parachute Regiment. And of course the 'war' in

Northern Ireland was still proceeding along its evil path when U2 wrote 'Sunday Bloody Sunday'. But the music and the lyrics finally produced, after collaboration with Bono, Adam and Larry, are, one might reasonably conclude, a broader reflection on Ireland and the world.

The battle constantly referred to in this song is personal:

> But I won't heed the battle call.
> It puts my back up, puts my back up against the wall.

That back might have been Edge's. Or Larry's. Or Bono's. Or Adam's, or Paul's. It might indeed be the back of any Irish man or woman on a Sunday Bloody Sunday when the Churches beckon, when you are identified, divided, hated, loved, dismissed, despised or merely patronized according to where you pray to your God.

Over angry, powerful music Bono sings:

> And the battle's just begun,
> There's many lost, but tell me who has won?
> The trenches, dug within our hearts,
> And mothers, children, brothers, sisters torn apart.
> Sunday, Bloody Sunday.

The Irish Troubles, to which this classic rock song is commonly thought to refer, had *not* 'just begun'. They were hundreds of years old. What *had* just begun in the lives of its composers was a different 'battle': the battle to reconcile their spiritual beliefs with their worldly endeavours. In Bono's childhood there lay the experience of Sunday Bloody Sunday when Bobby went to one church, he, Norman and Iris to another:

> The trenches, dug within our hearts,
> And mothers, children, brothers, sisters torn apart.

'Sunday Bloody Sunday's' final stanza offers a perspective

from which to reflect on Ireland, religion and most significantly of all, perhaps, on U2.

> *The real battle just begun,*
> *To claim the victory Jesus won,*
> *On a Sunday, Bloody Sunday,*
> *Sunday, Bloody Sunday.*

There *is* no definitive interpretation of an artistic achievement as immense as this U2 song. There are many other images to reflect upon in 'Sunday Bloody Sunday' and it is necessary to draw on them all to share the riches that are there. But of all the songs on what was to become the *War* album, this is the one that was most complete when U2 joined Steve Lillywhite in Windmill Lane.

Bono had always been generous to journalists – with his time. He was voluble, willing to talk stream-of-consciousness fashion for hours at a time, but the net result was like the music he wrote, impressionistic. Sometimes his words read as babble. He was curious about everything and everybody, including those who came to interview him. His impulses were generous, but the chameleon avoided clear-cut statements, didn't like to be pinned to the spot. His articulation of what 'Sunday Bloody Sunday' was 'about' is a perfect illustration of his public relations technique. Liam Mackey from *Hot Press*, one of Dublin's best young journalists, went to the cottage in Howth where Bono and Ali lived, to talk about *War*. They talked until dawn. After reading the 2,000-word profile-interview that came out of the meeting, it is hard to state precisely where the subject stands – on anything. Observing that many people have misunderstood 'Sunday', Bono attempts to outline his view on the Northern Troubles:

I mean, as much as I'm a republican, I'm not a very territorial person. The whole idea of the white flag [U2 now waved on stage] was to get away from Green, White and Orange, to get away from Stars and Stripes, to get away from the Union Jack. I am an Irishman and we are an Irish group – stop! But I'm frightened of borders, frightened of restrictions on those levels and I get scared when people start saying they're prepared to kill to back their belief in where a border should be. I mean I'd love to see a United Ireland but just don't believe you can put a gun to somebody's head at anytime to make him see your way. 'Sunday Bloody Sunday' is a day that no Irishman can forget, but *should* forget, which is what we were saying – 'How long must we sing this song?' When I introduce it I say, 'This isn't a rebel song.' The name comes up all the time and we're saying, 'How long must we have songs *called* "Sunday Bloody Sunday".' That's one area in which I agree with Bob Geldof – 'History is just one mistake after another.'

Read very carefully, a few times, a substantive point emerges from this statement; Irishmen *should* forget Bloody Sundays. But there are contradictions cloaking this central point, if it *is* the point, for example, being 'a republican' has connotations in an Irish context. If you are a republican you are very much in favour of the Green, White and Orange flag and the people putting the guns to people's heads *are* the Irish *Republican* Army. If you claim that you would 'love a united Ireland' you must accept that this aspiration is a denial of identity to those one million Protestants in the north of Ireland who emphatically *wouldn't* like to see a united Ireland. Which is why there are Bloody Sundays in the first place. In all of this the real richness and diversity of a marvellous song is lost in the proselytizing which is little more than well-meaning rhetoric, devoid of intellectual rigour.

War was not a concept album, more a concept title. The image was strong, aggressive, masculine, depicting its creators as more than the introverted mystics, the good, intense young men of their two previous albums. *War* looked out. It was grown up. The new album was as traumatic to record in studio as its predecessors, the lyrics as always presenting the major problem.

Bono was a restless perfectionist, never satisfied that the mix was right, always pushing, driving for more, questioning every line, every note, every sound effect. He was chasing the song in his head and never seemed content that he'd found it in the studio. He was hard on everyone, but hardest on himself. His creative process was painful and complex, the lyrics a final, never-quite-right compound of the emotions, images and sounds with which he began. First, the *feeling*. Then, the *image*. Followed by a melody, laid over sound. All of this tortuously converted into lyrics, rock 'n' roll poetry that in his own mind rarely served fully to tell the tale. On *War* he got closer than ever before to resolving this problem. With Edge on 'Sunday', on 'Surrender' and on 'Two Hearts Beat as One' (the album's single), the lyrics are more literate than they've been before, the metaphor more self-assured. 'Surrender' bears witness to the lingering doubts about the rock 'n' roll life, the threat of fame and ego. The protagonist is Sadie, but it might be Bono:

> *Sadie said she couldn't*
> *Work out what it was all about*
> *And so she let go.*
> *. . . . .*
> *She tried to be a good girl*
> *And a good wife,*
> *Raise a good family*
> *Lead a good life.*
> *It's not good enough.*
> *She got herself up on the 48th floor,*
> *Got to find out, find out*
> *What she's living for.*
> *Surrender, Surrender.*
> *Surrender, Surrender.*

The essential demand of Shalom's Christianity was that one surrendered one's spirit to God. To surrender self, ego, fame. But as the singer explains in 'Surrender's' closing lines,

> *The city's a fire,*
> *A passionate flame*
> *That knows me by name.*
> *The city's desire*
> *To take me for more, and more.*
> *It's in the street getting under my feet,*
> *It's in the air, it's everywhere I look for you,*
> *It's in the things I do and say,*
> *But if I want to live I've got to die to myself too some day.*

It is fame. *It* is ego. *You* is God. And if any Christian wanted to 'live' he would have to 'die' and be re-born.

War closes with Psalm 40, a stirring chant that has become the evocative farewell to U2 concert-goers over the years. 'How long to sing this song?' '40' pleads. The line is from the Bible and 'Sunday Bloody Sunday'. It could be applied to any person, country or circumstances. Universal, eclectic, evoking everything and yet substantiating no particular political or religious point of view, '40' is quintessential U2, the essence of Bono, at least.

Embroidered by Steve Wickham's electric violin, Kenny Fradley's trumpet and Kid Creole's backing singers, the Coconuts, *War* was a major rock 'n' roll album, sophisticated, complex and much more mature than anything previously contemplated by the band. Edge's overall contribution was identified by the ever-perceptive Bill Graham who, writing in *Hot Press*, defined U2 on *War* as 'The Edge Orchestra'.

War, with its songs like 'Sunday' and 'New Year's Day', ostensibly about Poland and Solidarity, filled a gap in the rock 'n' roll market. While other contenders ignored such things U2 were deemed to be taking a stance politically. This was an illusion. *War*, like all U2 music thus far, was rooted in the emotions, had to do with personal experience rather than political or social commentary. In 'Two Hearts Beat as One' this is bluntly and honestly declared in the opening lines:

> *I don't know.*
> *I don't know which side I'm on,*
> *I don't know my right from my left,*
> *Or my right from wrong.*

On taking sides, the song continues:

> *I don't know*
> *How to say what's got to be said,*
> *I don't know if it's black or white,*
> *There's others see it red.*

War won critical acclaim when it was released in March 1983. Rock writers felt that this was a significant advance for a band destined to be a force in the business. This short review in the respected London magazine, *Time Out*, is, in both tone and content, a perfect précis of critical reaction worldwide:

A marvellous third offering from the Dublin-based foursome and, as singer Bono has made clear in press pronouncements, this is 'the one', not only the band's most assured performance to date but also a bid for massive commercial success. Cue for introduction of electric violin, horns and more complex production, not to mention Kid Creole's Coconuts as vocal backup and a toned down act for 'TOTP'. A process of, ah, sophistication which, thankfully, in no way detracts from U2's power. While Bono's voice seems occasionally to strain in the upper registers and there's nothing here to match the sheer devotional joy of 'I Will Follow' or 'Rejoice', *War* contains their most impressive songs yet. Witness the attack of 'Sunday Bloody

Sunday', no rebel song but a forthright reflection on the tragedy
of Northern Ireland, the thrilling bass-line on 'New Year's
Day' and 'Surrender'. Urgent, political and melodic pop.
(Richard Rayner)

Steve Iredale wasn't around when the band recorded *War*.
He had gone home to Kiltimagh, Co. Mayo, to fall apart. Steve
joined the band as a general roadie in the summer of 1981
when they were making *October* in Windmill Lane. Just over a
year later he'd had enough. There was no way he was going
into that studio again. He'd had enough of studios after *October*.
He'd had enough of U2 now.

Steve was born in Kiltimagh in 1960. His family were
English, from Huddersfield in Yorkshire, and had come to
Mayo when his father took a job as an engineer in the local
woollen industry. The Iredales had lived in Kiltimagh along
with six other English families for four years when Steve was
born.

Steve was sent to a mixed boarding-school at Wilson's
Hospital in Multyfarnham near Mullingar when he was eleven.
Six years later he left with honours in English, geography and
science. He'd always been a music fan, particularly fond of
Horslips. He met up with them while still at school and travelled to the odd gig, helping out as a trainee roadie during his
last year in Multyfarnham. He was a bright, pleasant, resourceful lad whom Michael Deeny, Barry Devlin and their
Horslips colleagues were glad to have around. When the band
went touring in the States Steve went off to look for work. He
would like to have gone to university but he was the youngest
of four, all of whom had been expensively put through school.
The money for university wasn't there.

Ireland had no use for its bright, educated, resourceful young
people when Steve came to Dublin looking for work in the
summer of 1977. He tried Aer Lingus and R T E without either
luck or encouragement. He bummed around farms in the

Midlands and worked for a jeweller in Portarlington. Finally he secured the Good Job we dream about for our children, trainee manager in Burgerland in O'Connell Street. For the first time in his life Steve committed himself to a job. Hamburgers looked promising. He kept in touch with Horslips when they were in town. But music was a dream, glimpsed on the occasional trip to Grafton Street where the scene was happening.

Burgerland burnt down in 1978 and Steve was out of his long hours, badly paid Good Job. That night, consoling himself in the Bailey, the scene's 'in' pub, he met Pat Maguire, Horslips' crew boss. He was offered the roadie's job with Deeny's band. When Horslips split two years later, Steve had proved his worth. He'd risen to the responsible position of sound man-cum-tour manager. He was twenty.

Along the way Steve met up with U2. Horslips' PA system was being serviced in McGonagles and U2 were being used to do the job. They were different, Steve observed. He could say precisely why: other bands around basically accepted what you told them. That's an amp, that's the mike, here's your sound. Now go. U2 questioned everything. They were a bit of a pain in the arse. But he respected them, even though he knew that they weren't quite sure what they were looking for out of the equipment. He noticed Paul McGuinness too. For one thing, McGuinness was always *there*. Most managers only appeared at pay-up time, but Paul was nosing around before and during the show. One night in the Baggot stuck in Steve's mind. Normally the monitors on stage, the sound boxes, were turned towards the audience. Here Bono, Edge and Adam had reversed the process, turning the monitors towards themselves. Larry wanted his turned as well. McGuinness wanted to know why. He asked Steve. This band takes nothing for granted, it would appear, Steve replied. Every time I see them they're trying *something* new.

Joe O'Herlihy. (*Colm Henry*)

Frank Barsalona of Premier Talent backstage. (*Donna Silverman*)

Bono: from *Boy* to man. (*Donna Silverman* and *Colm Henry*)

TOP Larry and Adam, off duty, as themselves.
ABOVE LEFT Larry the rock star. ABOVE RIGHT Adam in the wilderness.
(*Anton Corbijn*) (*Anton Corbijn*)
BELOW LEFT Dave Evans. (*Colm Henry*) BELOW RIGHT Edge. (*Anton Corbijn*)

Bono and Ali. (*Anton Corbijn*)   Aislinn Evans. (*Conor Hogan*)

Garret Fitzgerald and wife Joan visit Windmill Lane before the Irish general election in 1982. U2 was recording the *War* album. (*Myles Byrne*)

ABOVE LEFT Anne-Louise Kelly.   ABOVE RIGHT Steve Iredale.

                                       BELOW RIGHT Barbara Galavan.

BELOW LEFT Dennis Sheehan. (*Dionne Eskolin*)   BOTTOM RIGHT Tom Mullally.

Edge at Slane Castle during the *Unforgettable Fire* recording. (*Colm Henry*)

Bono, Edge and Brian Eno at Slane. (*Colm Henry*)

Edge entertains Eno in Malahide.

U2 then ... (*Adrian Boot* and *Colm Henry*)

. . . and now. (*Anton Corbijn*)

Larry and Ann. (*Colm Henry*)

Larry at home with jukebox and labrador J.J.
(*Colm Henry*)

Ready for a day's biking.
(*Colm Henry*)

ABOVE Happiness is working for the best rock 'n' roll band in the world. Tom, Timmy, Joe and Larry's new roadie Sammy O'Sullivan on stage at Edinburgh, July 1987. (*Eddie O'Hare*)
BELOW Bono and Edge with film director Neil Jordan during the making of *Redhill Mining Town* video in spring '87. (*Anton Corbijn*)

Rock 'n' roll 1987. (*Colm Henry*)

Seeing them some months later at a gig in the Stardust Ballroom, headlined by the Greedy Bastards, Steve noticed the impressive result of U2's experiments. The Greedy Bastards represented class, featuring people like Phil Lynott, Gary Moore and Steve Jones from the Sex Pistols in an ever-changing combination. In such illustrious company U2 more than pulled their weight.

Just as he noticed them, U2 and McGuinness spotted Steve. Choosing people to work for you was vital. U2 went for intelligence, a capacity for hard work, someone who got the job done, not someone who told you why it couldn't be done. They didn't hire dopeheads, loudmouths or poseurs. Decency mattered. Deeny and Devlin confirmed U2's impression of Iredale. He started as a roadie on the making of *October*. It was a tense time. Nobody worked harder than the band. If anyone did it was the new roadie. He served alone. Joe O'Herlihy was home in Cork with Marion and the boys. The road crew that worked on the *Boy* tour were English and now off the payroll. It was Steve who made the tea, went out for food, moved gear around the studio; Steve who got the fifteen sheets of galvanized iron to throw around the studio for sound effects on 'Brick Through a Window'. He went for chipboard for some other song; bought new percussion instruments for Larry; put the chairs in the hallway at Windmill to hold the tin that Lillywhite and Larry ended up using when the new percussion kit didn't work. Steve picked visitors up at the airport, and dropped them back out the next day. He ran errands for mothers, brothers and dads. And then he went out for fish and chips at three a.m. Then he started to get pissed off. But he stuck it.

Through the *October* tour, shifting beds, fetching Cokes, looking after friends, doing a bit of back-line, Steve's resentment grew. He always got things done, but this was no way to live. He was proud, well-educated, smart and confused.

He liked the band, respected the organization, was excited, inspired by the music. He knew that *everyone* had to serve the band, knew that in the end U2 was about the performance and the creativity of the four lads. They had to be cosseted, protected, looked after, for theirs was the biggest burden of the lot and *everybody* – Paul, Joe, Pod, and now Dennis and anyone else who went out on the road or into a studio – *had* to work towards the ideal, for the people who made everything possible. He knew it, but Steve didn't like his part in it, the role in which he'd been – unthinkingly, he felt – cast.

Before the *War* recording he went absent without leave. He didn't shout or fight, just got lost. He was missed and sent for. Bono and Edge talked with him in the cottage in Howth one day. He poured it out, all of it. He asked to be fired or given a position of real responsibility. Paul McGuinness stayed out of it and Steve resented that. McGuinness took the view that who they had working closely with them was ultimately the band's decision. He could be a ruthless delegator. He didn't interfere, one way or the other. That was tough. Not mean or sly or uncaring, but tough-minded, a quality that existed at the core of the thing called U2. Compassion was indulged everywhere – except at work. And that applied to everyone, Paul, Adam, Larry, Edge and Bono most of all.

Steve Iredale was appointed stage manager for the *War* tour.

As U2 were finishing the album a general election was taking place in the real world outside. Garret Fitzgerald was the liberal democratic candidate leading the Opposition Fine Gael party. A few months before, Bono and Fitzgerald had met at London airport when the singer introduced himself as both were waiting for the Dublin plane. Both voluble and well meaning, Bono and the politician hit it off on the journey home. The story made the Irish newspapers. Dan Egan, Fitzgerald's clever aide-de-camp and Fine Gael's press officer, didn't miss a trick. His leader's image as an absent-minded if somewhat garrulous professor needed a populist streak. Bono served. Egan set up a photo-call during the election campaign. Fitzgerald, accompanied by his wife, Joan, visited Windmill Lane to encourage his rock-idol friend. The pictures that resulted of the two garrulous national heroes in conversation were eagerly grasped by desperate news editors and splashed on every front page in the country. Fitzgerald was elected Taoiseach the following week.

Chapter Fifteen

RESPECT

If there had been a doubt about U2, it was to do with the band's ability to make hit records. Nobody doubted U2's capacity for hard work or the quality of their live rock 'n' roll show. With *War* U2 proved themselves capable of producing accomplished commercial albums and were thus real contenders, deserving the respect of all in the rock 'n' roll business. Island Records and Premier Talent had, it now seemed, backed a winner. U2 set out on their *War* tour in spring 1983 bearing new responsibilities. They were no longer a baby band admired for good intentions and hard work. The informed view in rock 'n' roll was that Paul McGuinness's band stood a real chance of becoming the next big thing.

There comes a point in great artists' careers when the qualities that distinguish them from their peers become assets rather than reasons why they will 'never be big'. U2's time was 1983. The big acts in the UK business, Depeche Mode, the Human League, Gary Numan and A Flock of Seagulls, were setting new trends using video technology and synthesizers to create images and music. Rock 'n' roll was changing. The old idea of 'breaking' a band on the road was passé in the 1980s. Hit records and videos and a single image were the routes favoured by ambitious rock bands and their managers. Touring the way U2's strategy demanded took too long, was too much hard work and was much more expensive. Live rock was a touch old-fashioned. Until *War*, U2 were considered not smart for choosing the long, hard, expensive route to the summit. Post-*War* they were respected for doing so.

The success of *War* had not brought wealth to U2. Profits from the album equalled Island Records investment on *Boy* and *October* and the tour support that went with that commitment. Like Frank Barsalona's Premier Talent, Chris Blackwell's Island had been a source of support and encouragement. Real money would come at the next level of growth to which U2 now aspired. The strategy conceived by Michael Deeny and Horslips, applied to his baby band by Paul McGuinness, was based on steady growth. It took you so far, but after that, in the area U2 were now in, strategy became less important than talent and the hunger to go all the way. Lots of bands were hungry for success, enough to satisfy themselves that they'd 'made it', to prove those who'd junked them on the way *wrong*. Only the great bands *stayed* hungry once the world was convinced of their talent. For the few, the Beatles, the Stones and The Who, the trick was proving it to themselves. They weren't hungry for success, they were starving for greatness, believing that they were the best, not merely one of the best. It wasn't about money or hit records. It wasn't even about being respected in the business, although that was nice. The hunger that drove the great bands forward and upwards had to do with self-respect, with closing the gap between success and what you knew you could achieve, the music and performance you knew was still within you.

It was clear when U2 hit the road with the *War* album that the band was hungrier than ever. They played a twenty-seven-date, sold-out tour of Britain before arriving in the United States to begin a three-month crusade in April. The fervour with which U2 embarked on this tour made the word crusade appropriate.

Tom Mullally came from Cork. He'd been around the music scene for a few years. Tom started out working for Joe O'Herlihy in the sound man's P A company in Cork. He knew nothing about music or the business to begin with. But he was a good worker, a quick learner and as tough-minded and independent as his red head of hair suggested. Tom had done a dozen jobs, including a spell in the Irish army as a military policeman. That lasted six months. On the rock 'n' roll scene he drifted from Cork to Dublin, ending up in 1983 with a band called Sweet Savage, who were good enough to support Phil Lynott and Thin Lizzy on an English tour. Tom was doing the back-line. Lynott and Lizzy shocked him. There were drugs, heavy stuff, girls and fights. The girls were exploited. So were the crew. Drink was a day-long sickness. This was rock 'n' roll the way the wicked legend depicted it. Tom was a game lad, he had the normal appetites and tastes. He was twenty-three. But he hated the sleaze, the sheer soullessness of the Lizzy scene, the badness of it. There was no dignity. He did his job, honestly and well.

After the tour Lynott sacked his crew. They'd had a row over money. Tom was invited to join Lizzy. It was a shot at the big time, a way forward and, maybe, out. Tom ignored his instincts and accepted the offer. Fuck it, it's a chance. Two days after he started, he quit. Lizzy were only at rehearsals in Dublin, but the vibe was desperate.

Joe O'Herlihy had used Tom for U2 gigs down the years. There was a possibility of something permanent coming up. The *War* album had hit and U2 needed another body on the road. Tom got the job for the *War* tour. The choice had nothing to do with Cork and friendship. It was about the work that had to be done, the hours that had to be put in and being able to resist temptation. If you were serious, as Joe was, as Rory Gallagher had been, and as Tom's prospective employers were, you hated the sleaze. Rock 'n' roll was work. Tom Mullally, Joe assured the band, was a worker.

Paul McGuinness was thirty-two. He would soon be celebrating five years in the rock business. This had to a large extent been an endurance test, but sitting on the tour bus as U2 rode the freeways from North Carolina to Denver, Los Angeles to New York, Paul drew immense personal satisfaction from the scene around him. His modest suburban home in Ranelagh was still his office. He was not rich or even prosperous yet. But U2 the concept had grown into something worthy of the respect it now enjoyed. The religious thing was, he felt, over, certainly no longer a threat to the band. *War* proved that the excitement generated by live U2 performances wasn't their only weapon. The gap between studio and stage had been a legitimate cause of much concern. Paul too had wondered. *War* was the antidote to such doubts. Now he knew that they could make albums that were sophisticated, commercial *and* still faithful to their experiences, Paul felt there was no way they could fail. Yes, he could see the attractions of using video and hit singles to break through, certainly in terms of the quality of your life, but touring, although longer, harder and more expensive, was safer, and when the hit record did come your support was much more firmly based.

The crew serving the band was another source of pleasure and reassurance for McGuinness now. Dennis Sheehan, Joe O'Herlihy, Steve Iredale and Tom Mullally shared U2's attitudes to the rock 'n' roll business. That they were Irish wasn't that important, although it was pleasing. What really mattered was the enthusiasm, intelligence and professionalism that Dennis, Joe, Steve and Tom added to the U2 cause. Dennis was tour manager and as such the boss on the road. Paul the ruthless delegator had assured Sheehan that he and the band would comply with the tour manager's decisions about how they travelled, where they stayed and how much they spent. The tour budget was Sheehan's responsibility. Ellen Darst was another valuable professional acquisition for the formidable organization McGuinness was building around the band. Ellen was an ambitious, experienced woman who knew the American music business from the inside out. She too lent intelligence and conviction to the cause.

The cause was not *War*. Although this was the *War* tour and ostensibly *about* promoting the album, that was not how the strategy worked. This tour was *about* the future, the *next* album, not the one just made. That's the way U2 had always worked; by firing up people who first saw them in some small club or college venue, and by always looking forward, never back to where they'd been. Looking forward in spring 1983, Paul McGuinness was preoccupied by two ideas. He wanted to produce a U2 video that would capture the excitement of the band's live shows, and he wanted to re-negotiate their deal with Island Records which required them to make two more albums for a £50,000 advance with the moderate royalty deal they had to accept when Bill Stewart signed them after the Stadium three years ago. It hadn't been about money then but more the opportunity to grow and develop. Now that the band had grown and developed to potential greatness the money began to matter more. Freed of the more onerous tour duties by Dennis Sheehan, Paul reflected on his plans as U2 floated through small-town America.

U2 celebrated Bono's twenty-third birthday after the show at Yale University in New Haven, Connecticut. They had had some champagne and a few beers after the show. The party continued on the bus which was heading towards New York where they were due at the Palladium the following night. In business Paul was obsessively formal, as meticulous as he'd been about his boyhood rituals, whether giving presents or collecting rocks. His meetings with the band were proper, mannered almost. The other side of Paul appeared at parties when the business was done and it was time to relax. At the proper time. Then Paul was gregarious, emotional, occasionally indiscreet, the degree to which he had to discipline himself to be Paul McGuinness, manager, being reflected in the uninhibited pleasure he took from socializing. Good company and a few drinks were the safety valves out of which relief poured. Correct was the word most often used about McGuinness the manager. He could be just as convincingly laid-back when it was time to relax.

New Haven brought back memories to those celebrating Bono's birthday. U2 had played Toad's Place in the town eighteen months before on the first leg of the *October* tour. For many reasons, personal and professional, tensions were then high between the members of the band. Bono was carrying the strain more than anyone. For months he had been uptight about everything, including the music being played behind him. He'd turn and glare at Larry, Edge or Adam if a drum pattern changed or a guitar deviated from the line. He was hyper the last time they played New Haven. Towards the end of the gig Larry's snare-stand broke. All Bono knew was that Larry had stopped playing. He forgot about audience and performance and turned, enraged, to find Larry grinning sheepishly. Bono charged, hurling his awkward bulk at the drummer, who took evasive action by jumping off backstage. Bono kicked the drum-kit over. As it crashed around the stage the audience roared approval. They thought this was part of the show. Bono ran after Larry. As he got to the rim of the stage Edge reached out and grabbed him by the hair. The guitarist rarely lost his cool, but now the Welsh passion so slowly roused boiled over and raged at Bono. Edge wanted to kick the singer's head in. Pod prevented that. Bono stayed out all night. The anger drained away to be replaced by the remorse he expressed when he came home at breakfast-time. They laughed and put it down to pressure and the dangers of unreliable snare stands. Success had now increased the pressure, especially on Bono. The venues were bigger, more people came to watch, and U2 shows were big news wherever they played. The most respected critics came to judge one of the most respected bands. The responsibilities were greater now than they had ever been.

Those who said that Bono *was* U2 were absolutely wrong. But live, for that hour every night, Bono was the point of contact between audience and band. His ability to perform, to give voice and physical expression to the anguish, joy, anger, pain and optimism in the music was what made U2's live shows unique. He knew it, Adam, Edge and Larry knew it. And loved him for the courage he revealed every time he went on stage. He wasn't smooth, it didn't always work, there was embarrassment and sometimes downright shame while they waited for the audience to respond, to come to them, to join the U2 celebration. Nothing was spared to ensure that this moment arrived sooner or later every night. They'd always cared, now, going into 10,000-seat arenas, U2 cared more than ever. It was Bono's job and he thought about it all day.

The band's working day began in mid-afternoon with the sound check. Some other bands, especially those with hit albums, flew through the sound check, relying on the crew to get things right. But each venue was different and U2 knew from too many bad experiences as a support band how important it was to prepare in the afternoons. Joe O'Herlihy would set up the equipment and test it throughout the day. The band would then fine-tune it to their liking. Bono would enter the empty arena in the afternoon from the back, from the punters' angle. He would look and listen to check that everyone who paid could see and hear. Especially those up in the 'nosebleeds' with the cheapest tickets. Was there a pillar in the way and why? Did that monitor on stage block the view in Row 93? Move it. The monitor, that is. Sound was a funny thing, no ear heard the same sound alike, no machine ever invented could gauge exactly right. The human ear, *his* human ear, was Joe's guide. Bono and Larry would double-check. Adam and Edge would be on stage tinkering with the machines, adjusting here and there. Everyone worked for a couple of hours, making sure the show was set up.

Bono would now be scouting routes for his nightly plunge into the audience. Emotionally, his spectacular journeys through theatres were trips into the unknown. Physically, he liked to know where he was going, and how he would get back to the stage. No other rock 'n' roll performer had ever ventured out the way Bono did. He had always engaged the audience physically. In a small club it was simple, a matter of eye contact or stepping from the stage. But as the venues got bigger, the task of breaking down the physical barrier between musician and ticket-buyer became harder. It was this Bono was after, the Iggy Pop concept of oneness between audience and star taken further, given more meaning. Bono's trips were symbolic, but none the less vital for that. They were, too, a variation on the born-again belief, the breaking of artificial barriers. Bono's adventures along balconies, into stalls, up scaffolding, along routes that no rock star had dared to travel before, were spectacular, a guarantee that U2 would be re-membered, that the show, this show, on this night, in this arena, *every night*, would be special.

Steve Iredale or Dennis Sheehan helped Bono plot his route. Steve was doing Bono's mike lead and would accompany him wherever he went. At each venue Steve would check for possible routes. What doors needed to be opened? How big was the drop off that balcony? Was that scaffolding safe? How will Bono get back to the stage? Bono was scared of heights, but when he was performing he was lost, unaware of anything except the emotions he was transmitting and receiving from the people he was playing to. He usually started travelling on 'Electric Co.', a surging, angry guitar-led rock song written in the early days about a friend of his treated by electro-convulsive therapy in a Dublin mental institution. As soon as he heard the opening riffs, Steve Iredale got ready. He was never sure where he was going or what would happen. Bono had lost his balance a few times, fortunately landing on his feet. The microphone cable had wrapped around his neck once, almost choking him. But he kept singing, driven by some manic instinct to touch people in a way they'd never been touched before. On the *War* tour Bono carried a white flag through the halls, a symbol of peace to soften the image of violence painted by the album's title. This made his forays more dangerous than ever.

At the Queen Elizabeth Hall in Vancouver, things almost went seriously wrong. There was scaffolding running off the balcony that looked as if it reached to the floor. It didn't: two feet beneath the balcony it stopped. Bono stepped out. There was nothing between him and the concrete floor twenty feet below. Everyone assumed that the performer knew what he was doing. Only he and Steve felt the sickening fear when the void appeared. Steve grabbed his belt and hung on as Bono's heavy body swung over the audience below. There was no dignified way back but somehow, still rocking and prancing, holding his white flag aloft, Bono made it back to the stage.

Concern was growing among band and crew at the hysteria Bono was generating in the theatre each night. He would hurt himself, or someone else. What would happen if one of the kids, pilled up, drunk or merely carried away by the proximity of a hero, decided to follow Bono's example? There would be no Steve or Dennis to help *him* or *her*. Dennis voiced the crew's worries before U2 played the US Festival in San Bernardino in May. This event was to last three days at an open-air site in the desert. U2 were due to play the second day. The Clash would play the day before, David Bowie the closing day. A quarter of a million people were expected. Hysteria was guaranteed, it wouldn't have to be generated. Dennis Sheehan was worried, really worried. He went out the day before to check the site. The stage was mounted on scaffolding that ran six storeys high. A plastic canopy stretched across the top. This was the kind of vantage-point Bono would want to occupy, especially with all those people to reach out to. The promoters said no climbing. Dennis conveyed the instruction. Bono started climbing anyway. Steve and Dennis, frightened but committed to staying with him, followed. At the top Bono turned and triumphantly saluted the teeming crowds below. The previous day the Clash had announced that they were performing under duress. The British band had had a row with promoter Steve Wozniak over money. U2 had made it clear where they stood at the beginning of their set. 'Nobody twisted *my* arm, I *wanted* to be here,' Bono declared when the band reached the stage. The populist tone was set. Now, six storeys up, messiah greeted multitude. Bono set off to cross the canvas to descend on the other wing of the scaffolding. Dennis Sheehan was angry. Suddenly the canopy began to tear under Bono's weight. Dennis, who hadn't dared add to the strain by following Bono all the way, had a dreadful vision as the singer crawled back to safety. Bono and Ali had been married less than a year. Suppose something happened on an escapade such as this? Ali would be wheeling Bono around in a chair for the rest of their lives. It was madness and Sheehan was determined to stop it.

Dennis hit Bono hard in the dressing-room-trailer afterwards. He had no right to take these risks. It was irresponsible, unnecessary, crazy stuff. Paul McGuinness intervened, a rare occurrence at the nightly inquest. Dennis was being a bit hard. No, Dennis insisted. He loved U2, loved what they were about, loved the feeling they put into their music. He, who'd seen it all with Zeppelin, loved what people got from U2. He knew it was real, a desire to give, to join with the people out there. But Bono should be beyond this stuff. People didn't come for that anymore. They came for the *music*. It *was* great music. Bono didn't have to go to the audience. They would come to him. He didn't *need* it anymore. Dennis spoke as an old pro, a serious guy. The room went quiet. The point was made.

Four days later, U2 arrived at Red Rocks, ten miles outside Denver. While playing Denver during the *October* tour, Paul and the band had gone sightseeing to Red Rocks, a spectacular configuration of sandstone boulders that jut out from the earth, forming a natural amphitheatre. Eight thousand feet up from Denver, itself one mile high, Red Rocks was used for summer concerts by many of the best contemporary American popular-music acts. Nine thousand people could picnic on a summer's day while listening to the concert.

Paul McGuinness had something more elaborate in mind. The Red Rocks site struck the film-maker in him as the perfect location for a U2 video. He could imagine Bono silhouetted against the skyline from a perch on one of the sandstone boulders. They would play a concert, shooting the video simultaneously and end up with dramatic film and a live U2 album, perhaps called *Under a Blood Red Sky*, after the dramatic ambience at Red Rocks. It was a brilliant idea but, because of the logistics of performing in this inaccessible place, expensive. U2 had £30,000 IR. in the kitty, which was nowhere near enough. McGuinness proposed a deal to Island Records and Feyline Presents, the local promoters, offering each a third of the profits in exchange for an investment of £50,000, one-third of the cost. Steve Lillywhite was brought in to produce the album and Gavin Taylor of *The Tube*, Independent Television's prestigious rock show, was asked to direct the video.

Red Rocks was U2's moment of truth. It represented a huge

financial gamble on one event: outdoors, logistically difficult, with expensive and cumbersome technology that could be rendered useless by the elements if things went wrong. Things went so wrong from the moment they arrived at Red Rocks as to be almost unbelievable. Three days before the show it began to rain. As the rain got heavier, a cold fog descended on the mountain. The day before the concert a tornado struck forty miles north of Denver. As they hauled the film and sound equipment across the muck, now ankle-deep on the site, the crew were hit with lashing rain, sleet and speckles of snow. It was the worst weather to hit Denver in June this century.

The band went up to the site the night before to sound check. The sandstone rocks emitted radio waves which complicated Joe O'Herlihy's and Steve Lillywhite's engineering. But larger problems began to manifest themselves. Those in charge of the sound and film technology wanted to quit this crazy place. Their equipment would be destroyed and with all that electrical cabling around, there was real danger of somebody dying. Paul McGuinness flew in from a business trip to New York the day before the concert. Kathy had come out from Dublin for the great occasion. Paul called Dennis Sheehan, Joe O'Herlihy, Steve Iredale and Steve Lillywhite to a meeting in his Denver hotel. He wanted to know the score. Barry Fey, the promoter, had also been away. Now he was back he wanted the whole thing called off. They could shoot their video indoors in Denver. Dennis Sheehan didn't believe in taking risks. He remembered Les Harvey and knew that talk of death around rock venues was not idle sensationalism. Now, however, he reassured McGuinness. He, Steve and Joe had checked everything out. They would have to do without some lighting and there was a risk that some sound equipment would be damaged by the heavy rain, but the site *was* safe. Lousy, demoralizing to work in, full of mud, cold and fucking wet, but nobody would die, except of pneumonia.

McGuinness now faced a choice. He could hang in there and hope that in this dreadful atmosphere people would travel from Denver to see the show and that U2 would play the kind of concert that would be memorable enough to showcase on video. His option was to cancel, haul the equipment off the mountain and settle for the kind of video more usually produced in the music business. There was no hint of equivocation in Paul's manner as he instructed his crew; provided it's safe to do so, we play the gig. If any production people complain about the weather, refer them to our contract and ask them where it says we only play on nice days.

The elements got worse on the day of the concert. Paul stayed away from Red Rocks, keeping to his hotel room in town. He put out a radio announcement promising a free U2 concert at the Colorado University Events Center the following night for anyone who missed the Red Rocks show because of the weather. This was a typical McGuinness response. The worse things got, the better he behaved. Offering the free show the following night hardly made his potential audience *more* likely to brave the elements. He risked having no audience at all to inspire his band. But the free concert was the honourable course to take even with his arse out the window for much more money than he had.

Kathy left him alone. He wouldn't discuss the crisis, he never discussed crises while they were happening. What was the point? Red Rocks was Paul's idea. Now it had become a massive gamble.

The band had stayed on site all day talking to their own crew, who were the only people there, apart from Lillywhite, who shared their determination to go on. As fans arrived, Bono, Adam, Edge and Larry splashed out through the muck and puddles to greet them. This might have been Criccieth in Wales six years ago, Bono reflected. He recalled that awful yet wonderful weekend when, drenched and hungry, sick and tired,

The Village had been escorted to the boat by a local Bobby. Disaster could be good for the spirit, if you survived and didn't buckle.

Eight thousand people came out to Red Rocks. U2 took the stage, the sun setting behind them, the towering sandstone rocks silhouetted on the skyline. This was not a concert but a gathering of people bonded by a moving sense of having faced and conquered adversity together. While U2 played their marvellous music – 'Gloria', 'I Will Follow', 'Sunday Bloody Sunday' and 'Electric Co.' – the euphoria of band and audience gripped at the throats of the hardened pros around the Red Rocks site. Rock 'n' roll was mostly fantasy, its heroism like its pain nothing more or less than a notion in a lyric. Rock 'n' roll was a grandiose illusion at best. But what they were doing here at Red Rocks was real. No video could do it justice. For Dennis, Joe, Steve and Tom this was what U2 was about, real people making real music. Kathy McGuinness watched the concert on a TV monitor under the stage, where Steve Lillywhite was recording the album. Halfway through, they knew Red Rocks had worked, as the mood seeped down to their damp little hole in the ground. Kathy and Steve felt like crying, but held off and smiled instead. Outside, five cameras captured the scene while a helicopter hovered, filming, above. Nobody could find Paul McGuinness. The rain had eased. And now Bono climbed on top of a boulder, steam rising from his soaked skin. He stood outlined against the darkening sky, lit by the propane torches set atop the rocks sending flames shooting skywards. McGuinness's imagined shot was now made life. He would have to watch the video to see it. For he *was* crying, tears of relief and pride, the private tears of a man wary of showing emotion to a hard old world.

As they made their way home, the eight-thousand cast of Red Rocks heroes echoed the sound of '40' which rang through the sandstone valley as they descended.

Doug Stewart, the American production coordinator at Red Rocks, was quoted in a local newspaper: 'I go to hundreds of concerts a year and I know no matter how many concerts I go to for the rest of my life there will never be another one where the interchange of energy between the audience and performers will ever be any stronger than it was at this show. It was just absolute magic.'

Red Rocks proved that the band were gutsy in the best rock 'n' roll tradition. This triumph over adversity underlined, once again, one of Paul McGuinness's greatest qualities, his courage. He hadn't lost his nerve when confronted by circumstances out of his control. As far as the future was concerned, something even more important became clear during the Red Rocks crisis. This was that Dennis Sheehan, Joe O'Herlihy, Steve Iredale, Tom Mullally, McGuinness and his band, had found the nucleus of a road crew as good at its job as the public heroes were at theirs. With nothing more than professional pride at stake, Dennis, Joe, Steve and Tom worked like dogs for three days enforcing U2 values on the hired Americans around them. Many of these veterans of the rock world were tough, phlegmatic characters not given to emotional involvement with the stars they served. Inspiration was not a factor in their lives. Yet bullied, cajoled and in the end respecting the genuine dedication of the Irish crew, the hired help pitched in to make the damn thing work. In the circumstances, winning this battle mattered as much as anything else that happened at Red Rocks. A new bond had been forged between U2 and those who until now had merely served. The original concept was expanded. U2 now consisted of more than four musicians and their manager. It was a small, watertight organization, founded at Red Rocks.

High on Red Rocks, the band set out on the final leg of the US tour. The question of Bono's invasions of audiences was still unresolved. The night of 17 June at the Los Angeles

Sports Arena placed the matter on the agenda again. On 'Electric Co.' Bono was off up the stairs behind the stage, around the balcony, white flag in one hand, radio mike in the other, with Dennis crawling behind. Bono was almost opposite the stage when a fist-fight broke out beside him. Someone grabbed for the flag. He climbed on the rim of the balcony threatening to jump if the fight didn't stop. It didn't. He jumped. The audience twenty feet below caught Bono. Dennis followed, landing on bodies. Madness erupted. Others jumped as their hero had just done. Nobody caught them. Bodies piled up on top of the seat, Bono's struggling underneath. He'd gone too far. The flag was ripped, hands clutched at the singer who, aided now by Dennis, was desperately trying to escape. As his shirt was ripped, Bono lashed out blindly with his fists. Someone hit back. Security arrived, scattering fans frightened by the hysterical scene. Adam, Edge and Larry kept 'Electric Co.' going as Dennis and the security men hustled Bono towards the stage. The white flag, torn, its pole snapped into tiny pieces, lay in the aisle, a casualty of the crazy scene. Emotions ran high in the dressing room afterwards.

Next morning the two Los Angeles daily newspapers raved about the show, reflecting the views of critics across the United States all through that spring and early summer. But both LA critics questioned the sense of Bono's crazy journey through the arena. That was not what U2 was about, they asserted, echoing Dennis Sheehan's stricture of some weeks before. Sheehan gave the reviews to Bono, who read everything written about U2, and hoped the message would at last sink in.

U2 returned to Dublin to headline A Day At The Races, a spectacular day-long concert before 25,000 people in the Phoenix Park. Simple Minds, the Eurythmics and Big Country featured also, but it was U2 that people really came to see. There was a wonderful sense of coming home among the travellers. Dublin was reality, Los Angeles and Red Rocks, places that one dreamed about even whilst you were there. It wasn't until you got home that you could measure your achievement, regain your sense of self and tot up the score. Edge had an even more personal reason for his feeling of well-being. He and Aislinn were to marry on 12 July. Remembered voices and familiar faces clogged the backstage area of the park. Dave Fanning, the archetypal Dubliner, unimpressed, cheerful, treating fame, achievement and success as the half-joke they were. Irreverence incarnate, Fanning was good for you. Bill Graham, smiling, disorganized, sweating slightly, was another reminder, another way of gauging what you were, how you felt, what it all amounted to. All the families came to the Park. Bobby Hewson, happy, cracking jokes, slightly pissed; Norman, erect, pleasant, proper, shaking his head now and then when, bemused, he thought of Paul-Bono; Jo Clayton, elegant, formidable, beginning to be convinced about U2; and Brian, quiet, amused, Cecilia and Larry Sr, taking the Fanning line on all of this, happy for Larry Jr, glad he was the *musician* he'd always wanted to be; Mr and Mrs Evans glowed with pride, Gwenda more than Garvin, who remained dignified through it all.

All of those who knew the U2 story most intimately now gathered behind the stage trying hard to grasp the meaning of what they knew, what they could see before them in the gathering dusk of Dublin's historic, much loved park. How could you measure glory and acclaim on this scale? Did it *mean* anything at all or was it just combustion? It *was* exciting to see the crowds and hear the noise. But once the frenzy ceased it was impossible to answer rationally any of the questions prompted by this seemingly glorious day. The band had survived and matured, the young look had left their faces. There was a knowingness about the boys now that suggested they had been someplace different, tougher, more worldly than Dublin. The innocence was gone, self-sufficiency in its place.

Bono stilled the audience to dedicate a song to Thomas Reilly, the victim of a sectarian murder in Belfast the week before. Thomas's brother Jim was the drummer with the Belfast Band, Stiff Little Fingers, whose leader Jake Burns had held out hope for U2 when they'd sat forlornly in a van at Fishguard a lifetime ago. Bono sang 'I Fall Down'. After this, U2's public voice dragged his father, Bobby, from the wings and they danced before the old music-hall trouper's biggest audience yet. As people had at Red Rocks and halfway across the world, the crowd of 25,000 Dubliners left the Phoenix Park with the chant of '40' flowing through their minds. Backstage mayhem broke out as everyone tried to reach the drink, and the heroes who made it possible.

Chapter Sixteen

FIRE

Talking to Bill Graham immediately after the Phoenix Park concert, Bono declared that U2 had come to the end of a stage in their journey. It had taken six years to get from Mount Temple to the park. They began with nothing that could be said to matter in the rock 'n' roll business. Nothing at least that was deemed to have any value. Except for Larry, they really couldn't play their instruments. They had no consciousness of what had gone before them, no one, no band they wanted to ape, no sound, ethnic or contemporary, inspired the formation of U2. Musically there was no tradition nor was there, when you examined it closely, any real social, national or religious identity. U2 came from nowhere. As Steve Averill pointed out when suggesting the name U2, it was nebulous, abstract, universal, meaning whatever you wanted it to mean. *You too* was a pun on the times and the society the band grew up in. The name a brilliant, intuitive stroke, product identification *par excellence*.

Six years later, Adam, Edge, Larry and Bono had an identity; they were U2, soon to be honoured by *Rolling Stone* magazine as Our Choice: Band of the 80s. They projected an image of ordinariness. This was an emotional aspiration rather than a fact. Maybe they wanted to identify with their generation, but their backgrounds were too varied and distinct, their experience of life and the world too broad to allow them to fit comfortably into a social class or a national character.

U2 was an Irish band, a Dublin band. To some extent this was true, but not absolutely true. Adam was born near London of English middle-class parents. He grew up in the twilight world of boarding-schools as far removed from Dublin as you could be and still lay claim to citizenship. Edge was also born in the Home Counties of parents whose Welshness was as richly authentic twenty-five years after settling in Malahide as it was the day they arrived in Dublin. Bono was Irish, he insisted upon it and was entitled to. But half-Protestant cool, half-Catholic gauche, growing up in lower-middle-class Ballymun in the shadow of deprived, tower-block New Ballymun, Bono had identity problems like the others. He became the Great Chameleon, angel, lover, fighter, man of peace who co-wrote *War*. The man who aspired to a United Ireland, but wouldn't put a gun to anyone's head to achieve this Republican–Nationalist fantasy. Larry looked easier to categorize, straightforward Larry, shy of fame and therefore identified as a dumb blond. If rock 'n' roll was the tribal chant of the global village, Larry was the village idiot for wanting privacy, for insisting that *he* was a musician, a drummer, full stop. But ordinary? The story of Larry Sr and Maureen O'Rourke, the bright working-class man who bravely rejected the seminary after seven years and the sad–gay young woman living alone for most of her life – ordinary? Larry Jr's determination to be a drummer, to be the drummer *he wanted* to be, not the one they tried to make him be, to show that kind of spunk in Harmonstown Avenue where all the inclinations are to settle for anonymity – ordinary? To overcome the presumed shyness and announce yourself on the school notice-board? If U2 had a common denominator it was that nobody in the band truly belonged where they found themselves. Larry was no exception. Until he found U2.

Paul McGuinness, born on a Royal Air Force base in West Germany, was as uncannily displaced as the four young men he led into the rock 'n' roll jungle. His mother was from the Cork–Kerry border land. Her son fetched up in Dublin, a film director-producer manqué sitting in late-night drinking dens, dreaming of a baby band with which to take on the world of Jagger, Presley and Bowie. If you looked again at Steve Iredale, a Yorkshireman in Kiltimagh, Co. Mayo, or Dennis Sheehan, decent and responsible, from Dungarvan, Co. Waterford, veteran of Led Zeppelin and the mad excess of 1970s rock 'n' roll, you could see that they too were displaced, that Steve and Dennis only found what they were looking for in the thing called U2.

What had been established by the time U2 reached the Phoenix Park was that U2 existed. Existed in other people's minds. U2 was real, more than an imagined identity for the people belonging to the band. The success of *War*, the triumphant tour of America, the citadel of rock 'n' roll fame and true appreciation, and finally the glorious homecoming to the park and the kind of respect so grudgingly given by a city steeped in worldliness, these were the achievements that gave substance to U2, that made the band and those that served it feel that they were no longer displaced persons.

That was what Bono described as the end of U2 Mark I. After six years of struggle, personal and professional, after many battles, a major victory was now secured. U2 existed.

The following week Paul McGuinness interviewed Anne-Louise Kelly for a job that had no title but whose duties would come under the heading of PA. Anne-Louise was twenty-one, a young woman with a pretty, open, freckled face, petite, of high intelligence and pleasantly confident manner. She had been recommended to McGuinness by the director of her course in the College of Communications in Rathmines, which Anne-Louise had left a few weeks before. Her interview with Paul lasted less than ten minutes. He worked on instinct when it came to people, and Anne-Louise was offered a job she wasn't sure she wanted.

She had been born in Brighton on England's south coast. Her mother was English, from Eastbourne, her father an Irishman who practised and lectured in law in England and Nigeria. Her parents retired to Dublin when Anne-Louise was four. She was educated by the nuns at Presentation Convent school, after which she worked in Dockrells, builders' suppliers, for a year to earn the money to study at the College of Communications. The diploma she left with entitled her to hope for a job in community radio. Lots of young people had such diplomas. Indeed, qualifications of much higher standing could be found in the drawers of suburban homes all over Ireland in 1983. There were forests of degrees and diplomas, but there were few jobs. Anne-Louise was really interested in drama production, which had been her specialization in college. But nothing was happening for her or the thousands of other young people who, aware of the national depression, left the education system, demoralized by the mood of 1980s Ireland. It was at that point that Anne-Louise met Paul McGuinness. She took the job, glad to have a weekly wage to look forward to. She thought she'd stay till Christmas.

In fact, Anne-Louise Kelly stayed forever. Over the next four years she acquired power, influence and responsibility within the U2 community, matched only by McGuinness and the band. By the time she was twenty-five Anne-Louise was sitting alongside the five principals in the U2 boardroom, a trusted and respected equal of the men more publicly associated with the cause.

McGuinness had met her that first day in his home-office in

Ranelagh. When they concluded their informal agreement, he took Anne-Louise upstairs to a spare bedroom that served as the U2 office. The room contained a phone, a weird desk and a portable typewriter that was in need of repair. There was an awkward silence. He wasn't quite sure what he required from a personal assistant. She knew nothing about the music business. Bits of paper lay everywhere, contracts were stuffed down the back of the old couch that dominated the room. Anne-Louise couldn't type, but she could organize. She started with the stuff behind the couch.

McGuinness introduced Anne-Louise to the band later that week. She'd never really heard of them, but they seemed pleasant lads. Bono and Larry stood out. The singer was a touch raucous, all *bonhomie*, 'great to meet you'; the drummer was quiet, shy and watchful; he filed in last and was first one out the door.

The results of Red Rocks were variable. The video was OK, the sound of the music less than good. They had taken the precaution of recording the Red Rocks set again in Boston and at an outdoor gig in West Germany in case anything fouled up in Denver. When it was finally released, *Under a Blood Red Sky* contained only two songs, 'Gloria' and 'Party Girl', from Red Rocks. Marketed as a low budget album, it went to No. 2 in the UK charts. Jimmy Iovine who produced at Boston and at the Rockpalast in Germany was credited on the sleeve. Reflection on the *Sky* album was coloured by the $50,000 compensation U2 were forced to pay for Bono's unauthorized rendition of 'Send in the Clowns' during the live recording.

U2 were preoccupied with their next album in the early months of 1984. They wanted Brian Eno to produce it, but when approached he had turned them down. The band persisted and finally after a couple of meetings Eno agreed to come to Dublin with Danny Lanois, a Canadian sound engineer with an international reputation. Eno was a cult figure in the rock world. His reputation had been established producing David Bowie and Talking Heads. Away from rock 'n' roll he was an artist. It was difficult to describe his work, which was avant-garde and concerned with light and sound. There was, it was claimed, something called Eno-ambience.

Ambience was also the word most closely associated with the music he produced. He had pedigree, class, a certain mystique. Brian Eno appealed to U2 because they were ready to begin the second phase of their career. They were seeking challenge and exploration rather than consolidation. They didn't want their next album to be *Son of War*. Such a record might well reach No. 1 in the charts, but it would represent stagnation. They were after growth. Professionally this was smart thinking. It was also quite brave: *War* had just spent its twelfth consecutive month in the UK charts.

In March 1984, *Rolling Stone* writers chose U2 as Band of the Year for 1983. The accolade was a response to the *War* album and the magnificence of the tour that followed it. But *Rolling Stone*'s writers were perhaps signalling something that transcended U2's measurable achievements; these, the people who thought most, and most intelligently, about the idiom of rock 'n' roll and the culture in which it was rooted had identified in this Irish band a seriousness of purpose that was rare. U2 seemed to want to change and expand the idiom, were committed to *give* to rock music rather than take, to change the thing they loved rather than exploit it. The *Rolling Stone* voters had shrewdly understood where U2 were coming from. As yet nobody knew where they were going, but their presence was vital and interesting. In the age of nihilism and contrived 'cool' when, if it looked anywhere at all, rock 'n' roll was looking backwards, one young band had the guts and imagination to explore and develop something that had become jaded.

The *Rolling Stone* award came at a handy time for Paul

McGuinness. He was re-negotiating U2's original deal with Island under which two albums were still due at the old price, $50,000, and the old royalty. 'The music business in its specifics and even in its broader strokes is not a terribly complicated business.' The words are Owen Epstein's, U2's New York lawyer. He, along with Ossie Kilkenny, a Dublin accountant who'd worked for U2 from the start, were McGuinness's cohorts in the Island re-negotiations. Epstein claimed of rock 'n' roll: 'It's a business that requires you having a sense of images and marketing and the relationship between publishing, recording and touring. If you are a very smart person you can pick it up very quickly. But not all of it, not the subtleties. Paul was obviously very smart.' Epstein was thirty-five years old when the new deal was being negotiated. He had started in law working for labour unions, but he found the entertainment business more congenial. He met McGuinness through Frank Barsalona. Chris Blackwell was also 'a great pal'. Epstein described himself as a 'deal-maker'. Making deals was an art form, the way he described it.

Ossie Kilkenny headed a successful Dublin accountancy practice. Ossie had style. He combined the gravitas traditionally associated with his profession with a sharp, amusing, streetwise manner. Ossie knew the score. He was educated by the Franciscans at Gormanstown College, a reputable boarding-school twenty miles from Dublin. (There are no disreputable boarding-schools in a country where a decent education is a privilege for the few rather than a right for everyone.) Ossie played R-and-B badly as a young man in a band called the Chosen Few whose vocalist, Paul Brady, later became a major recording artist, composer of 'The Island', the classic anti-war song. Whilst educating himself at University College, Dublin, at night, working in a bank by day and playing with the Chosen Few in the early hours, Ossie acquired his degree. When he started to practise accountancy, his friends in show biz often came for advice. He represented the Boomtown Rats and still acts for Bob Geldof. Chris de Burgh is another client. Shakin' Stevens, the Smiths and Dexy's Midnight Runners are also on Ossie's books.

McGuinness and Ossie were friends. Both were smart *and* gregarious, and both knew and liked Epstein. This was the formidable triumvirate that Chris Blackwell faced as he tried to hold onto Island's major act. The 1980s had been rough for Blackwell, U2 apart, and all they'd shown so far was promise. But they were the coming band, one hit single or big album away from the top of the First Division. Blackwell could screw two more cheap albums out of the existing contract, but he knew that the ball game had changed since the Stadium in 1980. Blackwell, McGuinness, Kilkenny and Epstein were friends and remained friends over the three-month negotiating period. But business is business, as they would say.

Paul McGuinness declared that U2's primary concern in any new arrangement was control of the music. He, Kilkenny and Epstein managed to get that. In addition they negotiated one of the cleverest deals in rock 'n' roll history. For their next four albums U2 would receive $2 million an album and double the royalties they'd previously received. U2 could appoint their chosen producer. Island would be bound to accept – unseen – the album produced. Each album would be promoted by three videos at a cost of $75,000 each which would be paid for by Island. That was the good news. The spectacularly good news, that as part of this new four-album deal U2 got all their publishing rights back, followed a couple of months later. The value of this was, and remains, inestimable. There were dozens of other bits of good news to do with mechanical royalties, methods of payment and record promotion. The bottom line was that U2 were financially secure for life and in control of their work – past, present and future. The old horror stories about rock 'n' rollers, from Elvis through the Beatles, Elton

John and the Rolling Stones, being ripped off would never be told about U2. A final caveat was added to the U2-Island Records deal; it would still apply even if any member of the band left. 'Three-quarters of that deal for a band without Bono' was, Epstein declared, 'sensational'.

McGuinness, Epstein and Ossie Kilkenny flew back to Dublin via London on Concorde. They toasted their success in champagne. How Blackwell travelled home is not recorded.

As the financial outlines of the deal had become clear over the previous weeks, McGuinness had kept the band in touch. The lads were near the end of *The Unforgettable Fire* recording at Windmill. Like its predecessors *Fire* was a nightmare to record. This time there was no Steve Lillywhite to act as honest broker between ambition, the search for perfection, and reality, what was possible in a recording studio. The task of synthesizing ideas, images, music and performance on this album had strained relationships to breaking point.

U2 had moved to a handsome suite of offices above the recording studio at Windmill. The meeting to unveil the deal was called in the boardroom during a lull in the storm downstairs. McGuinness and Epstein presided. The band listened in silence to the news that at twenty-four years of age they would never have to work again. When McGuinness and Epstein concluded, Bono spoke. Money could destroy them. It was corrupting. It would separate them from their friends, detach the band from their roots. The deal was good news, but no reason to get carried away. They had a record to finish downstairs. The others nodded agreement.

Holy shit, Epstein thought, I don't believe this. The following night Paul and Kathy McGuinness gave a party to celebrate the deal. All the parents were invited, together with friends like Barry Devlin who had helped along the way. The news, they all agreed, was wonderful. If you were going to be corrupted, some joked, this was the way to go. Deeper down,

Jo Clayton, Bobby Hewson, Norman, Gwenda and Garvin, Brian and Larry Mullen Sr were more than anything *relieved*. Like Paul McGuinness, they knew that money wasn't everything. But it was the way the world kept the score. Money was freedom. Money was power. As Paul reminded everyone, money would underwrite their ambitions, allow them to continue employing the best people, to concentrate on the music, to survive and create on their own terms.

Unforgettable Fire was, like *War*, a concept title. It was inspired by an exhibition the band visited at Chicago's Peace Museum. A series of paintings and drawings done by survivors of the bombing of Hiroshima and Nagasaki were exhibited under the title *The Unforgettable Fire*. The collection was regarded as a national treasure in Japan. Bono, Larry, Adam and Edge were deeply moved by the dreadful images of life after atomic warfare. Alongside *The Unforgettable Fire* collection, the Peace Museum housed work dedicated to Martin Luther King and his non-violent struggle for black emancipation.

It was those images and the emotions they triggered that U2 now tried desperately to capture in Windmill Lane with Eno and Lanois. Two weeks before recording was due to begin the band had wanted to cancel. They had moved from a feeling of confidence about the project to a state of panic. They were intimidated by the prospect of Eno. The songs weren't working out as they'd imagined. 'Wire' was a mess. Bono was working on a song called 'White City' that wasn't happening. They couldn't get a tight version of 'Pride', a song dedicated to Martin Luther King. In the end they decided to go ahead. Secretly the band of the year were terrified that they didn't have the music to do justice to a great idea.

When Eno arrived he and the band decided to start from scratch. Edge and he gelled straight away. Edge was U2's musical intelligence, a first-class mind applied to the technology of rock 'n' roll. Eno was a similar animal. They began to find the right sound. The horror of nuclear devastation, the dignity that Martin Luther King possessed: emotions like these were a major challenge to an idiom like rock music, created, informed and inspired by notions far less profound. But Edge and Eno got it. Bono was there as well. He shouldn't have been, Eno thought. Bono should be writing the lyrics, which were *long* overdue. But Bono was not just about lyrics. Bono heard melodies and sounds in *his* head. U2 wasn't a simple matter of Edge equals music, Bono equals lyrics and Adam and Larry look nice. They knew that. Eno was finding out. Edge was the mediator between the two heaviest protagonists, Eno and Bono. Much of the preparation and recording of *Fire* took place in Slane Castle. The angst began when the project moved to Windmill Lane at the critical concluding stage.

Finally, time ran out. An extra month of studio time was booked. Eno agreed, reluctantly, to stay; Bono, reluctantly, to go and write lyrics. Adam took a dim view of it all. He was a professional musician. You do the bloody work. If you're in charge of lyrics you write the fucking lyrics. The ambience in Windmill Lane was interesting if you were into that kind of thing.

Ironically Adam, the least confident about Eno's arrival, was maturing best through the experience. For many reasons Adam had endured the roughest U2 ride. He'd been a social outcast for a long, lonely period during the years on the road with *Boy*, *October* and *War*. His allies had been Paul and Steve Lillywhite and the crew, all of whom loved him, really did love him, for his humour, intelligence, good manners and delightfully laid-back attitude to the whole game of being big. Adam was serious when he worked, fun when he played. He had suffered also for not being a bass virtuoso, for not having the confidence in his playing that he might have had. Encouraged, nurtured, by Lillywhite, Adam was a fine musician.

But his confidence in his playing was liable to evaporate in hostile territory. Eno's studio might, he feared, be that territory. Events proved that Adam's confidence wasn't the only fragile property on the premises. Understandably, this made him feel better.

The news that filtered through about being millionaires had the effect of making the band try harder to meet the responsibilities the deal thrust upon them. From all the conflict and creative tension came an impressive album, which contained two great rock 'n' roll creations, the epic 'Bad', and 'Pride', a glorious evocation of Martin Luther King that managed to capture in sound the nobility of this great man's life and the poignancy of his death on a motel balcony in Memphis. U2 no longer dealt in matters merely personal, no longer projected youth and innocence. They had grown and their gifts had matured accordingly. There was something else, something that appealed to those at *Rolling Stone* and elsewhere who cared about rock 'n' roll; rock and the culture that inspired it had never really been taken seriously by anyone outside its colourful ghetto. Rock had been patronized, laughed at, and occasionally patted on the head by presidents. Its tragedies made the front pages, evidence for the prosecution. Nobody took the music or its heroes seriously; the greatest of them: Dylan, the Beatles, The Who and the Stones, had found that out. Now in 1984 even the heroes didn't believe in themselves. Nihilism was the vibe of these times.

Until U2. This band was doing more than selling albums and packing arenas. The four boys from Dublin were making a revolution, not outside in society, but here, within the rock 'n' roll culture itself. Because rock wanted to be taken seriously, wanted to grow up, U2 mattered now more than bands that had sold more records and achieved wider public acclaim. 'Pride' helped rock 'n' roll grow up, won it respect and self-respect. Born under pressure at Windmill Lane in Dublin,

'Pride' was conceived at a sound check in Hawaii. Joe O'Herlihy always taped sound checks. There was not one sound check in U2 history that Joe didn't get. To the casual observer it looked as if nothing was happening, as if it was all just fiddling and fucking around. But sound checks were work. Edge would experiment with a chord sequence, Adam throw in a bass line, Larry, tuning his drums, would suddenly hit on a new sound or pattern. Joe would log everything. When asked, he could find the bit they wanted, the glimpse of inspiration, the moment when, with no pressure on, the muse unexpectedly called. That's how 'Pride' began. The song was completed, as all this band's best work was, live, in concert, music *of* the real world brought to its creative peak *in* the real world.

Whatever U2 achieved in studio, the band's greatness lay in performance, where Bono endowed rock 'n' roll with the performing gifts of the great actor. At its most powerful, rock 'n' roll is a mixture of music and performance art. Whether the song demanded passion, sorrow, joy, anger, love or a poignant blend of all emotions, conflicts and experiences, Bono live at the head of this band delivered in a way that few if any before him had. If there was nothing especially profound in the concept of 'Pride (in the name of love)', nothing deeply imaginative in the lyric written on the run, it didn't matter. What mattered about U2, what made their music and this song in particular so special, was the powerful blend of ideas, sounds, images and performances. The idiom of rock 'n' roll had never been challenged so comprehensively before. U2 were seeking more from the idiom than their contemporaries. The music they wanted to create had to make you want to dance, but should also encourage you to think, help you to reflect. 'Pride' was the closest they had come so far.

The feeling within the U2 camp was that 'Pride' would become the No. 1 hit single they had never had. Alas, when it was released in autumn 1984 it peaked at No. 3 in the UK charts. In the United States 'Pride' failed to make the Top Ten, a disappointment that was put down to Island Records lack of marketing muscle in the most important district of all. *Fire* went straight to No. 1 in the UK album charts when it was released in October. In the States *Fire* topped the college and progressive charts but failed to dominate their mainstream equivalents. Hit singles that capture the casual record-buyer are the key to selling albums in the quantities necessary to top the American album lists. When the USA sales of *Fire* were finally collated it was discovered that U2 had sold one million albums over a two-year period. This contrasted with a public perception that three or four million records had been sold. They were still reaching U2 fans, and there were more of them all the time, but the universal popularity of someone like Bruce Springsteen, who shifted albums in tens of millions, still eluded U2.

The title track, 'The Unforgettable Fire', was released as a single the following spring, reaching No. 8 in the UK. The song was musically rich, with keyboards and a beautiful arrangement for strings by a gifted Irish musician, Noel Kelehan. It succeeded in its objective, which was to evoke the terror of nuclear holocaust. The relationship between music and lyrics was, however, tenuous and difficult to grasp in terms of the presumed subject matter. Some people close to the band, aware of the passions invested in born-again Christianity, regarded 'The Unforgettable Fire' as a metaphor for the experience Bono, Larry and Edge had gone through during the *Boy–October–War* period of their lives. In that context the closing lines in 'Fire' read more understandably:

> *Don't push me too far,*
> *Don't push me too far,*
> *Tonight.*

'A Sort of Homecoming', viewed from the same personal

perspective describes, perhaps, the compromise struck between Christianity and rock 'n' roll. 'A Sort of Homecoming' contains the following reflection:

> *Oh, Oh, on borderland we run,*
> *And still we run, we run and we don't look back.*

U2 embarked on a world tour which began in Australia and New Zealand in the autumn of 1984. Steve Iredale was promoted to production manager. Timmy Buckley, Joe's assistant from the old days in the Arcadia, Cork, now took over as stage manager. Tom Mullally, another product of O'Herlihy's 'Cork Academy', became Larry's drum roadie. Back in Dublin, Anne-Louise Kelly had accepted a permanent position running the U2 office in Windmill Lane with a staff of five people. The Island money was being used to build a structure that would serve the band. In just over a year Anne-Louise had established a close relationship with McGuinness and the lads, who now regarded her as a close friend, trustworthy, protective, an elder sister (although at twenty-two she was actually younger) who had nevertheless the executive ability to deal in a world where sharp practice was the norm.

Australia was a disaster. U2 played to 60,000 people over five shows in Sydney and more than 30,000 turned up to see them in Melbourne. Sadly, the music created with Eno's assistance in Windmill Lane simply didn't work live. 'The Unforgettable Fire', with its orchestral feel, wouldn't translate to the stage. 'Wire' was also impossible in concert. The truth was they'd spent too long in studio and had allowed themselves less time than they needed to prepare the live show. All of this was compounded by the presence of Timmy and Tom, new crew members still learning the job. Sound checks in Australia were spent trying to solve problems with musical arrangements rather than checking the systems for that night's show. The shows were ecstatically received, but the band, perfectionist, with its own standards now well established, knew that a major problem existed. It was during this crisis that 'Bad' became something more than the marvellous piece it was on record. Bono announced it as a song about heroin addiction in Dublin, but heroin isn't mentioned in the lyric. 'Bad' is about pain. Sung by anyone else it would be a melodramatic tear-jerker. Invested with Bono's powerful gifts, 'Bad' is genuinely moving, savage and bitter-sweet, musical theatre at its awesome best. Bono had stopped invading audiences. He still craved the contact, the bonding of performer and ticket-buyer and now, during 'Bad', which was wonderfully flexible, he used his massive stage presence to draw the people towards him. Every night, some girl would be plucked from the darkness to be hugged symbolically on stage. Now it was more controlled, more stagecraft than primal surge, more affecting, better. And safer. From adversity Down Under, U2 gained a victory of some significance in the discovery of 'Bad'. Less than a year later, this song, stunningly performed at Wembley during Live Aid, would serve to steal the greatest rock show of all time for U2.

In Australia the development of 'Bad' seemed small consolation for the band's inability to adequately perform 'Unforgettable Fire', the title track from their new album. Impatient and angry, Bono turned on the U2 crew to vent his perfectionist spleen. The relationship between band and crew is critical everywhere, but nowhere more than in the U2 operation. They are the best live band because they care the most about that aspect of their professional lives. Everything connected with the show must be perfect. Sound, vision, lighting, security, ticket price, quality of T-shirts on sale, all were of utmost importance. The tour programme had to be readable, not a way of extracting an extra pound from fans. The food and drink concessions, were they all right? Larry would ask. Sometimes a pretty young girl would hang around a gig all day. If any of the crew, U2 personnel, or hired roadies used his position to lure the young girl away, he might well find himself looking for a new band two or three days later. Larry would spot the move. Joe or Dennis would be quizzed. Those girls were there because of U2, nobody was to take advantage of that. Those were the rules. Joe or Dennis would lay down the law to new recruits when they arrived. The message was clear: you're working for U2 now boys, we don't give a fuck what you do with other bands or what you do in your private life. But around this band, no dope, no girls, no boozing. The wages are good, this band will sit and eat with the crew and treat you with respect. That works both ways. Got it? This pep talk didn't abolish drugs, sex or drink from the fringes of the U2 tours. What it established was a code of behaviour that was breached furtively when it was breached at all.

After six weeks in Australia and New Zealand, U2 returned to Dublin to solve their tour problems. They were due in the United States in February and it was clear that a new set would be needed. Some dates in Europe had to be cancelled while the music was sorted out. Problem number one was the breakdown in communication between band and crew. Joe, Steve, Timmy and Tom Mullally had borne the brunt of U2 frustration, or more precisely, Bono's temper. Dennis was the mediator. A conference was called in Windmill Lane. Grievances were aired uncompromisingly. The decision arrived at would apply to all future tours; Adam would take over from Bono as crew-band liaison man.

Adam was a pro, reasonable, rational, with a grasp of the technical problems the crew faced. He was aware of the difficulties of realizing a studio production in the uncontrolled environment of the live stage. Bono was a genius. His gifts as performer and creator served the cause. He was as well spokesman, catalyst, the spirit of the thing called U2. Thus his role was defined in the new arrangement which acknowledged the crew's professionalism and restored lost dignity.

On the New Zealand leg of the autumn tour U2 had met and employed a Maori named Greg Carroll. Steve Iredale met Greg walking down the main street in Auckland when the strapping, handsome young man stopped the production manager and asked for the U2 jacket he was wearing. Steve explained that the jacket was part of his job and not for giving. OK, Greg smiled, it was just a try. At the Auckland concert, Greg turned up again working for one of the support bands. He was friendly, with an open, good-natured face. He seemed bright as well. U2 borrowed Greg for a couple of gigs. He worked swiftly and efficiently and seemed to have an instant rapport with Bono. Before leaving New Zealand, Paul McGuinness, Dennis and Steve sat down to explore the possibility of offering Greg the job of roadie to Bono. On the strength of his intelligence, willingness, and easy-going nature – essential if he was to work for the man under the most pressure – Greg joined U2, with special responsibilities for Bono.

Following a tour of Britain and Europe and two months after completing a short series of concerts in major US cities, U2 left for a four-month trip to the States in February 1985. Although without a hit single, and aware that the change of mood on their new album left some questions about them still unanswered, U2 still enjoyed critical acclaim. They were an important band, and theirs was the best live rock show in the world. Their set was now a *tour de force*, containing the best songs from their four albums. The show was superbly paced, the hysteria of previous years now transformed into sheer power. The music and the presence of the band on stage could still captivate the biggest arena and make it throb with emotion. The messages were more complex, the medium more mature, and the band was learning every night.

Under the headline, 'Our Choice: Band of the '80s', U2 featured on the cover of the March 1985 edition of *Rolling Stone*. This honour placed U2 alongside the great rock 'n' roll figures of other eras, the Beatles, the Stones, Bob Dylan and The Who. This was an extraordinary accolade for a band still maturing, still struggling to climb the barrier between respect in the music business and the kind of mass popularity enjoyed by the greats of the past. U2 had yet to have a No. 1 hit single. Their albums were still only average sellers. 'Pride' had failed as a single in America. *The Unforgettable Fire* was selling to U2 fans, people who had seen them live, but there weren't enough of them to push the album to No. 1 in the charts. U2's one ostensible claim to greatness lay in the immense theatrical and musical power they generated in their live performances. For that, live music being the essence of the rock 'n' roll experience, they were entitled to respect.

Describing U2's music, identifying the ideas it was struggling to express and lauding the band's revolutionary decency, *Rolling Stone* concluded 'for a growing number of rock 'n' roll fans, U2 has become the band that matters most, maybe even the only band that matters.' This analysis crystallized the long-held feelings of those who followed and understood U2. The preferment of U2 in this almost aspirational manner suggested that those who mourned the idiom's retreat into triviality believed, or at least hoped, that this band, their music and the values that informed it, could make rock 'n' roll relevant again, as influential in the 1980s as it had been in the days of Lennon, Dylan and Townshend.

It was because U2 represented rock 'n' roll's best hope of achieving relevance rather than for their album sales that they were identified as 'Band of the 80s'. For too long rock's 'best hopes' had been bloated and self-indulgent, neither capable of, nor interested in, confronting the real world as experienced by real people. Of course, it couldn't *all* be real. Like other mass art forms, rock music was, indeed had to be, quintessentially escapist. Fantasy and illusion had their places, but without *any* roots in common experience, rock would be rendered utterly trivial, a way of getting, in Geldof's memorable phrase, 'rich, famous and laid'. Based in Dublin, living in real houses on real streets, meeting real people and socializing with them in pubs, clubs and restaurants, and perhaps above all exposed to the benign worldliness of Dubliners unimpressed by rock 'n' roll fame and fortune, Bono, Edge, Adam and Larry lived in the real world. Here they found the raw material for their work which was virtually unique in 1980s rock 'n' roll for giving expression to the feelings of ordinary people. Ordinary people *everywhere*, for Dublin was part of the global village and its spiritual life, its fears and anxieties, as well as its pleasures and aspirations, were universally shared. In their efforts to reflect real 1980s experience, U2 were challenging their contemporaries in the business who failed to acknowledge rock music's obligation to address the issues of the day.

In fact, they were doing more than that, something which constituted a musical revolution. For rock 'n' roll was not traditionally concerned with *ordinary* experience, but with a romanticized version of it. Rock music expressed alienation. As defined by, among others, Dave Marsh, biographer of Springsteen and The Who, rock was 'a voice and a face for the forgotten and the disenfranchized'. In terms of rock's traditional place in popular culture and consciousness, this claim was undoubtedly valid. The question in the mid-eighties was, however, this: *Who were the forgotten and the disenfranchized?* Rock's primal rhythms had always lent themselves to protest, and the major bands and singers of other eras had been, by definition, anti-establishment. Alas, by 1985 things had changed. The problems were different, and if rock 'n' roll was to offer a 'voice and a face for the forgotten and the disenfranchized', it would have to change as well.

Dave Marsh's definition of rock music's function echoed something The Who's Pete Townshend had said when attempting to explain the passions that moved his band in the 1960s: 'It was all dope, dope, dope and horrible vibes of aggression and bitterness. Out of that we were saying, "We are the mirror for the desperation and bitterness and frustration and misery of the misunderstood adolescents; people in a vacuum."' The 1960s illusion was a belief that you could personally be free, that inhibition was the problem.

When rock 'n' roll looked into the mirror in the 1980s, the reality that stared back was radically different. Pete Townshend grew up in a world where getting a job was easy, a world of burgeoning materialism where austerity was a word sociologists used to describe the conditions your parents grew up in. The 1960s promised a solution to larger problems too: racism was being fought, Martin Luther King was winning, freedom was on the march. Britain was liberating its black African colonies, America and the Soviet Union were agreeing nuclear test-ban treaties, people seemed to be getting richer. And everyone was getting laid. Or would be soon. The Beatles were awarded MBEs, the world was almost free and rockers could indulge themselves by focusing on 'the misery of misunderstood adolescents'.

Things had changed by 1985. Now we knew about the tyranny of personal freedom, the dreadful empty oppression of sexual promiscuity. We knew about the depression that ambushed you on the other side of a drug-induced high. Martin Luther King was dead – murdered – racism as popular as ever and the nuclear arsenal multiplying by the year. Austerity was back in the form of mass unemployment, with a vicious, paradoxical twist: those who were employed earned more than ever before and were probably living in your street, their every new material gain, their extra winter holiday, providing a bitter reminder of how *you* had failed.

Austerity in the 1980s was random and cruel, isolating its victims in a sea of plenty.

Austerity of that kind led to despair. Despair inspired nothing. Made you feel empty, helpless, without hope. Despair was an adult experience. If the 1960s were about teenage frustration, the 1980s were the years of adult despair. Here was the 1960s generation that Townshend had awakened, the generation that had fucked a little more, spent a little more, suffered teenage austerity a little less, the generation reared on an illusion, the real *Me* Generation, discovering the bitter truth: far from being solved, the problem hadn't even been defined.

The old constraints had been removed. Sexual promiscuity lurked in every suburban living room, flickered tantalizingly from every television screen. Sexual fulfilment was *the* modern fantasy, talked and written about and lied about everywhere. Should priests and nuns be celibate? Should fourteen-year-old girls have the pill? Should you forgive your husband? Your wife?

Of course most of today's parents didn't *do it*. But they sure as hell *thought* about it. And despaired of being personally happy. For sexual gratification was the ultimate in materialism, the grandest of all illusions. Parents didn't do it but they watched Joan Collins, who was so much more potent for being present, constantly present, in your living room. Jean Harlow and Marilyn Monroe you had had to go out to see, were occasional trips. Collins came to you weekly, at home.

Townshend's frustrated generation had grown up in amazing times. Their heroes, John Kennedy and Martin Luther King, had been exposed. The idealistic, idealized president had been a clinical sexual athlete. The dignified black evangelist who would have emancipated his race had been a secret raver. Nixon had been a liar and a crook, Elvis a pervert, Mao Tse-Tung a sponsor of mass murder; Harold Wilson gave the appearance of being a slippery little spiv. By the 1980s it was possible to publish and sell several million copies of a book that identified the Pope as the central character in a conspiracy to cover up the murder of his predecessor. The same book, heavily promoted in the local bookstore, revealed papal links with the Mafia and made a claim that to many of the 500 million people who looked to Rome for spiritual guidance may have been even more shocking: that through a holding company the Vatican was the world's leading manufacturer of contraceptive sheaths! The same Pope who denounced contraception was making millions *from* contraception.

Thus in the 1970s and early 1980s, as the Me Generation grew to adulthood, the ground was cut from under anyone who believed in *anything*. There *were* no heroes; no ideology remained untainted. There existed no faith that wasn't somewhere at the core a lie. There were no moral certainties. The Me Generation was rendered morally impotent, unable to impose old values on children conceived when there was hope.

There was, of course, one last resort: money. Jobs, cars, houses, videos, holiday homes, cocktail cabinets, stereos, super-stereos – all of this you got by working hard. Personal advancement through hard work had become the refuge of the rock 'n' roll generation for whom hope, in the sense that they had once experienced it, was no longer a valid emotion. The promises hadn't been kept. The world had not, nor would it ever, become a better place. The best they could hope for now was Margaret Thatcher's return to Victorian values, Ronald Reagan's faith in fundamentalist religion.

To grow up in the 1960s was to believe – or at least to *feel* – that the world could be transformed, expanded, set free by sex, hallucinogens and the songs of Bob Dylan and Frank Zappa. To grow up in the 1980s was to know the absurdity of this illusion, was to believe – or at least *feel* – that happiness had more to do with collective responsibility than individual freedom.

To grow up in 1986 was to wonder if it was too late. Heroin was on every street, in every office, classroom and college campus. In the past the drug addict rotted in the worst part of town, died in the pages of newspapers. Now drug-induced misery was semi-detached and suburban, lurking somewhere in the shadows of your neighbourhood. And in the era of AIDS, sex was no longer free. In 1986 you could die as a result of a brief liaison with the boy or girl next door. Dylan's times had changed.

When they sang their songs of 'Pride (in the name of love)', of heroin being 'Bad', of 'The Unforgettable Fire' that would follow nuclear war, U2 gave 'a voice and a face' to people other than those imagined by Dave Marsh when he wrote of 'the forgotten and disenfranchized' rock music traditionally played to. U2 played to all decent people who were in an indecent world, the newly forgotten and disenfranchized. Rock 'n' roll heroes had always left the suburbs and small towns they grew up in. Success was Getting Out for Lennon and McCartney, Jagger and Richards and Dylan. An essential part of becoming urban and sophisticated was the rejection of the values held by those who reared you in the neighbourhood you had fled. There was no soul, no spirituality in the suburbs. U2 rejected this urban life, legitimizing suburban existence, identifying its concerns and expressing them vividly and powerfully through rock 'n' roll. This was a revolutionary artistic achievement, imaginative and brilliantly realized. The ideas themselves weren't new. What was original and inspiring was the expression of common human experience, real and contemporary, through the idiom of rock 'n' roll.

The elevation of U2 by *Rolling Stone* magazine was confirmation that revolutionary cultural changes had taken place. The most decadent child of all, rock 'n' roll, had survived and matured to become in the mid-1980s the defender of truth and decency, the most vigorous agitator for a spirituality lost in the changing times. In U2 it seemed rock 'n' roll was born again. Their time had come.

U2 played Madison Square Garden on 1 April, two weeks after their *Rolling Stone* acclaim. The show, at this famous old venue, sold out. They were relieved. The initial pleasure of the article had brought in its wake an awareness of the responsibility now thrust upon them. U2 would be judged by the highest standards from now on. Every concert review would measure them for greatness and cast doubt upon them if they failed to deliver. That, the band felt they could handle. They'd been in enough crises to relish the concert-hall challenge by now.

But looming ever larger in their thinking was a challenge they were less sure they could meet: they were due to begin work on a new album in the autumn. Album-making had always been the nightmare, the part of being in U2 that wasn't fun. If the band was to fulfil the claims now made on its behalf, if it was to justify the title 'Band of the '80s', the next album would have to be more accessible than anything they had so far produced. To emulate the Beatles and the Stones and others with whom they now stood, they would have to write great songs, songs, as Bono put it, 'that people could whistle on the way to work or sing at parties round the fireside'. This was a challenge far greater than they had ever faced.

Edge woke up about eleven a.m. They'd done the press conference the day before, so he had time to potter around his hotel room. He felt nervous and distracted, as he always did on major concert days. He watched some daytime television and had a room-service breakfast. At one o'clock the band met Dennis in the lobby to go to the venue for the sound check. This was early, but New York was always different, more to see, more calls to take, the largeness of the characters, the stories and the deals tending to shrink time and wear you out. For Edge the early afternoon arrival at the venue was the first real release of adrenalin. You saw the fans' vigil outside. As you swept past you realized what people endured to see *you* play. Inside it was all security men, crew and equipment. You sensed the hierarchical nature of all of this and felt again that *you* were responsible. The feeling didn't elate Edge, it intimidated him.

The sound check was relief, work, absorbing, with its problems and adjustments deflecting idle thoughts. The period between sound check and concert was the worst time of all. You were back in the hotel and yet not really there. The adrenalin runs cold through your blood. You can't concentrate on conversations. Everything, everyone, even your family, is an intrusion, half resented, half accommodated. Food is picked at, a necessary ritual, observed rather than enjoyed. Then the dressing room; the visits to the toilet, the fear, more well wishing, now seeming further away than ever as you retreat into your private world. The Garden was a good show as Edge remembered it afterwards. At the time he felt nothing except relief when it was over. He recalled thinking the moment they hit the stage that the place was smaller than he'd imagined. Sometimes, on really great nights when the music worked the way *you* knew it should, you could relax on stage and savour the experience of being in a band. But such nights were rare. The Garden was good, but it wasn't rare.

The best seats at Madison Square Garden were occupied by the band's families and friends from Dublin. First-class tickets were provided to transport those closest to them from Ballymun, Artane and Malahide to the great occasion in New York. The presence of loved ones added a necessary pinch of reality to the day. The sight of Jo Clayton, Bob Hewson, Garvin Evans, Cecilia Mullen, Bill Graham or Dave Fanning after months on the road was a reassuring reminder of what was real and precious in their lives. The visitors, having fun, treating it all as 'gas', served to remind Paul, Adam, Bono,

Larry and Edge that it *was* all gas. Forming a protective circle amid the après-concert celebrity scrum, family and friends from Northside and Grafton Street days served also to keep the madness at bay. Touring boredom relieved temporarily by drugs, booze and sex was less likely in the presence of mothers, brothers and real friends. As U2 moved ever closer to being really famous, the sensitivity they showed to those closest to them was a measure of the common sense and decency that governed everything they did. It proved also that their self-protective instincts were in place and functioning. Where U2 were heading, this was no small thing. Graveyards and clinics all over the world bore testimony to the dangers of being The Band of any era.

Chapter Seventeen

ARRIVAL

U2 weren't a front-page story in Ireland. They were known and appreciated by those who were interested in rock 'n' roll and by observers who kept their eyes open in search of things that were about to 'happen'. The population at large had a vague sense that something called U2 existed. The band were rumoured to be doing great things for Ireland in the real world. It was Madison Square Garden that put a shape and four faces on U2 in their own country. Jim Aiken, who was promoting what was billed as the Homecoming concert at Croke Park in June, flew a party of Irish journalists to New York for the Garden concert. As well as the leading music-writers, Aiken invited some of the smarter social columnists and a correspondent from RTE. When this group returned home suitably impressed by the Garden hysteria, they saturated Irish newspapers and airwaves with the news that U2 had arrived. An Irish band was now the greatest act in rock 'n' roll. Within a few days everybody knew about 'the four lads from Mount Temple who'd taken the world of rock 'n' roll by storm'. The Homecoming concert quickly sold out. Up on Grafton Street Brummie read the early editions of the evening papers with Bono and U2 splashed across the front pages.

'Fucking hell, lads,' he laughed in awe, 'Bono's a national hero.'

In fact U2 were more national phenomenon than heroes of any identifiable kind. The post-Madison Square Garden publicity had, taking the *Rolling Stone* piece as a guide, depicted U2 as a band that sings about 'such topics as God and politics'. The headline on Christopher Connelly's *Rolling Stone* story had read 'Keeping the Faith' and had identified 'Sunday Bloody Sunday' as a song about 'a massacre of civilians by the British in Northern Ireland'. For all its prescience in identifying U2 as the band who would most vividly and faithfully carry the banner for rock 'n' roll, *Rolling Stone* had failed to distinguish between the group's work and the statements issued in interviews. U2 music came from the soul, was rooted in the emotions rather than any particular religious faith or political ideology. What was exciting was the music and that, like all great creative work, came from the subconscious rather than the rational mind. U2 didn't play or sing about God or politics. Their music reflected how they, and millions of others, *felt* about the world. But journalists continued to place them in a box marked God and Politics, and this was the image that Ireland, like the rest of the world, received of its new heroes.

Bobby Hewson was one of the millions absorbing the message the media communicated. He had taken early retirement from the Post Office and lived in a beautifully located apartment overlooking the harbour at Howth. He played golf, indulged as enthusiastically as ever in amateur dramatics and, inspired by his sea-view, had begun to paint again for the first time since Iris's death. Outwardly he remained unimpressed by his son's achievements. 'Don't mind that young fella of mine,' he would laugh when told of Bono's role as guru to his generation. They had grown closer since Bono's marriage to Ali. Bobby loved her, appreciating that she understood his daft 'young fella'. Father and son, now reconciled, rarely crossed swords. One thing did bug Bobby and he raised it with Bono after U2 had returned from some tour or other. Bono had conveyed the impression in an interview with an American magazine that he'd been born 'on the wrong side of the tracks'. A local newspaper had picked up the story which Bobby read with growing rage. Phrases like 'streetwise' and 'tough neighbourhood', meant to describe The Village and its adventures, helped paint a picture of Cedarwood Road that offended Bobby. We didn't realize, friends and acquaintances in Dublin would say to him, what a tough background you came from. We were reading in the papers about your son. Listen, Bobby would try to explain. But it was no use. People believed the papers.

Such minor misunderstandings apart, Bobby Hewson was proud of his son, though still concerned that the U2 thing would evaporate overnight as, legend had it, rock 'n' roll fame was liable to. U2 ended their American tour in Florida in May. They took a few days' rest on Marcus Island. Bobby joined his son. Fame and touring meant that they had little time together nowadays. They went for a walk in the luxurious retreat and talked as fathers and sons rarely do. So much can be taken for granted when life is lived normally. Bobby had read all the rock 'n' roll horror stories, about wasted lives, money vanishing. There was nothing, he knew, as sad as yesterday's hero, no one so unsympathetically regarded by those who'd loved him when the going was good. Walking in Florida, Bobby reminded Bono – still Paul to his Da – of these things. Paul reassured him. U2 weren't like that, the money was safely invested. They'd known about the traps from the beginning. Everything was OK.

'But if it all ended tomorrow, son, what would you do?' his Da asked anxiously.

'None of it means anything, Da, except the music. That's a

gift from God and it is his to take away. If that is meant to be, there is nothing we can do.'

For the first time Bobby truly understood the strength of his son's faith. He envied Paul and admired the humility that lay behind the public persona. 'And anyway,' Paul joked on the way back to the hotel, 'the money is invested in gilts.'

A week before Croke Park, U2 played in Milton Keynes in the south of England. They stayed at the Bell in Aston Clinton, a tiny village in Buckinghamshire, about fifteen miles from the venue. The Bell has one of the best restaurants in Britain. The night before the concert, Paul McGuinness and the band gave a dinner party for families and friends. Ali, Ann, Aislinn and Kathy McGuinness were there, together with the crew and some of their wives and girlfriends. Michael Deeny came down from London where he was in the music-management business. Deeny was amusing, stylish, slightly grand: very Trinity College. The food was exquisite, the wine Château Latour. No voices were raised, no bread rolls flung, nothing untoward disturbed the Bell's normal Friday night ambience. The gracious, good-natured scene served to remind the interested observer of the difference between rock 'n' roll myth and the reality of 1985. The sex, booze and drugs, the egotism and general indecency associated with rock 'n' roll in the popular mind were strikingly absent when the band of the 80s sat down to dinner. The talk was of the days, not so long ago, when the U2 van driven by Paul McGuinness had broken down on the M1 motorway which ran a few miles up the road from Aston Clinton. Evoked now, in this Michelin-starred restaurant, the greasy chip diners of other nights inspired nostalgic laughter. The great thing about being rich and famous wasn't so much the way you lived as the way you *didn't have to live anymore*. They drank to that and were in bed by one o'clock.

The day of the concert 29 June was warm and cloudy, a

typical Dublin summer's evening. Croke Park was full, with 55,000 people, packed and clammy, waiting impatiently for a glimpse of the heroes. The Homecoming concert had captured the nation's imagination. Politicians and other celebrities squatted in the VIP enclosures, not quite knowing what they were celebrating but knowing that there was *something* being celebrated. For the band, their families, the crew and theirs, for teachers, friends and neighbours, *this* was the evening the dream became reality. Croke Park cast the largest shadow on Dublin's Northside. In many ways this great old sports stadium cast a shadow over Ireland. It was the home of the Gaelic Athletic Association, the self appointed guardians of Ireland's official culture. 'Croker' was holy ground, the site, on a September Sunday in 1920, of the original Bloody Sunday. From this the more recent British bloodletting in Derry took its name. Croke Park was thus a symbol of imperialist persecution as well as a sports ground and concert venue. It was also a monument, guarded by fanatics who claimed to represent Irishness. The concept of foreign sports existed in these damaged minds. Music, too, was classified as either pure or foreign. Foreign games were those played by the British. Sixty years after Bloody Sunday, soccer and those Irishmen who played it were forbidden in Croke Park. Popular music, whether rock 'n' roll or any other kind deemed un-Irish, was also forbidden, until Neil Diamond came to Dublin in the 1980s. Diamond, promoted by Jim Aiken, was able to generate enough money to buy the principles of those who remembered Bloody Sunday. Soccer was still banned. Thus, Croke Park was effectively an unknown shrine to many Irish men and women who felt excluded from this bastion of pure Irishness.

Larry Mullen had gone to Croker regularly with his Da to see the Irish football and hurling. But for Bono, Adam and Edge the venue for the Homecoming concert was virgin territory, a large concrete hulk they had vaguely been aware of as they passed in and out of town during their Northside childhoods. A country divided by such symbols, its divisions ruthlessly enforced by those who knew their history, welcomed U2 that June weekend and smiled knowingly at the irony of the venue.

For band, families and audience, irony was but a passing mood. Croke Park was home and, for U2, real in a way that no other evening could be. Success elsewhere had an abstract feel to it. This was their city. The streets they travelled through on the way to the concert were the ones in Artane, Drumcondra, Fairview and Ballybough they'd grown up on. The faces of this day, familiar and intimate, neighbours at gates, fans from years ago outside the gig, schoolfriends, guys off the road you played on as a kid. It was overwhelming, scary in a way. They'd get no bonus points tonight for being a 'Passionate Irish Band'. The city was full of *them*. Tonight they would have to be world-class.

Dave Fanning introduced them. This was one of those rare nights when the music was as good as it should be. The stage felt springy, the boys felt the tidal waves of emotion sweeping up off the vast faceless throng of people that stretched out across the field in front of them. Pausing before 'Sunday Bloody Sunday', Bono tried to talk about the song's real meaning. Sitting in the Hogan Stand, named in memory of the footballer run to ground by the Black and Tans sixty-five years before, some reflected on the beauty of the scene they now witnessed. Music was a powerful healing force. That thought jostled restlessly with another: when the concert ended Ireland would still remember. Croke Park would close its doors again to things foreign to its keepers' spirits. Joe O'Herlihy knew Croker well, had followed the Cork hurlers he loved to Dublin many times. He knew the beauty of Croke Park on September Sundays when the All-Ireland finals were being played. Then you saw the Irish people as they really were, sporting, wonderfully humorous, enjoying the festival and pageantry. Men and women from city and country, laughing, cheering and groaning as the drama unfolded on the field. Everywhere the children, excited, shiny eyes gulping in tradition in helpings that were too large to be digested by young spirits. Croke Park's glorious past belonged to the hurlers of Cork and Kilkenny, the footballers of Kerry and Dublin. Sport was the essence of Irishness, sport, culture and music. The juxtaposition of things he loved in this historic scene caused Joe, the old rock 'n' roll pro, to cry now as he mixed the sound for his band. He, Cork, Catholic and as Gaelic as he had to be, wept through the Homecoming concert. Gwenda Evans, Welsh and Baptist, wept too.

Driving through town after the concert, on their way to the U2 party at Blooms Hotel, Bono and Ali got stuck in a traffic jam. It was carnival weekend and Dublin was full of revellers. A young man with a green, white and yellow tricolour spotted Bono sitting in the car. He ran across the narrow street and smashed his fist on the car windscreen. Pointing to the Irish flag he screamed, 'You bastard, Bono.' Denying history could be dangerous in late-night Dublin. Later, on the hotel balcony, Bono heard a row on the street below. A drunken couple were arguing about U2 and 'Sunday Bloody Sunday'. 'Fuck you, Des,' the woman said, 'that's not what it means.' Having missed the beginning of the dispute, Bono never discovered what it was they hadn't meant.

Edge and Aislinn stopped briefly at the party before going home to Holly, their new baby girl. Edge was sanity personified in rock 'n' roll, genius driving a saloon car, living in semi-detached peace, the suburban hero. Everyone spoke of his confidence, much of which was due to Aislinn. Like Larry's girlfriend Ann, and Ali, Aislinn had been there from the beginning of what seemed now like a glorious journey. The women didn't make any big deal of staying in the U2 shadows. They didn't do press interviews because their lives were private, but their existence wasn't denied, nor did it have to be as the old rock 'n' roll myth had it, 'to keep the fans happy'. In contravention of tradition, the couples lived normal lives in extraordinary circumstances. Arriving home in Rathgar, Edge was hailed from across the street as he reached for his front-door key. 'Great show,' a voice shouted. 'Come on over, we're having a party.' Edge declined, claiming, truthfully, that he was too tired. Inside, Aislinn, always on the look-out for big-time vibes, teased him. 'Go on, take them a bottle over and wish them well,' she urged. He decided to be a sport, taking a bottle of whiskey with him. The tiny front room of the neighbouring house was packed with teenagers. They screamed and dived at him and he realized his mistake. This, he thought ironically, was the kind of party he'd always wanted to go to when he was shy Dave Evans. Now he wanted to go home. They agreed, if he would first sing a song. He sang Bob Dylan's 'Maggie's Farm', playing a borrowed guitar. When he got back to his house he realized he still had the whiskey. They probably think I'm a miserable bastard as well, he laughed to himself. Knowing Dublin, he knew it would be all round town in the morning. 'Did you hear about yer man Edge?'

Two weeks after Croke Park U2 went to Wembley to play Live Aid. Bob Geldof had inspired, bullied and begged the greatest acts in popular music to donate one day of their lives to the cause of famine relief. 13 July 1985 was that day, when concerts played simultaneously in London and Philadelphia were broadcast live on television to the watching world. Videos of starving children ran in between sets from the legends of rock 'n' roll. Now Elton John, next an emaciated black child dying of malnutrition. David Bowie and Mick Jagger appeared with a video of the classic song 'Dancing in the Streets'. This was followed by the film of a crowded refugee camp in Ethiopia. Presiding over this spectacular collage of entertainment, darkened by death, stood Geldof, the archetypal rock 'n' roll hustler turned conscience of the western world. Scruffy, in blue jeans and T-shirt, designer stubble lending menace to his anger, Geldof symbolized the difference between compassion which could be dirty and bitter, and complacency with its grey suits and collars and ties.

Speaking to the writer, John Mortimer, months afterwards, Geldof denied that rock 'n' roll could ever be taken seriously, could ever be anything more than 'be-bop-a-loo-loo'. Warming to his theme, he pointed to a generation's response to contemporary rock 'n' roll heroes like Bruce Springsteen and U2. 'They actually look to Bruce for integrity and gravitas. They even think a group like U2 is the backbone of civilization and they say "U2 won't let us down."' Geldof was only slightly wrong. What 'they' looked to Springsteen and U2 for was something not easily defined in a glib phrase. It wasn't integrity and gravitas but a sense of decency and hope, qualities largely absent from modern life. Live Aid, inspired by Geldof the sceptic, confirmed that with a little help from its friends, rock 'n' roll, for long identified with wasted lives, with sex, drugs, booze and egotism, could, without losing its balls, agitate in favour of decency, compassion and real love as opposed to cheap sex. Live Aid was the most magnificent consciousness-raising exercise of the 1980s, succeeding in an afternoon and evening where clergy and charity professionals, preachers in empty churches and bureaucrats on expense accounts had failed for two decades. Live Aid may on another level have reminded rock 'n' roll of something decent in its own ethos that was worth nurturing.

For U2, a band whose existence was threatened not so long ago by the apparent conflict between the rock 'n' roll culture and decent Christian living, Live Aid swept away any doubt that remained about the choice they had made. More than any other single achievement, Live Aid secured for U2 a feeling of professional satisfaction. If they had been just another band with a certain audience and a stylized up-beat act tailored to that audience, if, in other words, they were what their critics said they were, then Wembley that day would have found them out. It didn't. They had gone into the greatest gig in history matched against legends like Bowie, Jagger and McCartney and come out ahead. Later, during a summer spent in the West Indies and autumn in showery, windy Dublin, Adam would feel a comfortable glow whenever he thought about Wembley. Remembering how scared they'd been, how Bono had gambled and won, he'd shiver a little and smile contentedly. Now he *knew* they had arrived, that U2 was a major band. He knew that the audience was there and wouldn't go away. They didn't have to fight every time, not at any rate in the desperately anxious way they had had to up to now. Maybe they weren't the band of the '80s. But perhaps they were worthy of consideration. He felt confident that, after all those inches, they had moved a couple of feet along the road. To go all the way, to achieve the stature enjoyed by the acts they performed alongside with such distinction at Wembley, U2 needed a great album and a No. 1 hit single.

They went back to work on Monday 11 November 1985, a dark, winter's day. They came to Larry's new house on the edge of the sea at Howth. The house was comfortable, detached, the residence of a successful businessman rather than a famous rock star. It was still unfurnished.

The boys crammed themselves and their equipment into a room no bigger than any other suburban living room. After a couple of months apart they were happy to be back together again. U2 was home for each of them. Like any home, you longed to break out now and then but after a while you wanted the comfort and security of your own people, your own things. It was perhaps more than anything this identity with the band, a sense of shared destiny that was the driving force behind U2.

U2's contract with Island Records allowed for complete creative freedom. This was responsibility. The plan was to work for roughly six months before sending for Brian Eno and Danny Lanois. The album was due in autumn 1986. According to this plan, in January they would move to Danesmoate, a large neglected manor house at Rathfarnham, six miles from the city. They would keep to an eight-hour day, more or less, beginning work at midday, breaking at four p.m. for lunch and working on until seven or eight p.m. Fridays they would have off to take care of other business. They would do no press. This was a time for lying low.

They began by listening to the sound checks from the *Fire* tour. Those empty hours of the touring day, travelling through strange landscapes, lying in anonymous hotel bedrooms were, in a creative sense, often the most fruitful. A line or a chord would sometimes drift, unbidden, into your head. Some lines, some chords hardly stayed, drifting away as mysteriously as they'd come. Others lodged. Excited you. They were the ones you tried at the next sound check. Did they work? Could they be developed? What did the others think? 'Pride' had been conceived like this. The process begun in Howth that grey day in November 1985 was to end, not, as they imagined, one year later, but in March 1987, when their next album was released. Howth was about looking for clues.

U2 had committed themselves and their organization to the Conspiracy of Hope from the beginning in August 1985. Jack Healey, Amnesty's American director, was travelling to a meeting in Finland. He decided to stop off in Dublin to visit U2's manager, Paul McGuinness. They'd never met but Healey had seen the band at Madison Square Garden and had decided then that Bono's passion was real, not simply staged. Healey thought he'd try to get some kind of commitment from the band for Amnesty's twenty-fifth anniversary in 1986.

When he walked, somewhat tentatively, into Windmill Lane, Healey would have settled for a one-off U2 benefit concert. When he left an hour and a half later, he had a letter signed by McGuinness pledging *at least* one week of the band's time in 1986. With that unconditional commitment, the Conspiracy of Hope was conceived. Healey had been pushing an open door with McGuinness and U2. McGuinness was a long-time friend of Tiernan McBride, son of Sean McBride, one of Amnesty's founding members. The band knew very well the value of consciousness-raising contributions from the world of entertainment. They had first become aware of Amnesty as a result of watching a comedy benefit show, *The Secret Policeman's Ball*, on television in 1979.

Two years after joining U2 Anne-Louise Kelly had proved herself a capable businesswoman. Much of the day-to-day running of what had become an organization was delegated to her. Decisions, all decisions relating to U2, were made round the boardroom table at Windmill Lane. The four band members, Paul McGuinness and Anne-Louise sat at that table. There was no formal leadership, no voice dominated as of right. They were friends, they shared the same interests and objectives and, between the six of them, there was absolute trust. There were enough good minds to ensure that no soft options were taken.

Paul McGuinness had become a powerful and respected figure in the rock 'n' roll business. U2's success, now widely appreciated and acknowledged in Ireland, had earned Paul respect in Dublin. He was perceived as a man of substance, something more than an entertainment entrepreneur. He didn't cultivate personal publicity, indeed, the opposite was true. He possessed, as a consequence, a certain aura. Privately he enjoyed success, savoured it with the relish of a man who'd gambled and won. He could be impatient with people who failed to grasp how complex and demanding the music business was.

McGuinness was proud of U2's achievements and even more
so of the business-like, ethical manner in which they'd been
gained. He was on occasions arrogant, usually to the right
people. When people speculated about his relationship with
the band and placed him in the Svengali role, they were wrong.
Round the table at Windmill everybody knew the figures.
Power *and* responsibility was shared equally between band and
manager. He worked *for* them. Anne-Louise worked for the
five of them. She had to prove herself as they did. Two years
after arriving at his office-home in Ranelagh, Anne-Louise was
offered the Amnesty job by McGuinness. The letter Paul had
signed for Jack Healey was meant to open doors in rock 'n'
roll for Amnesty. If U2 had committed, the theory ran, others
would join the band of the '80s on a tour of the United States.
Sting, an Amnesty supporter for years, readily agreed. And
then Healey's optimism ran up against reality. Using the names
of U2 and Sting, he started knocking on doors. His plan was
for a two-week tour in June, west to east, San Francisco to
New York. The doors stayed closed: Dylan's, Stevie Wonder's,
Springsteen's. Healey was asking for a big one. This wasn't
like Live Aid, a glorious, one-day spasm. The Conspiracy
Healey was hatching meant *two weeks* on the road. The excuses
offered were many and varied. 'I don't have a band right now,'
'We're in the studio then,' 'My marriage is breaking up,' were
just some of the ways of saying no gently. Healey was dismayed
to discover that many of those approached had never heard of
Amnesty.

Working day and night over the next nine months, Anne-
Louise honoured U2's commitment. With help from Paul and
the band, who were preoccupied with their new album, but
mostly working alone, Anne-Louise proved that she had grown
at the same rate, if not faster, than her boardroom friends. Paul
McGuinness's Amnesty letter came to life in the form of the
Conspiracy of Hope tour which began in San Francisco on

3 June 1986. Supported by the U2 crew, the band of the 80s joined Sting, Peter Gabriel, Joan Baez, Bryan Adams, the Neville Brothers, Jackson Browne and Lou Reed on a six-city, fifteen-day sweep through America that would earn Amnesty $4 million and triple the organization's membership in the States.

This engagement, occupying the first two weeks of June, would be their only spell on the road between July 1985 and the spring of 1987, when they were due to begin another world tour. So altruism notwithstanding, the Conspiracy of Hope provided the band with an opportunity to remind the world that they were alive and well.

They spent six weeks preparing a set which they wanted to be memorable. There were a number of constraints to be considered; they would have just over thirty minutes on stage. The music they were working on for their new album was as yet raw and nowhere near ready for public appraisal. They didn't want to do a 'greatest hits' set, principally because it would have reinforced an image of the band that they had now grown impatient with. That image could best be described as U2, the good boys of rock. The public's perception of them as righteous, serious good guys was seen now as something of a professional trap. They had grown up personally and were determined that their music, especially the next album, would express ideas and emotions more complex than goodness. After Live Aid and the *Fire* tour they felt more secure, were ready now to deal with uncertainty, to deal with issues and concepts more personal than *War* and nuclear holocaust, more profound than the adolescent yearnings of *Boy*. Life for twenty-five-year-olds, wealthy now and famous, was about more than its simplest values. Life was funny, ironic, paradoxical and it often made you angry. Righteousness was no longer an adequate response.

The Conspiracy of Hope set reflected their desire to break away from their past. U2 had no new music of its own with which to go public – yet. So they spent the six weeks before going on the road doing something they had always shied away from, for fear of having their limitations exposed: learning to cover other people's songs. The result was an Amnesty set that consisted of three of the band's standards: 'Bad', 'Pride' and 'Sunday Bloody Sunday', and three rock 'n' roll classics: Eddie Cochran's 'C'mon Everybody', Bob Dylan's 'Maggie's Farm' and the Beatles' 'Help'. Confidence and maturity meant redesigning those songs to U2's style and musical strengths. It remained to be seen how audiences would react. But whatever worries there were about taking the new act on the road were eased somewhat by a dress rehearsal in their native city two weeks before opening at the Cow Palace, San Francisco. Inspired by Bob Geldof's Live Aid, Tony Boland, a Radio Telefis Eireann producer, had decided to try to help Ireland's jobless young by promoting Self-Aid, a rock concert at which the most successful Irish bands and solo acts would headline a day-long Festival of Hope. The basic message was, 'Don't wait for the government to help, you can help yourself.' This was to be the greatest gig in Ireland's history. Bob Geldof was due to play with the Boomtown Rats. Van Morrison, Paul Brady and Chris de Burgh were also on the bill. U2 had agreed to close the show. More, the band had lent its organization to Boland. Thus, with typical generosity, they moved from initial caution to absolute commitment, being perceived in the end virtually as co-promoters.

A couple of days before the show, *In Dublin* magazine, the anti-establishment street Bible, appeared on the news-stands with a bitter attack on Self-Aid. Over a cover photograph of Bono, *In Dublin* made its opposition clear: 'The Great Self-Aid Farce, Rock *Against* the People', the banner headlines declared. Ideologically speaking, Self-Aid was an affront to left-wing radicals who believed such a philosophy offered the establishment an easy way out of *its* responsibilities in the area of unemployment. This legitimate argument was expressed in somewhat lurid terms by *In Dublin*, one of whose page 2 headlines spoke of 'Self (aid) Righteousness!'

At the concert, 30,000 people rose to greet them. The old RDS arena was cold as May evening gave way to night. Van the Man, Geldof and Christy Moore had been on, now U2 pushed the audience towards climax with the familiar chords of Eddie Cochran's 'C'mon Everybody', their opening number. The band hadn't played live since Wembley, ten months before. They wanted to blow minds with their choice of music. They did. Bono addressed the crowd after 'C'mon Everybody'. He'd been lucky never to have been unemployed, but he knew how it must feel to 'stand in line' waiting for your 'pocket-money'. When he made speeches, as himself, the words sounded contrived, maudlin, almost insincere. He could rarely find the voice required, the degree of glibness necessary to make public-speaking work. But when he sang Bob Dylan's 'Maggie's Farm', the tone of savage anger was perfect. This was Bono and U2, music not speeches, passion not sentiment.

Self-Aid was the beginning of a new phase in U2's creative life. For the first time the music they played openly acknowledged rock 'n' roll's roots and traditions. By choosing the songs of Dylan, Cochran and the Beatles to introduce themselves anew to the public, they signalled that they were ready, strong enough now, to deal with rock 'n' roll on its own terms. It was time now to write songs using the heritage of their idiom, to look out on the world for inspiration.

A couple of months after Live Aid, Bono had met Keith Richards and Mick Jagger in a New York recording studio. The two old heroes were jamming away with acoustic guitar, singing old Stones numbers they did as party pieces. 'Sing us one of your songs, Bono,' Richards suggested, handing over his guitar. Bono had freaked with embarrassment. He *had* no songs. His immediate thought was 'Fuck, where's Larry, Adam and Edge?' That night, hot with shame, he locked himself in his hotel bedroom and wrote 'Silver and Gold' for the *Sun City: Artists Against Apartheid* album. It was the most lyrically accomplished piece of work he'd ever achieved. Describing the view from a South African prison cell, 'Silver and Gold' shows the distance the lyric writer has travelled since the days of stream-of-consciousness at the studio microphone:

> *And in the shithouse a shotgun,*
> *Prayin' hands hold me down.*
> *If only the hunter was hunted*
> *In this tin-can town.*
>
> *No stars in the black night,*
> *Looks like the sky fall down.*
> *No sun in the daylight,*
> *Looks like it chained to the ground.*
>
> *Broken back to the ceiling,*
> *Broken nose to the floor,*
> *I scream at the silence,*
> *It crawls under the door.*

Graphic, restrained, yet powerful, 'Silver and Gold' is the work of a maturing writer. Self-Aid was the performance of a band that had reached maturity in other ways as well. What had been shrill and callow, the primal scream of youth, was now powerful, resonant; passion, anger, felt *and* understood in terms larger, broader and deeper than those that had been merely personal. Analysis doesn't quite match having been at the R D S that night, where the power of the new U2 could be experienced. In the year since Live Aid and Croke Park, boys had become men. Maturity had not however doused the passion. At the end of the Self-Aid set the opening chords of 'Bad' sent a shiver through the darkened grounds. Out there friends like Dave Fanning, Pod, Gavin, Guggi and Day-Vid stood rooted to their places in the old R D S stand. They had seen a hundred U2 gigs but never anything as powerful as this. As 'Bad' reached its improvised climax, Bono gripped the mike, knuckles white, face contorted in anger; he had decided to answer U2's *In Dublin* critics. To the strains of Elton John's 'Candles in the Wind' he sang, looking fiercely out towards the crowd:

> *They crawl out of the woodwork*
> *Onto the pages*
> *Of cheap Dublin magazines.*

The hurt from two days before, bitter, raw, irrational, spilled briefly into the night. It was over in a line or two. But it had been there. Dublin still got to them. The response was mildly paranoid, proof that wealth and fame hadn't separated U2 from the world around them. This being Dublin, Self-Aid night ended with a party at which Bono and Eamonn McCann, author of the offending *In Dublin* polemic, and a long standing U2 fan, shook hands and cleared up any 'misunderstandings'.

On 3 June, eight bands, thirty-six musicians and two hundred tons of equipment set out from San Francisco on the Conspiracy of Hope. Along the way many popular heroes were due to make a contribution; Dylan and Jack Nicholson came to the Forum in L A. Yoko Ono and Muhammad Ali would be in Giants Stadium, New Jersey, for the final show. Robin Williams had promised to be at the Rosemont, Chicago. But the core group remained through San Francisco, L A, Denver, Atlanta, Chicago to New York.

Paul McGuinness was due to join the tour in Chicago. For now he was in Dublin where Kathy was giving birth to Max, their first son. Anne-Louise Kelly represented U2: it was her gig. Together with Paul's assistant, Barbara Galavan, and any member of the band she could grab, Anne-Louise had done most of the arm-twisting on U2's behalf. She'd also taken care of the logistics — she hoped. Bill Graham provided a powerful ally. Jack Healey had gone to Graham early on. Even though the cause was noble, the potential for hassle existed in a venture as ambitious as the Conspiracy. Bill Graham was there to underwrite the good intentions.

Graham was America's leading rock-concert promoter, and a powerful man. Over two decades and more in the business he had seen it all, been disgusted by some of it: the greed, the vanity, the sheer crass stupidity, the tragic deaths. He had often had cause to concur with the observation that fame is the stepmother of death, ambition the excrement of glory. The best and the worst in rock 'n' roll respected Bill Graham. His presence made the Conspiracy of Hope credible. He'd had no hesitation in agreeing to join. Bill knew what Amnesty was about, knew better than anyone else on the tour why evil had to be confronted. Graham's parents died in a German concentration camp. Post-war, he was left to wander Europe, a penniless teenage refugee. He arrived in America with nothing. Amnesty was his struggle. Even before the call from Healey, Graham had publicly opposed President Reagan's visit to Bitburg, the German cemetery where members of Hitler's SS are buried. The night after the visit, Graham's offices and warehouse were burned to the ground.

Two weeks on the road was nothing.

Socially, the Conspiracy of Hope tour was restrained. After the gig there was the dressing-room ritual of visits from friends, friends' friends, local VIPs (and their friends) who were important, or thought they were, and anyone else game enough to bluff security and the minders. This was show biz.

Back at the hotel the scene was more commercial traveller. Amnesty was on the road to make money, so musicians and crews stayed at Hyatts, Ramadas and Marriotts. Here they would gather in the lounge for a beer or a glass of wine before bed. The days of the rock 'n' roll orgy appeared to have passed. There were no groupies, just the everyday everyman chance of getting laid. The odd joint made the rounds as it does at the tamest suburban gathering. No smack. No coke. No big deal. Cocktail chat about the business, the next album (or why the last one bombed).

The Ramada Renaissance in Atlanta was in an industrial estate, or so Bono thought. Looking out the window you could have been anywhere. The skyline gave no clues. It was Monday, three gigs done, three to go, here, Chicago, New York. They had two days to kill before Wednesday's show. Bono felt good. After all those months lying low, working in a vacuum, it was invigorating to perform before an audience again. The new set had worked. People *would* accept the new U2, if it produced the right stuff. Three years ago U2 had opened for Sting and the Police at Gateshead. They'd been young contenders. Now they were the headline band and, as the Amnesty tour proved, accepted as such by Sting, Lou Reed, Peter Gabriel and the rest. And by the critics who'd responded as if they were U2 audiences.

Nevertheless, looking at the gifted musicians and performers on the Amnesty bill, U2 felt, at the beginning, the odd ones out. The backing musicians were virtuosos, Reed, Baez and Gabriel, all legends. Acceptance by these people was tangible proof that whatever it was U2 had – and they weren't certain of that most of the time – was currency, real currency in the business. If, like U2, you operated more on instinct than calculation, it was gratifying to discover that you had taken the right turn in the road.

In the circumstances, Bono could live with the view from the Ramada, Atlanta. He was looking forward to dinner. There was rather more to Bono than met the eye on stage or than was apparent in casual encounters. He *was* intense, heavy, intelligent, serious and committed to his idea of goodness. He *was* the angry young Irishman too. He had a highly developed sense of spirituality. But he adapted to the company he kept. Socially Bono was the great actor, his high intelligence and powerful spirit tuned to the wavelengths of those around him, or, to be more accurate, those he wanted to be around. This was the Irish gift of assimilation taken to its creative limits. Thus as a kid he won the hearts of mothers, teachers and neighbours. As a teenager at parties he would slope off from his street gang and chat up the pretty girl, the streetwise urchin transformed into serious young man. Outraged by his betrayal, the lads would try to tear off his disguise, Gavin or Guggi would wander over and utter some crude remark: 'Hallo, dirty bollox,' to try to shock the nice suburban girl. Bono would feign horror and disown his friends. The gift was now highly developed. With an intellectual Bono would be intellectual. With an accountant he would talk money. With the road crew he'd talk crew talk. With journalists he'd talk about the world. He was a sharp and wickedly funny exposer of other people's acts. But that gift was rarely revealed in public, was for the band and his closest friends who knew and understood where he had come from.

After dinner they moved to the lounge for a few drinks. Monday in Atlanta. A bar band was playing, telling the story of rock 'n' roll, complete with costume changes. The Amnesty crowd watched indulgently. It was midnight. Edge had gone to bed. So had Lou Reed. Bono was relaxed, not ready for bed yet, in the mood for devilment. 'Someone should liberate those instruments,' an Amnesty voice suggested as the bar band launched into their impression of Bruce Springsteen and the E Street Band. Fortunately, Springsteen brought the bar band's history of rock to its awful climax. The audience applauded. The mood of barely suppressed hilarity among the Amnesty crowd expressed itself as exaggerated applause. All the tension of touring, all the ice melted away as the Ramada band took their bow. Manu Katche, Peter Gabriel's brilliant drummer, together with Lou Reed's guitarist, negotiated a loan of the band's instruments.

'Could we play a little tune?'

'Sure, go ahead.'

Bono, high on the absurdity of the night, got up to sing. He started Lou Reed's 'Sweet Jane' and sang it to a raunchy young lady posing at the bar. She thought it was for real. Bono was moving in close, a lounge-lizard blending now with the atmosphere of late night provincial low-life, making his seedy play for the local *femme fatale*. She responded to his meaningful looks. As he reached her side she whispered, 'My name's not Jane, it's Rose.' Okay, 'Sweet Rose'.

Everybody played and sang. They jammed the night away, Baez, Gabriel, Adams, the Neville Brothers, Larry, Adam and Bono. At four a.m. the management moved them out, so they sang on in the foyer. The Ramada Atlanta was the social highlight of the tour, a night of marvellously uncontrived gaiety. Who needed drugs? Who needed orgies? This was childhood, good clean fun.

When they heard about it next day, Lou Reed and Edge were sorry to have missed the party. 'If you ever do that again, be sure to wake me,' Reed chastized Bono. Okay, we'll do it again tonight, Bono replied. Only this time it *was* contrived. The magic was missing on Tuesday night. But not the pleasure. Reed was one of Bono's heroes. He'd been no great record-collector when he was young, but one of the few good LPs he'd had was of the Velvet Underground, Reed's group. Streetwise was an overworked word, but in Reed's case it applied. He was worldly, damaged, but not beaten. He was smart and daring, and Bono was intrigued.

They talked on the road. About music, the power of rock 'n'

roll to influence things. There was a part of Bono that could have lived where Reed had lived, in the drug-induced twilight of New York City. Reed understood. Bono and U2 were a different generation. They were smart too, they weren't going to fuck up. Reed understood what their music was trying to say, understood, because he had lived it, the difference between freedom and responsibility. Bono called on him to sing that second night in the Ramada. Reed, after much persuasion, shyly consented, offering a rare rendition of 'Sweet Jane' and 'Vicious'.

On Friday when the Conspiracy of Hope reached Chicago's Westin O'Hare, Jack Healey relayed the good news; the tour had been more than an artistic and social success, it had been a triumph for Amnesty. They would make $3 to $4 million and, perhaps more importantly, thousands of young Americans had stopped on the way out of the concerts to pledge themselves to Amnesty's letter-writing campaign on behalf of political prisoners. Healey's battle would never be won, but after the Conspiracy of Hope the fight would never seem so lonely again. Reagan's America still had a conscience.

The Westin Hotel was not in the grand style. It functioned the way businessmen travellers wanted it to. The lobby was designed to discourage intimacy: high ceiling, low couches, lots of glass. You felt slightly diminished. Reception, a long desk raised a little to enable staff to look down on you, was equally devoid of the personal touch. The staff were formally polite with their 'Have a nice days.' People came, people left. The Westin was the black hole of experience. Anonymity was the motif. The Westin delivered on its promise; you got your food and board. All it demanded in return was the imprint of your credit card.

This suited Bono. The seventh floor of the Westin was a sanctuary from fame, the world, people with their prying eyes. At twenty-six he now understood that to be famous, to be a public man, was to be violated constantly. People stared. Some brazenly, others in amusement, many in adoration. Some talked to him, at him, about him. He felt *everything*. The looks, the talk. Everything he felt drained him. There were *no* casual encounters. Sitting in his car at traffic lights he could feel the eyes from the car alongside penetrating the flimsy shell of glass and steel he drove. In bars, conversations stopped, girls giggled nervously, men seemed vaguely amused. Fame edged you ever further from the centre, robbed you of the comfortable anonymity essential to observe. Fame forced you to avert your eyes. He liked to observe. He liked to look at people, watch them play their games. He liked to play himself, but it was getting harder. So the Westin was fine. You could get lost, store your emotions for tonight's performance. Daytime boredom was part of touring, an essential part.

Chicago was the penultimate stop. This was Ronald Reagan's America, where Rambo was *the* folk-hero. American Amnesty wasn't so much despised as ignored. The tour was an attempt to raise consciousness. Seduced by their rock heroes, the generation of young people whose parents had elected Reagan would be exposed to human rights, videos and literature, exposed to the reality of tyranny and oppression around the world and reminded that there was more to life than the material and emotional aspirations of the American Dream. There was more to life than air-conditioning and the weekly orgasm. There was, for the overwhelming majority on earth, more to life than Going For It.

What Geldof had done for famine-relief, the Amnesty tourists were now attempting, albeit on a smaller scale, to do for human rights. Like famine, political oppressions knew no ideological, racial, religious or cultural frontiers. It was a universal scourge. This was Amnesty's message.

Robin Williams, a star of situation comedies, including *Mork and Mindy*, on American television, made a guest appearance at the Rosemont, Chicago. He came on between Peter Gabriel and U2. Williams was greeted with rapturous applause by 18,000 people. Gabriel had ended a set of brilliant theatricality with a moving lament for Steve Biko, the young leader of Black Consciousness who'd been murdered in custody by South African police. Gabriel's 'Biko' was the emotional peak of the Amnesty concerts, the moment when entertainment overlapped with awareness, when the Conspiracy of Hope being played out in this arena came face to face with the reality of the world outside. During 'Biko' it was possible to feel, concurrently, hope and despair. Hope because Amnesty existed, because Gabriel so clearly cared and could for that fleeting moment make middle-America care as well. But despair also because you knew that good intentions, even 18,000 of them, weren't enough. Robin Williams' act did nothing to dispel such thoughts. The millionaire hero of sit-com wore a Tom Paxton cap and blue jeans. A squeal of delighted recognition escaped from the auditorium: 'What are *you* doing here?' it seemed to ask. 'Are you for Amnesty too?'

Williams drew waves of laughter. He swore a lot: 'Fuck this, fuck that, fuck everything.' Gee, Robin Williams says fuck! He referred to Ronald Reagan and Nancy and the White House. The greatest glee was when he said Reagan and fuck in the same sentence! It was childish and sad. Was American radicalism reduced to this? A generation ago Mort Sahl, Lenny Bruce or Dick Gregory would have been funny and truly relevant. Surely a president who admired Rambo, who thought Zimbabwe was a board game, was ripe for satire and parody? Was there not in contemporary American culture, in Sylvester Stallone, Joan Collins, George Bush enough material for any comic? If you were radical and funny, when better to be working than here in 1986? With his fucks and bastards Williams was a pathetic gauge by which to measure the state of American opposition to Ramboism. By their jokes you shall know them. Williams left to a standing ovation. American Amnesty's task was placed in proper perspective.

U2 restored the mood. Edge felt Chicago was their finest performance. The word he used was maturity. They were, he felt, starting to understand better what it was that was good about the band, realizing that there was something powerful musically, something innately worthwhile about *them* as performers. They didn't have to work harder, do anything sensational like hanging from the scaffolding round the stage, they didn't need gimmicks, physical or theatrical; the music and Bono's voice were enough. They had real confidence. They could harness their passions. Focus on what they wanted to say rather than on how they stage-managed it. Let the music talk.

In the Rosemont, Sting and the Police were to follow. U2 knew they would have to be special. They were. From the opening chords of 'Pride' through to 'Help', U2 transformed this evening of political consciousness with its vague and essentially meaningless abstractions into a personal experience. The Rosemont contracted as Bono reached out and drew Reagan's people in. 'Help, I need somebody. Help, not just *anybody*. Help, you know I need someone.' As in 'Bad', U2's version of the old Beatles classic was a beguiling blend of plea and proclamation. The words evoking human vulnerability, the music and the singer embodying the enduring strength and optimism of the human spirit. The suggestion was that help was at hand. You felt somehow strengthened by the music.

Later, in the dressing room, Dick Gregory defined reality. He was a ghost from the 1960s when Bono, Edge, Larry and Adam were barely born. A black comedian who had prodded America's conscience when Kennedy was in the White House and Martin Luther King was sharing his dream with a prime-time audience, Gregory now bore the marks of defeat. Here backstage at the Rosemont he represented another age. His blue suit was immaculately tailored, shirt neatly starched but half a size too big. His hair was grey, his face deeply lined, his eyes blankly watchful. Bono and Sting huddled respectfully with him in the centre of the room.

Gregory had once written a book called *Nigger*. 'When you hear them say it don't despair,' he told his mother. 'They will be plugging my book.' Gradually, through civil rights, Vietnam, Presidents Ford, Nixon, Reagan, the isolation and self-destruction of Teddy Kennedy, Dick Gregory had found himself moving ever further from the mainstream of American life. He was too much for Hollywood, Madison Avenue, too much even for black Americans *en masse*, who recoiled from his uncompromising confrontation with everyday, across-the-block racism. As new black heroes like the Rev. Jesse Jackson and Bill Cosby emerged, Gregory came to represent un-reasonableness. Work in show business became harder to find. More and more time was spent as a political activist.

Larry Mullen hated the strained artificiality of post-show dressing-room chat. He had yet to learn the conversational gymnastics of the cocktail-party circuit. He wasn't much good at the body language of polite encounter. He often felt the urge to clear the room, to utter an almighty roar: 'Fuck Off!' On occasions he acted on this impulse, to the great embarrassment of Bono, who loved his star-fucking as much as the next man.

Watching Bono now with Dick Gregory, Larry felt grudging admiration for his pal. He could certainly talk with the best of them. Meanwhile, waiting impatiently to get out of here and back to the hotel, Larry steered clear of new faces and talked to those he knew. 'How was the show?' That was what he wanted to know. He'd never heard of Dick Gregory and feigned only mild interest when told exactly who he was and what he'd done. The 1960s were history, ancient history, in politics as much as rock 'n' roll.

Back at the Westin, Bono talked about Gregory. The black

activist had told Bono and Sting that AIDS was a government plot hatched in Washington, a form of germ warfare being used by the Moral Majority to punish homosexuals and promiscuous heterosexuals, a Conspiracy of Revenge!

As the Amnesty jet flew down towards New York an end-of-term mood prevailed. As the Manhattan skyline grew clearer a pillow-fight broke out on the plane. Thus the rock 'n' roll class of 1986 expressed high spirits and the high of reaching New York where, before 55,000 people in the Giants Stadium, New Jersey, the Conspiracy of Hope would come to a glorious climax.

Sunday at the Stadium was to be a day out for show-business's liberal establishment. Yoko Ono, Elliot Gould, Joni Mitchell, Carlos Santana and Miles Davis had committed. Pete Townshend was flying in from London. Muhammad Ali and Bob Geldof would drop by. MTV would broadcast live for twelve hours from noon. It would be a Grand Occasion.

Seconds after the plane hit the runway there was a loud bang which silenced the happy company. People exchanged curious, slightly concerned glances. What was *that*? It was a burst tyre, a potential disaster that was forgotten by the time the company reached the press conference at Giants Stadium. The artists sat at a long table in a marquee in the stadium grounds. To the side and on a bench behind sat a small group of ex-prisoners freed by Amnesty pressure. Among them sat Fela, a Nigerian singer imprisoned by his government on trumped-up currency charges, and an attractive yet sadly worn-out-looking lady from Argentina. Alongside the casually elegant, comfortably confident music people and the business-like representatives of New York press and television, the dispossessed seemed out of place. Their clothes were new, cheap and thin, their faces flushed with nervousness, yet bearing the strangely indefinable marks of defeat, of a light somewhere deep inside having been extinguished.

On this hot, humid Saturday afternoon, the reality of political oppression contrasted sharply with good intention and the banal irrelevance of the media's interrogation. Sting, the cool, self-possessed, intelligent Englishman, spoke eloquently about the Conspiracy of Hope's modest aims. Bono beside him was less sure in response to a loaded and deeply misguided question from a lady writer who sought to link the IRA murder campaign in Northern Ireland to Amnesty's campaign on behalf of the politically oppressed. 'What about the prisoners in Belfast?' this lady asked. There are only two credible responses to this: a complete rejection of the premise on which the dumb question is based, or a long complex explanation pointing out *why* the IRA are *not* freedom fighters. Had this journalist *ever* heard 'Sunday Bloody Sunday'?

> *Broken bottles under children's feet,*
> *Bodies strewn across a dead-end street,*
> *But I won't heed the battle call,*
> *It puts my back up,*
> *Puts my back up against the wall,*
> *Sunday Bloody Sunday.*

Obviously not. Bono's answer diplomatically fudged the issue.

Further along the top table, Cyril Neville listened sceptically to the castigation of brutality and oppression worldwide. The press conference was running out of steam. Everyone was feeling pretty good. Nobody had mentioned America yet. 'If you're black and on the street in this country, you're politically oppressed,' Neville exploded. This was the first sign of *real* anger this afternoon, an ironic reminder of the score. An uncomfortable intrusion that was edited out of subsequent TV coverage and newspaper accounts.

Having arrived in Chicago on Friday for the last two dates on the tour, Paul McGuinness was delighted to find things going well. He was proud of U2, the band, the crew, Barbara, and, most of all on this job, Anne-Louise. Thus, on this warm Sunday morning in New Jersey, Paul could consider himself a tourist. At eleven a.m. he set out alone for Giants Stadium. U2 weren't due on stage for almost twelve hours. Paul was going to enjoy the day, have fun. It would be a fun day and maybe a useful one. All the powerful people in the business would be at the concert, it was *that* Sunday's buzz event in New York.

Although he projected a rather dry, serious image, the well-modulated public-school accent suggesting the right amount of gravitas, McGuinness was a convivial social animal. The greatest pleasure of having made it with U2, of having arrived, was the collegiality of life among the best and brightest. The food was better, the jokes more sophisticated, the gossip high-grade. Paul was looking forward to the day.

For Anne-Louise and the band left behind at Loews Hotel, this was an important working-day. They wanted everything to be spot on, but they had problems. U2 were due on stage second-last on a long bill. All through the Conspiracy tour they'd had a feeling of being in control of things. Nobody had taken liberties, none of the other acts had over-run. It had been a cooperative venture. Today was different. MTV, the rock-music television station, were broadcasting live from the stadium. In exchange for this unprecedented opportunity to reach millions with the Amnesty message, Jack Healey had to surrender power over the day's proceedings to the television people. This meant that the band playing second-last were at the mercy of any other act that over-ran. Their set could be cut short or interrupted by commercials, or almost anything could happen to screw up what was an important day in the life of U2. They wanted some kind of assurance. They wanted Anne-Louise to get that assurance from somebody. How long did they have on stage? Would their set be interrupted, or cut short?

By mid-afternoon, still no assurance was forthcoming. They

were trying to work out a set for one of the most testing gigs of their career, in a vacuum. They wanted Paul. Anne-Louise rang him at the stadium. He could do nothing much. The Amnesty tour was now out of control. Everyone was in on the act: Senator Bill Bradley was on stage making a speech. He'd just voted aid for the Contras in Congress, now he was advocating human rights on MTV. The Conspiracy of Hope had become a media event, an opportunity for politicians, movie stars, the well-meaning and the not-so-well-meaning to grab their fifteen minutes of prime time glory. There was nothing Jack Healey could do. There was nothing Bill Graham could do. Paul McGuinness, whose generous impulse had inspired the whole thing, was now just another guy with an 'All Areas' badge. And *everyone* had those.

Out in the arena Joe O'Herlihy, the band's sound engineer, was growing anxious; he needed to know what set they were going to play so that he could programme the sequencers. Back at the hotel the band were angry. Great performances didn't happen by accident and this had to be a great performance. They were a little resentful that Paul wasn't with them. He was pissed off that they were expecting him to perform miracles. Anne-Louise was in the middle.

They would have to wing it; before 55,000 in New York! Before an audience that would include some of the record and agency people who mattered, *really* mattered in the business. People like Frank Barsalona, who hadn't seen or heard them for over a year, who would judge them, their progress, their ability to play to an outdoor stadium, on the set. And they were having to wing it. On a bill where Miles Davis, Carlos Santana and some of the greatest performers in the game were going on *before* them, and Sting and the Police were going on *afterwards*! This day had all the ingredients of a bummer.

Fear was being out of control. The stadium floodlights were on, dusk was falling as they drew up outside. This was the moment you braced yourself for, when the adrenalin began to flow and the fear of failure ran through your blood. This was the moment you started concentrating on the reality that lay at the core of this movie you found yourself in. The stadium, any arena, was a mass of noise and faces, famous and familiar. Beyond, reality waited; the stage, the music, the audience, the reaction to your songs. You got more confident, were more acclaimed, became stars, the band of the '80s but you never rid yourself of the vulnerability. Performing was unique in that there was no formula, procedure or set of circumstances in existence that would guarantee that night's success. Every gig was different, every audience, every atmosphere, every venue. Chicago was history. So was Croke Park, Live Aid, Self-Aid and all the other triumphs. *This* was the one your life depended on.

The dressing room was a small, curtained-off corner of the stadium restaurant. The place was full of famous faces; people ate, talked and laughed and watched each other eating, laughing and talking. It could have been fun, if you didn't have to work.

Word reached them that Muhammad Ali and his two teenage daughters would like to visit the dressing room. In this room full of the famous Ali cast a shadow of true greatness over all. As he helped himself to a chicken dinner from the restaurant buffet, eyes, famous and otherwise, turned in his direction. A slow giant, he shuffled back to his table accompanied by his little girls and a tall, impassive Muslim minder. Everyone knew about the slurred speech, the confusion. Everyone had heard the rumours about the consequences of those last few fights. Now everyone in this room could see and feel the tragedy. Once the greatest athlete of his time, the bravest, the most gracious and the funniest, Ali sat now struggling to get the damn chicken onto his fork. His eyes were blank, dark pools of despair, yet his face was unmarked, glowing with an almost childlike innocence. The man who'd mocked racists, taunted them with the promise that they'd never get him like they got Joe Louis, was now as gotten as any man could be. Ali, the symbol of hope and defiance for his people, for *all* people who believed in beauty and courage, was now just another old fighter who couldn't get the fucking chicken on his fork.

A middle-aged man approached the table with his young son, maybe ten, twelve years old. 'Muhammad, please, would you sign his book?' the man asked tentatively, holding out an autograph book. Ali looked up, smiled and reached out for the boy with one arm and the book with his other hand. 'What's your name?' he whispered. The father had tears in his eyes. The signature given, Ali hugged the kid close to him and cuffed him lightly on the cheek. The man tried to say something but couldn't. Choking back his grief, he grasped Ali's arm and held on. 'Thanks, Champ.' Ali smiled again, a smile that was kind of helpless, as if telling the man that yes, *he too* knew that it was tragic what had happened to him, that yes, he knew better than anyone that he was got, the victim of his own innocence. It was almost show-time for U2. Ali towered above them, smiling that ghostly smile. He showed the boys his magic trick. As Ali left the room Bono shook his head, the pain of the encounter flickering briefly in the singer's eyes.

As they hit the stage Bono almost froze with shock. The lights should have been dimmed. Instead, the stadium flood-lights glared down upon him. No chance to feel for anything. He felt like a laboratory specimen with 55,000 technicians gazing down at him. He was naked. He exchanged a murderous look with Edge, grabbed the microphone stand and flung it behind him. Backstage, Paul McGuinness stood, impassive, knowing something was seriously wrong. Anne-Louise stood deeper in the shadows. Out there the audience rose and heaved forward. MTV had taken over. Peter Williams, U2's lighting man, had lost the power play with television. Nobody noticed, apart from the principals. The performance was superb, fuelled, as the R D S show had been, by anger and by pride. And by ruthlessness that demanded perfection, a quality the band looked for first in themselves and after that in everything and everybody around them. Frank Barsalona and Barbara Skydel sat proudly in the V I P enclosure, remembering the Ritz.

Afterwards, while Eamonn McCann and Terry O'Neill ligged with Geldof and other famous faces, the band of the '80s held an inquest in the dressing room. Bono wanted to know what had gone wrong. Outside, people talked about how great they'd been and wondered what U2 might become when they produced the magic on record.

Greg Carroll died tragically in a road accident in Dublin within days of returning from the Amnesty tour. He was killed when the motor-bike he was riding collided with a car on More-hampton Road a few minutes from the city centre. Madge Smyth, the band's dresser, received the news of Greg's accident. It was for her perhaps more than anyone a devastating shock. She and Greg were 'great mates', living in the same house and sharing a way of life. Madge, who had come to U2 from the fashion business, had joined the band at the same time as Greg. They were oddly similar, gracious, cheerful, modest and happy to be working for their band. Anne-Louise Kelly was sent for in the early hours. She was at St Vincent's Hospital when Greg died shortly after being admitted.

Greg had been with the band eighteen months. He looked after Bono, on stage and off. They were friends. Being a roadie was what you made of it. Being a rock 'n' roll singer was what you made of it. Greg loved his job. Maybe he wouldn't be working like this for ever, but he was young and it was fun. U2 was a small community, Greg loved them, they loved him. He'd been hired for his personal qualities, like almost everyone else around. He would learn his job as Paul and the band had theirs, as Joe, Dennis, Anne-Louise, Steve and Tom had.

Greg's large Maori frame radiated dignity and good humour. He wasn't a roadie. U2 didn't employ roadies. They employed people.

Greg's natural father was a government minister in New Zealand. In keeping with Maori tradition, Greg had been adopted at birth by his father's childless sister and her husband. Steve Iredale and Joe O'Herlihy took Greg home to New Zealand. Larry, Ann, Bono, Ali and Katie McGuinness (Greg's girlfriend and Paul's sister) attended his funeral.

Chapter Eighteen

THE JOSHUA TREE

When *The Joshua Tree* was released in March 1987 it was dedicated to the memory of Greg Carroll 1960–86. Greg had spent the last eighteen months of his life at Danesmoate with the band. The big Georgian mansion stood in Rathfarnham next door to St Columba's, Adam's old school. It was there that the album that answered the outstanding question about U2 was created. Brian Eno and Danny Lanois co-produced, flying in to Dublin to inspire, correct or simply comfort the band of the '80s. Greg was there every working day, as was Mary, who provided food.

The Joshua Tree was the album U2 *had* to make, the only one they *could* make, ten years on from Mount Temple. It was honest, as usual, reflecting the experience of twenty-seven-year-old rock 'n' roll musicians who wanted to compose songs that would be sung at parties. The new album succeeded magnificently. *The Joshua Tree* went to the top of the album charts within days of release in Britain, America, everywhere that popular music was played and appreciated. 'With or Without You' gave them their first No. 1 single in America. The second single released off the album, 'I Still Haven't Found What I'm Looking For', also reached the top of the charts in the States. In April, Bono, Larry, Edge and Adam were featured on the cover of *Time* magazine. U2 were the third rock 'n' roll band to reach *Time*'s famed front cover, the Beatles and The Who having been there before.

The Joshua Tree was a wonderfully crafted piece of popular art. All the power of previous records was on this album and as ever they had been original in their choice of sound. To these fundamental qualities they had added rich melody and a new lyricism that made their music accessible as it had never been before. Craftsmen look outwards rather than in, resist the urge to shout, invest the passion instead on mastering the instruments they work with. On *The Joshua Tree*, Bono's words, Adam's bass, Larry's drums and Edge's 'orchestra' work individually and collectively, as they never had before. With twenty-seven-year-old musicians this is how it should be, but rarely *is* in rock 'n' roll. Men and women who should mature, regress, craft neglected, art never aspired to. U2 are different. They love their work. The band of the '80s had broken on the road playing live, working. One month before *Time* magazine they had never had a No. 1 single. After all those years of sweat *they* hadn't achieved what half-arsed pop bands, creations of clever sound engineers, could manage time and time again. That hurt a little. Now that hurt was gone.

'Running to Stand Still', a lament for a Dublin woman addicted to heroin that closes Side One of *The Joshua Tree*, contains lines that tell a truth about the men who created the album:

> *You got to cry without weeping,*
> *Talk without speaking,*
> *Scream without raising your voice.*

The maturity U2 had reached, in their music and their lives, is present on *The Joshua Tree*. Where they look out, the view reflected is perceptive. America, the culture governing all who can be reached by rock 'n' roll (or *Time* magazine), is captured here in words, music, sound and images as vivid as paintings. 'Bullet the Blue Sky' evokes the plaintive soul of Central America, cowering from the giant at the door. The ugly face of cultural imperialism, the tourist in search of a good time, is here as well, in words as vivid as the rock 'n' roll that guides them:

> *Suit and tie comes up to me,*
> *His face red*
> *Like a rose on a thorn bush,*
> *Like all the colours of a royal flush,*
> *And he's peeling off those dollar bills*
> *(Slapping them down) one hundred, two hundred.*

Almost ten years ago Bono wrote 'Out of Control' on his eighteenth birthday. That song was personal, about 'boys and girls who go to school', the writer not quite knowing how to express the doubts and anxieties of teenage life:

> *I was having feelings*
> *Out of control,*
> *I had real pins and needles*
> *Out of control.*

Ten years on, the grown man knows exactly what he is seeing and feeling on his travels through Central America, and has acquired the literary craftsmanship to express it:

> *And I can see the fighter planes,*
> *And I can see the fighter planes,*
> *Across the mud huts as the children sleep,*
> *Through the alleys of a quiet street,*
> *Up the staircase to the first floor*
> *We turn the key and slowly unlock the door.*
> *A man breathes deep into a saxophone,*

Through the walls we hear the city groan,
Outside is America,
Outside is America.

Those words, describing the terror America's presence inflicts on the people of Nicaragua, were written for a piece of music created by Edge, Adam and Larry while they were jamming in a studio a few months before the final mix of 'Bullet'. It was Edge who composed the sound of menace. As a piece, 'Bullet' is art, the expression of human experience through rock 'n' roll, more profound and accessible than it has ever been. 'Bullet' was not one of *The Joshua Tree*'s 'songs'. It has yet to be issued as a single. Instead 'Bullet' provides a clue to where U2 might head now that their ability to top the hit parade is no longer the issue. One of rock 'n' roll's tragedies has been the idiom's inability to facilitate its great musicians and writers beyond a certain point in their artistic development. Speculating about his future, John Lennon voiced his fear of ending up in a creative cul-de-sac, trapped by the need to write instantly accessible songs that conformed to the idiom he'd grown up in. 'I don't want to end up like Elvis, playing to fat cats in Vegas,' Lennon insisted. He wanted to grow, and stay relevant, but nobody had yet proved that rock 'n' roll could nourish the talents of men and women beyond a certain age. Pete Townshend, another powerful, no longer angry, force, posed the same question about rock 'n' roll's limitations. The wasted lives of so many great musicians bore testimony, Townshend suggested, to artistic frustration, a kind of self-disgust, experienced when what you had to say could no longer be expressed through the idiom you'd mastered. This crippling dilemma awaited down the road for U2. If there was an answer, then perhaps they were the band to discover it.

Brian Eno and Danny Lanois had finally helped them master the studio. Eno was the link with the past, with Bowie and

Roxy Music. He had an original mind and a pedigree, and having his imprimatur on their music mattered. Lanois the engineer-musician was crucial to the translation of ideas into sounds. They sent for Steve Lillywhite for the last few weeks of recording. Steve mixed 'Bullet', 'With or Without You' and 'Where the Streets Have No Name'.

By his presence, Steve ensured continuity, his was the trusted verdict on the most important album of their career. On the final night of mixing, in mid-February, Lillywhite and the four lads sweated together in Windmill Lane. One critical decision remained: 'Bullet' ended with the words, 'outside is America'. But a second ending had been recorded which left the question of America's culpability for the listener to decide. This alternative line ran, 'outside is the world'. To confront or imply, that was the final issue? Lillywhite phoned Paul McGuinness for a decision. Paul decided on confrontation. 'America', not the world, would be identified.

They threw a party the following night out at Edge's house in Monkstown, where much of the final mixing had taken place in a fit-up recording studio. They played the record for their friends and waited for reaction. The Village were there, but not all of them. A few weeks before, Gavin had left the Virgin Prunes to begin a solo career. The Prunes had survived the 1980s as a cult performance-art band, popular in alternative pockets of the UK and Europe. Dick Evans had left in 1984, with Gavin and Guggi taking the major roles front of stage. They'd been booked to tour America when, two weeks before they were due to set off, Gavin pulled the plug. Pod was left unemployed. The bravest knight of all did not attend *The Joshua Tree* celebrations. Neither did Maeve O'Regan who was living in England, a committed Christian working for her beliefs. She watched U2 from afar, happy for Bono, astonished at the progress the band had made in the years since Mount Temple. In the months ahead Maeve would grow even more astonished as *The Joshua Tree* echoed around the world, reaching people who'd never heard of U2 before. They were, *Time* magazine claimed, leaders of their generation.

The 1980s had bred a new kind of hero, suburban rather than urban, real smart rather than street-smart, rooted in Dublin's sanity rather than rootless in LA, New York or London. Belonging somewhere – that was, in the age of the global village, everywhere.

The party in Edge's house might have been anywhere in suburbia. People drank wine, red or white, ate from the kitchen buffet. There was no champagne, no cocaine, nobody freaked out or got laid. Once upon a time you went to the city for drugs. Now the drugs travelled to the suburbs. 'Running to Stand Still' was set in Ballymun in the flats they built behind Cedarwood Road when Bono was growing up.

> *Sweet the sin,*
> *But bitter the taste in my mouth.*
> *I see seven towers*
> *But I only see one way out.*

Once upon a time Bobby and Iris Hewson sought suburban bliss in Ballymun. Today the seven towers of Ballymun Flats cast a shadow over the green fields that promised so much. Heroin is 'one way out' of the misery of new Ballymun. Lennon, Dylan, Townshend and Keith Richards all left suburbia in search of what they called life. Now life spreads out, touching us all, its empty premises seducing those who previously sought mere tranquillity.

The Joshua Tree did more than make U2 famous. It set them free. They no longer need to prove that they can top the charts. Drawing freely on rock 'n' roll tradition *The Joshua Tree* reflects the influences of Dylan, Lou Reed and Jimi Hendrix. Here is Bono, the great actor and mimic, at his most convincing as he reaches out for artistic maturity. The kind of fame U2 now enjoy destroyed most of their predecessors. The fame and the money were ends in themselves, the products of talent that had reached its creative peak and no longer knew where to go. This band will be different. They are still growing musically and personally. They still haven't found what they're looking for. Bono, writer, performer, image-maker, painter of vivid landscapes, will continue to be enriched by his experience. Edge, the genius composer of sounds, will interpret those images and the melodies that cascade around his partner's head. Larry will intuitively understand the drumming parts which will continue to be as distinct as the words and chords they put muscle on. Adam will play his bass, its chords providing inspiration for all who would travel from Castle Park to *Time*'s front cover. U2 are, finally, a group. Every stage of their journey has revealed a truth, about themselves or the times their music has attempted to reflect.

The penultimate song on *The Joshua Tree* is 'Exit'. It puzzled many reviewers and listeners. 'Exit' means out from the confusion of the past, out of the twilight world where Christianity merged with rock 'n' roll to form doubt. That is over. U2 have exited into daylight, certain now that music is a gift from God and that as musicians their responsibility is to use it. Exposed by fame to temptations of ego and the flesh on a scale that few people can imagine, their story is in essence just beginning. U2's greatest struggles lie ahead.

Irish artists have invariably been casualties of the culture that reared them. Those who didn't languish bitterly in exile were, like Kavanagh, Behan, O'Riada and 'Myles', destroyed by native indifference. They only became Official Irishmen in death, evidence, offered without shame to the world, that we were a gifted people behind it all. Behind it all: the sectarian Church serving as a life-support system to the Nationalist-Republican Parliament of official Ireland; spiritual mediocrity breeding political and philosophical pygmies whose reach was sufficient to castrate the more imaginative native sons. If you had ideas that 'didn't belong' and a spirit that was 'too large' you got out or drank yourself to death, penury attending the bedside vigil.

Ireland has changed a little. U2 are not alone, not quite. They belong to a generation of Irish artists which is fighting back, or at least trying to. Most still get out, like film-makers Pat O'Connor and Neil Jordan. Seamus Heaney won't die, he remains, along with Bono and the lads, living proof that these days you don't have to piss your talent up against the walls along the back of Grafton Street that witnessed Kavanagh's degradation. Elsewhere, Irish culture, of which sport is an integral part, produces great men like Stephen Roche and Sean Kelly, the world's best cyclists, and Pat Eddery, one of the finest jockeys the racing game has known. All these men possess qualities that are manifest in the nation, Unofficial Ireland, that bred them. They are gracious, humorous, confident, their view of the world formed by the world rather than the sick fantasies of the Ireland of another age. U2 are part of this, New Irelanders, using the resources that are their true inheritance rather than genuflecting before the worn-out symbols of Church dogma and Nationalist myth. The Irish are different not because they pray or because they fight, but because they are sensitive, imaginative, rich in spirit in that part of their culture that isn't soaked in blood. The new generation will forge its own identity.

Talking about how things used to be in rock 'n' roll, Tom Mullally pointed to the sleaze that infected the entourage of Phil Lynott, who'd tasted glory in the music business before U2. Did it have to be like that, Tom wondered back in 1983? Four years on he knows that rock 'n' roll *can* defy sick traditions. Tom is assistant production manager with U2 now, Steve Iredale's right-hand man. They are the best in the world at what they do. Dennis Sheehan and Joe O'Herlihy have likewise proved themselves masters of a craft that no Irishman had mastered before. They are all Irish, refugees from pasts that promised much less than they have achieved. All they needed was a new tune to dance to.

Appendix

OTHER VIEWS OF U2

DON'T BELIEVE A WORD:
THE LIFE AND DEATH OF PHIL LYNOTT
Fintan O'Toole

Leighlin, Clonmacnoise, Ferns, Kells, Bangor, Lismore, Clogher. The centre of the corporation estate of Crumlin was started in the year of the Eucharistic Congress and built in the shape of the Eucharistic Cross. The roads were named after the dioceses of the Irish Catholic Church. Out here it was new territory, a kind of Ireland – suburban and working-class – not known before. As if to magic away the uncertainty of what might emerge from these winding rows of pebble-dashed, two-up-and-two-downs, the planners gave them the shape and the names of the greatest institution of Irish tradition – the Church. Happy homes and happy families, with the huge vaulted church and the granite barracks-like police station to look down and smile, and not a whisper of rock and roll on the distant breezes.

> *I'm a little black boy*
> *and I don't know my place,*
> *I'm just a little black boy*
> *I just threw my ace*
> *I'm a little black boy*
> *Recognize my face.*

(Phil Lynott, 'Black Boys on the Corner')

Phil Lynott was born on 20 August 1951 and brought up on Leighlin Road, but his happy family was not the kind which the planners dreamt of. His father had never been around. He lived with his grandmother and his two uncles, Peter and Timmy. Timmy worked and kept the family going, not poor, just making ends meet. Granny was the matriarch. But Peter was the dreamer and Peter was the rocker. At Armagh Road CBS primary school, the topical taunt,

'Ya Baluba!', had an extra cutting edge when aimed at the little black boy, and Philip, though he suffered no serious racism, was more self-conscious, more angular, than the other kids. But with that self-consciousness was a new reason to be proud.

The music that Uncle Peter listened to was soul and rhythm and blues, black music, even if it was sung by whites. Philip grew up with the Yardbirds, The Who, the Animals, led by his hero Eric Burdon, and, beyond that, with the black soul music of the STAX label singers. Later, when his uncle Peter turned down the job of singing with the Black Eagles, the first Crumlin rock band, Philip would take his place.

The music never completely filled the gap left by his father. Philip looked for heroes, in books and in the cinema. At the Roxy and the Stella he acquired a taste for stand-up saviours, lone men pitted against the world. In his songs he would again and again return to the figure of the hero, of the Wild West or of Celtic mythology. Thinking of himself as an orphan, he had himself adopted by the heroic loners of his dream world. He called one of his first bands the Orphanage and wrote songs like 'Shades Of A Blue Orphanage' ('. . . the Roxy and the Stella/where film stars starred/that's where me and Hopalong Cassidy, Roy Rogers got drunk and jarred/and we might have been/the saviours of men/the captured captain in the devil's demon den.')

There were times, after he had grown up and become famous, when he went looking for his father. He looked in big cities of the western world. He even ended up once in Rio, where his father might have come from. In the end, he invented myths about his father, writing him into cosy domestic scenes in his songs, or transporting him into the realm of the legendary heroes. In his 1973 Thin Lizzy album, *Vagabonds of the Western World*, he had a song, 'Legend of the Vagabond', in which a mysterious traveller from afar meets and falls in love with a young girl, fathers a child by her and leaves on the night the child is born. 'It is written from that day to this, all male descendants/Of the fatherless child are blessed in the art of love/to win the heart of any, but cursed never to be in love/or they will grow old and wither.' Phil Lynott, the fatherless child, never grew old and withered. But he never stopped thinking of himself as an orphan.

DON'T BELIEVE A WORD

Father and I waved goodbye
As we went to look
Uncle Peter was writing a book
And his mama was starting to cook
And she's ageing.

('Saga of the Ageing Orphan')

*

Armagh Road primary school had no secondary school attached. The boys from ambitious families, the ones anxious to take advantage of the new benefits of free education, went to Drimnagh Castle, a hub of the new meritocracy. The others went to Clogher Road Tech. Philip Lynott went to the Tech and stayed until he was fifteen. He went on to Tonge and Taggart metal works as an apprentice, going to Bolton Street College of Technology on day release to study mechanical drawing. Except for the music, it was a normal Dublin working-class upbringing. But the music was everything. Shortly after he left the Tech, Philip returned to play a gig in the school hall, making a big splash, putting on the style. He loved the idea of being king in a world where the teachers' writ didn't run, where you could make it big without them.

In the mid-sixties Dublin had a bit of money, a lot of young people and a hunger for the new rock music. Music clubs blossomed, where bands played and the audience drank minerals. There was the Club A Go-Go, the Five Club, the Moulin Rouge, the Flamingo, the Seventeen Club, the Scene Club, Club Arthur, the Apartment. The clubs were small and the entrance was cheap but there was enough work around to keep a succession of new bands going. The bands played the clubs on a four-week circuit, returning to the same place and pretty much the same audience every month. There were also gigs at tennis clubs outside the city centre, in Templeogue and Terenure, and halls in Fairview, Donnybrook and Phibsboro.

Phil Lynott's first band, the Black Eagles, formed in Crumlin in 1968, with a line-up that would soon include the Thin Lizzy drummer Brian Downey, played in a few of the clubs while Downey and Lynott were still at Clogher Road Tech, as well as finding a place on the bill of the large rock concerts in Crumlin's Apollo cinema. By the time they left school, the band had split, but Philip had tasted the tang of rock and roll, and moved on to another local Crumlin band, Kama Sutra. In 1969 he became the singer with Brush Sheils' Skid Row.

Psychedelia hit Dublin in 1968, and Skid Row were its harbingers. The bands around the clubs until then, bands like the Vampires and the Strangers, still thought that 'Good Vibrations' and 'The Sloop John B' were far-out numbers. Skid Row brought echo chambers, liquid lights and smoke bombs and Little Mick's eight millimetre films. Little Mick would film the band in one club and show the movie behind them while they played at the next one. Skid Row were louder, weirder and hipper than anyone had ever dared to be in Dublin before. Philip was getting into the *I Ching*, Kafka and acid before anyone else. He was listening to the Fugs and the Velvet Underground when hardly anyone else in Ireland had ever heard of them. Philip, they said, was really sussed.

By the time Philip was pushed out of Skid Row – he had tonsillitis and Gary Moore could sing as well as play lead guitar – he had learnt a lot about style, about giving the people something different. He had also learnt the peculiar mixture of an arty romanticism and macho hardman strutting that would become his image for stardom. By the time he formed Thin Lizzy in 1970, with Brian Downey and the Belfast duo of guitarist Eric Bell and keyboard player Eric Wrixon (Wrixon was let go halfway through the band's first year and subsequently written out of the official biographies – the rock and roll business has no tears for the ones who don't make it), Philip had a persona to sell.

> *I am your main man if you're looking for trouble*
> *I'll take no lip 'cause no one's tougher than me.*
> *If I kicked your face you'd be seeing double,*
> *Hey little girl keep your hands off me.*

('The Rocker')

*

Macho is an exaggerated masculinity in which an aggressive toughness goes easily with a romantic posture, and Philip, by the time he was twenty, had adopted the style. He didn't mind fighting but he liked a stylish fight, one hard punch and walk away. He took on the classic Latin macho image, growing a thin Latin moustache and wearing toreador outfits, with short jackets coming to the waist, of his own invention. On him they looked good, and he earned extra money doing fashion spreads for women's magazines. In his songs he would refer often to Rudolph Valentino, and for Lizzy's follow-up single to 'Whiskey in the Jar', he released a classic Latin fantasy, 'Randolph's Tango', full of Latin moonlight and the boys at the ranch and a *senorita* looking pure as a dove, all in white. 'Don't go my Randolph, slow tango with me.'

As Thin Lizzy began to be successful, the macho confidence grew. Philip was the man who could handle anything, drink anyone under the table, get any woman he wanted. One of the things he thought he could handle was drugs. In the early seventies in the Dublin rock scene, there was dope and acid. Smack (heroin) was a distant rumour; cocaine had hardly been heard of. That stuff would come later.

In 1970, Zhivago's nightclub opened in Dublin, a new kind of place where you drank alcohol instead of minerals while you danced the night away. The clubs, where the Dublin rock scene had blossomed, fell into sharp decline, and bands like Thin Lizzy were much too heavy for the more sophisticated nightclubs, who preferred the control of discos to the wild frenzy of live rock. Lizzy were smart enough to see the change coming and moved out into the still-thriving ballrooms, building themselves a national following in the way that very few rock bands had done. There were 'heads' in the country too, and Lizzy, six months into their career, got a run on the ABC ballroom circuit, playing a one-hour set, sandwiched between the show-band's two sets. For this they got £150 a night. In the Dublin clubs, they had been getting about £35.

Particularly after Eric Wrixon had been pushed out, and the band reduced to a three piece, the rock business began to provide a passable, if by no means decent, living. In Dublin there were still the larger ballrooms, the TV Club, the Crystal and the Ierne, which could attract a crowd of up to eight hundred for their Teenage Friday Nights. In

June 1970, Thin Lizzy did a one-off deal with EMI/Parlophone, who pressed a single, 'The Farmer'. Even if it only sold 273 copies, it at least proved that they were a real rock band.

More importantly, they were an Irish rock band. Philip's black skin and lithe style had an exotic air and the band's thunderous sound was like nothing from the Ballroom of Romance, but his accent was unmistakable. In their early days Lizzy did Jimi Hendrix numbers and a loud, brash, twenty-minute version of 'Dancing in the Streets', the sixties' hit recently re-released by David Bowie and Mick Jagger. The songs lists the names of American cities, from Chicago to New Orleans. When Philip sang it, he shouted an extended litany of Irish towns, from Cork to Ballina, like a country-and-western singer singing the right song for the locality of the ballroom. If the harsh violent sounds of hard rock were a culture shock to the Irish, Thin Lizzy narrowed the gap and nationalized the music.

And everywhere the band went, there were women. For Philip the women were not just an occupational perk, they were in a real sense a part of the business. He had a woman every night and argued that it was good for the band's business. He brought the women to to the gigs, the women brought the men. Sex was a personalized form of PR for the band, a way of building up a loyal following. The macho style became more than a style, it became a part of his way of life. Like the drugs, it was a habit he would never kick.

> *Don't believe me if I tell you*
> *Not a word of this is true*
> *Don't believe me if I tell you*
> *Especially if I tell you that*
> *I'm in love with you.*

('Don't Believe A Word')

*

London was the place to be for a young rock band, and to get there the band needed management. Their first manager, Terry O'Neill, sold his rights on Thin Lizzy for £150 to Pete Bardon and Brian Tuite, who had connections across the water. The band moved to

London to heel up on Granny's Intentions, the band who, with Skid Row, had found the path for Irish acts into the big time and the big city. They signed up with Decca Records in November 1970 and five months later, released their first album, *Thin Lizzy*. But the money in London for live bands was considerably lower than the going rates in Ireland and until the beginning of 1973 when 'Whiskey in the Jar' became a freak hit for the band, they survived in England only on the strength of twice yearly Irish tours. At this stage, the band could command £300 a night in the ballrooms of Ireland, which meant that they could make £6,000 in three weeks of hard slogging at home. After everything was paid for, there was enough to subsist in London for the rest of the year.

Even after the success of 'Whiskey in the Jar', which reached number six in the British charts in February 1973, Phil Lynott wasn't rich. The money from the record was enough for a decent flat and better band equipment, but it wasn't until May 1976, when 'The Boys Are Back In Town' made the top ten in Britain and America, taking the album *Jailbreak* with it, that Philip became rich. Within a month he was seriously ill with hepatitis, forcing the cancellation of the band's crucial American tour. From then until his death, he never broke down again, and even though he was using both heroin and cocaine, his high energy made him believe that he could take it on and beat it, like anything else. He had it sussed.

He had the music business sussed too. When the bloated old rock order was toppled by punk in 1977, Thin Lizzy survived. Philip helped Bob Geldof, about to sweep into the charts on the coat tails of punk, to get established in London. He turned up at all the wild parties for the young bands who were just about to make it big. He had the stamina to out-party them all. While the others were being written off as boring has-beens, Philip retained the confidence of the industry. He could still cut it in the wild-man stakes. By the end of 1978 he was playing with the *enfants terribles* of the new wave, the Sex Pistols, in a pick-up band called the Greedy Bastards, in both Dublin and London. While the others were retiring to their country mansions to play the family man, Philip was riding the new energy and taking care of the business. He had been doing it a lot longer than any of the young pretenders and he wasn't going to stop.

Bands on tour have contracts. There's the money, of course, by now around £20,000 for the services of Phil Lynott, but there's also the extras. The little bands get a crate of beer in the dressing room. Further up the scale it's beer, and a bottle of brandy, a bottle of tequila and a bottle of white wine, chilled. Thin Lizzy reached the heights where it could be six dozen bottles of German pils, a case of champagne, a bottle of the best cognac, and what's a few hundred quid on drink out of a gig that's costing £20,000?

Cocaine keeps you sober. It boosts your energy and keeps you from falling apart, even if you're drinking most of the night and getting out on the road again early the next morning. It also hides the debilitating effects of heroin. And it keeps you going in a world of lonesome heroes who take on the world and beat it. It's OK so long as you can handle it, so long as you have it sussed.

> *Now I've been messing with the heavy stuff*
> *And for a time I couldn't get enough*
> *But I'm waking up and it's wearing off.*
> *Junk don't take you far.*
> *Tell my mama I'm coming home*
> *And in my youth I'm getting older*
> *And I think it's lost control.*
> *Mama, I'm coming home*
> *Got to give it up*
> *Give it up*
> *Got to give it up, that stuff*
> *Got to give it up.*

('Got To Give It Up')

*

On Sunday 5 January 1986, Heavy Metal Heather cashed in her chips. She told her story to *The Mirror* and for the next two days it ran under the banner 'The Private Hell Of My Rock Hero'. She wasn't called Heavy Metal Heather, which was the name she went by in the rock world, but 'Heather Mitson, the housewife who shared the life of doomed rock star Phil Lynott'. 'Housewife Heather Mitson had everything anyone could wish for – a loving husband, a pleasant home and all the comforts money can buy. But, like millions of other suburban housewives she dreamed and longed for the excitement and glamour that was missing in her respectable life.' When Phil Lynott died, Heather got in first with her story of life with the tragic star. Dozens of other women could have told the same story, but Heather got in first and had two days of fame as his 'ex-girlfriend'. It was the last star turn for Phil Lynott, the final bow to the public for whom he had played at being a hero. 'All I've done,' Heather told *The Mirror* on the Monday after his death, 'is to write his epitaph.'

> *Dear Lord take the time*
> *I believed your story now you believe mine*
> *Give me dignity*
> *Restore my sanity*
> *My vanity is killing me.*

('Dear Lord')

(from *Magill*, January 1986)

DEUS EX MACHINA:
THE BAND WHO GREW TO EARTH
John Waters

'We're not the Beatles, we're U2,' protested Bono from the stage during a recent U2 gig in New Jersey. It might well have been directed at the eighteen Irish journalists present: please don't let us be misunderstood; try to see the wood as well as the tall trees.

U2 are riding high right now, that much is true. And the media have latched onto them in a way which creates layers upon layers of irony around the fact that the band originally wanted to call themselves the Hype. And the message is coming back that what we've got here is a band that is VERY BIG. But something bothers me, just a little bit.

Like, how big is BIG. What does it mean to be 'bigger than Springsteen'? How BIG were the Beatles, anyway? (I really don't know – not because I was too young, but because at the time I wasn't all that bothered.) What I'm getting at is that, apart from telling us how many stretch limos they've got in their entourage, and how many bottles of champagne are devoured after every U2 gig, and aside from measuring them against less-than-relevant existing rock yardsticks, surely there is some objective, empirical way for journalists to go about telling us how big, how important, U2 are. To my way of thinking you don't have to be very significant to be more important than a third-rate reactionary versifier like Bruce Springsteen, and I was under the impression that somebody had shot the Beatles . . .

As, er, hinted at by Eamonn McCann in an article in this very magazine some weeks ago, U2 have been badly served by the press, particularly in their native country. For a while there I thought I was alone in being totally uninterested in hearing for the umpteenth time that, y'know, U2 – *our* U2 – are very highly thought of abroad there in Amerikay, that there's no end of 'celebrities' queueing up to shake their hands and that even Bob Dylan himself, bejapers, is only mad to be leppin' up on the stage and he to be singing a few bars of a song with the boys. Perhaps – fair dues – it's of some relevance to celebrate the fact that U2 have taken over the Number One spot in the US album charts – but then you hear that the spot was previously occupied by the Beastie Boys and you start to wonder. Perhaps being on the cover of *Time* is better than being on the cover of *In Dublin*, but I don't think so.

Me? I think U2 are the most important band in the history of popular music – about ten million leagues ahead of anyone else, past or present. Sometimes it seems like they exist to show just how mediocre everything else has been. The problem is that their success is being presented by the media as being within the terms of a Music Business which, if the truth be told, they are uncomfortable with, which they have subverted from the inside and shown to be barely able to comprehend or contain them. The Irish media have been more guilty in this respect than the British or American press, where it is occasionally possible to come across a half-intelligent article about U2. Perhaps it's Our National Inferiority Complex ... but no, that's when you criticize U2, so it couldn't be that ...

U2 are important not because they drive around in stretch limos, or get on the cover of *Time*, or get to play with Bob Dylan, but because of their music. That seems axiomatic, but sometimes you get to wondering if it needs to be said. They will remain important long after the media have run out of hyperbole and superlatives, long after the novelty of the success has worn off. U2 are important, not because they are successful but despite that success. Success, as the Music Business normally defines it, has always been a barrier between U2 and where they really wanted to go. That they have attained the prominence they needed to, whilst remaining for the most part untainted by the circus surrounding their success is a truly remarkable achievement. The media in recent months have been focusing on the shadow of U2's achievement and not enough on the substance. They have remarked on this themselves: 'Some of the recent pieces on us have concentrated perhaps too much on the U2 *phenomenon* ... and forgotten that above all we're a rock band,' Bono told Simon Garfield of the London magazine *Time Out* some weeks ago. 'The music is articulate in a way that I'm not.'

This latter remark is an echo of something which occurs again and again in interviews with U2. 'I think the music is better than the musician,' Bono told *Melody Maker* in 1984. 'I think if there's a difference between the art and the artist there's something up.'

There was always this thing about U2 – that they were bigger than the sum of their constituent parts, that they were dealing in something they didn't rightly understand nor fully want to. There is the old, oft-told story about Bono plugging Edge's guitar in exactly the way Edge does, setting up the amp in exactly the same way, using the same plectrum to play the same chords and ending up with what he himself described as 'a pitiful noise'. U2's sound doesn't seem to come from machinery or technique or from any source within the rock 'n' roll tradition.

On another occasion, talking about their methodology of writing songs, Edge described how the title track for *Unforgettable Fire* came about: the song had started with him messing about on the piano, and had been polished up finally in the studio with all the band and producer Eno present, but in between – the most important part – was where he and Bono had first got together to work on the song . . . 'It was the first twenty minutes in Bono's house that counted . . . it was the *mood* we were always in touch with, not necessarily the chords or the melody.'

The rather Zen notion of inspiration coming from some exterior source, from some external wellspring of imagination, with the artist as cipher, is by no means new in rock 'n' roll. John Lennon was fond of comparing it to the apple falling from the tree onto Newton's head, thereby leading to the discovery of gravitational force. 'I used to go though hell thinking I don't own any of my songs, and then it dawned on me that I never owned them in the first place,' he once told *Newsweek* magazine. 'The real music *comes* to me, the music of the spheres, the music that surpasses understanding. That has not to do with me, I'm just a channel . . . So for that to come through, which is the only joy for me out of the music, is for it to be given to me and I transcribe it like a medium. I have nothing to do with it other than I'm sitting under this tree and this whole damn thing comes down and I've just put it down.'

Something's up with U2, right enough. Something that surpasses understanding. Something that's got sod-all to do with stretch limos. Something magical. Something true. As it was in the beginning.

They always knew, you see – that's what makes them so different, so much BIGGER. The Beatles may have hoped. The Stones may have yearned. Springsteen may have tried. But U2 *knew* that one day they'd be the Biggest Band In The World.

In rock 'n' roll terms U2 were an immaculate conception. Theirs was a pearl which formed without the aid of even the obligatory grain of sand. They came to rock 'n' roll with little knowledge of its history or tradition, the better to avoid cliché and prejudice. Rock was a useful medium – maybe, they thought for a while, not the right one for them – but it was not a sacred cow. Having opted for it, though, they decided to exploit its machinations to the fullest extent, whilst retaining their single-mindedness, their certainty of vision. The Music Biz had, many times before and with absolute cynicism, itself attempted to market the naïveté and innocent passion of youth as a pop 'product', but here now were four possessors of just such a vision attempting to peddle *themselves* as a 'product', whilst at the same time hoping to retain their naïveté and innocent passion – and *succeeding*. It was some tricky tightrope, but U2 are still up there, tip-toeing away.

U2 are a band who grew to earth. A band who, as Bono once said, had their roots 'in space somewhere', they have approached rock 'n' roll on their own terms, from a position of ignorance rather than allow it to come to them on its terms.

They have done pretty much everything backwards. They have gone from writing music which was like nothing anybody had ever heard previously to music which hinted at the best of everything that had gone before. *The Joshua Tree* is as close to a perfect statement of where rock 'n' roll is at after over thirty years as anyone could wish to send to their relatives on Mars. It is a sign of hope, of redemption, in the barren desert which rock music had become: U2 have assimilated, refined, filtered the language of rock and distilled it into a piece of crystal. In other ways, too, they have done things in reverse: starting a band before they could play, writing songs first about spirituality and only later about love; becoming raunchier as they grew, instead of mellowing out like the rest. U2 were always inclined to go against the rock 'n' roll grain.

Much has been made, not least in the pages of this magazine, of the question of where the ultimate importance of U2 lies. Is it the indisputable fact that they make a fine noise? Is it because they communicate so directly and so well with millions of young people? Is it that they have conquered a corrupt and pretty much irredeemable Music Business on their own terms whilst retaining their own integrity intact? Is it their spiritual dimension? Could it be because of some as-yet unexploited political dimension?

Or is it because U2 are, above all, an Irish band? U2 make a fine noise. Their musical greatness primarily has to do with their sound – not merely in the technical, electronic sense, though that too – but especially in terms of the coming together of its diverse and complex units into something which is at once ineffable and hugely articulate. Much emphasis has been placed in the wake of *The Joshua Tree* on the fact that the band are now actually writing pieces which are more in the form of *songs* than they did formerly. This is quite true, but none the less they are not 'songs' in the sense that 'Yesterday' or 'Let it Be' are songs – it is difficult to imagine anyone having the empathy or the moral authority to cover a U2 song. They are, above all, a *sound*.

U2 do communicate in a unique way with their millions of followers. And their followers with them. It is as though they are different sides of the same coin, perhaps because U2's music *does* genuinely come from some sort of central wellspring in the human psyche – a truly universal folk music. U2's own belief in this closeness has on occasion highlighted the extent to which the band themselves are almost unconscious of their own status as 'stars'; during the *War* tour some years back, Bono, anxious to dispense with whatever barriers remained between band and audience, took to making sorties into the crowd, a practice which on one occasion ended in a minor riot. Though this has been instanced once or twice to support charges of incipient demagoguery against Bono, in truth it is probably a clear sign that U2's naïveté and good intentions remain intact. No other band has come anywhere as close to transcending the Music Business's obsessive need to turn musicians into icons.

Within the Music Biz, U2 have been a hugely subversive force. By their very stature and achievement, for example, they have in America coerced the ultra-conservative radio stations into broadening their horizons, and have opened up the airwaves to other bands who might previously have been excluded. In a broader sense, too, U2 have jammed the codes which allow the Biz to consumerize rock/pop music and left it less able to easily define, divide, predict and market according to its own dubious value system. U2 have, to a small degree at least, put control back within the grasp of the bands and the fans. Toppling the Beastie Boys from the number one spot, whatever its dubious aspects, was symbolic of this.

The spiritual and political aspects of U2's music are generally perceived as being contradictory, which of course they are. In his recent, fine article for *In Dublin* Eamonn McCann summed it up nicely when he asked: 'Is it possible that the very spirituality of U2's music, the quality that causes it to stir the soul even as it sets the limbs twitching, that this quality operates also to deprive it of direct access to the more mundane feelings and aspirations of the "masses"? In lifting the audience up, is the music rendered less relevant to issues which can only be handled by people who have their feet on the ground? This, even when the song is commenting directly and polemically on just such issues?' These are very good questions. I seem to remember that it was Plato in, if I'm not mistaken, Book III of *The Republic* who said that music is dangerous, not because it undermines law and order, but because it involves to such an extent the loss of self, the inability to contain feelings within the fences provided by language. This is what makes rock music a subversive force – that by the subtle manipulation of words, melodies and sound, it removes things from the rational onto the emotional plane, thus taking issues out of the realm of the idealogical tract or the political speech into what might be called the total dramatization of belief, thereby making them less susceptible to the manipulations of the many economists of truth who inhabit the body politic. Words are not mathematical symbols: sometimes they don't add up, sometimes they don't fully tell the truth. The best music does not lie – if it did, as

Lennon remarked, it would choke on itself. U2 make the best music in Christendom.

But this only goes half-way towards tackling the question of politics and how it relates to rock 'n' roll and specifically to U2. As Bono has acknowledged, rock is a living contradiction. At its best it has its head in the clouds and its feet on the dancefloor. In a recent interview with *NME*, he outlined some of the contradictions he saw: 'Elvis Presley singing gospel songs as he's drinking himself to death. Jerry Lee stopping a recording session 'cos a voice from God tells him to forsake the devil's music. John Lennon being in the world's biggest rock band ever and writing a song called "Help".'

I've got another one: U2, natives of a country colonized for generations, going to America, the great modern military and economic colonizer, and conquering it through the medium of a music which is itself colonized. You don't really have to go beyond this simple observation to explain why U2's audience is overwhelmingly white and middle class – something which has occasioned quite a bit of comment recently. The marketing methods of the essentially racist and sexist Music Biz have so far dictated that this is the way it will be. If anyone can succeed in breaking out of this absurd system of musical apartheid, maybe U2 can. They have kicked over the tables in the temple, now maybe they'll turn on the Pharisees . . .

Now that U2 are bigtime, every political animal with an axe to grind wants to fashion them into an implement for their own use. Garret FitzGerald, Charlie Haughey, the SDLP in the recent British elections, Amnesty, Self-Aid . . .

Because U2 are just about the most important and successful thing to come about in this country ever, it is not surprising that everyone should want to seek their imprimatur, get their nod of approval, bend their ear, touch their garments. We *want* to believe that they have answers to all our questions, that they can show us the way out of the mess. There used to be a thing in this country about Charlie Haughey that, because he made himself a millionaire, he could make the country prosperous as well – it's only now, perhaps, that we're beginning to realize that the two things are almost mutually contradictory. Similarly with U2, we think they can, because they have themselves become great, bring greatness in some vague way to their country as well, that they can be the panacea to all our ills, our *deus ex machina*, the catalyst which will ignite the spark to blast us out of the depths of despair. And U2, in turn, desperately want to *do something* for their native country, though they seem to have no idea exactly what.

Sometimes it seems that we expect too much of U2. They cannot abolish unemployment, renew the city centre, feed the poor or make the Hot House Flowers a hit band. The things which made U2 great – passion, idealism, naïveté, innocence, emotion – are not necessarily the best qualifications for a politician. There is no evidence that U2 know very much about politics and no reason whatever that they should. Their great strength has been the open and honest expression of the things that concerned them personally, the issues that impinged on their own lives. In so far as they are political at all, they are motivated more by a mixture of idealism and middle-class guilt. The issues which sometimes seem to preoccupy them – the state of Dublin's architectural heritage, for example, would not be the most pressing issues of the day for many of their fans. U2 have never been rebels – partly because they never had very much to rebel against and partly because rock's brand of token rebellion was one of the things they set themselves against.

U2's increasing political consciousness has many inherent con- tradictions. Their progress in this area has been made largely in full public view and has at times been traumatic. One of the problems is that U2's brand of emotional upsurge is in many ways antithetical to the proper propagation of the leftish politics which they instinctively espouse. Another thing is that U2 could never, *ever* be a socialist band. Their central credo, both in religious and political terms, has always been a celebration of the individual. They are, almost by definition, anti-collectivist. Though always wearing their spirituality on their sleeve, U2 have from the start professed their opposition to organized religion. Equally, though their politics are rapidly emerging as broadly left, Bono has recently been taking great pains to make clear his disenchantment with the ideological left as well as the right and centre.

There is, and with a bit of luck always will be, a place in politics for the passionate emotional hit, but of necessity it must be accompanied by the often tedious process of explanation and analysis, of groundwork and organization, of action and follow-through. Without such foundations, whipped-up fervour will always be at risk of being exploited for ends which may be ugly, evil, dangerous and wrong.

U2 are in possession of an enormous power. It is a moot point whether power can ever be a positive force, but at best it can perhaps be benign. U2 have made some mistakes, though nothing serious, perhaps just a few more contradictions. For example, even though they proclaimed *War* to be an anti-war album, the band could be seen in the videos strutting around on horseback waving flags, an exercise which looked suspiciously like a blatant exploitation of the more glamorous aspects of the imagery and symbolism of the very thing they sought to condemn. Or, for example, the fact that in live performances of 'Bad', their anti-heroin song, Bono is seen simulating the process of intravenous drug-taking, using the microphone in a very explicit manner; again, to my way of thinking, this does more to glamorize the procedure rather than the opposite. Bono has been similarly accused in relation to his usage of the national flag in live performances of the song 'Sunday Bloody Sunday', but here I think that, from U2's particular political standpoint at least, he's got it right. Recently at a New Jersey concert he reached into the audience, grabbed a huge tricolour brought by a fan and held it up. 'Do you see green?' he demanded of the crowd. 'Green!' they repeated happily. 'Do you see gold?' 'Gold!' the answer came back. 'White?' 'White!' Bono then threw the flag back at the fan who had brought it and screamed, 'All I see is fucking red.'

Which reminds me, for some reason, of Self-Aid . . .

I think I can, in all modesty, claim to have been the most outspoken critic of Self-Aid. At the time, I thought it was reactionary in its implications, regressive and wrong. I still think so. I was responsible for the cover of *In Dublin* showing Bono and the headline 'Rock Against The People' and for a couple of articles which criticized U2 for taking part in the exercise and giving it the full support of their organization. These objections have been characterized elsewhere and by one or two people who know different, as being personal and vindictive – they were not. I have nothing against either Bono or U2 and no reason to be personally vindictive towards them. In my view what was at stake was vital enough to risk the odium of a few members of the showbiz establishment; that an important social principle – that employment is not the responsibility of the individual in society – fought for for decades by many enlightened people, was being sold down the river in the interests of making a few reputations; and U2's magic and idealism was being used to give the idea currency and credibility. I'm glad I threw that particular brick – I'd do the same tomorrow.

U2's political naïveté is matched only by their potential as a force for political good. So far that potential has been under-realized. Their work on behalf of Amnesty has been admirable and Self-Aid at least showed that their heart was in the right place (I like them best when they're *angry*), but they're still only beginning to feel their way. They have, with some justification, been accused of vagueness and generalization in their songs, of approaching issues in a deliberately oblique way, of sticking to safe issues. On the other hand they have from different directions been charged with heavy-handedness in their political statements during their recent London concerts.

When U2 learn to sublimate their developing political consciousness into their music the result could be devastating. When they do, I suspect it will manifest itself in a way which will be a million miles from the kind of token, this-week's-good-cause approach which rock has adopted in recent years, something not at all like the Live Aids and the Self-Aids, steeped as they are in rock's sense of middle-class guilt (was I the only one who always thought it ironic that the very same Music Business which saw Fleetwood Mac's Peter Green locked up in 1970 for attempting to give his money away to the Third World should in 1985 be setting itself up as saviour to the starving millions?).

The fact that U2 are an Irish band is of practically no significance whatever. There is a mutual guilt-complex about Ireland and U2 which could ultimately be destructive on both sides and which needs to be gotten rid of immediately. They seem to feel the need when abroad to invoke the spirit of their home territory at all times, as though they were in some kind of debt to Ireland and the Irish people. We, for our part, have made criticism of U2, even to a very minor extent, the Great National Sin.

The fact is that, although they come from Dublin and will always be in that sense an Irish band, U2 are top of the heap in a medium which is universal, or which, if it has an epicentre at all, is primarily an American medium. U2 have been aware of this from the start and the manner in which they went about tackling the American market is a prototype for every young European act to follow. They write about America better than any other rock band in and in their interviews give liberal mention to reference points like Flannery O'Connor, Truman Capote and Norman Mailer. They now say they want to get America out of their system and turn their attention to affairs in their own country, where the band's soaring success is matched to inverse proportion by the despair of their contemporaries – U2's Picture Of Dorian Gray.

If this is what U2 really want to do, then of course they should do it. But I wonder if their guilt-edged relationship with the home country is causing them to overrule the gut instinct which always served them so well in the past.

There is nothing here for a rock band; Bob Geldof is right. Nearly ten years after U2 we are still waiting for the local scene to throw up even a minor contender. It is still as difficult for a young band to get off the ground as it was in the early days of U2. U2 themselves have made admirable efforts to pull a few people up the ladder after them, but so far to no avail. U2 can best serve the interests of their native country by continuing to do it in the big bad world. If they return they are in danger – as the head of their own Mother label, Fachtna O'Kelly warned recently – of becoming part of a new establishment which could ultimately be as difficult to overcome as the one they themselves came up against.

We should be proud that U2 are an Irish band, but should not attempt to be possessive about them or try to parochialize them. Being Irish allowed them to bring to the tired body of rock 'n' roll a kiss of new life, a lyricism, a romanticism which instilled it with new strength, but this is not something which derives from anything uniquely Irish, rather it comes from deep within the Celtic Imagination of which Ireland is just one wellspring.

U2 also in their interviews frequently invoke the name of Irish writers such as Brendan Behan and Patrick Kavanagh and, whilst there is no gainsaying those connections, U2's songs, with their strongly biblical and elemental imagery – the metaphors built around strong naturalistic symbols like trees, fruit, seeds, flowers, the desert – are reminiscent much more of the work of the Welsh poet Dylan Thomas than of any Irish writer I can think of. Like Thomas, U2 provide a bridge between the religious and secular imaginations; and, like the Welshman, Bono's lyrical imagery is underwritten with the suggestion of an organic link between man and the natural world – what Thomas reffered to as 'the earthquake of the heart'. U2 owe us nothing at all.

Even yet, U2 themselves don't rightly know where it is they're going or what propels them. 'For a lot of people,' Bono told *Time Out*, 'we're *either* a spiritual band, *or* a political band, *or* just a rock band . . . But the real truth about U2 lies in the complications . . . you just can't sum it up though.'

Some day, however, it will be summed up. U2 will be old bluesers and we will know whether it was all just flights of naïveté or something rather special, or a little bit of both. U2 have not touched down, they glide six miles over solid ground, like something out of the corner of your eye that you can't quite focus on.

One day the full truth will reveal itself, to U2 and the rest of the world.

Though not necessarily in that order.

(from *In Dublin*, 25 June 1987)

Epilogue

Until *The Joshua Tree*, 'U2 were the biggest underground band in the world.' So spoke Edge in late 1987 and he was right. Until then, U2 might claim millions of fans but they weren't household names, as well known to their fans' parents. Creatures of the music press, they still hadn't been introduced to the world's features editors and gossip columnists who determine the global celebrity ratings.

1987 was their year of fundamental change. After *The Joshua Tree* sold 16 million copies worldwide, U2 became global celebrities and ceased to be leaders of a private club. They graced the cover of *Time* magazine and every movement of every member of the band was minutely scrutinized. A Dublin nightclub incident might be headline news in Frankfurt or Los Angeles by the next afternoon. Henceforth all responses to U2 would prove the existence of an infinite number of parallel media universes. The problem for U2 was that sometimes they would have to live in all of them. Even believe in some of them.

Such experiences forced U2 to examine their own public meaning. Could they find any balance between their music and their fame? Was there any way to resolve creatively all these new contradictions? Or does the 'Zoo TV' gameshow end that pilgrimage with the decision not to resolve but instead expose and celebrate those contradictions?

That wasn't their attitude in 1987. In an American interview, Larry Mullen, the most earthbound member of the band, wondered: 'Isn't it incredible that, when you reach a certain stage, everything [you do] suddenly becomes important? Everybody has been talking about the U2 phenomenon and not so much about the music.'

This may have been the purest statement of the U2 party line, *circa* 1987. Bono cited John Lennon's rueful quip, 'Nobody told us there'd be days like this', and like so many acts, hurled into their first disorienting experience of celebrity hyperspace, U2 took refuge in the music. Especially in America, *The Joshua Tree* had been their first complete and unapologetic acknowledgement of their debt to America. But whereas a song like 'Bullet the Blue Sky' had theatrically criticized American public and political values, U2 were now exploring America's private history of the blues, gospel and rock 'n' roll, visiting Sun studios in Memphis to lay down tracks for their next album. It was one, perhaps the most reassuring, way of reminding themselves of their priorities.

Their success had the most unpredictable consequences in, of all places, Ireland. In their homeland, U2's achievements were unprecedented. Ireland's literary heroes were all safely entombed, but the country had never had to reckon with the contemporary fame of music or movie stars. The essence of their work, the music, could get missed in the scramble for instant analysis. In harsh economic times with rocketing youth unemployment and emigration, U2 were uncomfortably cast as symbols and role-models for Irish youth by pundits and politicians determined to find a multitude of often contradictory social meanings in the band.

Such expectations only added to the stress as they prepared

to play their two homecoming Dublin dates in the summer. The venue was Croke Park, an ageing Gaelic games stadium on the decaying Northside of the city. Within and without, all the contradictions of both Dublin and U2's fame were on display. In the drizzle, ticketless, unemployed young Dubliners slumped in the surrounding pavements and alleyways, drinking cheap cider, and later I would witness half-hearted, unavailing efforts to storm the stadium and get free entry. Inside, the guest list would include the government press secretary, the Dublin city manager and socialites who would never venture inside a grimy Dublin rock club. Bono would try to make a point, prove *his* integrity and turn heads by inviting a group of motorcycle mates, a Hell's Angels platoon from Waterford whose long hair and leather jackets would clash with all the well-groomed habitués of the hospitality tent.

The first night almost had its disaster. A young guy climbed on to the roof of a stand, over 200 feet above the football pitch. At a time when rock performances were becoming more computerized and less spontaneous, only Bono had the instinctive gift to talk him down, but then again, only U2 had sent him aloft.

This was an Event with a capital E, no time for U2 to show their more lyrical side. They survived and won but there were moments when the band seemed as if they were about to be drowned by the intensity of the audience's desire; as if only U2 could promise and deliver them the sun, moon, stars *and* a job. The second night was far more controlled, but afterwards there were still moments of tension. Bono's car got stuck in a traffic-jam and he was bitterly rebuked by a young Northerner for his wealth and anti-Republican politics. The band had hoped to round off the weekend with a carnival, a laser-light show over the city, but the technology failed and there were disturbances and a police baton charge in the city centre. Some Irish spirits even U2 just couldn't exorcize.

A fortnight later, they played a far more relaxed show in the Republic's second city, Cork. Boats ferried the crowd across the River Lee to the stadium and a far more affectionate audience gave them room to breathe. U2 were buoyed up, not buffeted, by an Irish audience and played a more smiling show in which, for once, they weren't fighting to escape from the crossfire of impossible national expectations.

Then it was back into the arms of America. U2 weren't just touring. *The Joshua Tree* experience was now merging into their most controversial project – the album, film and ultimate promotional nightmare and monstrosity that would become *Rattle and Hum*.

At first, it was their way of maintaining the momentum. Keep the songs fresh and flowing. Document every idea before it dies on the notebook or at the soundcheck. U2 were still obsessed by America, and Bono, especially, didn't want to delay. They all wished to prove U2 could use their new status; that they wouldn't coast but instead stake out new artistic ground.

But then there was also the idea of a new live album. *Under a Blood Red Sky* had been released as far back as 1983, before both *The Unforgettable Fire* and *The Joshua Tree*. With U2 the most bootlegged band in rock, might it not make sense to present their own official live album to their fans?

The notion of a film added a further potential source of conflict. Paul McGuinness believed the 'Red Rocks' video now looked 'very dated . . . Every time someone on television wants to show U2 live, you always get these four rather shiny-faced adolescents clambering around. It really has to be replaced.'

Along with contributions from Island and Paramount Pictures. U2 sank $5 million of their own money into the project. They recruited a Steven Spielberg protégé, Phil Joanau, to direct the film, and his team began work on the autumn leg of the tour. Meanwhile Jimmy Iovine, who had produced *Under a Blood Red Sky*, took charge of the accompanying record.

Both record and film were released in the last months of 1988. As an album, *Rattle and Hum* was a commercial success, eventually selling over 14 million copies, but, especially in America and Britain, the band walked into a critical firestorm. Later, U2 would argue that their artistic intentions had been misread, but they also acknowledged that their signals had got jumbled: the spontaneous scrapbook nature of the record got lost in the hard sell of the film.

The record went against the tide of fashion. In Britain, the Smiths were the critical flavour of the moment and indie guitar rock had erased rhythm 'n' blues signatures in favour of styles borrowed from the Byrds and the Velvet Underground. Belief was also profoundly suspect: the *Melody Maker* reviewer reviled U2 for daring to add a gospel choir to their live version of 'I Still Haven't Found What I'm Looking For'.

Such rancour could have been expected: U2 and most London critics long had different agendas. But the band were far more sensitive to American responses. U2 thought they had recorded a tribute; instead, they often got arraigned for theft. Their enthusiasm, especially Bono's, was deemed to signify a lack of proper humility. How dare these arrogant Irish outsiders march in and appropriate the American heritage!

The live tracks did offer hostages to fortune. For all his charm with interviewers, Bono could still let his mouth run ahead of his mind. The man who orders 'Edge, play the blues' on 'Silver and Gold' and who claims, in the first words of the album as he introduces 'Helter Skelter', 'Charles Manson stole this song from the Beatles, we're stealing it back,' obviously set himself up for jibes about his apparent self-importance.

Yet the new songs were as strong as any they had recorded. America was essential to Bono as the best place to explore and parade his own contradictions. He would commend Wim Wenders' remark that America had colonized all our minds and argue that 'sexuality and spirituality co-exist in American music in a way they don't in Irish or British music.'

The Irish had spirit but the Brits had sex, and America was the only place he could hope to fuse both. This attitude was also a response to the Jansenism and body-hatred ingrained in Irish Catholicism, whose ceremonies contained none of the fervour of gospel music.

But the search for roots was also part of another set of Irish musical trends. Van Morrison was recording with the Chieftains, and the Waterboys' Mike Scott had decamped to Ireland to start the raggle-taggle movement with the Hothouse Flowers. The Pogues were at their peak; Sinead O'Connor was also drawing from the well of traditional music; and there was a general notion that Irish music could be linked to rock 'n' roll through Appalachian bluegrass music and early country 'n' western.

U2 weren't immune to those ideas in vogue. Curious about Irish traditional music, they had become friendly with folk musicians like Christy Moore, Clannad and the Dubliners' Ronnie Drew. Touring in America, they had recorded a song called 'Jesus Christ' for a Woody Guthrie tribute. Later, Adam would play bass on one track of accordion-player Sharon Shannon's debut album, while Bono would contribute a song to a double-album and television documentary, 'Bringing It All Back Home', which explored the relationships between Irish and American music. So it was no major surprise that the second track on *Rattle and Hum* was a ballad, 'Van Dieman's Land', sung by Edge, that lamented the forced emigration of Irish convicts to Australia.

I still believe the album's new songs were underestimated and would be better appreciated if they were set alone on their own album. 'Desire', 'Hawkmoon 269' and their collaboration with B. B. King, 'When Love Comes to Town', were all founded on Larry Mullen's most stirring drumming performances so far. Then there was the slow country-blues, 'Love Rescue Me', co-written with Bob Dylan, 'Angel of Harlem', Bono's enchanted tribute to Billie Holliday, while the inspiration of John Lennon pervaded 'God Part II'.

The tale they were telling was also more complex than their detractors noticed. Bono's lyrics were still about romantic surrender – to lovers, heroes and his version of America. Yet he was also trying to escape stereotypes. 'God Part II' angrily rejects nostalgia, with Bono shouting 'I don't believe in the 60s, in the golden age of pop/You glorify the past when the future dries up.' 'Love Rescue Me' was his appeal to escape the sanctifying pressures of fame, with its key couplet: 'Many lost who seek to find themselves in me/They ask me to reveal/The very thoughts they would conceal.'

Nor had they completely abandoned earlier styles. Both 'Heartland' and 'All I Want Is You' could have featured on earlier albums and the stunning latter track, which closed *Rattle and Hum*, showed how their latest influences could add a new emotional depth and maturity to their older styles.

But these issues got lost in the hype and the resulting backlash. In Ireland, audiences would view the film and note Bono's angry attack on the IRA during 'Sunday Bloody Sunday', but many critics instead watched and deplored the band's visit to Graceland as if they had no right to commune with the spirit of Elvis Presley. U2 had become the victims of over-exposure. After *Rattle and Hum*, they would not tour either Britain or America for three years.

Instead in autumn 1989, they set out for Australia, New Zealand and Japan on the 'Lovetown' tour. B. B. King was welcomed as support and dubbed the 'Mayor of Lovetown', and the tour's main musical fascination lay in the band's efforts to fuse their various styles into a seamless live show.

They hadn't vegetated earlier in the year. Bono and Edge had written and produced 'She's a Mystery to Me' for Roy Orbison, while Bono had appeared at a benefit for Dublin's Abbey Theatre, reciting the poetry of W. B. Yeats over his own taped backing. But there had been one cloud – Adam Clayton had been arrested in August for possession of cannabis. Luckily the court was understanding. In return for paying £25,000 to a refuge for battered wives, the bassist was spared a conviction that might have stopped him touring.

The tour, though, had its own difficulties. The U2 of the 'Unforgettable Fire' era had cruised at high altitudes, but the new material made extra demands. As the effective band-leader, Bono was still trying to expand the band's range, but as their frontman he also had his own problems to solve. In the view of many, he was over-projecting and over-emoting to reach and touch those in the furthest seats of the vast arenas U2 were now playing.

But their fans didn't notice, and in December the tour passed through Europe before closing in Dublin. Instead of an outdoor venue, they played four post-Christmas dates at The Point, a new 6,000 seater which they hoped would give them the intimacy they had lost at Croke Park. But their Irish agenda became secondary as the Berlin Wall collapsed and Eastern Europe rid itself of Communism. Instead, U2 got to play the first pan-European rock concert as their New Year's Eve show was broadcast live all over Europe, including a Roumania that had just freed itself from the tyranny of Ceauçescu. In a special gesture of celebration, the band bought space in magazines for an inlay for anyone who had taped the concert.

But U2 watchers were more bothered by Bono's remark about the band stopping and retiring for a while. Did this mean they were about to burn out and collapse like so many earlier superstar bands? No. Instead U2 were entering the phase of re-evaluation and rebirth that would lead to both *Achtung Baby* and the 'Zoo TV' extravaganza.

Bono had been the American of the group with Edge cast as the European. As long ago as the contrast between *War* and *The Unforgettable Fire*, their music had shuttled back and forth across the Atlantic. Now the fall of Communism had given them a heaven-sent artistic opportunity to curtail their American obsessions and re-explore Europe. For once, they didn't base their recording at home in Ireland, instead relocating to Berlin's Hansa studio, where David Bowie had once radically redirected his career.

To escape emotional clichés, the concept of U2 had to be scaled down and expectations re-channelled. They wanted to deflect attention from Bono (the rock saviour) and prove themselves still capable of artistic rebirth through their response to the new sounds of the late Eighties, especially the rock dance of the new Manchester bands and the searing guitar outrage of My Bloody Valentine, led by fellow Irishman Kevin Shields. U2 still didn't lack commercial ambition, but they were also still sufficiently proud and hungry to want to prove they could outsmart their younger contemporaries.

The first single arrived in autumn 1991. 'The Fly' was an intentional shock, corrugated guitars wrapped around their most radical rhythms with a vocal from Bono that seemed phoned in from Sverdlovsk. All American signatures had been discarded, and later Bono would happily claim that 'The Fly' 'was the sound of four guys chopping down *The Joshua Tree*'.

In November, *Achtung Baby*, its title a coinage of their Cork soundman, Joe O'Herlihy, was released worldwide and U2 were seen to have shed another layer of skin. The rhythm section juddered in at oblique angles for U2, and Adam Clayton, previously the most subliminal element in their sound, now took frontstage. Many of the tracks were dirty, throwaway pop songs, as if the band were collectively recalling their youth, listening to Marc Bolan and David Bowie. The former puritans were now sexually explicit, with Bono preaching submission – 'on your knees, boy' – on 'Mysterious Ways'.

Yet they hadn't completely obliterated their lyricism. Three ballads, 'One', 'So Cruel' and 'Love Is Blindness' formed the emotional core of *Achtung Baby*. Hearing them, many recalled that, earlier in the year, Edge's marriage had broken down, and saw that as one backdrop to the record.

Generally, reviews were positive and U2 were seen as rescuing themselves from the black hole of stadium rock. But in contrast to the promotional overkill that surrounded *Rattle and Hum*, U2 spurned interviews. Nobody could anticipate the second stage in their strategy: 'Zoo T.V.'

It was another idea partially bequeathed by David Bowie. Moonlighting on his 'Sound and Vision' tour, U2's lights designer, Pete Williams, had realized there was a new generation of interactive technology and decided to push it to the maximum. The result was a show that finally freed Bono.

All his friends knew that Bono was a charming chameleon, a lethal mimic and a far more comic character than was seen on stage. In a 1992 interview, Edge even speculated that 'maybe over our career, our ability to create music that shows the full range of the personalities of Bono and the other members of the band was very poor.'

What was true was that live, U2 had refused elaborate light shows and had become completely dependent on Bono's ability to magnetize an audience. The result was both a distortion and an inflation of his public character as both Bono's and the band's sense of humour was lost.

'Zoo T.V.' let Bono be playful again. The juvenile naif who once toyed with cigarettes in Dublin's Baggot Inn now had a television station full of tricks to toy with. Now the kid who had once sidled up to Irish premier Garret Fitzgerald on a London–Dublin flight could ring up the White House and make fun of George Bush. 'Zoo T.V.' let him be lightning conductor, circus clown and ringmaster and finally abandon the suffering romantic hero of yore. Finally U2 had discovered it was both far better fun and far better art to play with your contradictions.

Index

Index

INDEX

READ MORE IN PENGUIN

In every corner of the world, on every subject under the sun, Penguin represents quality and variety – the very best in publishing today.

For complete information about books available from Penguin – including Puffins, Penguin Classics and Arkana – and how to order them, write to us at the appropriate address below. Please note that for copyright reasons the selection of books varies from country to country.

In the United Kingdom: Please write to *Dept. JC, Penguin Books Ltd, FREEPOST, West Drayton, Middlesex UB7 0BR*

If you have any difficulty in obtaining a title, please send your order with the correct money, plus ten per cent for postage and packaging, to *PO Box No. 11, West Drayton, Middlesex UB7 0BR*

In the United States: Please write to *Penguin USA Inc., 375 Hudson Street, New York, NY 10014*

In Canada: Please write to *Penguin Books Canada Ltd, 10 Alcorn Avenue, Suite 300, Toronto, Ontario M4V 3B2*

In Australia: Please write to *Penguin Books Australia Ltd, 487 Maroondah Highway, Ringwood, Victoria 3134*

In New Zealand: Please write to *Penguin Books (NZ) Ltd,182–190 Wairau Road, Private Bag, Takapuna, Auckland 9*

In India: Please write to *Penguin Books India Pvt Ltd, 706 Eros Apartments, 56 Nehru Place, New Delhi 110 019*

In the Netherlands: Please write to *Penguin Books Netherlands B.V., Keizersgracht 231 NL–1016 DV Amsterdam*

In Germany: Please write to *Penguin Books Deutschland GmbH, Friedrichstrasse 10–12, W–6000 Frankfurt/Main 1*

In Spain: Please write to *Penguin Books S. A., C. San Bernardo 117–6° E–28015 Madrid*

In Italy: Please write to *Penguin Italia s.r.l., Via Felice Casati 20, I–20124 Milano*

In France: Please write to *Penguin France S. A., 17 rue Lejeune, F–31000 Toulouse*

In Japan: Please write to *Penguin Books Japan, Ishikiribashi Building, 2–5–4, Suido, Tokyo 112*

In Greece: Please write to *Penguin Hellas Ltd, Dimocritou 3, GR–106 71 Athens*

In South Africa: Please write to *Longman Penguin Southern Africa (Pty) Ltd, Private Bag X08, Bertsham 2013*

READ MORE IN PENGUIN

A SELECTION OF MUSICAL HITS

The Big Wheel Bruce Thomas

'The former bass guitarist of Elvis Costello and the Attractions, Bruce Thomas has written about life on the road for a successful rock band with a drummer whose excesses fulfil our every expectation of every rock drummer and a singer whose behaviour remains utterly enigmatic throughout. Thomas is obviously a witty and perceptive man, who handles his one-liners well' – *20/20*

Sweet Soul Music Peter Guralnick

'As important for what it says about America, class and race issues, and the sixties as for its outstanding musical insights. Sooner or later it is going to be recognized as a classic' – Robert Palmer in *The New York Times*

Shots from the Hip Charles Shaar Murray

His classic encapsulation of the moment when rock stars turned junkies as the sixties died; his dissection of rock 'n' roll violence as citizens assaulted the Sex Pistols; his superstar encounters from the decline of Paul McCartney to Mick Jagger's request that the author should leave – Charles Shaar Murray's *Shots from the Hip* is also rock history in the making.

Mystery Train Greil Marcus

'There has never been a more well-written, imaginative, scholarly, infuriating, crackling, gladdening book about rock music ... Greil Marcus uses a handful of modern popular artists ... to illuminate and interpret two centuries of the American Dream' – *Sunday Times*

Dylan: Behind the Shades Clinton Heylin

'The most accurately researched and competently written account of Dylan's life yet ... Heylin allots equal space to each of the three decades of Dylan's career, and offers a particularly judicious assessment of his achievements in the post-conversion Eighties' – Mark Ford in the *London Review of Books*

READ MORE IN PENGUIN

A SELECTION OF MUSICAL HITS

Sinéad Jimmy Guterman

Sinéad O'Connor is internationally famous for her haunting, passionate vocals and outspoken political views. Here is the story of the woman and her music: from her unhappy early years in a broken home and a Catholic reform school to her triumphant arrival as a major pop star of the 1990s.

Stone Alone Bill Wyman with Ray Coleman

Ruthless, cynical, electrifying and exuberant – the Stones played a revolutionary soundtrack for the Sixties. Offstage, bass guitarist Bill Wyman has always been 'the silent Stone'. But here he gives us the intimate and gripping story of the 'bad boys' of British rock and the era they helped to shape.

Pet Shop Boys, *Literally* Chris Heath

'They have defined something intangible in an all-too obvious era of pop music. Their Englishness, their balance – and their cynicism – combine to produce an effect of brilliance, self-regarding and self-referential' – *Sunday Times*. 'Witty, straightforward and painstakingly precise ... a compelling read' – *Time Out*

The American Night Jim Morrison

'A hellfire preacher, part-terrified, part-enraged and mainly fascinated by the drawbacks that being merely human entails ... refreshing' – Robert Sandall in the *Sunday Times*. 'A great American poet' – Oliver Stone

Bare George Michael and Tony Parsons

'A fascinating study of fame, power, and insecurity ... *Bare* paints a picture of a modern-day folk-hero against the stark background of contemporary Britain. Funny and incisive ... *Bare* heralds a new chapter in celebrity biography' – *Arena* magazine